THE SENSIBLE WORLD AND THE WORLD OF EXPRESSION

Northwestern University
Studies in Phenomenology
and
Existential Philosophy

General Editor Anthony J. Steinbock

THE SENSIBLE WORLD AND THE WORLD OF EXPRESSION

Course Notes from the Collège de France, 1953

Maurice Merleau-Ponty

Translated from the French with an introduction and notes by Bryan Smyth

Northwestern University Press
Evanston, Illinois

Northwestern University Press
www.nupress.northwestern.edu

Printed in the United States of America

10 9 8 7 6 5 4 3 2 1

Library of Congress Cataloging-in-Publication Data
Names: Merleau-Ponty, Maurice, 1908–1961, author. | Smyth, Bryan A., translator, writer of added commentary.
Title: The sensible world and the world of expression : course notes from the Collège de France, 1953 / Maurice Merleau-Ponty ; translated from the French with an introduction and notes by Bryan Smyth.
Other titles: Monde sensible et le monde de l'expression. English | Studies in phenomenology and existential philosophy.
Description: Evanston, Illinois : Northwestern University Press, 2020. | Series: Northwestern University Studies in phenomenology and existential philosophy | Includes bibliographical references and index.
Identifiers: LCCN 2019042473 | ISBN 9780810141421 (paperback) | ISBN 9780810141438 (cloth) | ISBN 9780810141445 (ebook)
Subjects: LCSH: Merleau-Ponty, Maurice, 1908–1961. | Phenomenology. | Perception (Philosophy) | Movement (Philosophy) | Expression (Philosophy)
Classification: LCC B2430.M3763 M6613 2020 | DDC 194—dc23
LC record available at https://lccn.loc.gov/2019042473

For Bob, Mae, and Jack

Contents

Acknowledgments ix
Translator's Introduction xi
Note on the Translation xliii
Typographical Information liii

Course Notes from the Collège de France, 1953

Preparatory Lecture Notes 3
Working Notes 129

Translator's Notes 167
Bibliography 237
Index 253

Acknowledgments

This volume would not have been possible without the painstaking work of Emmanuel de Saint Aubert and Stefan Kristensen in transcribing the original notes and putting together the original French edition. In addition, both Emmanuel and Stefan responded to numerous questions concerning the text, and this has helped me considerably. Likewise, Jérôme Melançon generously answered countless questions and offered a great deal of helpful advice. David Morris read parts of a draft version of the translation and offered many constructive comments. I am also very grateful for the feedback received from two anonymous reviewers. Suggestions from all of these sources have improved the translation. But many of the questions that translational work like this raises never issue in consensus, and I bear responsibility for any and all shortcomings that remain.

At Northwestern University Press, Trevor Perri was extremely helpful and patient in the initial stages of the project, Mike Ashby provided meticulous copyediting, and Anne Gendler, with assistance from Laura Ferdinand, very ably and supportively ensured that the production process went smoothly. Special thanks to Faye Thaxton at Classic City Composition for meeting the many typesetting challenges posed by this work.

At the University of Mississippi, Steven Skultety helped me with a question concerning some Greek, Molly Pasco-Pranger with one concerning Latin, and Valerio Cappozzo with one involving Italian.

As always, Anne, Fyntan, and Aurélia Mae have been present throughout, and have helped in all of their own special ways.

Translator's Introduction

Phenomenology of Imperception? Merleau-Ponty and the Problem of Expression

Presented in this volume is a translation of the notes that Merleau-Ponty produced while preparing his Thursday lecture course—titled "Le monde sensible et le monde de l'expression"—during his inaugural year (1952–53) as chair of philosophy at the Collège de France,[1] along with a translation of a selection of related working notes. Until the publication of these notes, little was actually known about the content of this course other than what is conveyed through the fairly brief (approximately two thousand words) official course summary that Merleau-Ponty composed after the end of the course.[2] Indeed, something similar is true for all the courses Merleau-Ponty gave at the Collège, and for a long time this situation presented serious obstacles to a genuinely insightful—rather than a more or less speculative—understanding of the development of his thought during the last decade of his life. In recent years, however, lecture notes from several of these courses have been transcribed and published, with many more potentially yet to come, and this has proven enormously valuable with regard to tracing out the philosophical trajectory that led from Merleau-Ponty's early published works—*The Structure of Behavior* and *Phenomenology of Perception*—through *The Adventures of the Dialectic* to the unfinished manuscript of *The Visible and the Invisible.* Although often and in many ways textually problematic, owing to their status as personal notes, these previously unpublished materials now represent crucial elements that must be taken into account when engaged in the tasks of reading, interpreting, and assessing the Merleau-Pontian project. And as an initial step in the reinvigoration of his research agenda that followed his release from the academic responsibilities that he had had at l'Université de Lyon (1945–49) and l'Université de Paris (1949–52), while also incorporating some of the sources that he had dealt with in his lectures at both those institutions, this is certainly true of the course in question here. Situated midway between *Phenomenology of Perception* and *The Visible and the Invisible*, "The Sensible World and the World of Expression" offers insights which—as the conjunctive title of the course itself would even seem to suggest—serve to bridge his earlier and later work. In linking "the sensible" and "the expressive," that is, this course sheds light on why and how Merleau-Ponty moved from his earlier phenomenological concern with perceptual experience to his later efforts aimed at working out the ontological implications of his phenomenological approach in terms of a new dialectical understanding of the relation between nature and culture.

In this introduction, I do not intend to lay out a fine-grained recapitulation of the course, nor to reconstruct its position within the development of Merleau-Ponty's thought in any detailed way. Rather, I merely try to provide fairly clear accounts of the main impetus behind the course, and of its principal thematic content. My goal here is not to provide readers with any sort of condensed substitute version of the course but simply to offer some reflections that may help them in preparing for a more productive engagement with a text that, owing to its fragmentary form, can be challengingly understated with regard to its own import.

There are thus two main parts to this introduction. (1) I begin by considering how Merleau-Ponty formulated his overall goal for the course, something that can be done most instructively by taking a step back and situating it in the context of Merleau-Ponty's synoptic assessment of his research agenda at the time of his candidacy for the position at the Collège, and the prospective vision that he had for his work as a whole.[3] (2) I then describe how Merleau-Ponty sought to fulfill his goal for the course in terms of the main themes of his lectures and their overall sense.

Context and Goals

At the time of his candidacy for the Collège de France (i.e., early 1952), Merleau-Ponty presented his previous major works—*The Structure of Behavior* and especially *Phenomenology of Perception*—as having developed a new methodological approach to perceptual experience, and he presented his subsequent and projected work as endeavoring to extend the earlier results by taking up and applying that method to the higher-level cultural or intersubjective phenomena of language, history, and knowledge in a way that would ultimately culminate in a new theory of rationality and truth.[4] This view was basically congruent with the claim that he had made—somewhat defensively—in November 1946 that with regard to questions concerning rationality, *Phenomenology of Perception* was only a "preliminary" work, "since it hardly speaks of culture or of history." Taking perception as a "privileged" because "primordial" "layer [*couche*] of experience," he characterized this work as having aimed at defining a method for approaching "present and living being" as this is found in "man's relation to sensible nature, and [in] the relation of man with man at the level of the sensible," a method that could then be applied subsequently "to the relation of man with man in language, knowledge, society, and religion."[5] "There is," as Merleau-Ponty had put it, "a whole cultural world that constitutes a second layer above perceptual experience," and which remained to be explored through the same style of "radical" reflection.[6] Looking back in 1952, he thought that some of the essays collected in *Sense and Non-Sense,* as well as *Humanism and Terror,* had taken important steps in this direction and that in taking up its itinerary and method, these essays would help "to establish definitively the philosophical meaning" of *Phenomenology of Perception.*[7] Something similar could be said of *The Prose of the World,* which he had been working on more recently. But Merleau-Ponty also thought that he had yet to rigorously work out [*élaborer en toute rigueur*] "the philosophical foundations" of these contributions.[8] By implication, these would also be the philosophical foundations of *Phenomenology of Perception* itself, and in very general terms the task of working them out *en toute rigueur* formed the substantive content of Merleau-Ponty's research agenda circa 1952.

So it was not the case that in his work after 1945 Merleau-Ponty was simply building on the methodological basis laid out by *Phenomenology of Perception* with regard to the sensible world. That may be true to an extent, and it may have been an impression he was not loath to convey. But it would be more accurate to say that this work was undertaken as the extension and continuation of the metalevel "phenomenology of phenomenology" that constituted the final part of *Phenomenology of Perception.* Here Merleau-Ponty had specifically tried to provide the self-referential methodological closure that would shore up the phenomenological project philosophically such that it could be taken as providing its own foundation in the sense of the Husserlian maxim, "Die Rückbeziehung der Phänomenologie auf sich selbst."[9] Ultimately this would amount to an account of the subject of philosophy as grounded in and structurally homologous yet irreducible to the subject of perception—not unlike the way in which, for Kurt Goldstein, the biologist relates to the organism she studies: "Biological knowledge appears as a form of biological being," Goldstein thought, in virtue of "reproduc[ing] in a conscious way the approach of the living organism."[10] Yet Merleau-Ponty's view of philosophy may have been *too* similar to this. For as found in the descriptions of perceptual experience in *Phenomenology of Perception* that are supposed to provide the methodological model for approaching cultural phenomena, the subject of perception is the subject of what Merleau-Ponty frequently calls *natural* perception.[11] This subject is an isolated one that effectively remains within its "individual inherence,"[12] such that whatever active contribution it makes to perception is understood in terms of its "precognitive functions of organization and structuration,"[13] where the "*pre*cognitive" status of these functions implies a strict kind of natural priority. This view issues from a "methodological abstraction,"[14] the content of which is precisely tantamount to the bifurcation of the experienced world into distinct natural and cultural "layers." While perhaps understandable for the sake of gaining an initial hold on perceptual experience, this perspective introduces a fundamental problem inasmuch as the methodology it proposes for approaching cultural phenomena is modeled on an abstraction that excludes something that is essential to such phenomena.

Let's step back for a moment. For Merleau-Ponty, what is of central interest in all the cultural phenomena that he had in view was their *expressivity*, their sublimation and transcendence of the sensibly given, whereby they go beyond the latter while still engaging the real, and this expressivity was in turn taken to be based upon a certain *spontaneity*. In contrast to ("natural") perception, which on its own "could only teach us a '*bad* ambiguity,'" in the sense that it left us with an equivocal and thus ultimately senseless and unintelligible "*mixture* of finitude and universality, of interiority and exteriority," there is "a '*good* ambiguity' in the phenomenon of expression," in the sense that it involves "a spontaneity that accomplishes what, considered in terms of the discrete elements, appeared to be impossible, and which brings together the plurality of monads, the past and the present, nature and culture into a single tissue [*un seul tissu*]."[15] This spontaneous taking up and unifying of the otherwise merely juxtaposed aspects of the perceptual encounter is "the very productivity or freedom of human life," which, "far from denying our situation, utilizes and turns it into a means of expression,"[16] thereby generating in a quasi-teleological way the cultural world in its various dimensions, up to and including knowledge and truth. Thus satisfying, at least on the face of it, the methodological desideratum that Merleau-Ponty had formulated at the end of *The Structure of Behavior*—to wit, to "define transcendental philosophy anew in such a way as to integrate within it the very phenomenon of the real"[17]—this gives rise to the need to come to terms with the "wonder" [*merveille*] of human spontaneity in general[18] and in particular the need "to clarify what it is in ourselves that accomplishes the spontaneous movement of knowledge."[19] By effectively answering the metaphysical questions that his phenomenology of perception had raised, this clarification would supply the outstanding philosophical foundations that Merleau-Ponty was seeking, and in a nutshell this was the heart of his research itinerary in the years immediately prior to his election to the Collège de France.

The problem is now easily seen. For on account of the methodological abstraction that renders the cultural distinct from the natural, and which thereby effectively denies any human spontaneity or productivity *in* "natural" perception, this clarification was unachievable. Indeed, in the postwar years the spontaneity of cultural expression remained a mysterious blind spot for Merleau-Ponty that was sometimes reflected rather conspicuously in metaphors of *fulguration.* For instance, "In the coexistence of men, to which these years have awakened us, morals, doctrines, thoughts and customs, laws, works and words all express each other; everything signifies everything. *There is nothing outside this unique fulguration of existence.*"[20]—"Sometimes there is that flash of fire, that streak of lightning, that moment of victory, or, as Hemingway's Maria says, that *gloria* that obliterates everything."[21]—"The glory of the self-evidence . . . of dialogue and successful communication."[22] These moments of blinding light serve to conceal that the expressive spontaneity in question had *not* been clarified, that the ambiguous relation between the sensible and the expressive remained "bad" because it was not yet grasped in its dialectical unity, and this was arguably so precisely because the methodological abstraction of natural perception precluded any understanding of that spontaneity as being positively rooted there. To be sure, there are numerous indications to the contrary in the descriptive analyses of *Phenomenology of Perception,* including in his incipient discussions of linguistic expression, and these can be seen as placing pressure on that abstraction. But inasmuch as these countervailing moments did not overturn the abstraction, they were ultimately left in a kind of muted, undeveloped philosophical limbo. Merleau-Ponty thus struggled unsuccessfully to come to terms with the spontaneity of expression on account of having located it uniquely at the cultural level as the means by which expression is *given* to the sensible. In effect, he had tried to understand expression on the basis of *im*pression or, if you like, the impressivity of natural perception. But the desideratum issuing from *The Structure of Behavior* to the effect that transcendental philosophy should integrate within itself "the very phenomenon of the real" could be fully satisfied only by recognizing that the spontaneity in question is *already* present in perception, that expressivity is not a distinguishing feature of cultural phenomena, that nature and culture do not need to be *brought* together, for in the relevant respect they are already together in a dialectical unity, and that it is with this unity (or "single tissue") that we need to come to terms.

This is indeed a recognition to which Merleau-Ponty came, and it stood behind and motivated what he set out to do in "The Sensible World and the World of Expression." At the very outset of his notes, he laid out the following two goals for the course: "deepen the analysis of the perceived world by showing that it already presupposes the expressive function" and "prepare the analysis of this [expressive] function through which the perceived world is sublimated, produce a concrete theory of mind."[23] In one sense, these goals reflect the structure of *Phenomenology of Perception* as presenting phenomenological analyses of the perceived world that are then followed by a metalevel phenomenology of that phenomenology. At the same time, however, it rejects that division as reflecting an arbitrary abstraction that is unfaithful to the phenomena. It will be seen below that Merleau-Ponty was still stung by the critique that Jean Hyppolite had made of *Phenomenology of Perception* in 1946, to the effect that there was "no cohesion [*solidarité*] between [the] description of perception and [the] conception of 'the being of sense'"—that is, that the phenomenology of phenomenology did not follow from the phenomenological analyses themselves on the basis of a coherent internal connection.[24] Merleau-Ponty heartily rejected this criticism at the time, and continued to do so, based on his conviction that "all that we are is implicated in our manner of perceiving." But on the basis of that same conviction, he could now see more clearly that there was indeed a lack of cohesion along the lines pointed out by Hyppolite (who may, however, have been right for wrong reasons), precisely in the sense of the split between nature and culture that was operative in Merleau-Ponty's approach—a split that could be healed, however, *by returning to perception and disclosing its inherent expressivity*. Thus, still at the outset of his lectures, Merleau-Ponty offered some striking critical comments on *Phenomenology of Perception* to the effect that it "remained governed by classical concepts"—most notably, those of perception and consciousness—and that as a result the work made itself liable to misunderstanding, with Hyppolite's objection being a key case in point.[25] By way of figuring out a sound (if somewhat belated) response to this objection (among others), radically rethinking perception and consciousness on the basis of a renewed engagement with the sensible and in terms of expressivity is Merleau-Ponty's overarching preoccupation in the lecture notes below.

So while it is still correct to say that "The Sensible World and the World of Expression" stands on the basis of *Phenomenology of Perception* even while trying to rework the philosophical implications of that earlier work concerning expression (i.e., the phenomenology of phenomenology), the key innovation here is that *Merleau-Ponty is also revisiting the phenomenological analysis of the perceived world itself.* It's not just that he continued to grapple with the problem of how the sensible is taken up expressively. Rather, he came to see that the way he had framed this problem made it unsolvable and that, to the contrary, perception as the encounter with the sensible was already expressive, that expression properly speaking did not enter *Phenomenology of Perception* only in its final part, that the entire work was actually—as the many countervailing indications had suggested—expressive through and through. He came to realize, in other words, that he didn't get the phenomenology *of* phenomenology right, because he didn't get the phenomenology itself right in the first place. So he was still building his phenomenological method, not building *on* it. In this sense, the specific *unifying* concern with the sensible and the expressive that is indicated, albeit obliquely, by the conjunction in the present course's title marks a pivotal point in the trajectory of Merleau-Ponty's thought, a turn that is crucially germinal, if as yet inconclusive, with regard to important subsequent developments concerning history, nature, and ultimately the hyperdialectical ontology of flesh.[26]

Here we can return to Merleau-Ponty's two goals for the course. These goals were reflected in the outlines for the course that he put together after the first few lectures,[27] and the emphasis was very much on the first of his stated goals, to "deepen the analysis of the perceived world by showing that it already presupposes the expressive function," rather than the second goal, which was preparatory with regard to questions concerning higher-level forms of expression such as language, history, rationality, and truth. Merleau-Ponty never intended to deal with these broader questions in this course. Rather, the content of "The Sensible World and the World of Expression" was meant only to reach the "passage from natural expression to nonlinguistic culture"[28]—that is, the passage from expression at the level of the sensible to cultural expression that is not yet language. Merleau-Ponty planned to consider this passage in terms of visual art (painting and cinema), while with regard to those larger themes (i.e., language, history, rationality, and truth), his intention was to take them up over the following two years,[29] and the secondary goal of "The Sensible World and the World of Expression" had to do with setting the stage for that. As it turned out, though, Merleau-Ponty fell behind in his lectures, as philosophy professors are so often wont to do, and he also altered his initial plans (see pages xxi–xxiii), with the result that the number of lectures allotted to that secondary goal was reduced considerably. The passage from natural expression to nonlinguistic culture was thus ultimately given very short shrift, while the emphasis on the primary goal was even greater than originally envisioned. Merleau-Ponty adhered to this goal and focused on the question of "natural expression" itself quite closely and carefully, perhaps even struggling at times, and the reader would do well to bear this in mind.

Overview of the Course

Inasmuch as this can be based on Merleau-Ponty's notes, the course can be more or less broken down into four (unequal) parts: (1) a general introduction and overview, (2) phenomenological accounts of space and movement, (3) discussion of the body schema, and (4) a brief discussion of nonlinguistic cultural expression in visual art, along with some even briefer indications concerning higher-level cultural expression. The first three parts correspond to Merleau-Ponty's main goal, while the fourth pertains to his secondary goal.

General Introduction

The first three lectures presented a general introduction in which Merleau-Ponty laid out his objectives in relation to outstanding problems in his earlier work (as elaborated in the previous section) and presented his working definition of expression—or, more precisely, of expressivity—as "the property that a phenomenon has through its internal arrangement to disclose another [phenomenon] that is not or even never was given."[30] With this, Merleau-Ponty's philosophical concern is less with the disclosure of phenomena that happen to be nongiven at some particular moment, which is basically what goes on in the phenomenological analysis of intentional horizonality, than with forms of totality that, as such, can in principle never be given. And his primary concern is with human existence—"man" in Merleau-Ponty's terminology—as a form of totality that encompasses body and mind, or perception and intellection. Products of human labor, for example, broadly construed, would express this totality directly. Human perception, however, is more akin to "intellectual work or painting," in that these activities give expression to human existence *indirectly* "by talking about things or about the world as well, such that here it is not only man expressing himself in [a] product, but moreover [a] product that expresses the world." There is an orientation toward truth in art no less than in science, he thought, and this can also be found in perception. Indeed, it is ultimately rooted there. Although perception is characterized by a kind of "mutism" that excludes any actual or literal "*talking about* things or about the world,"[31] there is nonetheless an implicitly understood "natural language" through which the body is able to act as an "organ of mimicry."[32] This "mimicry" of the sensible is expressive, however, in that it takes up the sensible in worldly terms; that is, as the sensible *world*, in virtue of the body's own *Umweltintentionalität.*[33] It is as a *mimetically expressive* encounter with the sensible that perception lies at the origin of truth, that it is the birthplace, so to speak, of "a truth of the world."[34] The relation between the sensed and the perceived is ambiguous in this expressive mimicry, but it is a "good" ambiguity rather than a "bad" one because, as a form of expressivity, perception involves a "reversal" that meets the upsurge of the sensible and ensures its unity with the perceived on an equiprimordial basis.[35] This reversal is not yet the "retrograde movement of the true," which, adapting it from Bergson, Merleau-Ponty associated with higher levels of expression.[36] But it is the anticipation of this movement, and as such it is the dialectical element that was insufficiently elaborated in the account of the sensible laid out in *Phenomenology of Perception*.

This already says a lot, and in many ways this initial presentation of the notion of expression—and of "natural expression" in particular—prefigured the outcome of some of the more detailed discussions yet to come in later lectures. But to judge from his notes, Merleau-Ponty devoted much more time within his three introductory lectures to working out and presenting the implications that this rethinking of perception would have with regard to perceptual consciousness, and by extension to consciousness in general. The main thrust here is to sketch out a radically different understanding of consciousness from the idealist view of it as constituting its objects as discursive significations or values, and as possessing them in an absolutely clear and immediate presence that is at the same time, owing to the complete asymmetry of the relation, an absolute distance. In contrast to this, Merleau-Ponty portrayed perceptual consciousness as embedded or situated in the thick of the world, and thus as a perspectival opening to concretely existing beings. The proximity of the latter is not a matter of an ideal presence before consciousness but rather of their encroachment (*empiètement*) on perceptual consciousness, the fact that they affect me from within, while their distance stems from the fact that in encroaching on me, they do so from without; that is, they remain beyond and thus always exceed me in this way.

The reversal involved in the mimetic expressivity of perception has to do especially with this distance of the sensible. As Merleau-Ponty describes it here with the language of *écart*, which he was using for the first time, there is a certain normativity inherent in perception, in that what is given in perceptual consciousness are (only) "divergences" from implicit or nonthematic "levels"; that is, differences or deviations from typical norms that are located in the contextual background of perception, where most of the time they pass unnoticed and are simply taken for granted.[37] It is primarily in making this *diacritical* reference back to "levels" that perception is expressive. For these levels are, as Merleau-Ponty put it more than once in his notes, sites of *imperception*.[38] They may be integral to perception and to perceptual sense, but they are never *given* in perception. Here we might note that Merleau-Ponty fully subscribed to the basic Gestalt-theoretic account of perception, taking as axiomatic that it involves the experience of a figure on a background, in which the sense of the former is never apprehended in isolation but is rather conditioned by the latter, which thus forms an integral part of perception.[39] But inspired by the likes of Freud and Marx, who recognized that, because of psychological and ideological factors of repression and projection, conscious experience is much less straightforward than is generally assumed, Merleau-Ponty saw fit to describe perceptual consciousness as "inverted"—or even "mystified"—because it "does not make its background explicit."[40] Merleau-Ponty was more precise when, along these same lines, he characterized consciousness as "cross-eyed"—it has one eye, so to speak, on the figure and the other on the background, but it is essentially unable to focus on both at once—implying that, in a certain strict sense, perception occurs rarely, if at all.[41] Merleau-Ponty may have been suggesting this when he claimed—surprisingly, perhaps, but quite matter-of-factly—that his earlier (otherwise flawed) phenomenological approach to perception did at least show "that there are very few perceptions, and that most of the time perceptual life is movement slipping from one to another."[42] As he provocatively suggested in a working note, "consciousness is, if you like, synonymous with imperception."[43] There is a lacuna introduced into the picture of perception when the naively assumed determinacy of the background drops out, and filling in this lacuna will be the main philosophical job of perceptual expressivity.

It is also in terms of this expressivity that Merleau-Ponty will be able to settle accounts with Gestalt theory. Although at the descriptive level Merleau-Ponty fully embraced Gestalt theory's structural view of perceptual experience in terms of figure and background, he had long held that as inductive empirical science, Gestalt theory had failed to adequately pursue (let alone answer) the philosophical questions that this description raised. In his view, Gestalt theory had sought to explain phenomenal variations on the basis of objective causal processes and structural laws supposedly discovered in artificial experimental settings—Merleau-Ponty probably had this in mind (and Wertheimer's phi phenomenon in particular) when, taking a jab at Gestalt theory, he characterized it as reducing the phenomena of movement, for example, to cases of the kind of "flickering" observed in stroboscopy.[44] His point was that on account of its realist assumptions, Gestalt theory had a tendency to draw conclusions about perception that controverted its phenomenality. So while according to Merleau-Ponty there may be, strictly speaking, "very few perceptions," it is also the case that "there are far fewer illusions than Gestalt [theory] would have us believe."[45] It is by rethinking perception in terms of expression—or more specifically of *expressive imperception*—that he wanted to navigate an empirically and phenomenologically sound middle way between the naive poles of realism and idealism.

Merleau-Ponty had long felt the need to redress the philosophical shortcomings of Gestalt theory by rejecting the realism and the corresponding conception of consciousness that it uncritically presupposed. But the operative split between nature and culture in his earlier thinking had prevented him from pushing through consistently toward the radical conceptual overhaul of consciousness that he undertakes here in "The Sensible World and the World of Expression." Freed from that constraint, he had come to recognize that the proper philosophical task was to unpack the context of perceptual experience genetically—that is, in terms of the mutual responsiveness of subject and world—and to do so in terms of the body's mimetic expressivity understood as a form of praxis. *This turn to bodily praxis in perception marks Merleau-Ponty's decisive break with Gestalt-theoretic realism.* But in making it, he does veer closer, perhaps uncomfortably so, to transcendental idealism. Philosophical proximity to the latter is, of course, a familiar worry for Merleau-Ponty, one that he already tarried over at length in *The Structure of Behavior.*[46] But even in 1952, he still reiterated the main claim underlying that discussion—namely, that such idealism is less false than merely superficial.[47] For in concrete terms, there *is* something like a *Sinngebung* in perception, even if it is a mimetic one that somehow "predates itself in the [sensible] manifold."[48] It does not stem from the constitutive activity of consciousness, however, but rather from the praxical activity of the body when, in returning to the world through the reversal that it enacts, it establishes or projects "existential signification."[49] As Merleau-Ponty put it, mimetic expression "has to do with a perception that is more and more 'intelligent,' less and less 'sensory' . . . In short, it has to do with a praxia."[50] And as involving a kind of "projective preadaptation" to the sensibly given, Merleau-Ponty recognized that this is what his previous approach to perception had discounted. "It's of all this work of praxis, *far more extensive than I had thought,* that we must develop an understanding."[51] And inasmuch as this understanding of the praxis of perception would bear upon questions concerning the *subject* of perception, pursuing it would be a (if not *the*) fundamental part of working out the "philosophical foundations" of Merleau-Ponty's phenomenological project. And with the exception of the final lecture, this is basically what occupied him for the remainder of the course.

Merleau-Ponty's Plan for the Course

Merleau-Ponty had originally intended to devote his final two lectures to matters of higher-level cultural expression (language, history, truth, etc.), and these were to serve as a transition to the follow-up courses he anticipated. And these final two were to be preceded by four lectures concerning nonlinguistic expression in painting and cinema. This would have left a core of five lectures devoted to working out a praxical understanding of perceptual expression in more general terms, which was to be done on the basis of the experience of space and, especially, of movement. As noted above, however, the course did not unfold as envisioned in that original plan. At least to judge by his notes, all of those final six lectures were squeezed into the very last *one*, and the number of lectures devoted to the core discussion more or less doubled (to ten). While at least one possible reason for this may be gleaned from Merleau-Ponty's notes (which will be noted presently), there may well be other factors about which, at least for the time being, we cannot even speculate.

The ten lectures that followed the three introductory ones reflected, albeit informally, the structure of *Phenomenology of Perception*, in the sense that they first laid out phenomenological description and analysis of perception and then turned to consider the subjectivity that is thereby implied. But with perception now being understood in expressive terms, the difference is that the first part now already involves the kind of self-referential concern with expression that characterized Merleau-Ponty's earlier phenomenology of phenomenology, with the result that the second part turns more directly to an account of perceptual expressivity in practical—or, better, praxical—terms. It is as if the line within *Phenomenology of Perception* between the phenomenology of perception proper and the phenomenology *of* the phenomenology of perception lay not at the beginning of part 3 but rather at its end, at the very culmination of the book; namely, the deference to "heroic" action and the enigmatic insinuation that *that* is what actually accomplishes philosophy,[52] and as if Merleau-Ponty were now finally undertaking to clarify just what exactly that would mean.

In this course, the concern with praxical subjectivity was cashed out in terms of the body schema. The latter was certainly not a new idea for Merleau-Ponty, but it was one whose sense had changed significantly along with that of perception, inasmuch as its role therein is now understood in a much more active (or *en*active)—because expressive—way. It is noteworthy, however, that in his original plan for the course, Merleau-Ponty did not allot any time at all for an explicit discussion of the body schema. This is almost certainly one of the main reasons, if not *the* main reason, for the unexpected way that the course unfolded. It is not clear why this is so, nor why he decided midcourse to include it as the basis for his account of the praxis of perceptual expression. To be sure, it makes excellent philosophical sense. But it would seem to be the case that going into the course Merleau-Ponty saw no need for it—there is no mention at all of the body schema in the detailed notes for the general overview provided by the first three lectures, even while these notes do broach all the *further* issues of linguistic and higher-order cultural expression. It may be the case that while in the process of elaborating his new expressive understanding of perception he came to see—possibly prompted by questions from his auditors—that this understanding, shorn as it was of any "natural" basis, would be on thin ice without addressing the corporeal basis of the expressive function, and that without doing that first he could not properly advance to the further discussions that he had planned. In any case, it is worth noting that the official course summary deftly conceals through a retrospective illusion this aspect of how the course took shape.[53]

Space and Movement

Merleau-Ponty's treatment of perceptual expression in terms of space and movement occupies about half the entire course (approximately seven lectures), and it is arguably here that what is most fundamental and innovative in his new thinking is worked out. This applies especially to what he says about the perception of movement as expressive (which takes up about five of the seven lectures). For what he says concerning space is explicitly intended to play a merely propaedeutic role with regard to his treatment of movement, specifically by clearing away "objective" preconceptions concerning the notion of "place" that, by reinforcing the mistaken view of movement as passage from one preexisting place to another, would set up obstacles to the proper phenomenological intuition of movement. Merleau-Ponty says many interesting and important things about the perception of space in this course, and it is worth considering it fairly closely here, but the role of this discussion is secondary by design, and this should be kept in mind.

Concerning space, Merleau-Ponty was interested in reaffirming the sort of "primordial spatiality" at the level of perception that he had brought to light in *Phenomenology of Perception* as having priority over objective space. More important, he wanted to go further to show that the dimensionality of that perceived spatiality is an expressive achievement of bodily praxis. As in his earlier work, Merleau-Ponty focused chiefly on spatial orientation and (visual) depth perception. But whereas there he had implicitly prioritized the lived spatiality of the body (or "bodily space") over the spatiality of the perceived world, and was thus left, concerning space, with a "bad" ambiguity, here he lays out a specifically *situational* understanding of "place" as stemming from the body's expressive projection of "virtual space" as a "system of correspondences between properties of my actual field and what these properties would be for me situated elsewhere or for another."[54] And this expressive projection is to be understood in terms of what Merleau-Ponty is so fond of describing as a dialectical "gearing together" [*engrenage*] of the body and its milieu. Thus, in revisiting the renormalization of spatial orientation as described in George Stratton's well-known experiments involving uninversion goggles, as well as in Max Wertheimer's tilted-room experiments, both of which he had previously discussed critically in *Phenomenology of Perception*, Merleau-Ponty affirmed that neither the sensible landscape nor the body itself is intrinsically oriented, and he sought to clarify how spatial orientation emerges precisely from their mutual *engrenage*.

What is crucial about his discussion of perceptual renormalization—which is, of course, meant to have implications for the genesis of perceptual normativity in general—is that it draws particular attention to its *elective* aspect. Perceptual renormalization occurs, he claims, through the reestablishment of background "levels," and this occurs when given perceptual elements are *taken as* levels—space is thus set up through "the *choice* of reference points."[55] But rather than as any sort of intellectual or otherwise reflective operation, this "choice" is described by Merleau-Ponty in terms of a bodily praxis of inhabiting. "What brings it about that there is an up and a down, a here and a place, are not objective points but a certain hold of my body on the world, a confidence and ease of my body in the world, the fact that I inhabit it."[56] In this way, the correspondences or equivalences of my virtual space "only appear through [my] *choice* of abode."[57]

The sense of "choice" here is not to be misunderstood. Merleau-Ponty invokes that term as a way to denote the fact that situations are, objectively speaking, indeterminate, and that their acquiring a determinate form in experience ultimately involves a moment of contingent activity on the part of the experiencing subject. Here Merleau-Ponty is specifically concerned with perception, and the activity in question concerns perceptual synthesis, the determination of the overall "configuration" of the perceptual landscape. Given sensible elements do not of themselves form a determinate configuration, because their registering as either figure or background is not a property intrinsic to them. Rather than to their givenness, then, that property pertains to their *takenness*, so to speak—that is, to their *Auffassung*, or more specifically to the *Situationserfassung*, how the situation is grasped, construed, or apprehended by the perceiving subject. For Merleau-Ponty, perceptual synthesis is a kind of lateral "existential" (rather than top-down "intellectual") synthesis, which, although occurring prereflectively, nonetheless appears to involve a degree of creativity or inventiveness. But the "choice" effected by the subject is never arbitrary—it is strongly motivated and conditioned by given circumstances in which, paradoxically, it "predates" itself. Perceptual synthesis thus involves a dialectical "feedback" or "exchange" between self and world—between "subjective" desire and "objective" circumstance—which, still in a broadly Gestalt-theoretic sense, is geared toward "optimal functioning"; that is, toward the "privileged state" of an existentially optimal relation between self and world.[58] It is this mutual responsiveness of "chance" and "choice" in the establishment of background norms or "levels" that provides the "situational" sense of place concomitant to the "bodily inhabitation" of a perceptual landscape, and elucidating this dialectic is the goal of the "genetic" analysis that Merleau-Ponty is interested in here.

In this regard, Merleau-Ponty made several notable allusions to Paul Valéry's analysis of attention.[59] But here again we might also think of Goldstein. For this optimal relation is achieved through something fundamentally akin to Goldstein's notion of the organism's *Auseinandersetzung*—its back-and-forth "debate" or, as it has been conventionally translated, "coming to terms"—with the world. Indeed, at one point Merleau-Ponty describes the optimum as emerging from a "*struggle* of factors of *Auffassung* against objective figural conditions."[60] Such is how the perceiving subject intervenes creatively in the process of perceptual synthesis. There need not be (and typically there is not) any particularly pronounced tension or discrepancy (as in the Stratton and Wertheimer experiments). But Merleau-Ponty's point is that the "choice" of background is in general part of a dialectical "exchange" between the means and the end of perceptual synthesis, in which an imminently felt sense is brought to a more determinate form through a kind of *Sinngebung*. Now, it may be that this *Sinngebung* can be regarded as "the work of the elements themselves."[61] But *how* given elements variously function as means of perceptual synthesis can be understood only with reference to its end, and this is tied in an at least a quasi-teleological way to the existential optimum of the perceiving subject. The genetic context of perceived space is thus inescapably as much about its whither as its whence. As in the genesis of depth perception, in which vision, faced with disparate images, is "polarized toward the future,"[62] there is in spatial perception in general *a temporal encroachment of the synthesis to come,* the presence of a futural imminence that implies a kind of generativity.

It is along the lines of this generative dialectic of perceptual expression that Merleau-Ponty laid out his situational understanding of place. "Place is [a] relation of self and the world through my body, not [a] relation between parts of the world. Place is first of all <u>situation</u>."[63] Thus characterized by spatial and temporal encroachment, this sense of place enables Merleau-Ponty to transition smoothly to a consideration of perceived movement, where the expressive generativity in question is more readily seen. For as he put it, "if place is [a] particular tension in the dynamic [of] self [and] world, [then] *it's already movement*."[64] That is, in the same way that space does not exist in itself, but is rather a matter of situational place that stands as an expressive achievement of the perceiving subject, likewise movement is nothing more (nor less) than a phenomenal encounter in which the perceiving subject is similarly (i.e., expressively) implicated through its "choice" of background levels or anchors. Far from movement being premised upon space as a necessary precondition (i.e., as that *in which* it occurs), Merleau-Ponty proposes that movement is an equiprimordial *modality* of the (primordial) spatiality of bodily inhabitation.[65] In this view, perceived movement is the expressive unfolding or becoming of the spatial landscape, and as a function of the overall configuration of the latter it will, rather than indicating an isolated feature of a thing, disclose generatively its situated being.

Merleau-Ponty developed this view of movement across five lectures, and his discussion is effectively driven by the problem of the identity of a moving thing. Rehearsing ideas from Zeno, Merleau-Ponty first shows how any attempt to address this problem in objective terms is met with results that paradoxically sever the movement from the thing. Taking the cue from his discussion of space, Merleau-Ponty sees that the way forward requires approaching movement in rigorously phenomenal terms that (as such) admit encroachment, and in this way he is sympathetic to Bergson's attempt to resolve Zeno's paradoxes by deriving the integrity of phenomenal movement from one's own duration. But according to Merleau-Ponty, in doing so Bergson was implicitly setting up the perceiving body as the site of mediation, yet without developing an explicit account of it, and particularly of how it effects encroachment, with the result that his response to Zeno remained an instance of idealism.

For Merleau-Ponty, taking a more rigorous phenomenological approach meant taking up the descriptions—but nothing more than that—afforded by Gestalt-psychological research. Here the main point is that perceived movement is a "figural moment" in the sense that it appears the way it does only against a certain background or within a certain configuration, variations of which, even when all given elements remain unchanged, can significantly alter (or even eliminate) the perceived movement. Two points follow from this "field" character of perceived movement. On the one hand, it means that perceived movement is not based upon the perception of a thing as occupying a sequence of intermediate positions—indeed, it precisely precludes that.[66] And this is the case even though, on the other hand, objectively considered—that is, considering the visual perception of movement in terms of retinal stimulation—all perceived movement is stroboscopic; even in cases of "real" movement the identity of a moving thing is never objectively given.[67] This is why, for example, Merleau-Ponty challenges Wertheimer's claims about "pure movement" (i.e., the phi phenomenon). For not only does it seem nonsensical, like the flip side of Zeno, to speak about movement without an object, but also and more to the point, such cases do not differ essentially from the perception of "real" movement anyway, since even there no bona fide (identical) object is present, and so it too could just as well be regarded as illusory. Better, according to Merleau-Ponty, to drop any talk of illusion and instead take all cases of perceived movement as expressive phenomena that can potentially serve to disclose, in terms of configuration and background, the otherwise nongiven identity or *being* of the "moving thing." Given the relative ease with which attempts to formulate an "objective" account of perceived movement devolve into paradox, such is how Merleau-Ponty sought to use the expressivity of perceived movement as a way to recover the dialectical relation between self and world that was effectively missing from his earlier phenomenological approach to the sensible world.

Merleau-Ponty pursued this through analyses of various experimental observations and results that he took up as showing how perceived movement can be understood only as a function of the structural configuration of the perceptual field as a whole. He seems to have been particularly intrigued by the then-recent work of Albert Michotte on the perceptual experience of causality, and particularly by cases of auto-locomotion in which perceived movement, by giving expression to a nongiven interiority, was even more clearly a matter of ontological disclosure than simply of locational change.[68] But even here it is never a matter simply of given figural conditions. Partly echoing Johannes Linschoten's critique of certain laboratory results as being skewed by the artificiality of their experimental setup, Merleau-Ponty insisted on the ineliminable role of the perceiving subject's *Situationserfassung* and the irreducibly subjective personal and historical factors that that invokes. The perception of movement thus does indeed involve a *Sinngebung*. But rather than an intellectual one on the part of the "I think," it issues from the perceiving subject as an "incarnate total being."[69] Inasmuch as the subjective factors pertaining to the perceiving subject so construed are themselves embedded in the perceptual landscape, the (nonrepresentational) meaning bestowed by this subject effectively serves to consummate the "self-organization of the field."[70] Observations concerning the latter represented the valuable contribution that Merleau-Ponty wished to retain from Gestalt psychology. For they show, for example, that configuration can never simply be a matter of association with past experience, since that past experience itself was possible only on the basis of the configuration. But the same observations also convinced Merleau-Ponty that configuration could not be taken, as Gestalt thinkers tended to take it, in objectively causal terms, and so the active moment of embodied perceptual praxis is the key step that Merleau-Ponty takes beyond that theoretical framework—resulting in a view that today we might describe as a kind of embedded enactivism.

As with spatiality, then, the perception of movement involves a supple and virtually inarticulable exchange between given "figural moments" and a perceptual *Sinngebung*. There is no relation of causality between them, and neither has priority over the other. For Merleau-Ponty, what occurs in the perception of movement could be described as the reciprocally motivated expressive passage from sense to meaning that forms the crux of a "good" perceptual ambiguity: "Figural moments operate inasmuch as they satisfy an apprehension of meaning, and [meaning] only appears as embodied in [the] figure."[71] This dialectical balancing act between passive "chance" and active "choice" stands at the heart of perceptual expression. "Taken up in a *Situationserfassung* that is motivated by it and which motivates how it looks, the 'objective' constellation becomes incarnate in it. No causality, [but rather] motivation, i.e., meaning preserves and goes beyond the objective conditions, [it] recognizes them as coming from it, but [it] only appears as their completion."[72]

But while this is by its nature difficult to articulate, the upshot, which Merleau-Ponty adapts from Linschoten, is as clear as it is remarkable: "The apprehension of meaning and the apprehension of movement are the same thing."[73] To perceive movement is to actively gear into a certain situational configuration of the total landscape and bear witness to its unfolding—it is not fundamentally about displacement; that is, this or that thing changing its location, but rather the expressive disclosure of nongiven being, and it is in virtue of the holistic logic of this expressivity that the perception of movement coincides with the experience of existential significance. "Movement and meaning [are] inseparable [and] synonymous,"[74] and therein lies "the miracle of perception," as Merleau-Ponty put it, its expressive schematizing of sensibility and its bridging with signification that ultimately underwrites any real purchase that discursive truth might have: "It makes us see the meaning of the spectacle rather than seeing according to a meaning [that is] posed arbitrarily."[75] Merleau-Ponty thus drew a structural analogy between the perception of movement as a "*tracing*" and *reading* as an event of diacritical praxis.[76] In the same (or at least a very similar) way that the reading of a sentence—as a series of linguistic signs in which "there is [a] *Deckung* [coincidence or overlapping] of the intentions carried by the beginning and by the end, and possibly retroactive correction"[77]—implicitly refers through semantic differences to the linguistic field as a whole in disclosing expressively the meaning that guided it, so too the perception of movement as ontologically disclosive refers through imperceptible divergences to the landscape as a whole and is thus an "event . . . of everything" with "an evental unity that extends across time."[78] Achieved through the praxis of perceptual tracing, it is within this evental unity, marked by existential self-world as well as temporal encroachment, that the dialectical exchange at the root of expression is ironed out, so to speak, and a "good" ambiguity is realized.

But who is the subject of this praxis? As with spatial perception more generally, which he tied to bodily inhabitation, Merleau-Ponty is clear that all of this is mediated through the body. But not, of course, in any strictly biological sense. Rather, Merleau-Ponty takes up the notion of body schema as the locus of the "bodily magic" of motricity that stands behind the body's "power to trace," its "power of inventiveness" that supports perceptual expression.[79] Drawing inspiration from Valéry, Merleau-Ponty likened the latter to an *awakening* in which "the mind becomes body and the body becomes mind,"[80] and this sense of a "natural thinking,"[81] a "perceptual thinking,"[82] or of "a perception that is more and more 'intelligent,' less and less 'sensory,'"[83] is central to the prediscursive schematizing role that the body plays in perceptual expression.

The Body Schema

At this point in the course, Merleau-Ponty had delivered ten lectures and had fallen significantly behind with regard to his initial plan. And as noted above, it does not seem that he had originally intended to devote several lecture sessions to a discussion of the body schema. The idea may well have been implicitly present in his thinking, but it was not until the end of the eighth lecture that his notes betray any intention to deal with it explicitly.[84] This may be related to a certain dissatisfaction that he seems to have felt with regard to his discussions concerning movement up to this point. The Gestalt-theoretic observations that he was working with were, as is entirely typical for experimental psychology, abstract and artificial. But this meant that the cases of movement that he had considered were really just cases of what he came to call *premovement*,[85] in the sense that they were limited to the visual field and did not engage the body as a whole concretely. They thus turned out to be an inadequate basis on which to deal with the aspects of encroachment that he took to be bound up with expression. Owing to its relative simplicity, this may have been a beneficial way to begin. But it would seem that Merleau-Ponty came to think that it did not on its own support a compelling account of perceptual tracing as a bodily praxis. He briefly considered other sources—scientific as well as artistic—that foregrounded intersensory equivalences and actual movement in perception. It would seem that the point of using these sources was to highlight the abstractness of the Gestalt-theoretic results. In any case, they served to bolster the motivation to consider the body schema directly. In effect, then, at this point in the course Merleau-Ponty returns to his critique of Bergson in order to lay out the "the theory of the perceiving body" that Bergson had neglected to develop. As a "'machine for living' the world"—as Merleau-Ponty, adapting a Valéryan motif, intriguingly put it—the body must engage in "real" movement, but in such a way that it is projected from within with an undivided evental unity.[86] If it can substantiate this by showing that one's own movement is itself an original kind of expressive praxis that prefigures the temporal encroachment of perceptual tracing, then an account of the body schema would make a stronger case for the claim that perceptual background levels are established through motor projection, and hence that the expressive perception of movement occurs through praxical possibilities of the body.

Merleau-Ponty's consideration of the body schema is based to a very large extent on Paul Schilder's important work, which he was rereading, or else, quite possibly, reading closely and directly for the first time.[87] There are also many references to Henry Head, especially his "taximeter" analogy concerning the automatic intersensory translation between the visual and the tactile[88] (although like many others, these references are nearly always secondhand via Schilder), along with numerous other sources that provide corroborative pathological contrast cases, including, at least in passing at several points, Gelb and Goldstein's case of Schn. In considering these cases, it is of the utmost importance to bear in mind that Merleau-Ponty continued to adhere to Goldstein's fundamental methodological postulate according to which sound conclusions bearing upon "normal" existence can be drawn on the basis of pathological cases only on condition that the latter are taken as definite intelligible modifications of "normal" existence, in such a way that the pathological phenomena considered appear as "expressions of a change in the total personality of the patient."[89] More than anything else, it is this uncompromising epistemic commitment to viewing embodied existence holistically as a psychosomatic totality that enabled Merleau-Ponty to sketch out an *expressive* account of the body schema—or better, of the body *as a schema*—that ultimately went beyond Schilder's own views,[90] even though it borrowed significantly from them (including with regard to libidinal and interpersonal aspects) and relied on Schilder's book for most of its empirical sources.

Owing perhaps to the seemingly unexpected way that the theme of the body schema entered his lectures, Merleau-Ponty's notes on it are somewhat rougher and less detailed than his notes on other topics, and so his actual lectures here presumably rested to a greater degree on extemporal elaboration. But still, his main claims can be at least partly reconstructed. The body *is* a schema inasmuch as it is a totality that, as an absolute spatial "zero point," inhabits external space and forms a system with it, while also involving, internally, a (taximeter-like) system of immediate intersensory equivalences. It is a schema, in other words, as the locus of perceived movement. Standing as the concrete point of mediation between movement and perception, the body qua schema is what undercuts any dualistic distinction between object and subject, between body and mind. Merleau-Ponty thus likened it to "a 'natural' idea," "a thinking given to itself," "an implicit intellection," "a knowledge that we have [solely] because we are."[91] The protointellectual content of the body schema has to do with existential normativity, which it realizes through the establishment of "levels" in the perceptual landscape—a distinctly "anthropological" form of projection on account of which the structure of the perceived world is rooted in the body schema as a motor power.[92] This may be the clearest way to grasp the body schema as our "machine for living"; to wit, as that through which, as discussed earlier, perceived space takes shape. But it is not just about space. Indeed, time is perhaps the more fundamental dimension here. "My body is not only a device for producing anchorages in space. It is also [a] device for producing anchorages in time."[93] Merleau-Ponty is particularly interested in "my body not only as [an] actual body but as [a] possible body, as [a] 'machine for living,' as [a] machine for making time."[94] This seems to be what is most crucial. There is a normatively oriented imminence, or futural temporal encroachment, operative in the body schema: as a motor power, it is "always oriented toward privileged positions [or] norms," such that—as evinced, for example, by Kohnstamm's phenomenon[95]—"the body schema and the body are situated not where they are objectively but *where we are preparing to put them*."[96]

It is on this basis that Merleau-Ponty presented the body schema as having the same open, centrifugal unity as praxis understood as a dialectically hybrid (practical-theoretical) notion of agency that, going beyond the mundane level of ordinary action, involves the "projection of the whole man" in reference to the horizonality of the world. Specifically, the body qua schema is the protointellectual background of praxis so construed.[97] Far from merely being a postural schema that involves an immediate bodily self-awareness, then, or even the sedimented record of past experience, for Merleau-Ponty here the body schema, as the locus of motor possibilities, is the dynamic organ of anthropological projection through which the sensible world is joined organically with the world of expression.

This function of anthropological projection is an expressive modification of the function of "projection" that had already played an important role in *Phenomenology of Perception*,[98] and it may be considered as being both more and less "projective" than that. More, in that the structure of the perceived world as a whole falls within its scope. But also less, in that as a feature of embodied praxis, it is dialectically embedded in the perceived world and, as with perceived movement, "predates" itself there. As with movement, in other words, this new projective function is characterized by a supple dialogue of *mutual anticipation*, and higher levels of expression are founded not so much on perception as the experience of an originary kind of *being* as on perception as an originary kind of *praxis*. Although elementary bodily movement differs from perception, and even more clearly from thought and language (although he does not discuss these latter in any detail here), Merleau-Ponty's claim is that they correspond to different "levels of motility" that are nonetheless dialectically related inasmuch as the "same basic function" of expressive projection is operative in all of them.[99] This is key to maintaining the unity of the body schema, and thus for overcoming—concretely and not just verbally—the tenacious vestiges of mind-body dualism.

Similarly to Merleau-Ponty's argumentation in *Phenomenology of Perception*, the strongest evidence for this view of the body schema comes from selected pathological cases. Merleau-Ponty wants to take the distinctive phenomenal features of such cases as expressing disarticulations of the body schema that lead to a diminishment of projective praxis, and hence disturbances with regard to its being "geared together" with the world, its schematic role of mediation, and in particular its being the locus of spatial and (especially) temporal encroachment. So whereas earlier he had based his approach around agnosia (no doubt following Goldstein's lead), inspired by Head and Schilder he now sees a generalized notion of apraxia as the paradigm pathology or disturbance. Although there was (and still is) a diverse clinical taxonomy, Merleau-Ponty tended to use the term broadly to refer to any situation in which, in the absence of an appropriate motor background, "intellectually defined tasks no longer call forth the praxical organization that would accomplish them."[100] This can manifest at the different levels—clinical apraxia (in its various specific senses), agnosia, and even aphasia—but each case can be taken as evincing a diminishment or breakdown of the projective function of expression, and in this way as substantiating the view of the body schema that Merleau-Ponty has sketched out in general (or "normal") terms.

Aphasia would be the real litmus test here, and there are numerous allusions to it in this regard. But as noted, Merleau-Ponty does not discuss issues of speech and linguistic expression in any detail in these lectures. So his analyses here are limited largely to showing how agnosia is grounded on apraxia. This grounding is borne out in relatively simple, temporary postural cases like the so-called Japanese illusion (or other similar experiments described by Schilder involving a disarticulation of visual and tactile experience), in which a form of finger agnosia arises when the immobility of the fingers positioned in the appropriate way renders the body schema "indistinct."[101] There is a "deintegration" of the hand from the body as a whole that is integrated within the world in praxical terms. Studies of this illusion also show, however, that the practical presence that is normally supplied automatically by the body schema can be at least partly reconstituted through other means, and that therefore the agnosia in question here (and this holds generally) is in no way *reducible* to the apraxia—it can (and does) occur otherwise and is thus relatively autonomous of it. In general, Merleau-Ponty is at pains to avoid any reductionist implications concerning the relation of agnosia (and aphasia) to apraxia. As with the case of Schn., then, he reads such substitute or compensatory performances (i.e., what Goldstein called *Ersatzleistungen*) as also being expressions of the "same originary power" of projective praxis.[102] Again, it must be kept in mind that for Merleau-Ponty, following Goldstein, pathological cases can shed light on normality only if, in fundamental holistic terms, they too are ultimately "normal" in the sense of establishing existential normativity in and through their *Auseinandersetzungen* with the world.

This is especially important in more interesting cases, such as Gerstmann's syndrome, a disorder stemming from a lesion in the left angular gyrus that results in finger agnosia combined with right-left confusion, acalculia, and agraphia. This constellation of symptoms, which was first identified in the 1920s—but which is not, it should be noted, universally accepted as a distinct pathological condition—provides a more complex view of the connection between agnosia and apraxia, in that it involves spatial, numerical, and even (in terms of agraphia) quasi-linguistic dimensions. But although the etiology obviously differs from cases like the Japanese illusion, the analysis is not essentially different. Indeed, given the loss of the practical presence of her body to herself, what a person with Gerstmann's syndrome shows even more clearly is that—and here Merleau-Ponty was citing Johannes Lange's work on finger agnosia—"the hand is dedifferentiated not as instrument but as object." In general, what is absent in finger agnosia "is the capacity to change the hand as instrument at any moment into an object *and by this means to transform it into a more complete instrument*."[103] Hence the further deficiencies. For Merleau-Ponty, then, the analysis of Gerstmann's syndrome reveals the hand as bearing "an indefinite number of symbolic systems; it is not defined by its factual, physical presence . . . but [rather] inasmuch as it incorporates such and such significations."[104] And what applies to the hand, applies to the body as a whole. The hand does not think, but it realizes thought in the world. "So we don't think with our hands, but we don't think without the transfigured body, [the] bearer of significations, that is the body schema."[105]

Merleau-Ponty's notes refer to many other details and describe other cases, but these selective glimpses give a good sense of how he wanted to show that human motility is an expressive power, that it is never entirely absent (except perhaps in dreamless *sleep* as a possible limit case of "total apraxia"), that embodied praxis admits of degrees corresponding to "degrees of articulation of the body schema" (or degrees of *wakefulness*),[106] that it operates at different levels, and that, most important, "higher forms of expression ([the] manipulation and recognition of symbols) *are still facts of praxis or of motility*."[107] Just as in human perception "the apprehension of meaning and the apprehension of movement are the same thing,"[108] likewise for the perceiving subject, "to be able to move in the human sense and to be conscious are the same thing."[109] The mobility of the body inaugurates a transformative dialectic that ascends, through gesture to language, from "natural" to cultural expression, such that it makes eminently good sense to say that "the joining of the sensible world and the world of expression comes about through movement."[110]

Visual Arts

Of course, Merleau-Ponty did not fully demonstrate that claim in these lectures. Although he came a long way in terms of casting light on the pivotal junction between given sense and lived meaning, his discussion here was nonetheless limited and thus, strictly speaking, inconclusive. And he was well aware of this. For it could be fully conclusive only if it took up issues concerning language and, ultimately, truth. But owing to time constraints, these had to wait. Although he gave some indications concerning the dialectical origin of language in the body schema, and "how the order of Λόγος can be understood only as [a] sublimation of corporeality,"[111] without a more complete examination of the "double movement" of expression[112]—of what Bergson had called the retrograde movement of the true, the fact that "the experience of the true cannot avoid projecting itself into the time that preceded it"[113]—the account of expression remains in suspense. For while this double movement of projection is implicitly more pronounced in linguistic expression, it also tends to be more concealed there, and so there is a strong temptation to infer the existence of an independent "logical necessity that would give life to it from within."[114] Pushing back on this view of linguistic expression as fully autonomous of embodied praxis is precisely what Merleau-Ponty wants to do, but he cannot do it here.[115] What he does do, though, is sketch out a helpful segue in terms of the visual arts of painting, sculpture, and cinema as forms of prelinguistic cultural expression.[116] The idea is that breaking up the transition from "natural" expression to linguistic cultural expression into two steps will better illuminate the dialectical links and avoid the error of treating linguistic phenomena as essentially disembodied. The discussion of the visual arts, in other words, is meant to serve as a wedge by which to establish the account of natural expression on the terrain of culture.

As noted above, Merleau-Ponty had originally intended to devote four lecture sessions to the visual arts, but as things turned out he got to it only in the final (fourteenth) lecture. Little wonder, then, that his notes for this lecture as we have them are relatively long. He had a fair bit of material, and much of it is quite interesting. But given the role of these discussions as an argumentative wedge, there is nothing fundamentally new here. Rather, it is mainly a matter of marshaling some corroborating evidence and other considerations that help to show that his account of natural expression holds for what are distinctly and indisputably cultural artifacts.

With painting and sculpture, the main issue is how something that is stationary can express movement. The idea is that this is not a question of inference or cognitive judgment but of the projective perceptual reading that occurs through the body schema. The artwork is not *indicative* but rather "emblematic" of movement when, owing to its configuration, it produces a "transformation" in embodied perception. Rodin's discussion of sculpture is key here in confirming for Merleau-Ponty that movement is not primarily a matter of objective displacement but of lived meaning. Indeed, as an artist, Rodin seems to have had an intuitively eloquent grasp on what some Gestalt psychologists studied in artificial experimental settings and reported on in long, dry scientific articles. Merleau-Ponty combined Rodin's views with art-historical considerations from Bernard Berenson and (especially) Heinrich Wölfflin's conception of "painterly representation" in early modern art. The upshot here is a confirmation of the expressive view of perception that Merleau-Ponty had laid out, in which movement is presented indirectly or diacritically "through divergences with respect to a norm that is itself never given." The expressivity of painting and sculpture thus lies in its presenting the world "*through variations in modulations of our being toward the world.*"[117]

Finally, Merleau-Ponty turned to cinema. Earlier lectures contained some specific discussions of tempo in cinema,[118] but here at the end Merleau-Ponty addresses what is at issue more generally. Whereas painting and sculpture were (merely) about the expression of movement, the development of cinema illustrates the dialectic of expression inasmuch as here movement comes to be taken as a universal *mode* of expression. Movement is no longer simply *what* is expressed, but it is used as the means for expressing "*invisible* cultural things." It is still a matter here of an embodied perceptual encounter, and this is still a diacritical response to a sensible configuration. But owing to evolving techniques, movement in cinema effects perspectival changes that vary our relation to the world as a whole. In comparison with painting or sculpture, then, there is in cinema a higher or "universal" degree of expressivity: "We articulate *the visible* according to significations that transcend it,—but which were already at work within it."[119] It is this dynamic play of cinematic emblems that prefigures in a particularly clear way the logic of linguistic expression.

Concluding *Avertissement*

There is an obvious parallel that might be drawn between the title of this course, "The Sensible World and the World of Expression," and that of Merleau-Ponty's last published article, "Eye and Mind," or his final, posthumously published work, *The Visible and the Invisible.* And there is surely some substantive basis to this, which, with the publication of these notes, could now be explored in some detail. But even though this course occupies a special position in the development of Merleau-Ponty's thought, these notes reflect a thinking that is very much a work in progress. We should therefore be cautious about reading and interpreting them in the retrospective light of what we think we know about Merleau-Ponty's final work, or in isolation from his other courses at the Collège de France. Indeed, we should be cautious about drawing any firm conclusions from them at all. As Merleau-Ponty wrote in concluding the official course summary, and as alluded to above, he will be in a position "to determine definitively the philosophical meaning of the above analyses" *only after examining linguistic expression.* That is, only then would he "be able to decide whether the dialectic of expression implies that a mind is already present in nature, or that nature is immanent to our mind, *or [else] to search instead for a third philosophy beyond this dilemma.*"[120] Now, it is definitely this latter tack—which resonates with his recurrent metaphor of *awakening* as heightened existential integration that issues in expressive speech[121]—that Merleau-Ponty pursued and that ultimately led to his later work. But although it is clearly germinal, we cannot ascertain directly from these pages alone whether the radical rethinking of phenomenology as a philosophy of expression—and in this specific sense, as a phenomenology of imperception—that we see sketched out here is in fact an integral part of how Merleau-Ponty sought to overcome that dilemma. From history and institution to dialectic and nature, there is, even beyond language, much more that must be taken into account. So just as our understanding of Merleau-Ponty's final work is due for potential revision in the light of newly published (and as yet still unpublished) materials, the broader significance of these lectures likewise remains to be worked out.

Notes

1. Although initially a long-shot candidate, Merleau-Ponty was elected to the chair (left vacant by the death of Louis Lavelle in September 1951) in February 1952, and he officially assumed the position at the beginning of April, following a brief but unusually controversial bureaucratic confirmation in March (concerning the details of Merleau-Ponty's election, see Stephen Noble, "Maurice Merleau-Ponty, or the Pathway of Philosophy: Desiderata for an Intellectual Biography," *Chiasmi International* 13 (2011): 86–88). Merleau-Ponty delivered his inaugural lecture—later given the now-familiar title "Éloge de la philosophie"—on Thursday, January 15, 1953, and began his lecture courses the following week. He typically gave two courses per year at the Collège, each meeting weekly for fourteen or fifteen weeks, one on Mondays and the other on Thursdays. For 1952–53, the Monday course was "Recherches sur l'usage littéraire du langage," Merleau-Ponty's notes for which have been published as *Recherches sur l'usage littéraire du langage: Cours au Collège de France, Notes, 1953*, ed. Benedetta Zaccarello and Emmanuel de Saint Aubert (Geneva: MétisPresses, 2013). An English translation of this volume (*Investigations into the Literary Use of Language: Course Notes from the Collège de France, 1953*) is in development and will be published by Northwestern University Press.

2. See *Résumés de cours: Collège de France, 1952–1960* (Paris: Gallimard, 1968), 11–21 (*Themes from the Lectures at the Collège de France, 1952–1960*, trans. John O'Neill [Evanston, Ill.: Northwestern University Press, 1970], 3–11); hereafter abbreviated as *Résumés*, with French/English pagination. The reader may profitably consult this summary in conjunction with Merleau-Ponty's lecture notes here. But it should be borne in mind that the summary presents a somewhat cleaned-up view of the course from the perspective of Merleau-Ponty's original intentions, and that references there tend to be made in a rapid passing or even

merely allusive fashion. Also, the O'Neill translation contains some errors and infelicities. In particular, there is a significant omission of a series of words at the very end that results in a grammatically correct but confused and very misleading sentence. Merleau-Ponty wrote, "On pourra alors décider si la dialectique de <u>l'expression signifie qu'un esprit est déjà présent dans la nature ou que</u> la nature est immanente à notre esprit, ou plutôt chercher une troisième philosophie au-delà de ce dilemme" (underlining added). By omitting the underlined series of words, the O'Neill translation has, "We shall then be able to decide whether the dialectic of nature is immanent in our spirit, or whether we should seek a third philosophy beyond this dilemma," whereas it should read, "We shall then be able to decide whether the dialectic of expression implies that a mind is already present in nature, or that nature is immanent to our mind, or [else] to search instead for a third philosophy beyond this dilemma."

3. As contained in (i) the 1951 document titled "Titres et travaux: Projet d'enseignement," reprinted in *Parcours deux, 1951–1961,* ed. Jacques Prunair (Lagrasse, Fr.: Verdier, 2000), 9–35; and (ii) in the letter that Merleau-Ponty sent to Martial Guéroult, later published as "Un inédit de Maurice Merleau-Ponty," *Revue de métaphysique et de morale* 67, no. 4 (1962): 401–9; reprinted in *Parcours deux,* 36–48 ("An Unpublished Text by Maurice Merleau-Ponty: A Prospectus of His Work," trans. Arlene B. Dallery, in *The Primacy of Perception: And Other Essays on Phenomenological Psychology, the Philosophy of Art, History, and Politics,* ed. James M. Edie [Evanston, Ill.: Northwestern University Press, 1964], 3–11). Hereafter these texts are abbreviated as TT and *Inédit,* respectively, with English pagination following French where applicable.

4. TT 27–35; cf. *Inédit* 41–42/6–7.

5. "Le primat de la perception et ses conséquences philosophiques," in *Le primat de la perception et ses conséquences philosophiques, précédé de Projet de travail sur la nature de la perception, 1933, La Nature de la perception, 1934,* ed. Jacques Prunair (Lagrasse, Fr.: Verdier, 1996), 68 ("The Primacy of Perception, and Its Philosophical Consequences," trans. James M. Edie, in Edie, *The Primacy of Perception,* 25); hereafter abbreviated as PrP, with French/English pagination.

6. PrP 85/33.

7. *Inédit* 41/6.

8. *Inédit* 42/7.

9. See *Phénoménologie de la perception* (Paris: Gallimard, 1945), xvi (*Phenomenology of Perception,* trans. Donald A. Landes [London: Routledge, 2012], xxi). Hereafter abbreviated as PhP, with French/ English pagination.

10. Kurt Goldstein, *The Organism: A Holistic Approach to Biology Derived from Pathological Data in Man* (1934; repr., New York: Zone Books, 1995), 306–8; Kurt Goldstein, "Remarques sur le problème épistémologique de la biologie," in *Selected Papers/Ausgewählte Schriften,* ed. Aron Gurwitsch, Else M. Goldstein Haudek, and William E. Haudek, 439–42 (The Hague: Martinus Nijhoff, 1971), 441. I discuss Merleau-Ponty's methodological relation to Goldstein in "The Primacy Question in Merleau-Ponty's Existential Phenomenology," *Continental Philosophy Review* 50, no. 1 (2017): 127–49.

11. E.g., PhP 209, 260, 371/185, 234, 336. See also TT 23.

12. TT 23.

13. TT 20.

14. TT 22.

15. *Inédit* 48/11; all italics added.

16. *Inédit* 41/6.

17. *La structure du comportement* (Paris: Presses Universitaires de France, 1942), 241 (*The Structure of Behavior*, trans. Alden L. Fisher [Boston: Beacon Press, 1963], 224).

18. *Inédit* 48/11.

19. TT 22.

20. *Sens et non-sens* (Paris: Nagel, 1948), 269 (*Sense and Non-Sense*, trans. H. L. Dreyfus and P. A. Dreyfus [Evanston, Ill.: Northwestern University Press, 1964], 152); italics added. Hereafter abbreviated as SNS, with French/English pagination.

21. SNS 330/186.

22. SNS 171/98.

23. See [17](I1).

24. See [18](I2).

25. See [17](I1).

26. It would be worthwhile to further develop how this turn is partly a turn back to *The Structure of Behavior*, such that the specifically "existential" character of *Phenomenology of Perception* may henceforth appear to be somewhat aberrational with regard to the overall trajectory of Merleau-Ponty's thought. Even if that is the case, though, his subsequent work could still be seen as pursuing certain thematic vectors of existentialism more profoundly, and thus as not necessarily marking a break with it, as many periodizations of Merleau-Ponty's work would suggest. But that discussion must be reserved for another occasion.

27. See [39] and [40](III7)–[40]v(III7); cf. [95](X5) for some later revisions.

28. See [36](III4).

29. The themes of Merleau-Ponty's courses the following year were indeed speech and history, although in the year after that they dealt with institution and passivity—it is the availability of his lecture notes that would allow for an understanding of such developments in his thought.

30. See [18](I2), [28](II4).

31. See [29](II5), [33](III1).

32. See [37](III5); cf. [23](I6).

33. See [28](II4).

34. See [18](I2)–[19](I3), [28](II4).

35. See [26](II2); cf. [9] (131–32 in working notes).

36. See [36](III4); cf. *Éloge de la philosophie: Leçon inaugurale faite au Collège de France le jeudi 15 janvier 1953* (Paris: Gallimard, 1953), 49 ("In Praise of Philosophy," in *In Praise of Philosophy and Other Essays*, trans. John O'Neill [Evanston, Ill.: Northwestern University Press, 1988], 29), "what we are calling expression is just another formula for a phenomenon to which Bergson never tired of returning—the retroactive effect of the true." Hereafter abbreviated as *Éloge*, with French/English pagination.

37. See [20](I4), [27](II3)–[29](II5).
38. See [22](I5a), [27](II3), [30](II6).
39. See [22](I5a), [29](II5).
40. See [33](III1).
41. See [22](I5a), [29](II5), [33](III1).
42. See [22](I5a), [29](II5).
43. See [17](I1).
44. See [62](VI5).
45. See [62](VI5); see also [65](VIII1).
46. Recall also Jean Beaufret's criticism of *Phenomenology of Perception* in November 1946 at the Société française de philosophie, following Merleau-Ponty's lecture "Le primat de la perception et ses conséquences philosophiques": "The only reproach that I would make to the author is not that he has gone 'too far,' but rather that he has not been sufficiently radical. The phenomenological descriptions which he uses in fact maintain the vocabulary of idealism. In this they are in accord with Husserlian descriptions. But the whole problem is to know whether phenomenology, fully developed, does not require the abandonment of subjectivity and the vocabulary of subjective idealism as, beginning with Husserl, Heidegger has done" (PrP 103/41–42).
47. E.g., TT 20.
48. See [53](IV9).
49. See [21](I5)–[23](I6); cf. [189] (152–53 in working notes).
50. See [23](I6); Merleau-Ponty's underlining. Cf. [48](IV4), where Merleau-Ponty invokes the idea of a "natural thinking."
51. See [23](I6); Merleau-Ponty's underlining, italics added.
52. See PhP 520/483. I discuss this at some length in *Merleau-Ponty's Existential Phenomenology and the Realization of Philosophy* (New York: Bloomsbury Academic, 2014); see also my "Heroism and History in Merleau-Ponty's Existential Phenomenology," *Continental Philosophy Review* 43 (2010): 167–91.
53. See note 2 above.
54. See [23](I6), [37](III5).
55. See [50](IV6); italics added.
56. See [43](III10); Merleau-Ponty's underlining.
57. See [49](IV5); italics added.
58. See [43](III10), [52](IV8), [55](V1).
59. See, e.g., [51](IV7) and [56](V2).
60. See [71](VII7); italics added.
61. See [70](VII6). Note that the term "elements" is uncertain in the transcription.
62. See [51](IV7).
63. See [43](III10); Merleau-Ponty's underlining.
64. See [58](VI1); italics added.
65. See [44](III11).
66. E.g., see [66](VII2), where Merleau-Ponty glosses an observation made by Wertheimer: "When I look at my pencil shifting laterally, I see it in movement exactly to the extent to which I do not see the successive positions."

67. See [65](VIII1).
68. See [70](VII6), [73](VIII1).
69. See [71](VII7)–[72](VII8).
70. See [75](VIII3).
71. See [82](IX1); Merleau-Ponty's underlining.
72. See [76](VIII4); Merleau-Ponty's underlining.
73. See [72](VII8); Merleau-Ponty's underlining. See also [82](IX1).
74. See [84](IX3).
75. See [76](VIII4); Merleau-Ponty's underlining. See also [72](VII8).
76. See [70](VII6), [72](VII8), [78](VIII6), [86](IX5).
77. See [86](IX5).
78. See [80](VIII8) (underlining removed); [73](VIII1).
79. See [88](IX7), [53](IV9) (Merleau-Ponty's underlining). See also [56](V2).
80. See [52](IV8), [56](V2).
81. See [48](IV4).
82. See [94](IX11 or X4).
83. See [23](I6).
84. See [81](VIII9).
85. See [88](IX7), [183].
86. See [60](VI3).
87. Schilder first published *Das Körperschema: Ein Beitrag zur Lehre vom Bewußtsein des eigenen Körpers* in 1923 (Berlin: Springer), and this is what is listed in the bibliography of *Phenomenology of Perception.* An English translation, *The Image and Appearance of the Human Body: Studies in the Constructive Energies of the Psyche,* was published in 1935 (London: Kegan Paul), reprinted in 1950 (New York: International Universities Press), and it was this later edition that Merleau-Ponty was working with here (hereafter abbreviated as IAHB). A French translation by François Gantheret and Paule Truffert was published by Gallimard under the title *L'image du corps: Étude des forces constructives de la psyche* in 1968.
88. See [98](X7).
89. See Kurt Goldstein, *Human Nature in the Light of Psychopathology* (Cambridge, Mass.: Harvard University Press, 1940), 35–38.
90. As Schilder wrote, "Our study is primarily a study of the body-image which lies on the *impressive* side of our psychic life" (IAHB 15; italics added), even while noting that "impression and expression form a definite unit which we can separate in its parts only by artificial analysis."
91. See [101](XI1).
92. See [112](XII5); cf. [176](5) (139–40 in working notes).
93. See [201].
94. See [181]v(1)–[182](2).
95. See [99](X8), [110](XII3).
96. See [107](XI7); underlining removed, italics added.
97. See [108](XII1).
98. Described there by Merleau-Ponty as "the power of delineating boundaries and directions in the given world, of establishing lines of force, of

managing perspectives, in short, of organizing the given world according to the projects of the moment, of building upon the geographical environment a milieu of behavior, a system of significations that express outwardly the internal activity of the subject" (PhP 130/114–15).

99. See [115](XII8), [118]; cf. [113](XII6), [120](XIII2), [124](XIII6).

100. See [112](XII5), [121](XIII3).

101. The Japanese illusion is touched upon at several points in Merleau-Ponty's notes, with the most detailed discussion occurring at [114](XII7) and [117](XIII1). See also [106](XI6).

102. See [124](XIII6).

103. See [127](XIV3); underlining removed, italics added.

104. See [127](XIV3); underlining removed.

105. See [128](XIV4).

106. See [118]. Merleau-Ponty explored the theme of sleep two years later in the Monday course beginning in 1955 (titled "The Problem of Passivity").

107. See [116](XII9); italics added.

108. See [72](VII8); underlining removed. See also [82](IX1).

109. See [124](XIII6).

110. See [116](XII9).

111. See [128](XIV4).

112. See [130](XIV6)–[131](XIV7).

113. See *Éloge* 49/29.

114. See [136](XIV12).

115. His concurrent Monday course in 1953 was titled "Investigations into the Literary Use of Language," and his Thursday course the following year was titled "The Problem of Speech."

116. Although Merleau-Ponty's later discussion will touch on sculpture, all of his references to this discussion in his earlier lectures as well as in the course summary mention only painting and cinema.

117. See [134](XIV10); underlining altered, italics added.

118. See [84](IX3)–[85](IX4) with regard to Jean Epstein, and [87](IX6) with regard to Maurice Jaubert's score for Jean Vigo's 1933 film *Zéro de conduite.*

119. See [136](XIV12); italics added.

120. See *Résumés* 21/11; translation altered (see note 2 above), italics added.

121. This metaphor recurs throughout the notes. E.g., "The perception of depth is [an] awakening, it's mind that becomes body and body that becomes mind" [52](IV8); "the degrees of wakefulness [correspond] to the degrees of articulation of the body schema" [188]; "Man wakes up [*se lève*] and man speaks" [130](XIV6). Cf. *Éloge*: "The philosopher is the man who wakes up [*s'éveille*] and speaks" (100/63).

Note on the Translation

This is a translation of the transcription established by Emmanuel de Saint Aubert and Stefan Kristensen of Merleau-Ponty's notes for "Le monde sensible et le monde de l'expression," his 1952–53 "Thursday course" at the Collège de France, that are deposited as NAF 26993 X at the Bibliothèque nationale de France (BNF). This translation follows the French edition in most fundamental respects. The main section contains Merleau-Ponty's "preparatory lecture notes" themselves, which for the most part are organized according to the fourteen lectures that he gave, and this is followed by a smaller section that contains a selection of "working notes" (see page 129). Unlike the French edition, however, page breaks have been inserted in the first section between the notes for each lecture. In some cases, these insertions disrupt slightly a continuity obtaining at the level of content, but overall they augment the tractability of the notes for the reader. (It should also be noted that there are some pages that, on account of their content, were inserted into a certain lecture by the BNF, even though they were not originally part of Merleau-Ponty's own paginated notes.)

The French editors of "Le monde sensible et le monde de l'expression" strove to present Merleau-Ponty's notes in a virtually verbatim form, and meticulous effort was made to keep the page layout as close as possible to that found in the actual notes themselves—I have done my utmost to preserve this latter effort in the present translation as well. The French edition also includes numerous annotative notes of various sorts (e.g., clarification of bibliographic references, explanation of special terms, noteworthy cross-references to other works by Merleau-Ponty). I have certainly consulted these and have drawn profitably from many of them, but the present translation includes a new and expanded set of annotative notes. In general, these are intended to facilitate a more critically insightful and productive reading.

Following the French edition, the pagination established by the BNF is indicated in square brackets, and it is followed in parentheses by Merleau-Ponty's own manuscript pagination, where this exists (which it does in most but not all cases of the preparatory notes, but not in any of his working notes). The BNF pagination is expressed in sequential Arabic numerals, while Merleau-Ponty's manuscript pagination typically conjoins the Roman numeral corresponding to the lecture with the Arabic numeral that corresponds to the page itself. The letter *v* after a BNF page number indicates its reverse (i.e., verso) side, while the letter *a* after Merleau-Ponty's own pagination indicates an attached page, with *b* indicating a further attached page. Located directly within the text, these page references are separated out by backslashes and have been set in boldface for clarity. Thus, the original pagination of the notes is usually indicated in the form /**[29](II5)**/, for example, but in some cases it may appear like /**[40]v(III7)**/, /**[54](IV9a)**/, or simply /**[118]**/. Rest assured, this is not nearly as complicated as it may initially appear.

Some further technical and typographical information concerning the text (for ease of reference, a table summarizing this information is provided on page liii):

Marginal and other additions on the part of Merleau-Ponty are clearly indicated in the text, separated out by backslashes.

The few words whose transcription was uncertain are indicated in curly braces, while {?} indicates an illegible word.

All words with a horizontal line through them represent text crossed out by Merleau-Ponty. Larger passages crossed out by him are either clearly indicated as such editorially or were omitted from the French edition altogether and thus not included in this translation.

All underlining (and occasional but infrequent double underlining) is Merleau-Ponty's own—the corresponding text has not been italicized in order to be able to distinguish emphasis from other uses of italics. Symbols used by Merleau-Ponty—for example, =, ≠, &, →, and the like, as well as numerical digits—are also retained as such.

Concerning punctuation, commas have been frequently added in accordance with normal English usage (e.g., following "e.g."). I have not, however, added periods to the ends of sentences (or sentence fragments) where Merleau-Ponty did not have one, nor have I capitalized the first word of a sentence where the notes appear that way (such cases are, at any rate, relatively few). In some cases, an em dash has been introduced (in square brackets) as a generic piece of punctuation to separate terms within a series of words that do not form a continuous phrase (this reflects Merleau-Ponty's own frequent use of dashes in these notes). All other en and em dashes, and the spacing (if any) around them, reflect as faithfully as possible Merleau-Ponty's idiosyncratic use of them in his notes.

As for quotation marks and scare quotes, when Merleau-Ponty quotes passages from others, the French guillemets become double quotation marks, and double quotation marks within guillemets in the original become single quotation marks. When guillemets are used as scare quotes, they become single quotation marks. It is not always clear, however, in what way such words are being used. In general, guillemets are treated as scare quotes except where it is clear that he is directly quoting the words in question from an immediately identifiable source (whether mentioned explicitly or not).

The French editors made certain additions that were placed in square brackets. Where these lie outside the text proper (e.g., headings, titles), I have kept them in square brackets, and I have made no further additions of this sort. In the very small number of cases where the French editors' additions are internal to the text (e.g., adding an implied term), however, I have placed them in angle brackets to distinguish them from additions that I have made and placed in square brackets, and from Merleau-Ponty's own occasional use of square brackets (the few cases of which are indicated in the notes).

Turning to some more general translational issues, whereas the French edition made minimal textual additions, the present translation adds a very large number of terms within the text itself. These additions have been made in order to facilitate as clear and unambiguous a reading of Merleau-Ponty's notes as possible, which are for the most part written in an unevenly abbreviated style. As noted, with scarcely any exceptions, this style is conveyed directly in the French edition, and although challenging at times, it can have a certain value for the reader. It is only possible because there it is simply a matter of transcription, not translation. When engaged in the process of translating notes like these, however, there is nearly always an unavoidable need to ascertain more precisely the intended meaning of the transcribed words. It is not possible, in other words, to translate the notes as they stand without engaging in some disabbreviation, for there are simply too many uncertainties and ambiguities at the level of the words themselves. And it seems only fitting to have this aspect of the translational task show up in the result itself. Most of the additions in question involve either the insertion of definite and indefinite articles, at least in cases where this choice was sufficiently clear (the reader might bear in mind, though, that translating from French to English very often involves *dropping* definite articles, and this is certainly true here as well), the disambiguation of certain grammatical references, the reiteration, where necessary, of implied terms, or the clarificatory unpacking of telegraphic phrasing. A small number of additions involve the insertion of an omitted term (e.g., a verb), and in such cases the choice is made so as to be as inconspicuous and uncontentious as possible. To be sure, not all of this is strictly necessary—in many cases additions are motivated primarily with an eye toward consistency across the text rather than out of a need internal to a particular passage. No doubt some readers might have preferred a "leaner" translation, but I am confident that the overall gains in terms of flow and readability outweigh any objections of that nature.

I have also made deliberately liberal use of English contractions, for this seems to convey well the informal and often fragmentary style of the notes.

Merleau-Ponty's notes contain numerous terms and phrases in German, as well as a few in ancient Greek and occasionally Latin. Although for the most part these are left untranslated in the French edition, translations have been given here in square brackets. The term *Sinngebung* (bestowal of sense) is relatively familiar and appears frequently, including on one occasion as *Sinn-gebung*, and so the translation is not supplied in every instance. (With regard to terms that are drawn from Husserl, by the way, I have consulted Dorion Cairns's *Guide for Translating Husserl*). The term "Gestalt" is not treated as a foreign term and is thus not italicized.

Merleau-Ponty often quotes from English and German sources, usually but not always translating these into French. In some cases of English sources, I have simply included the passages in their original form (and have noted this). In other cases involving English or German sources, where Merleau-Ponty's own French rendering may be in some respect questionable, I have, as appropriate, provided the original passage in a note. Similarly, in cases where Merleau-Ponty cites only a word or two, for example, I have provided the fuller sentence or sentences by way of contextualization in a note. In these and many other ways, the notes in general aim to provide supplementary information that can enable the reader to make better sense of the text.

In addition, several seemingly mistaken words in the original notes (e.g., conjugation errors) that are indicated by "[*sic*]" in the French edition are given a corrected reading, with this indicated in a note, and several minor transcription and other errors (e.g., orthographic or citational errors on the part of Merleau-Ponty unnoted in the French edition) have also been corrected.

As is conventional, when the translation of a term raises some sort of question or issue, either in general or in a particular instance, the original term is provided, italicized, in square brackets. To avoid at least some of this clutter, however, it might be worthwhile to flag a few particular terms here (for the most part in alphabetical order).

The term *apparition* is usually translated as "appearance." But this is to be understood not in the sense of the way something appears but rather the fact of its initial appearing (or coming into appearance) at all. In most cases this could be equally well translated as "emergence," and in many cases it is translated that way to avoid possible confusion with *apparence*. All potentially confusing cases of *apparition* are noted in the text. The term *émergence* is also (and always) translated as "emergence," but without comment.

The term *contre épreuve* is always translated according to its sense as "supplementary proof," as opposed to something potentially misleading (even if technically correct) such as "countertest," while "verification" translates *vérification*.

The adjective *corporel* or *corporelle* is usually translated as "bodily," but in those cases where a more technical sense is involved, it is translated as "corporeal." The term *la corporéité* is translated as "corporeality." The compound term *schéma corporel*, however, is always translated as "body schema." Merleau-Ponty's expression *le corps propre* is always translated as "one's own body" rather than, for example, as "the body itself"—neither rendering is ideal, but the former choice is a better fit with the contexts in which it is used here.

The plural term *les données* occurs fairly frequently and occasionally in the singular. Although to some ears it can sound a tad awkward, in general I try as much as possible to stick close to the literal and phenomenological sense of givenness by rendering it as "what is given" or, if there is a qualifier, "the . . . givens" (e.g., "the sensuous givens"). In certain contexts, however, it can be safely and appropriately translated as "impressions," or as "the given facts."

The term *écart* is usually translated as "divergence," except where noted in the text.

The term *intégration* is always translated as "integration," and I have indicated the original term when and only when it is used with a preposition (which is invariably *dans*). This is because the term *insertion*, which always takes a preposition here (usually *dans*, but *sur* in one case), is also usually translated as "integration." In no case does Merleau-Ponty's use of the term *insertion* correspond to the usual English sense of "insertion," which implies something's being entered into something else from without. Rather, the sense here is always of the first thing (already) *being included integrally* within the second, and in all cases but one I have opted for "integration" over "inclusion" to capture this sense best: instances of *insertion dans* are translated as "integration within," while *insertion sur* is translated as "inclusion within." The difference is not major. More important is the fact that in each case the preposition is translated as "within"—to capture the sense of being both *with* and *in*—rather than simply "with" *or* "in," or something more misleading like "into." All instances of the term *insertion* are noted in the text. The two instances of the term *désinsertion* are rendered by "deintegration," the connotation of which, at least in this context, is more appropriate than "disintegration," a term that invariably renders *désintégration* (and similarly for cognate terms).

In his discussions concerning perceived movement, Merleau-Ponty makes frequent use of the term *le mobile*, which could be translated simply as "moving thing." But Merleau-Ponty also contrasts this term with *le mouvant* in a way that reflects the distinction between something that is or gets moved (*le mobile*) and something that moves itself (*le mouvant*). Avoiding cumbersome circumlocutions, the expression "moving thing" seems better suited to render the latter, *le mouvant*, even if imperfectly, and accordingly I have rendered *le mobile* as "thing in motion."

Outside contexts concerning cinema, Merleau-Ponty's use of the term *montage* presents challenges—see note 8 in lecture 4 for a rather longish explanation as to why I have chosen to translate it here as "schematic typology." This is the one case in this work in which I have used a seemingly artificial construction in order best to convey what I take to be Merleau-Ponty's intended meaning.

Merleau-Ponty's discussions often deal with *praxis*, which is of course translated as "praxis." But he also very often refers to *praxie* (plural *praxies*), which is translated as "praxia" (plural "praxias"), which in contrast to praxis refers much more specifically to coordinated, goal-directed motor actions, especially as these come to our attention through their absence in pathological contexts of apraxia. Merleau-Ponty often uses the adjective *praxique*, which could relate either to praxis or praxia and which I render as "praxical" (rather than simply "praxic") in order to relate it closely to the term "practical" (*pratique*) while also maintaining its distinctiveness. Along the same lines as his use of *praxie*, Merleau-Ponty also uses the terms *gnosie* and *phasie*—that is, the general intellectual and linguistic capacities of which the more familiar terms *agnosie* (agnosia) and *aphasie* (aphasia) are, respectively, the pathologically privative forms. These terms—*gnosie* and *phasie*—are translated here, respectively, as "gnosia" and "phasia," and the corresponding adjectives *gnosique* and *phasique* are translated as "gnosic" and "phasic."

The term *le regard* is commonly translated as "glance," and I follow that practice in some cases here, but it is more often rendered by "looking" owing to the need, at least in these contexts, to avoid the furtive sense that the word "glance" seems unavoidably to carry, without resorting to "gaze," for example, which tends to have misleading connotations of its own (although it is appropriate on two occasions below in connection with Jean Epstein and Lev Kuleshov).

The specific way in which Merleau-Ponty uses the noun *reprise* here is to denote a "taking up" of something, and I have always translated it accordingly, even though in certain cases—usually those in which *reprise* is qualified in some way—the result may sound a bit awkward. But this seems like a lesser problem than the potentially misleading connotations that would follow from alternatives like "resumption" or even "uptake." I have noted such cases in the text. The term *assomption* is translated as "taking on," cases of which are also noted in the text.

In his discussions concerning perceived movement, Merleau-Ponty also makes use of an overlapping ensemble of terms that include several substantive cognates of the verb *tracer*, including *la trace, le traçage, le traceur* (although these latter two are infrequent), and, most notably, *le tracé*. This last term in particular presents some translational challenges. In general, it can mean a route, path, or course, for example, or else a tracing, drawing, or plotting (this list is by no means exhaustive). Roughly and in general, there is the sense of a continuous line or pattern being laid down or followed. *Tracé* could thus be "path traced out." But that is basically what Merleau-Ponty will mean by *la trace* of a movement, a trail of spatial points, or at least something (like a gesture) immanently emblematic of that. With *le tracé* Merleau-Ponty seems to want further to invoke the active passage through which the points are connected, or that which serves to connect them, or even to recognize movement in a stationary trace, through a perceptual "reading." But this leads to a certain ambiguity. At one point Merleau-Ponty glosses a claim that all perceived movement is a *tracé* as follows: "I.e., [an] inscription or sedimentation of time in space, [the] taking shape of the internal in the external,—*or conversely* [the] deciphering and taking up of this trace by my temporality" (see below at [87](IX6); italics added). *Le tracé* thus in effect does double duty (and in this way is central to the course), referring both to the path laid out by a moving thing as this is being laid out and to the embodied perceptual synthesis of that path qua trace (or the misguided attempt to synthesize it intellectually—Merleau-Ponty alludes critically to attempts to grasp movement through a "*tracé sprituel*"). It thus seems to me that the optimal (albeit far from perfect) rendering of the term *le tracé* is thus "tracing," denoting either the tracing of its path that a moving thing does or the tracing (or perhaps retracing) that occurs when that movement is taken up perceptually. Either way, it should be borne in mind that, for Merleau-Ponty, perceived movement is a field phenomenon in the sense of being part of the figural organization of the perceptual field as a whole.

Last but certainly not least, there is the term *sens*. It is well known that this is a central and importantly polysemic term in Merleau-Ponty's thought, connoting as it does "meaning," "sense" (in all senses), and "direction." The underlying notion here is of a perceived and affectively valenced situational orientation or polarity. It is central to Merleau-

Ponty's concern to disclose phenomenologically the fundamental connections that link rationality to sensory experience, horizonal projection, and historical orientation, and it is arguably not a stretch to say that much commentary on his phenomenology effectively amounts to an interpretation of the nature and scope of the philosophical weight that Merleau-Ponty wants this term to carry, and the work that he wants it to do.

There is no single English word that is semantically isomorphic to *sens*. In any case, the task of the translator is not to render the term in the abstract but rather to convey as well as possible how it is used in each particular case. With Merleau-Ponty, there tend to be some relatively easy cases—when, for example, it is used to denote the *direction* of a road, or the *sense* of smell, or the use of a word in a certain *sense*, or to the *meaning* of a proposition—and some relatively hard cases. The latter are typically those involving a perceptual experience with regard to the lived significance of which the distinction between *sense* and *meaning* is more noticeably ambiguous. It is precisely this ambiguity itself—evincing as it does the dialectical exchange within this experience between the sensible as that which is given *to* the perceiving subject as relatively passive and the expressive as that which is given *by* the perceiving subject as relatively active—that is of central philosophical interest for Merleau-Ponty in these lectures, and in these cases the translator must judge (reflectively, in the Kantian sense) which of the two terms works better. (Note that in the translation below, "sense" and "meaning" only render *sens*, and all other verbal forms of "meaning" (e.g., *vouloir dire, signifier*) are indicated in the text.)

Decisions concerning these hard cases are certainly not made any easier by the fragmentary style of these notes. But the situation is not as fraught as it might seem. In the present translation, I have hewed to a heuristic maxim to the effect that in cases where a certain use of *sens* leans to the passive side of experience and is more a matter of phenomenological givenness as that is ordinarily understood, then I render it as "sense," while in cases where it leans to the active side and is more a matter of existential signification, then I render it as "meaning"—thus, for example, the *sense* of space, the *meaning* of a diagram. (In cases where this maxim is inconclusive, *sens* is translated as "sense.") The qualifier "existential" is crucial here, for Merleau-Ponty does deploy an important distinction, which should be borne in mind, between *sens* and *signification* (translated as "signification") as such, a distinction that is germane to worries about intellectualist misunderstandings when *sens* is translated as "meaning"—it must be kept firmly in mind that acts of *existential* signification are not acts of reflection or intellection.

More generally, it is imperative to note that however *sens* may be translated in the hard cases, the connotation of the English term used, be it "sense" or "meaning," will itself necessarily be altered—the point, after all, is that Merleau-Ponty is fundamentally rethinking the polysemy of *sens* along specific phenomenological lines. So while they can and should facilitate it, no translational choices can disburden the reader of the reinterpretive work vis-à-vis the sense and meaning of "sense" and "meaning" that this rethinking implies.

My overall aim with the translation and the accompanying notes has been to provide as clear and as fluid a readability of Merleau-Ponty's notes in their substance as possible, with the only ambiguities and unclarities remaining being those that are inherent in Merleau-Ponty's notes as such and not in the language nor, as much as possible, in the style in which he wrote them. It should be noted that this style includes the use of gender nonneutral language, which is accordingly preserved in the translation.

Typographical Information

[ ] Square brackets	Additions made by the French editors outside the text proper (headings, titles, etc.) Additions by the translator within the text proper (English words for readability, or original French terms, in italics, where appropriate)
⟨ ⟩ Angle brackets	Additions made by the French editors within the text proper
{ } Curly braces	Uncertain word
{?}	Illegible word
[—]	Generic punctuation introduced to separate terms within a series of words that do not form a continuous phrase
/backslashes/	Used to separate out pagination and marginalia
underlining	All underlining (including double underlining) is by Merleau-Ponty
~~strike through~~	Short passages crossed out by Merleau-Ponty (longer crossed-out passages are indicated editorially)

COURSE NOTES FROM
THE COLLÈGE DE FRANCE, 1953

Preparatory Lecture Notes

Table of Contents of the Preparatory Lecture Notes

First Lecture — [17–24]

[INTRODUCTION] — [17–40]

I. General goal	[17]	9
II. Reference to work on perception	[17]	9
III. The concept of expression and perceptual consciousness	[18]	11
IV. Passage to creative expression [and] productivity	[21]	15

Second Lecture — [25–32]

Summary of the first lecture	[25]	18
Consciousness and perceptual consciousness (as expression)	[26]	19
Consequences concerning the 'internal perception' of the psychic, the social, or the institutional	[29]	22

Third Lecture — [33–44]

Development of a theory of rationality	[36]	27
Aim of this year's course	[36]	27
Outline of the course *(first version)*	[39]	29
Outline of the course *(second version)*	[40]	30

I. SPACE AND MOVEMENT — [41–95]

1) No priority problem	[41]	32
2) Sense of 'up' and 'down,' right-left, height-width	[41]	33

This table of contents is translated directly from the published French edition. The pagination indicated in square brackets is that established by the Bibliothèque nationale de France, while that on the right refers to the present volume.

Fourth Lecture — [45–54]

SPACE [45] 37

1) Height and width [47] 39

2) The near and the far [51] 42

a) Convergence [51] 43

b) Apparent size [52] 44

Note I [54] 46

Note II [54] 46

Fifth Lecture — [55–57]

The near and the far [55] 47

a) Convergence [55] 47

b) Apparent size [56] 49

Sixth Lecture — [58–64]

MOVEMENT [58] 51

I. Movement in-itself or objective movement [58] 51

II. The subject [is] implicated in movement [59] 53

III. Movement as phenomenon [61] 54

Seventh Lecture — [65–72]

1) All movement is stroboscopic [65] 58

2) Movement is a figural moment [66] 59

3) Movement as disclosive of being [69] 61

4) Interpretation: organization and perceptual logic [70] 63

Eighth Lecture — [73–81]

Experiments [73] 66

4) Overall interpretation: organization of the field and perceptual logic [75] 68

a) [Figural moments (according to Gestalt [theory])] [75] 68

b) Interpretation (beyond Gestalt [theory]) [77] 70

1) Exchange between meaning and figural moments [77] 70

2) Perception and symbol [78] 71

3) The perceiving subject [78] 72

4) Perceived movement [80] 73

Ninth Lecture — [82–88]

[The] nature of perceptual organization — The logic of perception [85] 78

[The] nature of movement [87] 79

Tenth Lecture — [88–99]
Generalization [88] 81
Example [analysis of J. Paliard, *Pensée implicite et perception visuelle*] [89] 81
Role of the following lectures [95] 86

[II. BODY SCHEMA] — [96–131]
[Reading notes on Paul Schilder, *The Image and Appearance of the Human Body*] [96] 86
(1) Prelogical unity
(2) Background of praxis
(3) Relation to [the] external world
(4) Relation to language and to the thought of others

THE NOTION OF BODY SCHEMA [97] 88
1) Its integration within [*insertion dans*] space [97] 88
3) Its unity [97] 89
2) Its intermodal unity [98] 89
4) The body is [a] schema because it's [a] motor power [99] 90

Eleventh Lecture — [101–107]
1) The body as nonideal totality [102] 93
Totality of its senses [102] 93
Totality of its limbs or organs [103] 95
2) This unity is that of a praxis [106] 97

Twelfth Lecture — [108–116]
2) Unity of praxis [108] 100
3) Apraxia and the relations [between] praxia [and] external perception [112] 104

Thirteenth Lecture — [117–125]
[Relations between praxia and gnosia] [117] 109
[Introduction of the problem: Japanese illusion] [117] 109
[Initial presentation of the problem] [118] 110
(1) Originality of praxis [121] 114
(2) Praxical disturbances sometimes lead to gnosic disturbances [121] 114
(3) Relations between praxia and gnosia [123] 115

Fourteenth Lecture — [125–136]

4) Body schema and relations with others [125] 118

5) Body schema and thought, and speech [126] 119

The hand [126] 119

Language [128] 121

[III. EXPRESSION AND MOVEMENT *(sketch)*] — [131–136]

1) Painting [expression of movement through something stationary] [131] 123

2) Cinema [universal expression through movement] [134] 126

First Lecture

/[17](I1)/

SENSIBLE WORLD AND WORLD OF EXPRESSION

I. GENERAL GOAL

Sensible world = things
World of expression = cultural things, 'use objects,' symbols. (I didn't say: universe of language)
Double goal: — deepen the analysis of the perceived world by showing that it already presupposes the expressive function.
— prepare the analysis of this [expressive] function through which the perceived world is sublimated, produce a concrete theory of mind.[1]

Thereby reestablish the unity and at the same time the difference between the perceived world and the intelligible world through a redefinition of consciousness and of sense. Classically (Descartes, Kant), [the] unity is ultimately founded on the understanding. The difference is simply a fact, inconceivable except through myths. For us it is a matter of finding another sort of unity: everything is perception, the mode of access to being that is present in perception is present everywhere. But perception in the restricted (sensory) sense calls for its own expression.

II. REFERENCE TO WORK ON PERCEPTION

We attempted an analysis of the perceived world that brings out what is original in it in contrast to the universe of science or of objective thought.
But nevertheless this analysis remained governed by classical concepts such as: perception (in the sense of [the] positing of an isolated, determinate object, considered as [the] canonical form of our relations with the world), consciousness (understood as [a] centrifugal

power of *Sinn-gebung* [bestowal of sense] that finds in things what it put there), synthesis (which presupposes elements to reunite) (for example, [the] problem of the unity of *Erlebnisse* [lived experiences]), [the] matter and form of knowledge.

To be sure,

we showed that there are very few perceptions, and that most of the time perceptual life is movement slipping from one to another, — we showed that we don't constitute the perceived world, — that the synthesis is not to be made, [that it is] always already made, — and that there is no matter without form and vice versa.

But the definition of the new themes (the field as opposed to the perceived thing, 'passive synthesis' as opposed to constitutive consciousness, the Gestalt as opposed to matter or to form) was still worked out in relation to these classical concepts, and was thus often negative. As in Husserl (or the Gestalt theorists, for different reasons).

As a result, the thesis of a primacy of perception was at risk of being distorted, if not for us, at least for the reader.

1) He [i.e., the reader] might think that it was [the] primacy of perception in the old sense: primacy of the sensory, of the natural given, whereas for me perception was essentially a mode /**[18](I2)**/ of access to being: access to what is *leibhaft gegeben* [given bodily, or given 'in the flesh'].

2) He might think that that work was only a phenomenology — [an] introduction that left the question of being untouched, whereas I didn't differentiate between ontology and phenomenology, [he might think] that the study of the being of sense that remained necessary after this phenomenology would be independent of it, whereas in my view all that we are is implicated in our manner of perceiving. Cf. Hyppolite at the philosophy society: no cohesion [*solidarité*] between [the] description of perception and [the] conception of "the being of sense."[2]

3) Consequently he might think that being was reduced to the 'positivism' of perception. Cf. German authors talking about 'psychologism,' opposing speculative philosophy to phenomenology as positivism (Fink).[3] Our insufficient development (but you have to start somewhere) risked distorting the relation to being that we had in mind. In reality this relation is distant: the thing itself is never captured [*prise*] by the philosopher: it is the concretion of an infinite experience, it is therefore not possessed. It is unquestionably before us, but as something we can't lay our hands on without losing it (cf. the sense of language: taking words one by one, one loses it; looking for it, one misses it). It thus appears that our study of percep-

tion 1) did involve a view concerning the being of sense 2) that this view did not reduce everything problematic to what is positive in perception since the positing of being within perception itself was paradoxical.*

/[*in margin*] *actually the disagreement with the Heideggerians is not only due to this insufficient development: there may be a philosophical formalism beneath their refusal of psychological analyses, the assurance that philosophy has its domain conceived as a certain realm, beyond the ontic realm. Heidegger saying in *Sein und Zeit* that the distinction [between] philosophy [and] psychology is immediate:[4] as a philosopher the facts can teach me nothing, inductive generality presupposes essences. For me this is formalism: the facts prepared by [the] ontological presuppositions of science can only return these presuppositions to me, but even the 'scientific' fact always exceeds this ontology and eventually puts it in question. In any case, philosophy has to think it as a modality of the existing thing. Failing which, philosophy risks falling back into the ontic, on this side of science. E.g., Heidegger's etymologies have to justify themselves before the critique of linguists in order not to be imaginary linguistics. Just because philosophy is radical, and in order to be radical, it must conquer and justify its dimension by making all the rest understandable, and not just set itself up there straightaway. No numerical distinction between philosophy and psychology and sociology, because [there is] no formal a priori. A hermeneutics of facticity can't be without facts./

We will avoid the equivocations by taking up (and completing) the established results with the help of the concept of expression.

III. THE CONCEPT OF EXPRESSION AND PERCEPTUAL CONSCIOUSNESS

Here we will define expression or expressivity as the property that a phenomenon has through its internal arrangement [*son agencement interne*] to disclose another [phenomenon] that is not or even never was given. The tool, the work, express man in this sense. Intellectual work or painting too, but [this is] more complex: they express man by talking about things or about the world as well, such that here it is not only man expressing himself in [a] product, but moreover [a] product that expresses the world, man bearing witness to himself through the emergence [*apparition*] of this relation:

/**[19](I3)**/

It's in the second sense that perception is expression, expression of the world, and it proves itself as human [perception] only inasmuch as it contains this emergence of a truth of the world.

This requires us to conceive perceptual consciousness completely differently than the notion of consciousness would demand, to place within it a proximity of the object and a distance from the object that are equally disregarded in the notion of consciousness.

More precisely:

To be conscious [*Avoir conscience*] = to make appear, before the obscurity of the subject, a being which is thereby raised to value or to signification. No matter how it is conceived, ~~this consciousness has no cracks~~ this consciousness can only deal with its significations. Nothing can affect it except by awakening within it one of the significations that it conceives. Receptivity is the death of this consciousness. Hence at once both [an] immediate presence of this consciousness to its objects: nothing separates it from them, it reaches them without distance, — and at the same time, since with regard to them it is absolute survey [*survol absolu*], and they cannot turn against it, it is altogether distant from them.[5]

This implies a conception of meaning as essence = that which responds to the question: what? = definition. All consciousness is the grasping of an essence of this sort or its application to a particular case: E.g., even hyletic data for Husserl are the occasion for an *Auffassung als* . . . [apprehension or construal as . . .] which is the imposition of an essence — Husserl does say that not all constitution can be of this type, that there is an *Urkonstitution* [primal or originary constitution] which leaves essences behind, but [he] gives hardly any description of it.[6]

This makes for [a conception of] consciousness that constitutes its object in total clarity: the essence is in principle clear and the individual [object] to which it is applied likewise can't fail to be clear, since it has access to consciousness only on condition of offering it a meaning. Consciousness can only connect a signification to a signification. This consciousness is ready-made to be put into words, translated in language, it is already [the] positing of a statement, speaking consciousness.

In sum, this is a monadic consciousness, not the crude monadism that locks up each [consciousness] within the things it senses itself, but a more radical monadism that insists that consciousness is immediately present to everything, everything outside, and hence that /**[20](I4)**/ there is no horizon remaining beyond it. For this consciousness anything other than itself is absolute non-sense [*absolu non-sens*], because [this consciousness] is [the] positing of meaning and because here meaning is [a] strict unity, because it is essence or nothing. Consciousness does everything or else is nothing. It is certainly not individualized, but it is unique.

SECOND LECTURE
Contrast this idea of consciousness with perceptual consciousness informed by the concept of expression

1) It does not deal with values or significations but with existing beings, and is itself not absolutely cut off from the being that it presents to us, which encroaches on it, surrounds [*entoure*] it. As a consciousness that perceives, I am part of the world and I occupy a point of view in it. I am near things but not through a completely ideal presence: I am near the thing because it takes possession of my body in order to be perceived by it (color imposes a certain vital rhythm on me, sound [imposes] a certain adaptation of the organ, etc.), or again because in its absence my body is capable of giving it a quasi-presence. I am near the thing in virtue of an expressive relation between sensible things and the perceiving organ. [A] proximity that is not impalpable like the one just discussed — And which also goes with a different distance, for the perceived only reveals itself in this way through its vibration in me, it is thus always beyond.

2) Here meaning is not [an] essence. Of course, the existing thing is not an inarticulate, inexpressible mass. It has its internal logic, hence its quasi-categories. But as [something] perceived, it offers a sense as tacit that reveals itself in the exceptions where it is lacking rather than through its own positing, [a sense] that is a part of the internal framework of the landscape [*une armature du paysage*] rather than an essence. E.g., the circle for perception and the definition of the circle: the sense of the circular is a certain mode of curvature (change in direction at each instant but always in the same way*). Example of negative sense: vertical and horizontal are not given to us thematically but primarily by the cases where they are disrupted and as levels (and this idea can be generalized). But what's a level? It's a typical activity [*activité type*],[7] it's the universal context [*cadre*] of an action in the world. Perceptual consciousness often consists in noticing divergence in relation to a level, and this divergence is the sense which is thus configuration [or] structure.

> /[*in margin*] *This sense is less possessed as such than it is practiced: perhaps it can't be defined, but every aberrant fact is lived as deviation in relation to it. Thus perception adjusts imperfect circles, goes toward good forms./

3) Perceptual consciousness is not [the] positing of a statement, it /**[21](I5)**/ is tacit, it does not concern free-floating significations that exist for themselves as such: but rather significations like those in a painting: a touch of green placed here makes a cheek smile without us knowing how,

in virtue of a syntax that we practice without having an explicit understanding of it. The perceived world is full of magical regions that assign unforeseen properties to the beings that enter them because they are the habitat of an affective category. It's the definition of the perceived world to assign properties to the object that pertain not only to what it is but also to its place. Hence bound, non-speaking significations, [or] structures.

It's again the notion of expression that enables us to understand [points] 2 and 3 [above]: for the adoption of a level presupposes the expressive relation between the perceived and ourselves, presupposes our settling into it, that is to say, the raising of certain of its elements to the status of dimensions,* — hence bound [or] configurational signification presupposes even more clearly that the sensible thing speaks a certain language to us which we understand just as if a linguistic agreement were established between our perceptual system and it, as if we spoke its language without having learned it = expression.

> /[*in margin*] *having systematic value, i.e., in relation to which the others have sense and our action is organized or unfolds. Thus the internal framework [*l'armature*] of the perceived = expression of us in it and of it through us. Every figure with an 'interior' and an 'exterior' presupposes that I am in a situation in the world, i.e., that I express myself in [the world] and that I express it./

We are thus seeking first of all to reconsider in terms of expression our results concerning the sensible world: thus

quality
space – movement
world

while emphasizing the rejection of the notion of consciousness and what to replace it with (cf. attached page I5a)

/[22](I5a)/

ATTACHED PAGE

REJECTION OF THE NOTION OF CONSCIOUSNESS

So perceptual consciousness is certainly not consciousness in that sense: pure unfolding of an in-itself before a for-itself.

Gestalt [theory]: the simplest formation is a figure on a background. This means [*veut dire*]: the very positing of the figure as in-itself, as something determinate, always presupposes the simultaneous presence of a background. The background forms part of the definition of the being (without it [there is] no figure, no outlines).

Consequently there is always something inarticulate and implicit in that of which there is consciousness.

Inasmuch as we are in touch with it [*on le touche*] ([inasmuch] as it is figure), we are not in touch with it [*on ne le touche pas*] (since there is the implicit background), and inasmuch as we are not in touch with it ([inasmuch] as we let the background be without thinking about it), we are in touch with it or we reach it (there is figure).

Perception and imperception.

Theory of inverted consciousness: consciousness is by definition cross-eyed (Freud – and Marx as well): the fact that one is conscious of *this* means [*veut dire*] that there is also *that* which is unspoken.[8]

And nevertheless it is not severed from the true, since what it doesn't say is present as background: teleology of truth.

This [is] to be taken up again in the face of revealed truth which is the truth of language, the statement, [and is] to be contrasted with it.

/**[21](I5)**/ [*continuation of page* [21](I5)]

IV. PASSAGE TO CREATIVE EXPRESSION [AND] PRODUCTIVITY

But at this point this is for us only [an] introduction to the world of expression, that is, one example of an expressive activity that will subsequently be mind [*l'esprit*].

For there is [a] double function of the body. As a given organization, as sensory fields it responds to what presents itself, — but the same body is also a body that moves itself and in this it is no longer limited to responding, it returns /**[23](I6)**/ to the world in order to signify it or to designate it. Individuals with apraxia show us through its absence an activity that is present in everyone, albeit scarcely visible, that constructs 'virtual space,' [a] system of correspondences between properties of my actual field and what these properties would be for me situated elsewhere or for another. To point already presupposes this virtual or cultural space. Here expression does not detach us from the bodily situation, since on the contrary it takes up its entire sense, it learns my own situation to such an extent that it finds in it the means for thinking other [situations].*

> /[*in margin*] *Mimicry of the world by the body, and corresponding layer of significations = cultural space as well as all use-objects.
> In particular, perception of symbolic objects (maps, drawings,

> artworks, cinema: excellent example [—] real movement and [movement] on film).
> All this has to do with a perception that is more and more 'intelligent', less and less 'sensory.' Yet nonetheless with a perception in the sense that 1) it's not a matter of [a] discursive function nor of [a] mechanical subsumption 2) it is a matter of the application of a principle that is not always thematized. In short, it has to do with a praxia./

It's of all this work of praxis, far more extensive than I had thought, that we must develop an understanding. It invests objects not only with gnosic predicates such as those of virtual space, but also with all cultural predicates.

In speaking here of praxis I don't want to imply [an] ~~anti-intellectualist~~ irrationalist philosophy: in order for there to be perceptions there must always be a 'natural' core. But I do want to point out [a] relation to the object that is not originally gnosic. Deepen the notion of gnosia through that of praxia. It's a matter of grasping mind [*l'esprit*] in its nascent state.

Cf. motor theories of perception, prolepsis,[9] what do they mean? That there is a spatial ubiquity in gesture, [in] the manual exploration of objects, [in] movement, which runs its course like a temporal ubiquity in consciousness ~~of time~~ which gives me the past through the series of retentions, that there is a synthesis other than exterior synthesis, that there is a synthesis that occurs in the situation and through it, through the fact that each perspective is the other perspectives as such. This cannot be understood in terms of gnosia or thetic knowledge. It can be understood in terms of praxis. Praxis [is] to be distinguished from action in the sense that Bergson, for example, gives to it.[10]

With this level of analysis [the] cultural component of the 'world' /**[24](17)**/ [is] initially defined as natural. In which sense the notion of world already has historical implications.

AT THE LIMIT: OTHERS AND LANGUAGE

This would bring us to language without us getting into it this year.

On account of what we'll have said about the notion of consciousness and its replacement, the problem of the other would be clarified. As well as that of the consciousness that stands behind language. Convergence here between the linguistic theory of the sign and our theory of meaning or consciousness. This will be the topic of the course in the following years. In particular, we will need to reconsider our whole theory of truth, [a] 'structural' theory of truth [that is] not indifferent to orientation or to logical sense, or to history.

Thus quality
space and movement
the world as Nature

Expressive taking up of these moments (which transforms them)
The tool
The artwork
The world as world of culture

Relation of Nature & Culture

Second Lecture

/[25](II1)/

THE SENSIBLE WORLD AND THE WORLD OF EXPRESSION

SUMMARY OF THE FIRST LECTURE

— Problem of perception facing reflective philosophy:
descriptive difference between perception and understanding
but, in terms of reflection, perception has no proper cohesion,
Descartes: the union of soul and body is original, to be thought through myths (gravity acting on heavy body), but that is lived, not thought.

— We tried to show that the perceptual order is original
if we remain in the above framework, that means [*veut dire*]: [the] interiority of the understanding [is] subordinated to [the] self-organization of the elements: empiricism, or even (Lachièze-Rey) "pantheism."[1] Aristotelianism.

— In fact, we specifically did not want to remain in the previous framework.
The perceptual order, for which we were making a claim, was not [the] passivity of the subject, [not the] antithesis of a transcendental idealism.
It was a new dimension of analysis, also applicable to the interiority of the understanding.
Henceforth everything was perception, but not in the sensory sense.
Logos of perception, implicit perceptual logic. An analysis was then to be devoted to the Logos of the understanding, which was therefore not reduced. But this analysis would be of the same type, analysis of the implicit, of structures, since the object of the understanding itself refers to the perceived thing, which forms part of its meaning. Double relation: the perceived exists to be thought, thought is of the perceived. [This] double relation [is] overlooked as much by empiricism or 'pantheism' as by transcendental idealism. Dialectical relation, not one-way.

The analysis of the perceived awakened us to a type of organization, [it] taught us a connection between the one and the multiple, —which should then /**[26](II2)**/ be used for approaching the understanding in its own structures. Everything is perception, but perception is all [*Tout est perception, mais la perception est tout*], which means that [*c'est-à-dire que*] our idea of perception must be enlarged in such a way as to make possible an analysis of the understanding.

It's this ambiguous, two-way relation, with reversal, that today we are calling expression.

Hence clarification by thematizing this concept.

The other day we were in the middle of showing [the] difference between [the] concept of consciousness & [that of] of perceptual consciousness understood as expression.

CONSCIOUSNESS AND PERCEPTUAL CONSCIOUSNESS (AS EXPRESSION)

CONSCIOUSNESS

Opening to value or signification. Pure power of *Auffassung als* [apprehension or construal as] [or] *Sinngebung* [bestowal of sense]

Proximity of what it intends: it is immediate presence to every being. Distance to what it intends: it is "absolute survey" (Ruyer),[2] it can never be 'captured' by the object.

Hence: meaning is essence, that which answers the critical question of *Was* [what], – *Wesen* [being or essence].[3]

Hence: this consciousness is already [the] positing of a statement, it always implies an I know that, it is already speaking.

Hence: it is monadic, not in the crude sense of the inherence of each in what it senses individually, but in the sense that, immediately present to everything, everything outside, it does not leave the horizons beyond itself open, [in the sense that] for it the other is absolute non-sense [*non-sens absolu*], [that] it is unique by dint of universality, not by dint of individuality (that's the conception of the early Husserl, and that of Sartre in *Transcendence of the Ego*).[4]

PERCEPTUAL CONSCIOUSNESS OR EXPRESSION

Opening not to values or significations but to beings or existing things. Consequently proximity and distance to the thing have an entirely different /**[27](II3)**/ sense:

Proximity: it's not ideal presence (intentionality in the sense of referring to an εἶδος [*eidos*]), absolute ubiquity. Consciousness is not cut off absolutely, being encroaches on it, surrounds [*circonvient*] it. As [a] perceiving subject I occupy a point of view in the world. It's from within the world that I perceive, and neither outlines nor geometric forms would have any sense otherwise. Relation of complicity between quality and my sensory field (the former suggests to me a certain affective and vital rhythm), (and conversely, because of this synchronization, in its absence I am able to obtain a quasi-presence of it: the image, [the] realization of quasi-sensible structures by my body on the basis of its integration within [*insertion dans*] [the] field). Proximity [that is] dizzying, not impalpable, [an] expressive relation [or] mixture.

Distance: used to come from the thing's being of another order, unable to look back upon the consciousness that thinks it. Here [i.e., in Merleau-Ponty's account], distance comes from the fact that the thing, precisely because it makes me vibrate bodily and reaches me from within, obsesses me, is always beyond this vibration that it communicates to me.

Hence: the meaning of the perceived ≠ essence

a perceived thing has a meaning, not as subsumed under an essence or signification, [not as] participating in an idea or in a category, — but as [the] modulation of a certain dimension: e.g., the sense of the perceived circle ≠ like that of the geometric circle, [a] locus of points, etc . . . . i.e., [a] constant relation [or] characteristic of all the points, but = 'mode of curvature' = 'change of direction at each instant always with the same divergence.' The circle = mode of divergence. That in relation to which there is divergence (the tangent to the point in question) is not laid out, [it] is implied as background. The divergence itself is thus not laid out [or] defined. Any point not following this pattern of movement is simply felt as deviant with respect to it. Likewise vertical and horizontal [are] not grasped for themselves but in the divergence of things from them. Thus as levels. Perception of them is imperception: it's when they're destroyed that we feel them (e.g., in the Wertheimer experiment when the whole field is oblique),[5] when they function /**[28](II4)**/ they're what we take for granted. Therefore perceptual sense = divergence with respect to [a] level that is not thematic. Therefore meaning here is not essence.

Hence: perceptual sense is not a statement, an I know that, it is tacit; it is not made of free-floating significations that exist for themselves and for their own sake — E.g., a green put into a face counts as a 'smile' (we make a cheek smile, Cézanne) like a word placed into a sentence changes its affective inflexion. In the sentence we can explain why, not in the painting. But it's not a matter of chance. There are equivalences there, a syntax of the context, a quality of the coexistence or of the spatial proximity. The perceived world is a world where the properties of an element depend upon its *situs* [location]. The signification of this element is therefore bound, not free-floating, tacit, not spoken, and {?} structure.

— These three properties of the perceived thing relate to expression
Expression or expressivity = [the] property that a phenomenon has to disclose, through its internal arrangement [*son agencement interne*], another [phenomenon] that is not and was never even actually given.
The tool, the work expresses man in this sense. But more precisely:
The intellectual work, the painting, the perceived, even the tool express man, but not directly: they express him by speaking about things or the world: tool, painting, etc. express [the] world and thereby express man.
The product only has the power to express man by expressing things. Only as the perspectival center of these views. Man is this relation between expression and expressed.

The human body is expressive in that it carries *Umweltintentionalität* [intentionality toward the environment or 'surrounding world'] in each of its gestures, it outlines and unfolds an '*Umwelt*' [environment or 'surrounding world'] and {even} a 'world.'[6] The identity of the thing is the equivalence of the various gestures that lead to it.

Now it's this expressivity that makes the 3 indicated properties of the perceived possible.

1) Opening to [the] existing thing and not to significations or values that have no bearer and, consequently, proximity and transcendence:
both [are] founded on [the] synonymy of certain gestures with /**[29](II5)**/ a certain landscape, on [the] rootedness of the body in the world, hence on [an] expressive relation between the exploring body and what it explores, e.g., quality.

⟨2)⟩ Meaning that is not essence: or that is only essence secondarily. Sense as divergence (as 'diacritical') with respect to a level. Adoption of a level = (Wertheimer experiment): raising of certain elements of the landscape to the dignity of dimensions having systematic value, the settling of our body into a norm (which is not given by the objective landscape but created by the fact that we take the walls, for example, as a privileged dimension, or our body as that to which this circle presents itself as [the] boundary of its range). In the two cases [an] expressive relation [is] presupposed between the body and the landscape, or [between] the landscape and me as its 'inhabitant,' I am here or I am in this setting [*cadre*], I express the world or it expresses me.

⟨3)⟩ Non-speaking sense, [the] 'mutism' [«*mutisme*»] of perception, — which is to be taken in the strong sense: not only does [perception] say nothing, but it is all the more opposed to language and to statements of the form 'I know that' since it is itself a sort of language: we understand the sensible as if between our body and it there were a pact prior to ourselves, [prior] to every institution, as if it spoke to us in a language we did not have to learn, [but] of which we have an implicit understanding [*dont nous n'ignorons pas la science*]. Hence [an] expressive relation from us to it.

— Hence reconsider and deepen our results dealing with the sensible world in terms of expression, and the notion of consciousness is thereby called into question.

CONSEQUENCES CONCERNING THE 'INTERNAL PERCEPTION' OF THE PSYCHIC, THE SOCIAL, OR THE INSTITUTIONAL

This calling into question places perception of the psychic or of the social in a fresh light: in perception, sense is never [the] pure unfolding of an in-itself before a for-itself.

Any positing of an in-itself (figure) presupposes, laterally, [the] positing of a background which itself is not ob-ject, [not] in-itself — the background or horizon forms part of the definition of the being. The simplest consciousness ([according to] *Gestalttheorie* [Gestalt theory]) is consciousness of a figure on a background: thus inasmuch as there is figure, there is also inarticulate background, inasmuch as we have being (figure), we don't have it, and inasmuch as we don't have it (background), [inasmuch as] we let it be without thinking about it, that's when we have it.

Theory of indirect or inverted consciousness: by definition it's cross-eyed, /**[30](II6)**/ all perception of *this* presupposes effective imperception of *that*. Freud: jealousy* /[*in margin*] *one could also take the example of love and hatred in mourning/ that is rivalry with the beloved over a third [person] appears as rivalry with this third [person] over the beloved.[7] But this is not for any reasons drawn from the content (homosexuality, initial polymorphism that leaves a trace and wants to hide from itself): [but rather] for reasons drawn from the structure of consciousness: to be aware of the beloved as beloved = identification with him and hence like him to go toward a third [person], if he goes there. To love X is to love Y that he loves, and this on account of identification. Perverse 'polymorphism' = intentionality of consciousness. Consequently one must not say: rivalry with the third [person] over the beloved is the appearance (heterosexual) and rivalry with the beloved over the third [person] is the reality (homosexual): for the second is identical with the first in a mediated way, and the second only takes place because the beloved is loved, it's through him (thus in a heterosexual way) that the third [person] is loved (in a homosexual way). And we can't say that the latent homosexual content is unknown: it is lived in the very love that one has for the beloved, inasmuch as it is identification (hence [the] possibility, in the case of rivalry, of a sort of sympathy for the rival alternating with jealousy in the usual sense: cf. [Jean-Toussaint] Merle, husband of Marie Dorval {acting} for Vigny)[8] The truth is not homosexuality all by itself, but homosexuality mediated within an immediate heterosexuality, the truth is that the rival is in no case indifferent [or] arbitrary, that he gives rise to reactions of removal or pursuit. Hence [there is] no unconscious, no inaccessible meaning: there is an ambiguous figure, i.e., sometimes [the] figure [of] homosexuality on a background of heterosexuality, sometimes the reverse, as in the ambiguous figures of the Gestalt theorists.[9]

Third Lecture

/[33](III1)/

Ext[ernal] perception = 'mutism' [«*mutisme*»]. Because [there is] no contact with an ob-ject. But [rather] modulation of a background without which [there is] no figure. Yet the background 'goes without saying' (*selbstverständlich* [self-evident]), [it's] not laid out. It's [a] level, i.e., unnoticed [*inaperçu*].

Hence perceptual consciousness = indirect (through the background) and inverted (inasmuch as it does not make its background explicit). And here we see [the] link [*lien*] between consciousness of things and consciousness of expression ('perception of the psychic') ('social perception')

Jealousy: figure: rivalry with a third [person] over the loved object
background: rivalry with the loved object over a third [person]

Freud: understands that homosexuality is truth, heterosexuality [is] appearance.
Deciphering of the unconscious, which overturns appearances.

Us:[1] not truth of homosexuality [and] mere appearance of heterosexuality. No un-conscious.

Rather: relation [between] figure and background: heterosexuality and homosexuality. The background is not truer than the figure, [not] uniquely true. Nor [is] the figure uniquely true. There is reciprocal implication [between] homosexuality [and] heterosexuality.
To be heterosexual is to be homosexual in a mediated way.
To be homosexual is to be heterosexual in a mediated way (inasmuch as the jealousy of the homosexual is his rivalry with the loved object over a third [person] of the opposite sex. Component that {?}).
What is called homosexuality or heterosexuality = sense of the possible structurations of the set [of] figure and background. The predominant structuration doesn't cancel the other, which remains in the background. It's lived in the love that

one has for the beloved inasmuch as it is always identification (and not merely a relation to an object).
Consciousness as consciousness of something [is] always deceptive or deceived: it is only consciousness of *this* by also being consciousness of *that*, but without taking the latter up. It's cross-eyed.

Mystified consciousness (Marx).[2] Like Freud, inverted consciousness: the fact that we see something proves that we're something else. And as in Freud [this is] understood in the sense of an external determinism that splits self-consciousness. We see in ourselves what we're not [*On voit de soi ce que l'on n'est pas*]: e.g., consciousness /**[34](III2)**/ of certain values indicates their absence in the social whole. Fulfillment [*réalisation*] in fantasies because they're not [truly] realized [*réalisées*]. Fantastical "compensation," "point of honor," "consolation, justification," religion [as the] "soul of a soulless epoch"[3] (Pharisaism: no value in the consciousness of being good, nor even in the consciousness of values).

[How] that [is] generally understood: ideology = appearance, effective social relations = reality, sole truth? — As in Freud, it's not so simple: the unconscious is lived even if only to flee itself in the 'figure.' In the same way, speculative philosophy is false as separate and true as reintegrated into the overall functioning. Just as heterosexuality is true as reintegrated into context. [Speculative philosophy is] true in the sense that it makes possible a relation of man with man. It is not absolutely true since it is essential to it to make itself autonomous, to separate itself, and so its falseness is indirect. Acting separately, outside of life, it is not an image of this life, it is not true as it knows itself, but as it can be thought with all the rest. Nonetheless it shows that the system needs external justification, that it is not at rest, that it is unsettled (some historical periods have no compensating ideology [*idéologie contre-partie*], only [directly] reflective ideology [*idéologie-reflet*]),[4] and in this sense [speculative philosophy] leads [the system] toward its overcoming. Movement toward something else and [the] locking of this movement outside of the world.

Thus there is consciousness of the true in the background of false consciousness. (And false consciousness in the background of consciousness of the true: alienation is only deferred, and the process of eliminating it is infinite.)

And this is due not only to [the] content but also to [the] structure of consciousness. Content: a content of homosexuality or of oppression hidden by a fantastical heterosexuality or [by] religion. Consciousness would remain inherently thetic or representational. In fact, this is in no way consciousness cut off from the true (which would be followed by consciousness cut off from the false, or [consciousness] without history, or pure [consciousness]). The mask is defined by [*est notion de*] what it masks (heterosexuality by homosexuality, – religion by oppression), precisely to be able to mask it. Hence [a] structural inversion that implies [the] presence of the true in the false (and of the false in the true). [There is] therefore no remedy which would consist in destroying appearance in order to reveal reality ([5]destroying heterosexuality in order to reveal homosexuality, destroying value in order to reveal the /**[35](III3)**/ social causes of our thoughts. One can destroy only by realizing: destroy the fantastical (i.e., dishonest) heterosexuality (which does not want to accept its homosexuality) in order to realize it (psychoanalysis), — destroy separate values (which as such are false) by realizing them. Hence truth is not behind ideologies but in their internal movement of realization [and] destruction. In short, consciousness of ambiguity is the opposite of ambivalence. Since it implies subterfuge [*artifice*], it is necessary to destroy the "point of honor" style of heterosexuality and of separate values, in order to realize them.

Thus ambiguous consciousness = not unconscious, not fate 'behind our back' (in that case there would be nothing more than to leave it totally up to the work of the other: [the] psychoanalyst understood as thaumaturge, [or the] organization understood as infallible). Ambiguous consciousness = there is another view of what we see, which places in the figure what we place in the background, relation of liberating dialectic with the doctor, discussions. The fact that we perceive others and not simply fantasies of ourselves, that we are open to other perspectives through the background that we know could become figure (the other [*autrui*] is whatever sketches out in our world other ways of grouping things [and] other boundaries [that are] grasped laterally in the perceptual spectacle)[6] suffices to prove that we are not cut off from the true.

Hence perceptual consciousness as consciousness of something more or less on [a] background is not self-consciousness through and through, [it] involves [a] duality [of] being [and] appearance (and not [an] immediate identity of appearance and being), [it] is relatively impersonal [*relativement on*], already generality, already anonymous.

Inasmuch as expression is also perceived, we thereby understand reciprocally that the perception of expression is anonymous [or] impersonal [*on*].[7]

Lateral expressivity (figure and background) → corporeity
→ sociality

The epistemological subject only comes to be [*se réalise*] within this framework and is not an a priori condition of these experiences.

/[36](III4)/

DEVELOPMENT OF A THEORY OF RATIONALITY

Requires that we clarify [the] analysis of

[the] expressive relation | [between] body [and the] sensible, natural, or mute world
| [between] man [and the] institutional, cultural, or speaking world

and [the] relation between these two systems:

at first glance:

double envelopment: Nature envelops culture
Culture envelops nature (Marx: all of our science of nature is cultural fact.) Rejection of this idea by 'new naturalism' (Thao).[8] Dialectic of nature.

The problem of rationality:

philosophical return to perceived nature and culture: how does this enable [us] to think this relation?

Brunschvicg: there is [a] naturalistic order of evolution, but there is [a] spiritual or eternal order that underlies it, idealism, participation in the One, true value of the reflective order.[9]

Us: even our reflection on perception belongs to culture. The truth of perceptual phenomena presents itself as truth of these phenomena in spite of the 'retrograde movement' of thematized truth. The latter must not blind us to the structural changes that it introduces. The complete examination of the 'world of expression' is also an examination of this examination. Consciousness can't ultimately be only of thematized truth, but of the latter + the perceptual {?}. Origin of the truth.[10]

AIM OF THIS YEAR'S COURSE

THIS YEAR

But the retrograde movement only occurs at the level of language.

Linguistic expression saved for another year, and with it the problem of rationality.

This year: [the] passage from natural expression to non-linguistic culture.

CENTRAL PHENOMENON

Double function of the body:

— the body as [a] given organization, [as] 'sensory' activity, [as] 'fields,' [as a] response to 'natural' aspects of the world

— and [the] body as [a] body that moves itself, and [that] returns ⟨to⟩ /**[37](III5)**/ the world in order to signify it [or] to designate it, [the body as an] organ of mimicry.

People with apraxia show [the] construction of a virtual space (beyond sensory functioning), [a] system of correspondences between [the] actual field and what would be spatial properties for other situations. The gesture of pointing [*monstration*] already presupposes this virtual space, this possible here as opposed to the actual.

The expression of the gesture is not the surpassing of my situation, but [the] taking on [*assomption*] of all its sense. It's in the [particular] case that I learn to see the εἶδος [*eidos*]. [The] use of maps, drawings, diagrams. [The] relation of expression and the expressed [is] reciprocal.

Nevertheless, even though [it occurs] in the same place [*sur place*], there is ascent [*ascension*]: cultural expression goes beyond natural expression.

It is tempting to invoke mind here. *Darstellungsfunktion* [representative function],[11] symbolic thinking,[12] etc. But since it's all or nothing, that would be a return to [the] philosophy of consciousness. Hence we can't constitute praxia on the basis of gnosia. The problem of the relations [among] apraxia, agnosia, [and] aphasia must remain open in order to provide [an] opportunity to grasp the opening to the virtual and to the possible in its primordial form.

Consider praxis as constituting, even with regard to the cultural world (and not just the natural world). Our perceptual consciousness, inverted consciousness, which lets a perceived thing appear or discloses it without possessing it, is already an activity of participation [*fréquentation*], a familiarity with . . . a praxis rather than a gnosia. Objects of a higher order, cultural objects [that are] expressive in the human sense, appear in the same way, through an equally tacit infusion of meaning: use objects, artworks, — this leads us up to the threshold of phasia, of language as presumptively universal expression. ~~(next year)~~ And which possesses itself, which presumptively possesses its sense.

Praxis as distinct from action in the Bergsonian sense.[13] Action: if not its solutions, [then] at least its problems are given, biological problems: habitat, food, preservation, reproduction. That presupposes given conditions. Praxis is the elaboration of the conditions themselves, preadaptations, initial projection of internal conditions of equilibrium, a priori of the organism. And this is what enables it to be the foundation of gnosia and language.

Hence outline (cf. below III7).

/[38](III6)/

Try to achieve in concrete terms [an] intuition of the movement of taking [things] up expressively [*le movement de reprise expressive*], of [the] coming together [or] of [the] consolidation of sense.

Next year: passage to the spoken world and to history.

Only after that: theory of rationality, ~~and in particular of subjectivity and intersubjectivity,~~ theory of truth.

/[39]/

COURSE I

12 lectures including today's (5. February [1953])

11 lectures

I) Space and movement:

Posing of the problem

Space and movement

1) Anchorage and level (Wertheimer) (analysis of 'straight' and of 'inverted'). Clarification through depth: relation [between] things mediated by relation [between] self [and] thing.

2) Movement [as] 'change of location' = variation with regard to an 'anchorage.'

The alternative: movement without moving object (Wertheimer)? Or movement as essentially implying a thing in motion? (Linke) All consciousness is consciousness of something. But this something can be *Etwas überhaupt* [anything whatsoever].

3) Relation [between] spatial field [and] qualitative field, spatial level and color level. Relation [between] spatial structuration [and] qualitative structuration — Interferences — Spatial structuration = expression. Relation [between] qualitative-spatial structuration [and] structuration of sense – perceptual logic.

4) The problem: perceptual field – sensory-gnosic mental field. Agnosias. Interpretation of agnosias in terms of field.

5) Agnosia and apraxia. Gnosia and praxia.

6 and 7) Perception of movement and expression: painting. Movement expressed by something other than itself.

8 and 9) Cinema: perception of the real movement of objects. It's [a] particular case of phenomenal structuration (stroboscopic movement), which exhibits not only movement of objects but also movement of the spectator with respect to the objects, i.e., cinema always presupposes [a] level of normality in relation to which panoramic views, tracking shots, editing, and cutting acquire expressive meaning. Here stroboscopic movement expresses something other than itself.

Complication of the expressive power of stroboscopic movement through [the] intervention of sound or music or speech: how they come into play. [The] expressive value of silence in a certain visual context [is] like [the] expressive value of the absence of anything seen [*vues*] in a certain auditory context.

10) The voices of silence and tacit expression. (Prelinguistic meaning). Problem of linguistic meaning. Relation to the problem of language and of history. Originality of linguistic expression with regard to 'mute' expressions.

~~11~~) Indirect consciousness and consciousness of something. Structuration and truth (Wertheimer).[14]

/**[40](III7)**/

OUTLINE OF COURSE I

11 lectures

Pick out [the] phenomenon of movement as

1) belonging to the sensible world and [as] already disclosing expressive relations there [between the] body [and the] natural world.

2) [Being,] besides [the] medium of other significations (painting, cinema), itself [the] means of an expressive power of a higher degree*

/[*in margin*] *= The perception of movement is already expression. The expression of movement or movement as means of expression is still perception. Sublimation of movement and of perception./

I. Space and movement

Movement implies a space. Which does not mean [*ne veut pas dire*] chronological or transcendental priority. They go together.

Space [as] anchorage or level. Analysis of 'straight.'

Space [as] relation [between] my here (incarnate self) [and] another here (over there). Depth shows that [the] relation [between] self [and] thing supports [the] relation [between] things.

II. Movement

Essential analysis: thought of a thing in motion

~~Existential analysis~~ Description:

Bergson: [the] model for objective movements is my movement. But for him [this is an] unanalyzable given.

Wertheimer: stroboscopic movement without [a] thing in motion.

Discussion

True meaning of the discussion: bring to light a bodily quasi-synthesis, — which is expression.

III. Relation [between] spatial field [and] qualitative field

Spatial structuration acts on qualitative structuration and is subject to its influence. Motor theories of perception.

And both are integrated within [the] structuration of the sense of the field. Perceptual logic.

IV. Relation [between] perceptual field [and] mental field. Perceptual and gnosic. Interpretation of agnosias in terms of field.

V. Gnosia and praxia. Agnosia and apraxia. Praxis opens a field of higher degree.

VI–VII. From perception as expression to expression of the perceived: the expression of movement in painting. Movement expressed by something other than itself. L[eonardo] da Vinci, the "flexuous line."[15]

VIII–IX. Cinema, initially [an] imitation of objective movement, becomes [an] expression of the movement of the camera in relation to the object, i.e., [an] expression of man, given a certain level of normality that gives meaning through divergence to panning, tracking, editing, [and] cutting. The movement [of the camera] expressing something other than itself owing to the hinge [between the] perceived world [and the] perceiving body, [or between] level [and] figure, that accounts for all 'association' or passive synthesis.

[The] intervention of sound, music, [or] speech making [this] expressive power more complicated: a visual emptiness full of sound or a visual fullness devoid of sound have [an] expressive power that they would not have without the intermodal background.

This suggests [that] cinematic expression [occurs] not through signs linked to significations, but through [an] internal relation from sign to sign within the intersensory or sensory whole, [within] the field [through the] expressive value of a sign's absence (non-vision or non-sound) (cf. linguistics).

X. [A] look at the passage from prelinguistic meaning to linguistic meaning. Gesture and speech. Voices of silence and the claim of language. Linguistic expression and 'mute' expression. Silent history and manifest history. Indirect consciousness and consciousness of something: structuration and truth (Wertheimer: structural conception of truth).[16]

/[40]v(III7)/

XI. The concept of world: sensible world and historical world.

/[41](III8)/

I. SPACE AND MOVEMENT

1) NO PRIORITY PROBLEM

I'm not posing [a] priority problem: 'we must have space to have movement because movement is [a] change of place' — Space [as] condition without which no movement — That without which.

This kind of analysis presupposes [its] solution: we look for [the] meaning of movement, [the] concept or essence of movement, i.e., [its] verbal signification. And on [the] pretext of [*sous couleur de*] knowing what we're looking for, we imply what we're going to find: for movement will be 1) either [a] source of positions and identification in the guise of [*sous couvert de*] time 2) or else, since that's only [a] trace [*trace*] of the movement, [it will be a] tracing [*tracé*] through [a] mental journey [*par parcours mental*]. Empiricism and reflexive analysis. The one [is] beneath the movement, the other [is] beyond [it].

It's precisely a question of knowing what movement means [*veut dire*], not what is contained in our verbal concept of movement. Grasp movement [in its] appearing. Kant saw this when he held that the tracing of a figure is not [a] mental tracing [*tracé spirituel*], but [a] bodily tracing [*tracé corporel*].[17]

This means [*veut dire*]: not reflection on theoretical implications (movement implying place).

Likewise we are not saying: chronological or transcendental priority (= according to conceptual relationships) of space with respect to movement. Simultaneous possibilities: the whole of space without determinations is no more thinkable than the latter without space. The point of view of the that without which (Aristotle ἄνευ οὗ οὐχ] [without which not] – reflexive analysis – Husserl) = criterial thinking, distrustful, on guard against error, which does not tell us the that through which, possibility in the positive [or] living sense.[18]

We are giving just enough indications concerning space so that our analysis of movement won't be hampered by prejudices concerning place [*lieu*]. We have to begin somewhere and there is no beginning in the phenomena, [there is no] initial phenomenon [or] one-way dependence. Basically [we are giving] indications concerning space that the analysis of movement will confirm.

2) SENSE OF 'UP' AND 'DOWN,' RIGHT-LEFT, HEIGHT-WIDTH

Just as I don't have to privilege [the] perception of space in relation to [the] perception of movement, I don't have to reduce [the] perception of space to its form irrespective of its contents.

E.g., space would be [a] pure tissue of relations between top [and] bottom, right [and] left, near [and] far. Since these terms indicate contents, space would be what makes their composition possible.

/[42](III9)/

But this space, composed of relations, hence relative (and homogeneous), is never actual. For here a place is [a] relation to other places, to which the same applies and so on, and nothing is ever somewhere [or] 'in place' [*en place*].

It's certainly true that places are relative: that we change them by choosing other points of reference. But this presupposes first of all a phenomenon of the absolute 'place' [or] of the [absolute] 'here,' without which the setting into relation wouldn't mean anything [*ne voudrait rien dire*]: big and small are relative, but in order for Socrates to be small in relation to the giant he must be big in relation to the ant. A standard must be posited.

Usual trick: [a] two-part analysis: space in itself and space for us. Space in itself with up, down, right, left, directions given in the spectacle. But that's not [the] truth of space: [the] truth of space is [the] mind making the internal framework [*l'armature*] of this content. For it, there is no up and down. And the proof that the perception of space is this mental act: [the] correction [*redressement*] of inverted objects (on [the] retina), binocular fusion, or [the] correction of retinal images [that were] uninverted [*redressées*] by [the] goggles.[19]

Reply: if it were a mental act we could not understand why stereoscopic fusion [is] conditioned by thresholds, below which [there is] diplopia, [we could not understand] why putting on [the] goggles → [the] uninversion [*redressement*] of retinal images is initially disruptive [*donne d'abord bouleversement*]. 'Above' and 'below' have no meaning for the mind. If it's the soul that sees, [then] it should see the same thing in all directions [*sens*]. The very idea that [directions [*sens*]] must be taken in a [certain] sense shows that the meaning of the perceived is not pure mental signification.[20]

Thus the standard can't be provided by the content to a mind that would be extraneous to it, [a] pure relation [or a] form.

Because 1) if it really were provided by the content, [then] it should be directly dependent upon it, which isn't the case.

2) if it has no sense at the level of the content, and if its whole meaning is made through relations in which the mind renders it explicit, [then] space will never begin, none of these relations will be set up.

There must be: spatiality sensitive to the content, brought about by it (the book appears to me upside down), – but not a simple function of the content.

In [the] Stratton experiment,[21] don't interpret [the] disruption [*bouleversement*], [the] gradual adaptation, [and the] correction as 1) {all} {of the} visual sensations [being] upside down, while tactile sensations are right side up 2) associative correspondence of the new visual with the old tactile allowing for the new visual to be interpreted in the language of the old tactile 3) training of the tactile by the heavier visual that "displaces" the initial space, makes it "go pale."[22] Until the tactile is interpreted in the language of the new visual look [*aspect*].

It's a question of knowing first of all how the visual field has an up and a down. The experiment correctly shows that it doesn't have them /**[43] (III10)**/ in itself. That they are relations. But not free-floating relations of thought [that would be] equivalent in all directions, not relations in a pure object placed before a pure mind. Up [and] down, right [and] left certainly form a system, not an aggregate, but a system that is not of the understanding, not [one that would be] immediately identical for different contents.

When visual images are restored, I no longer recognize [them], or [else] the top appears to me at the bottom. This means [*veut dire*]: not directions of the spectacle in themselves, but directions in relation to me. I.e., [the] previous spectacle and my body formed relations that make it such that the sky is in the direction of my head and the ground [is] in the direction of my feet. [That] my head [is a] celestial region [and] my feet [a] chthonic region, or [that] the sky [is] noble and the ground [is] accursed [*infernale*]. The initial disruption = the spectacle implies a certain orientation of my body and my body [implies] a certain orientation of the spectacle = mismatch of the previous body and the new spectacle. What brings it about that there is an up and a down, a here and a place, are not objective points but a certain hold of my body on the world, a confidence and ease of my body in the world, the fact that I <u>inhabit it</u>; there is a place because there is a <u>here</u> of [the] self which is not [an] objective body. Place is [a] relation of self and the world through my body, not [a] relation between parts of the world. Place is first of all <u>situation</u>.

Gearing together of my body and the spectacle. It will be asked: but why can't I perceive up and down correctly regardless of the position of the images on my retina? Doesn't gearing together presuppose an orientation of the behavior and an orientation of the perceived in itself? No. We are only saying that some aspect of the perceived calls for a certain hold of the body along a certain path, and [that] some orientation of the body [calls for] a presentation of the perceived that is not arbitrary. We do not extract up and down from the perceived or from the body or from the mixture of the two: we are saying that the orientation <u>arises</u> from a gearing together that does not occur in just any conditions whatsoever, that is systematic but nevertheless conditioned. The up and down that appear in these conditions are like [a] <u>general level</u> or <u>ground</u> that I <u>settle into</u> for optimal functioning. This level can be changed (hence relativity), but not by an intellectual activity: [rather] by an activity of taking on [*assomption*] or of inhabiting that each time makes it an absolute, the condition of being or of sense.

/[44](III11)/

Activity of taking on [*assomption*] = motivated. <u>Anchorage points</u> suggest themselves. They only have definite directions in a previous level (Wertheimer experiment).[23] But as such they represent a certain <u>divergence from the norm</u>, [a] divergence that tends to impose itself as a norm. To take them as norms is to stop seeing them as figures in order to see them as dimensions. That one level always presupposes another level = perception is inherently spatial, incarnate, situated, space is prior to all constitution, all perception is relative to a level.

Thus spatiality of height and width → primordial spatiality of me as inhabitant.

Theory of movement = variation, modality of this primordial spatiality.

3) <u>SENSE OF NEAR AND FAR</u>

Fourth Lecture

/[45](IV1)/

I. SPACE

What do here, there, where, locality signify [as substantive terms]? Such as we see them in the sensible.
To prepare us for consciousness of movement.
A preliminary question can be raised:

Logic

The appeal to what we see = necessarily confused results. If we want rigor, stop consulting [the] experience of space, — but [rather] science or exact concepts, i.e., logical [concepts]. Give a sufficient characterization of spatial statements through logical properties (a point on a straight line = membership of this point in a set of points) – In this way work out [the] rules of legitimate statements, bring to light fully formal implicative force – The appeal to intuition is only necessary because we have not formulated the characteristic axioms of the manifold under consideration – If we formulate them, [then] the appeal to intuition is limited to indicating at the outset the type of spatial being in question, which comes back into logical being as a special case.

But

Is it possible to construct [a] formal expression of space? (i.e., [a] logical equivalent such that not only everything we say about it would be true of the corresponding spatial relations, but [also] such that everything we find in these spatial relations would be represented in the formal relations)?
If not, [then] formalization does not yield [the] essence of space, but [a] partial symbolic substitute. We must therefore oppose space to our statements concerning space, restore space beyond them, consider logical positivism as [a] criterial thinking that defines not our access to what is true, but [rather] conditions for avoiding error, not actual spatiality, but its logical description [*signalement*].
The alternative posed by logical positivism: either sense, i.e., formal relations, or [else] non-sense [*non sens*] about which nothing can

be said. Philosophy can't be reduced to the λεκτόν [*lekton*, what is expressible]:[1] it's the confrontation between what we say and that about which we say it.

/[46](IV2)/

Another preliminary question, another formalism:

Transcendental logic:

Spatial existence is not logical existence. Symmetrical objects are logically indiscernible. Distinguished by orientation. Thus spatiality [is] intuitive. Nonetheless everything positive in this intuition is consciousness of [a] linkage [*liaison*] with regard to which what is linked is contingent. Linkage [is] the same for one symmetrical object or the other. Their duality in space concerns content. Formal intention establishes [the] form of the intuition. There is simply no way to lay out the form without 'content in general.' Everything starts with experience. But *this* content [or] *this* experience is contingent. E.g., up, down, right, left, near, far, height, width, depth = empirical determinations [or] contents that presuppose a linking power, i.e., linkage in general exhausts their meaning. Relational space. Here, there, [and] where [as substantive terms] have no sense other than [as] breaks in [a] totality. Space is not made of parts.

[This is] less [a] solution than [a] problem: it's true that space is not the sum of parts, [that it] is [a] totality, — and [it's] true that it's intuitive, not logical. But how [can it be] both at once? [The] theory of formal intuition reduces the form of the intention ('[the] way in which we are affected') to [a] production of the understanding. But then spatiality is always on hold: since the relational activity doesn't receive any meaning from the contents, spatiality = relation of an orientation [or] position to another which itself is [a] relation to another, and so on. Space [is] always possible (condition without which it would not be) and not actual. Hence space [is a] totality, yes, [it is] relational, yes, in the sense that it is not the sum of things in space, or of partial and absolute determinations (up, down, right, left, etc.), [in the sense] that it is [a] system and transposable. But to be transposable, the here [or] the place must be, and so it can't merely be [a] possible break in totality. If all knowledge begins with experience, [if] none can be defined outside of experience, [then] experience must be possible for me in a positive way. To be mutually transposable, height, width, and depth must first of all be, and not simply as possibilities of linkage in general. Connection of form and content that does not bind the form and does not make the content elective.

Thus return to experience with the question who perceives space? It's not the *I think*.

/[47](IV3)/

1) HEIGHT AND WIDTH

Up-down, right-left, and tracking of all objects in relation to these privileged dimensions.

They don't have [an] absolute sense. They don't have [a] purely relational sense.

They aren't in the content. They aren't only for the *I think*.

1°) I'm saying they don't have [an] absolute sense even in currently perceived space.

Up [and] down, right [and] left [are] relative to [the] position of the observer (reference to other possible observers).

But even for me, up [and] down, straight, oblique, horizontal, right [and] left are not absolute for a given position of my body. These characteristics can change when my body and the stimuli remain the same: Stratton's experiment, uninversion [*redressement*] of retinal images, inverted landscape at first, then still [a] tactile-visual discrepancy, but with body inverted, finally [there is] agreement and [the] reestablishment of normal vision. [It is] therefore impossible to relate verticality and horizontality to stimuli and to my factual body — Wertheimer: likewise space that is initially at an angle [*oblique*] becomes straight again, without the position of the body having changed.[2]

Thus → it's not the eye that sees, it's the soul. Perception = mental inspection. Space = relations that are transposable and indeed transposed by the understanding, not given with [the] content through [the] spatial value of points on the retina.

2) But that's not true either:

Space [is] relative, but not unconditioned: one can't see straight immediately after putting on Stratton's goggles, or by trying to do so through judgment in the Wertheimer experiment. We have to wait. Inertia or adversity. Mind [is] bound. There are no absolute spatial values of the points on the retina or of the 'sensations' that issue from them, but there are temporary spatial values that resist: the landscape initially appears inverted or oblique. It's not [an] act of *Sinngebung* that corrects it.

What does this wait signify? Stratton: the new visual positions have to be made to coincide with the previous ones through association. The new visual 'up' [has to be made to coincide] with the previous 'down' represented by touching. The experiment shows that these correspondences are gradually located. As the visual is dominant, it first of all follows that the new (visual) spectacle tends to impose its dimensions on the previous (tactile) spectacle which is, in regard to it, 'inverted': it's thus first of all the tactile /**[48](IV4)**/ that appears inverted. Then [a] more complete identification of the points of the field brings about [the] 'displacement' of the tactile by the visual which imposes its dimensions; but at this point, being the only thing considered, the visual field loses the characteristic of 'inverted' and vision becomes normal again.

Objection 1) this reeducation of touch by the new vision [and] the motor-visual experiences of establishing correspondence are not necessary: the Wertheimer experiment proves that normalization takes place without this. [Normalization] is thus systematic and not additive. And yet it's not instantaneous. It's not association. And it's not judgment.

2) Stratton's whole analysis operates as if the top and the bottom were properties of visual or tactile sensations; and as if, the visual {mass} being inverted in relation to the tactile, the problem were merely to make them coincide again. Yet the Wertheimer experiment precisely shows that orientation is not inherent in the contents, since the same content changes [orientation]. The question is not only to ensure agreement between {masses} of sensation oriented in themselves, but to know what this orientation is, which is not an absolute property of the contents, but no more [is it the] organization of mere thought, being tied to the sensible after all.

Thus the wait is not due to the necessity of time for some mental chemistry, but nonetheless stems from the fact that something other than me as [the] *I think* is involved. Just as my waiting for sugar to melt projects my time into things,[3] my waiting for normal vision proves that there is beneath me as thinking a quasi-thinking. What exactly is this natural thinking? What is it to see?

ANALYSIS

I tilt my head and it seems to me that I'm bowing [*je m'incline*] and that the world remains 'straight.'

I place myself in Wertheimer's apparatus and it seems to me that the room is inclined [*s'incline*], – then the room appears 'straight' to me.

What's going on in these three cases?

Straight and inclined in the Wertheimer experiment: 'normal' and 'abnormal.' 'What is self-evident' and 'what is strange' = agreement or disagreement. But of what with what? Shall we say of the current orientation of the landscape with its previous orientation? Or of the new orientation of the landscape /**[49](IV5)**/ with the orientation of my body [which] remained the same? But we know that neither the one nor the other is intrinsically oriented (critique of Stratton). How could there be disagreement between the current and previous orientation if orientation is nothing in itself, if it can vary for the same givens? In order for there to be conflict, there must be reference to a common term, in this case my body, each aspect of the visible must be linked organically to an aspect of my body for me, and these two aspects of my body must be mutually exclusive. But the orientation of my body for me is also not an absolute: Wertheimer's experiment shows that it can vary (my body [is] straight at first, then disappears as [a] reference). Thus we are not looking for the source of 'orientation' in it. 'Orientation' is tied exclusively neither to [the] aspect of the world nor to that of the body, [rather] it lies at their point of convergence. Each spectacle elicits or presupposes a body that sees from a position that is 'normal' in relation to it, each aspect of the body [elicits or presupposes] a 'corresponding' aspect of the world. The body appears 'straight' and the world [appears] 'straight' when the one is directly engaged with the other in [a] situation of optimal functioning. The body appears oblique and the world [appears] straight or the world [appears] oblique and the body [appears] straight when there is disagreement between the body summoned by the world and the world summoned by the body. We do not draw orientation from the visual 'content' or from the tactile 'content,' but from the confrontation of two systems [that are] called upon to form just one.

It may be objected: but why don't the two systems (visible-virtual body) (actual body-virtual body) coincide in all cases, or rather: why are there figural cases of the world as [there are] of the body, e.g., in the Wertheimer experiment, and thus an optimum, a situation of grip [*prise*], as well as situations of discrepancy or divergence? Because the relation [between the] body [and the] world whereby a movement signifies an unfolding of the spectacle, and inversely [whereby] the spectacle [signifies] a spectator, is not a relation conceived by a thinking [that] arbitrates between them, but a relation that we exist, i.e., these equivalences only appear through [my] choice of abode: I live in *this* world[4] and as a result I have *this* body, or inversely I have *this* body and thus I am situated in some particular way. This does not explain the appearance [*apparition*] /**[50](IV6)**/ of the optimum, of the [being] 'in gear' [«*en prise*»], but merely makes explicit the fact of the orientation of the world and of the body in their mutual presence. This fact = there are normal and aberrant [orientations]; or: there are privileged [orientations]; or again = it's from the midst of space that we perceive space, whoever can perceive space is necessarily surrounded or pervaded [*investi*] by space, [necessarily] has a body. The original sense of 'here,' from which any objective 'here' derives, is the presence to the world of a body and [the presence] to this body of that which perceives space. It's this settling into or this inhabiting that brings it about that any phenomenon can appear as divergence in relation to this level. Meaning of the notion of level.

Relativity of space: there is always the possibility of changing levels: the oblique room later appears vertical when I inhabit it, i.e., when I connect it to my bodily space. — But this relativity doesn't mean [*ne veut pas dire*] that [space] is only relations: for the choice of reference points is [an] activity of settling into space, and once the choice is made, [it] makes only one perception possible. Hence [it's] not simply [an] activity of relating through judgment [*opération judicatoire et relatante pure*]. Each constitution of a new level (Wertheimer) borrows from the previous one the determinate orientation of the elements upon which the anchorage takes place, and they owe this orientation to the previous level. Thus space can't be deduced, it's intuitive, without [it] being [the] property of the contents on their own.

/[51](IV7)/

2) THE NEAR AND THE FAR

What does the very striking impression of depth or relief mean [*veut dire*]. E.g., in the stereoscope or in three-dimensional cinema? The pleasure that we take in these spectacles? Like in the kaleidoscope? What is it to see, when it's not a *quale*? Reduction of this experience when we wonder what it means [*veut dire*], when we analyze [it].

First reply: it means nothing: depth is not visible. Because of the retina. But this isn't a reason. What we see isn't to be judged by what takes place on the retina.

Second reply: depth is not visible because it's not spread out, [because] the points conceal one another instead of being juxtaposed. Hence it's [a] reference to a widthwise vision. Construction of a universal space of ubiquity. There is no perspectival space of my own. There is no vision, or what we call vision is thought. Deciphered signs. E.g., discrepancy of the images in the stereoscope, convergence, apparent size, interpreted facts. All that is psychology of space: factual conditions in which [the] intellectual act occurs, contents or materials through which it occurs. Psychology of space {keeps} only this act. Incarnation = addition of a point of view to [the] mind. The point of view would impede vision if it were not overcome through [the] thought of this point of view.

All that comes up against the obvious fact of stereoscopic depth: these explanations are possible (reference to other experiments, or even [the] construction of a geometric diagram [*géométral*] that would account for [*rende raison de*] these perspectives). But we don't have the impression that they [actually] yield the experience of depth,[5] nor that space only begins beyond perspective.

a) CONVERGENCE

In the moment when relief appears there are more than just signs (more and less than an intellection of universal space). [There is a] discrepancy of retinal images, then abruptly relief. It all happens as if the discrepancy were not [an] established objective fact, but [a] fact /**[52](IV8)**/ for the looking [*regard*], this fact is only for [a] looking that seeks to see or to identify something, for [a] single looking through the two eyes, and its 'decipherment' is not an intellectual act, but [a] response to a solicitation, the eyes take hold [*s'installent*] in such a way that there is co-functioning and magically a single thing appears in depth. What is given specifies the body one must have and the body completes the given. It's exactly like inspiration: Valéry, or like the sexual act. "Exchange between the end and the means, chance and choice, substance and accident, prediction and opportunity, matter and form, power and resistance, which, like the burning, strange, intimate battle of the sexes, involves all the energies of human life, grinds them against each other, [and] creates" (DDD 138).[6]

The perception of depth is [an] awakening, it's mind that becomes body and body that becomes mind. What is the looking and the perceived relief? It's [the] teleological organization of a feedback:[7] received information calls forth from the motor system the movements that will arouse a sought result. But this feedback is not automatic, i.e., the movements that are set off are guided by [an] imminent vision, polarized toward the future, whereas radar only gives this impression in the conscious spectator. Furthermore, in contrast to radar, [this feed-back involves a] schematic typology [*montage*] [that is] general if not universal.[8] Hence intentionality, just weighed down [*alourdie*]: [it] isn't [an] ideal reference to space in itself. It's [a] progression toward a privileged state that wants what we want (cf. painter).[9] We don't visualize the sought relief, it exceeds our anticipation, and yet we don't go toward it with eyes closed, there is [a] logic of perceptual unfolding, style, the movement of our eyes and the three-dimensional look [are] reciprocally means and end.*

/[*in margin*] *see p. IV9/

b) APPARENT SIZE

Likewise apparent size is not [an] interpreted fact. With regard to an outline of [a] thing, it's [the] tension toward a relation of exact gearing together. Distance is measured by this tension. The apparent size results from [an] isolating stance and [the] interruption of perception. Perception does not involve determinate apparent size, but [the] presence of phantoms or things (and distant things are phantoms) and vectors which go from vision with [an] imperfect hold to [an] adequate vision, and which bring it about that the man at the horizon counts as [a] man, the road at the horizon [counts] as [a] road. /[*in margin*] (IV9a [Note] I)/ The 'deciphering' of the appearance is neither [the] invocation of experiences of touching at a distance, nor [the] construction of an invariable size in itself: it's [the] extension of the transition that I carry out for the objects spread out nearby, it's [the] perceptual power or reach of my looking [*regard*], and this extension appears possible to me as a matter of principle and because my perceptions pass into each other. My perspective is not the denial of the truth concerning space, projection onto a plane as in [a] camera obscura [*chambre noire*], [rather] it's [the] initiation into space, [the] implication of space, /**[53](IV9)**/ since each particular perspective is offered to me as [a] special case of my power of perceptual unfolding. It's the whole of space that I learn in my proximate horizon, the impossibility of limits, etc. The horizon is not [a] distillation of things, [but rather a] type of intellectual existence that's new with regard to thing[s] and relations. Cf. Kantian form. Pre-concept → cf. problem of historical sedimentation.
/[*in margin of several crossed-out lines*] cf. IV9a Note II/

/[*in margin of the following two paragraphs*] to be added to IV8/
Disparate images offered to [a] power of merging them that's unaware of itself as [a] power of movement in the 'real' world, and which doesn't know its 'end,' but which nonetheless is guided. There is no *Sinngebung* here, the sense appears as already there since it is the disparate images themselves which, offered to a seeing [*une vision*], draw it toward the goal: exchange between the end and the means, [between] chance and choice . . . The body is such a power of inventiveness, but subjected to conditions of nature (we don't perceive just anything whatsoever), and, when these conditions are brought together, [it] functions unfailingly. Here inventiveness = expressive relationship between the perceiving self and what I perceive = these disparate images exist in order to yield [the] stereoscopic object, [they] find their sense in it, but this sense

is strangely called forth by them, already in them. Three-dimensional vision precedes itself in the presented images which mutually call upon one another to merge. /[*in margin*] transcendental 'affinity' (Kant)/ Passivity — association — corporeality = encounter of the constituting with an unconstituted, in such a way that expression = *Sinngebung* but which predates itself in the manifold to which meaning is given, because from the outset this manifold was given to a moving body, [the] key to the world. The relation of expression = regressive movement of the true. I was already spatial (= situated) before any particular perception of space, I was already geared into space. I see relief = not as [a] 'visual given,' but as [an] implication of a becoming of action and perception in a presence, [as a] modulation of a bodily gearing together.

It may be objected: but precisely here there's no true relief, it's [an] illusion, thus [a] perception of relief that can be achieved without it, and construction [or] thought. Reply 1) that assumes that we only see what is; 2) nothing compels [us] to say that the organization here is equivalent to what it is when faced with true relief. Stereoscopic relief does not appear true to me. It's purer. It's more expressive. Cf. painting. Cf. three-dimensional cinema that afterward gave the impression that the world was flat or banal. The pleasure here is [the] pleasure of expression. Our body = given expression.

/[*in margin of the following two paragraphs*] Space and the idea of space/

In sum: depth [emerges] through [the] inhabiting of the world, [an] optimal level of vision, and horizons below and beyond.

[The] problem remains: how to go from this perceived space to the idea of homogeneous, universally ubiquitous space. Note that our perceived space is not without universality: our perspective has precisely the effect of presenting us with [the] possibility of other perspectives, [the] Kantian idea of a level of all levels, of an everywhere, of a world without us. But this universality [is] lateral, /**[53]v(IV9)**/ being that appears through [the] articulation of intersecting perspectives. Natural expression is never without remainder, [never] unattached, it is given to itself. To go from there to the idea of space, the perceived world itself must be treated in a way that builds into it dimensions, figures, and backgrounds, expressive possibilities [that are] in principle unrelated: language [and] cultural space are necessary. Culture and history are this effort that traces out history while trying {to reach} true expression.

/[54](IV9a)/

NOTE I

Perceptual constancy: is not real and is not ideal: I can't say that the road really remains as wide at the horizon as here, there is perceptual narrowing and shriveling, — nor that it remains the same ideally, i.e., in constructed space: I don't perceive in this space, in the space where I do perceive there is a truth of the appearance as appearance: it's a road at the horizon, neither ideally nor really identical to the road nearby, nor for that matter different.

NOTE II

This conception of apparent size and of perspective as non-deforming calls for general development: it's the whole problem of lived or existential synthesis. Temporal synthesis, [the] notion of [the] matter of knowledge or hyle, [the] notion of consciousness. Intellectual synthesis = frontal composition, the one who makes it is not of it. Existential synthesis = lateral composition, the one who makes it can only do so because he is of it. He is of it does not mean [*ne veut pas dire*] he is there like things: we are not in space in the manner of things: they're what locate us there through perspective. But if we didn't have [a] 'stem of [being] in-itself' [«*queue d'en soi*»], [a] body that can be looked at, inherence, [then] we wouldn't be able to look, and the universal would have no meaning for us. Conversion of our passivity, of our being exposed (to the look, to the world) into [a] contact surface with the being in which we are held and initiated.[10] [Hence reform of the notion of perspective and *Abschattung* [adumbration]: their reference to the geometric diagram [*géométral*] is not a pure constituting *Auffassung* [apprehension or construal]. Don't imagine consciousness as: sensuous givens [*données sensuelles*] + intentional *Auffassung*. For its part, the latter [is a] figure of *Urempfindung* [originary or primal sensation]. And the sensory givens [*données sensorielles*] are already intentional. The horizon comes into the act and the event, crossover synthesis [*synthèse d'enjambement*].]

Fifth Lecture

/**[55](V1)**/[1]

THE NEAR AND THE FAR

[We] have chosen to elucidate [*expliciter*] depth with regard to [the] stereoscope — to bring out what it is to see depth — [there is the] obvious fact of depth vision — and yet, upon analysis, it seems impossible: how could we see points situated one behind the other? We can't see depth. — We can only construct lateral vision – Geometric diagram – Space begins beyond perspective: the latter only provides material, signs through which a thinking of space takes place that is a thinking of everywhere and thus of nowhere – The point of view would prevent us from seeing if it weren't ruled by an idea of the point of view that is not attached anywhere – Convergence [and] apparent size [are] understood through 'natural judgments' as if we had divine knowledge of optics and geometry.

Is this true? Does this elucidation convey the whole sense of depth?

a) CONVERGENCE

We have the impression that in the moment when relief appears through the merging of images, we have more than signs and less than a space of ubiquity, [that] we enter into space through the discrepancy without leaving the point of view.

The discrepancy, the two images, ≠ two things; they are floating in front of things; and they don't become identified through 'merging,' the result of the synthesis is of another order [and] has a different consistency or solidity [*solidité*]; we have passage from 'phantoms' to the thing; they fit laterally into the final relief, they derive from it not as a theoretical consequence, not as [the] planar projections of [a] geometric diagram, but as weakened emanations, as memories of perception – The discrepancy = two non-superimposable aspects of the same thing; unity [is] given through the duality, behind it, and not in the two images as such (Koffka: the merging of the disparate things is due to their common function and not to their actual resemblance); how is all this possible?

When we see the two images as disparate images, [and] then that the relief absorbs them, it's because we start to look differently; it's because the two eyes start to function as means of a single looking [*regard*] – But it's the discrepancy itself that elicits the change of attitude from the eyes; there is solicitation of the co-functioning through the pair of images, the unified functioning is cause and effect of the imminent depth vision: the images imply [the] body that is necessary for seeing in depth and [that] the actual body realizes, but at the same time it's obviously the [visual] fixation that invests the images with this impending power;

Cf. feedback:[2] the 'information' received elicits [a] response that anticipates the state of the phenomenon at the moment of impact – But radar doesn't know what it does and only gives the impression of knowing it to the spectator who sees pre-adaptation; ocular movement is polarized by an imminence of vision, polarized by what's to come. From which it follows that the schematic typology of perception [*le montage perceptif*] applies to general situations – So it's intentionality [that's] just weighed down: progression toward a privileged state that we plainly don't represent to ourselves, but toward which we are guided inasmuch as it resolves tension.

/[56](V2)/

The movement of our eyes and the appearance of relief [*l'aspect relief*] [are] reciprocally means and end – the appearance of relief is not [a] represented end: we can't reach it by wanting it; there is no way of learning to see in the stereoscope, we just need to give ourselves up to it, we willingly look into the stereoscope and then end up wanting what our initial ocular movements want – There is thus no *Sinngebung*: it's the images that pull the looking toward their sense [that is] already there (relief appears as pre-existing, emerging from a haze of appearances that were hiding it): we settle into the relief and thereby we see it, we imagine ourselves in the relief and we thereby look in the way required to see it; the end itself gives the means and chance responds to choice.

Comparison with language: we settle into what we mean [*veut dire*], we speak with eyes focused on this private object, direct method, and thereby the other is drawn into the vortex and sees – Also: it's not necessary to want to speak, to think about the words that one is going to use, for then language slips away, it's the aphasic who looks for points of support – likewise it's not necessary to ask ourselves how to see in the stereoscope, we must let ourselves be guided by the style of the images.

Broadly speaking, comparison with inventiveness: Valéry often likened attention to focusing, and spoke of what's "amazing" [*«génial»*] in the glance:[3] "exchange between the end and the means, chance and choice, substance and accident, prediction and opportunity, matter and form, power and resistance, which, like the burning, strange, intimate

battle of the sexes, involves all the energies of human life, grinds them against each other, [and] creates" (DDD 138)[4] – Waking up: the mind becomes body and the body becomes mind – Body = power of inventiveness or expression, but subjected to precise conditions and, in these conditions, operating unfailingly (or almost: psychic diplopia) – The disparate images are only for blending together in relief, this sense is already present in them, relief precedes itself in them and it's what we move toward without seeing it yet, and without knowing through what means; transcendental 'affinity' and not subsumption; from the outset the images appear to a moving body that's [the] key to the world. Relief [is an] expressive response which, like all expression, predates itself because it's [the] modulation of a gearing into space that is primordial.
Remark: it may be objected: but relief is indeed a construction since there is none in the stere⟨oscope⟩. – Response: we can see what is not – and: in fact it's not true relief; [it's] purer [—] cf. three-dimensional film [*ciné-relief*]; [the] pleasure of expression.

b) APPARENT SIZE

Like double images, apparent size [is] created by [an] isolating stance and [the] dismemberment of perception – [It] no more exists in normal perception than diplopia for objects on this side of our [visual] fixation or beyond [it] – What is there in perception? Outlines or phantoms of things and tension toward a precise relation of gearing together – Distance [is] measured by this tension – toward [the] optimum – Perceptual constancy is not ideal constancy: I can't say that I think the road at the horizon as [being] equally wide as here, or the man at the horizon, [who is a] moving point, as [being] the same as [the] man nearby; nor may we say, as was said following Gestalt [theory] and [the] demonstration of constancy as [a] structural fact: there is real constancy, the road down there /**[57](V3)**/ has the same width as here – no, there is narrowing, perceptual shriveling – there is [a] truth of the appearance as appearance – there is this expressive structure of the horizon that is like that of the relief in the stereoscope, and which gives the same pleasure: this pale narrow trace, without detail, without color, tone on tone, it's the road, it counts as [a] road, not identical to the one here, nor [to one] elsewhere of a different width, [but rather a] phantom like the double image, [a] 'road seen from afar' – And how? Because the horizon is [the] limit of the synthesis of transition that links my experiences of gradual distancing, correlative of the 'scope' of my look – Perspective doesn't deprive me of space or of its truth, it is not [a] projection onto a plane of what can be seen from here as in [a] camera lucida [*chambre claire*], it is given as [a] sampling of the fullness of things, [a] slice of the world, [the] implication of space. The horizon is not a distillation of things, it's a positive structure of implication, a type of intellectual existence that is new with respect to things or relations [—] cf. Kantian form – exactly like memory is not a confused perception or [a perception] seen from further away, but a nested structure – pre-concept: generality of the horizon (there are things over there).*

In sum: like straight and inclined, depth [emerges] through inhabiting the world, [an] optimal level of vision, and horizons below and beyond.

Problem: how to go from this perceived space to the idea of homogeneous and universally ubiquitous space – Perceived space has inherent universality, it refers back to a level of all levels, to an everywhere, to a world without us – But it's lateral universality, intersecting perspectives, with being that shows through [*transparaît*] where they cross – Natural expression doesn't go beyond – it is given to itself – To move to the idea of space, expression is necessary that in principle doesn't operate like [a] given teleology, that grounds itself, that recasts and sublimates the given figures and backgrounds, language [and] cultural space are necessary – Simultaneous origin of history (history of culture) and of this expressive effort [that is, unlike natural expression,] without remainder.

> /[*at the bottom of the page*] *Image from Piéron:[5] [a] child standing at the entrance of a tunnel – [a] man at the end, objectively much smaller, [but] appears much bigger, because he catches [*intercepte*] [a] much larger fraction [of the retinal image] – There is no calculation – No tunnel seen from the side – no 'restoration' of the 'real' size of the man – no quantifiable relation – the man 'counts as' big and as [a] man because our perception is always 'extracted from' perceptual unfolding and from 'being toward the world' [*«être au monde»*] – Intellectual or frontal synthesis, the one who makes it is not of it, is not caught in it – and existential synthesis: the one who makes it is of it (I am spatial, not like things, but inasmuch as they turn some aspect toward me), i.e., he is exposed to space, exposed to looking and thereby can look, i.e., his inherence is [his] interface with the world, [his] initiation to space and to the universal. Lateral interdependence [*solidarité*] of my universality and my particularity, of my passivity and my activity: the perspective of things for me shows both that I emerge [*surgis*], and that I emerge from . . . [6]/

Sixth Lecture

/[58](VI1)/
MOVEMENT

We could deduce from the above – We know what place is; movement is surely passage from one place to another; occupation of a new place; thus it refers to coordinates or anchorage of the body in a 'world'; it's not a relation between objects, it's a modality of my relationship with [the] world, etc.

But to deduce is to go blindly from one content to another through combination – it goes against the contents that we have to lay bare: if place is [a] particular tension in the dynamic [of] self [and] world, [then] it's already movement, far from movement being a dependent concept – this is what we would conceal in deducing – [the] only [appropriate] method: take up the intuition of movement directly – what we have said concerning place is not [a] premise, but [a] simple propaedeutic, we have lifted certain obstacles to the intuition of movement.

I'm looking at the marble that's rolling on this desk – What's happening?

I. MOVEMENT IN-ITSELF OR OBJECTIVE MOVEMENT

There is movement, i.e., a series of moments and correlatively a series of positions as close together as you like – of the same marble recognizable at each instant –*

/[*in margin, added by hand*] *all exteriority on one side, all interiority on the other/

The perception of this can be understood in various ways (either as [a] reproduction of the fact in me, such as on my retinas, or as [an] intellectual synthesis of identification and mental tracing). In all cases, the movement, borne [either] by the positions of the thing or [else] by the mind, in space in itself or [else in] ideal [space], is perfectly clear, without anything strange or dubious [*sans rien de louche*], without any mixing of body and mind, without flesh, without any mixing of the before and the after, of the here and the there.

Yet we see that it's destroyed. Or at least that there's only the envelope or outline of the movement there, not the moving itself, not the perception – i.e., the presence of the movement.

What we actually have is [either the] factual identity of the thing in motion or [else its] identity through recognition – it's this [thing], the same [and] indiscernible, that's here, then there – And as a matter of fact there wouldn't be any real movement if there were destruction and re-creation, or discontinuous passage from one part into another [part] that must not be a different [part] – But in real or ideal space there is identity not in and through the movement, but outside the movement – The marble at rest remains – It's not it that moves – In itself it's always what it was – Or for me – I never grasp it in the process of moving – The movement is always before or after the moment I grasp it.

Zeno's arguments draw the consequences: in itself or for me as [a] reflecting mind, there is no movement – In space really /**[59](VI2)**/ composed of infinite parts, there is no movement, because the thing in motion is always faced with the same task of infinite exhaustion, and because it is always somewhere, – and in ideal space there is no movement: there is always a value of the spatial variable, and one of the temporal variable, we can multiply them, [we can] consider them as closely as possible to the preceding value, [but] at the very moment when they're about to differentiate: either it's done, or it's to be done, the substance of the movement isn't there – No movement before thetic consciousness, which freezes it – We can only see it out of the corner of our eye, on condition of not thinking, of not knowing what we see, [we can only see it] as appearance or illusion.

Hence: if there is to be movement, [then] it must be the case (1) that the something that moves be itself in movement (2) that the movement so to speak coming out of it [or] made by it not be [a] simple relation between a series of positions and a series of definite instants in a space and time of things, [a] relation between objects that leaves the positions and the temporal phases external to one another, and which is [an] external designation for the thing in motion, [rather, it must be the case] that the movement is absolute, [that it is] in the thing in motion and not elsewhere. Hence that there be [a] mixing of the before and the after, of the here and the there, encroachment [*empiétement*].

and that's only possible if (3) the movement is not [something that occurs] in itself, i.e., in the things, nor for me as [a] spectative subject of an objective world, but [rather] through a sort of mixing of me and the 'things.'

II. THE SUBJECT [IS] IMPLICATED IN MOVEMENT

That's what Bergson sensed – For him, what made movement impossible in Zeno's thinking is the actual and infinite division of both space and time, their additive composition based on infinitely numerous units, in the face of which the paces of Achilles and the tortoise become equal, and in which there is always a place where the arrow is at rest – And therefore to make movement possible it must be the case that time and space are divisible but not divided, that, formulated on the basis of the whole, they admit something 'between' positions and instants, which is not possible in the in-itself. Movement, which is [a] fact of the world, must therefore encroach on me as duration, [must] be [a] fact of consciousness as well – It borrows from consciousness its indivision, it occurs in the "internal aspect" [that] the path of displacement [*trajet*] [has] "for my consciousness" (*Matter and Memory* 210)[1] – So it's [an] "undivided fact" because its duration is "dense [*compacte*] and undivided like it [my consciousness]"[2] – Movement can only be detached from its path of displacement and grasped in its moving if it partakes of my duration, inasmuch as [my duration] alone is undivided.

But in order for there to be an "immediate perception" of movement as [a] "very clear fact" (213) in this way,[3] there must be an intermediary between my undividedness and the division of the in-itself, there must be a common measure between them, which is provided by my body, at once [a] thing and [something] grasped internally. It's this that will spread undividedness onto things and make movement possible. – And that's why all the examples of self-evident movement taken by Bergson, of [the] immediate perception of movement, are taken from the movement of one's own body: "a simple movement, like the journey taken by my hand when it goes from A to B" (210).[4]

But under what conditions can my body carry out the function of mediation? Inasmuch as it is at once a thing in motion in 'real' space and perceived from within in the undividedness of its movement – There must therefore be within it a consciousness of the unity of /**[60](VI3)**/ these two aspects – Now the unity, the undividedness of the movement, doesn't belong to my body as a thing, it's not its movement as it would occur in an objective space that's unified: it's [rather] its movement as projected by me in a single act that brings together its starting point and its ending point – In order for the consciousness of my body to make its movement as an objective body and that of objects possible, this undividedness of starting point and ending point must give rise to [a] description of an actual movement – If my body were for me a space like all others, the undividedness of the project would not give any more unity to its movements than to those of things – My body must therefore extend into space in its own unique way, and it [must] communicate with the whole world inasmuch as [it is an] extension of my body – My body must be like a "machine for living" [«*machine à vivre*»] the world,[5] that which distributes undividedness due to its privileged spatiality – Theory of the perceiving body that Bergson did not attempt.

/[61](VI4)/

Therefore Bergson explicitly considered [the] reference of movement to my duration as one duration among infinite possible durations, movement as what makes me wait, — and not [as a] direct reference of movement to a time of the universe

[and he] implicitly considered [the] reference of movement to my body as to that which 'generalizes' my duration

but as he did not thematize this, his theory of movement remains a matter of consciousness, he pointed out [a] condition without which there would not be movement (participation in my duration) without providing [the] condition through which there is movement (extension of my duration), he was not rooted in the order of phenomena, i.e., in things inasmuch as they are presented to me as things.

The analysis must therefore be taken up again at the point it was left, i.e.,

1) the thing in motion [*le mobile*] must be a 'moving thing' [*un «mouvant»*], identified in and through the movement, not separately from it

2) reciprocally the movement must emanate from the thing in motion, or be in it and not only in its interobjective relations with the outside

3) there must therefore be [a] mixing of the inside and the outside of the movement, of the before and the after, of the here and the there (not only 'in me' but also in the appearance)

4) finally there must be [a] mixing and not simply [a] juxtaposition of me and the things.

III. MOVEMENT AS PHENOMENON

There are descriptions of movement so understood in Gestalt [theory] and we are going to make use of them.

But there is often misunderstanding as to what Gestalt [theory] offers – we thus have to clarify the sort of contribution that we can expect from it.

(Piaget: Gestalt [theory =] anti-geneticism – innatism – Others[:] Gestalt [theory] = explanation of appearances through nervous phenomena – Others[:] Gestalt [theory] = explanation more generally in the sense of physics, stimulus-response relations of causality.)

None of these three contributions is what we're looking for in Gestalt [theory]. This would be to accept the Gestalt-theoretic philosophy, [which is] a bad philosophy.

1) With Gestalt [theory] we don't want to bring the problem of philosophy onto the ground of inductive proof: e.g., we can't prove inductively through Wertheimer's experiments that there is movement without [the] identification of a thing in motion – Wertheimer can prove that there is [a] phenomenon of movement without an objective thing in motion, [but] that doesn't imply that there is consciousness of movement without consciousness of [a] thing in motion – If Gestalt [theory] brings something to this question it's only as description, therefore [only] inasmuch as it provides access to phenomena [and] shows variations of our experience that may be necessary for suspending our thesis of the objective world [and] disclosing to us movement in its nascent state . . . But for all that the question of movement is not brought onto the ground of experimental psychology [or] objective science – It's a question of [the] context of our lived experience, not [of] a higher authority – Psychology [is] necessary but insufficient – [It] asks questions but doesn't answer them inasmuch as it seeks 'causal' explanations.

/**[62](VI5)**/

2) We don't regard the results of Gestalt [theory] as providing the elements of which [the] perception of movement would be made, such that there would be nothing more to do than to complete Gestalt [theory] – We regard them as [an] introduction to the study of the perceptual field – Gestalt [theory], operating in artificially simplified conditions, succeeds in showing that even in these conditions the totality of the field (and not psycho-physiology in the traditional sense) is involved – A fortiori it would be contrary to the very intentions of Gestalt [theory] to make up the total field with the processes that it studies – E.g., there are autokinetic movements of a point of light in the dark ranging to 30° – This fact is not found in illuminated space – It thus reveals, not [an] element of the total functioning, but factors in it that go beyond this 'elementary' process – Likewise [the] space outlined by a stroboscopic movement always appears larger than [the] same objective space bounded by two simultaneous lines – In fact, in our filled space, movement hardly expands perceived space – The analysis is thus not a real analysis – There are far fewer illusions than Gestalt [theory] would have us believe – Even Gestalt psychology

yields residual phenomena, parasitic on normal functioning, *Ersatzleistungen* [substitute or compensatory performances], like psychopathology (Schneider's movements don't show a process that would be found in normal counting, but what replaces it: they highlight the *simultan überschauen* [simultaneous survey [of wholes]][6]). But these residual facts have disclosive value inasmuch as they make us see [the] normal functioning that we no longer see because we see it all the time – The work of describing this field remains to be done.

3) Accepting neither inductive thinking nor the analysis of laboratory situations as self-sufficient forms of thought, we therefore don't accept Gestalt [theory] as psychology – or [as] psychologism. – But it turns out that [Gestalt theory] itself, leaving to then come back to explanatory thought and psychologism, – opened a field that goes beyond it, the phenomenal field – It introduced, between a priori reflection and empiricism, a reflection on the contents, a philosophy of the facts. That's what we retain from it, — which is not to be confused with the explicit philosophy of the Gestalt theorists. Gestalt [theory] poses a philosophical problem, — which is not the one it considers in its 'philosophy.' In its philosophy, it seeks to explain the universe of lived Gestalten. The problem it presents to the philosopher is not that one: it is, e.g., to know what is signified philosophically by the genetic contiguity of: stroboscopic movement and *Singularbewegung* [solitary motion] or *duale Teilbewegung* [dual partial motion][7] – Philosophy tries to think even these genetic relations – They show it that movement is a special case of the organization of the field (for there must be a reason such that we go from one to the other) – They thus invite it to look for [the] motivation of the movement in the overall situation of the field, and to describe [the] subject of perception in such a way that it is sensitive to this situation – In this sense the Gestalt-theoretic exploration of genetic varieties of organization excludes 1) realism of movement [and] 2) idealism of movement, and [instead] points to an investigation to be undertaken: [the] apprehension of movement as [a] modality of a total contact with the field[8] – But this investigation is not undertaken by Gestalt [theory] and has nothing to do with its 'philosophical' tests, which would consist in treating 'optimal' movement and 'imperfect' forms as varieties of a single process of distribution, and in reducing the privilege of the 'something,' of the true or [the] real to a special case of "*flimmern*" ["flickering"].

With these reservations, what do we get from Gestalt [theory] as contact with nascent movement?

/[63](VI6)/

[The] idea that movement = related to [the] apprehension of [a] figure on [a] background, or conversely [that] any apprehension of [a] figure on [a] background is [a] possible movement, [the] identification of the thing in motion is of the same order as [the] identification of a figure at rest with itself across time, [what is] absolute in the movement is of the same order as [the] descriptive characters that distinguish the 'figure' – movement belongs to the 'figural' properties – it's like the figure itself [in] that it produces a spatio-temporal separation – Movement [as the] becoming of a figure[9] – The 'inside' of the movement is inseparable from an outside like the inside of a figure doesn't go without an outside – Hence the ultimate question: what must the subject be [that] can perceive movement thus understood? Of what order is the perceptual logic or the perceptual 'thought' that brings this configuration about? Comparison between perceptual logic and linguistic logic – Perception as natural expression – And passage from this theory of movement as expression to 1) expression of the movement through the stationary (painting, plastic arts) [and] 2) universal expression through movement (cinema).

We'll begin with facts that reveal movement as [a] figural moment[10]

Seventh Lecture

/[65](VII1)/

So [there is] no movement in a world in itself (Bergson, Zeno) – But only in a world given to someone – Study this movement phenomenon.

What hinders our seeing it: we are obsessed with what we believe we know about the objective world – There is movement, and our perception of movement appears as deriving from movement in itself – Pseudo-evidence of the senses as receiving *eidôla* [images][1] of the movement: touch registers real movement, vision [registers] a copy of the spectacle on the retina – The best way to eliminate this prejudice is to look directly at what the functioning body [*corps fonctionnant*] receives from supposedly real movement.

1) ALL MOVEMENT IS STROBOSCOPIC – Even in cases of real movement, there is only the successive activation of distinct regions on the retina, not [the] identity of a thing in motion – something analogous to stroboscopic movement[2] – The latter is by no means [an] 'illusion': attention and [visual] fixation enhance it, [and] uninformed subjects take stroboscopic [movements] as real in [an] experiment where they're mixed.

Or more precisely: real movement has distinct properties: Rubin's experiment,[3] real movement of [a] homogeneous black surface [is] invisible through [a] slit in [a] screen through which [the] edges of the black surface are not visible – What is essential to the phenomena of real movement is thus the 'screen effect' that takes place between [the] edges of the thing in motion and what it hides and reveals – This effect (as between [the] edge of [a] window and [the] landscape) does not occur with stroboscopic movement – But it is of the same order as the persistence of the 'background' beneath the figure, or of objects beyond the limits of the visual field; it stems from the architectonic of figures and backgrounds, but the separation of figures is done by man, not given with the stimuli. Hence real movement, even when different from stroboscopic [movement], is not given as movement on the retina. The screen effect can be reproduced with stroboscopic movement (cinema does it) which would then seem like real movement. This 'reality' is therefore a matter of endogenous organization, and this organization can be studied **/[66](VII2)/** in stroboscopic movement where it is clearer.

2) MOVEMENT IS A FIGURAL MOMENT
Wertheimer's experiments:[4] by increasing the switching speed [i.e., the time interval between projections], there is empirical passage from succession to optimal movement and to simultaneity (that doesn't mean [*ne veut pas dire*] that the essence of the movement isn't original, that something new isn't established at the optimal stage, but it does mean [*veut dire*] that the philosopher is required to understand the genetic context, that the movement is [a] response to [an] intermediate experimental situation, that therefore like [these situations], [the movement] must be a totality and not a sum, [a] turning from a successive totality to a simultaneous totality).

there is [a] phenomenological difference between cases where the extreme positions exist separately, and cases where the movement is 'the best' and where the two extremities are embraced within the movement: here the unity "*fließt* [*nicht*] *direkt aus dem Erlebnis*,"[5] for [the] repetition *ababab* we have *phi ab* – There are visual experiences [*visions*] of movement distinct from those in which we see the intermediate positions or the object: by inserting [a] small strip on the path of displacement there is neither [the] completion of the missing part, nor even a shimmer of white, [rather] there is pure "*Hinüber*" ["passage across"].[6] Placing [a] stationary object in between gives rise to 'tunnel' movement that is not of this nor of any object[7] – When I look at my pencil shifting laterally, I see it in movement exactly to the extent to which I do not see the successive positions.[8]

[9](That does not mean [*ne veut pas dire*] that there is "movement without a thing in motion," for it could be thought and in a certain way it is[10] – There is a perceptual *Etwas* [something] that moves – Wertheimer's formula: dynamic as well as static givens, is insufficient.[11] That's mental physics – but that proves that the identity of the moving thing is different from an /**[67](VII3)**/ identity over and above the movement, [that it is different] from a recognition of the same in spite of the movement. What's the nature of this [identity]?

Ternus's experiments:[12]

In B [one sees a] sliding circular arc, which implies fusion of non-identical points and non-fusion of identical points[13] – In A we have identification of identical points,[14] but not due to this identity: [but rather] because [the] angular shape isolates the three upper points – i.e., by its very structure the circular arc makes probable a sliding that follows its extension – It's not only a matter of the identity of the two successively projected figures (initial and final): that also exists in case A. The two can be superimposed. It's a matter of the possibility of [a] shifting which, in case A, would require deformation, whereas in case B it's implied in the very form of the figure, in its internal possibilities.

Thus 1) The movement of the arc is therefore not the sum of the movements of its parts, it's the whole as such, a non-additive whole, that moves – The movement flows from the whole arc (or cross)[15] as such – The apprehension of the movement is the same kind as that of the figure, [of the] becoming of a figure, and the identification is the same kind as that of a stationary figure with itself: i.e., temporal effect of the separation. In this sense, movement is included in the structure of the figure.

but reciprocally 2) the structure of the figure is only constant by means of the movement, only in it – We don't first of all see the same figure and then that it moved: we see it pass from [its] initial to final position, it's recognized through the identity of its /**[68](VII4)**/ possibilities, the figure is [the] locus or trace of a certain type of movement, of certain dynamic properties.

Another experiment[16] which shows the perception of a movement emerging from the perception of a [rectangular] frame as at rest (although objectively it moved) due to its function as frame, hence movement here [is] induced magically in a stationary point on the basis of the structural properties of the whole in which it is situated,[17] and of which it is not even a constituent element, as in the previous case.

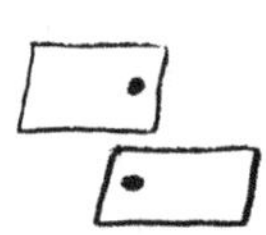

objectively

phenomenally

The enclosing [frame is] considered stationary and so the movement reverts to the point. This means [*veut dire*] that to see these figures is not to see a rectangular field and a point, but [to see] the overall arrangement of the two, in which from the start the point is assigned an a priori mobility because it is inscribed, and to distribute the change in such a way that the field value of the field is respected – Or rather, since the appearance of a movement of the point is immediate, and does not result from a calculation, there is no objective localization of the rectangle in a constant point of absolute space, along with [an] objective shifting of the point between different locations in absolute space, [rather] there is [an] immediate apprehension of the rectangle as 'the rectangle' with its field or background function that carries a sort of qualitative stability, and [an immediate apprehension] of the point as a 'fragile' or 'sensitive' being, its movement merely being emblematic of this 'sensitivity.' I settle into the rectangle as [I settle] into that little illuminated rectangle at the cinema that ultimately governs and haunts me, in which I live, and the point within it has a sort of essential lightness. Movement is tension within my level. It's just the other side of /**[69](VII5)**/ the same process through which I settle into a *Bildwelt* [image world]. What distributes movement and rest in the appearance is not a calculation that would determine the quantity of displacement allotted to the point in order for the frame to remain objectively identical while nonetheless retaining the total apparent displacement, [rather] it's a system of equivalences between rest and movement [as] qualitatively defined.

[18][Similarly in real movement, even though with [the] screen effect only the movement of edges is visible, [this movement] gives rise to [that] of the center in virtue of [the] figural organization.]

3) MOVEMENT AS DISCLOSIVE OF BEING

The well-known illusion concerning rings[19] carries over into the phenomena of movement [—] "these figures modify the field that surrounds them in a way that expresses itself dynamically in the determinate form of movement, [and] statically in the look [*allure*] of the optical illusion" (Koffka)[20]

movement toward the right with opening and widening[21]

zigzag movement transformed into movement of [a] ball in [a] gutter[22] (and this [occurs] even if the figure is inverted to eliminate the influence of experience).[23] Therefore [the] configuration of the field contributes to the genesis of the movement.

Better: cases where the structure of the movement follows from that of the thing in motion itself. Where there is truly "perception of causality" (Michotte),[24] Hume and Kant only thought of causality through triggering[25] – But there are all kinds of other effects: the launching effect[26] (movement of [object] A toward [object] B, stopping of [object] A, starting of [object] B, preferably at [a] lower speed [than object A], stopping of [object] B* /[*in margin*] *it's not approach and withdrawal [*rapprochement et écartement*] – [object] A has the initiative[27]/) on condition that: the two objects coincide at the moment of "impact," that they are both present during the entire process, that it occurs in central vision (otherwise [the] tunnel effect [occurs]),[28] that the paths of [object] A and [object] B are not so long as to exceed a certain "radius of action" [«*rayon d'action*»] after which the object travels "on its own account,"[29] – that the movements are not too slow (otherwise [there is] induced movement of [object] B toward [object] A)[30] – Launching in flight[31] with threshold of differences in speed – if [the difference] is too small, we get [the] entraining effect[32] – [The] impression of launching [is] weakened when the paths of [the] objects are parallel or form an angle, [and is] strengthened when the launching object is faster – in cases of increasing speed ratios there is triggering = autonomous movement [in object B] but which nonetheless is not spontaneous. = Low-intensity launching [*Lancement larvé*].[33]

/[70](VII6)/

Furthermore [the] description of launching by propulsion (bowstring and arrow – metamorphosis of movement),[34] [of launching] by expulsion,[35] [the description] of traction[36] [and] of transport.[37] Contrast between transport and launching: in transport [object] B 'does' nothing, [it] is only changed through 'displacement,' and it's only in [object] A that there is truly 'physical movement.' In contrast, in launching there is a movement in two steps, it's the movement of [object] A that launches [object] B, there is metamorphosis [of] wind [and] cloud, cf. identity of a sound when its intensity is made to vary, [its] belonging to a single *Weltlinie* [path in space-time].[38]

/[*in margin of the following paragraph*] VIII/

Phenomenon of auto-locomotion[39] – Rectangle extending toward the right, then stopping, the left side returns [to its original relative position] – 'caterpillar,' 'earthworm,' head and tail – Change of form [as the] source of a [lateral] shifting = crawling – if right and left sides move away from each other at equal speed, [and if the] left side then comes back toward the right at the same speed while [the] 'head' [i.e., the right side] continues to move forward [more] slowly, [then] there is swimming (inert head, movement through rear of the body).[40] This auto-locomotion ≠ global displacement + internal movement: it occurs when there is rapid movement of [the] H[ead] with slow movement of [the] T[ail], then slow movement of [the] H[ead] with rapid movement of [the] T[ail]: [lateral] shifting [*translation*] and change in shape are thus juxtaposed – In auto-locomotion there is [a] continuous ampliation [*ampliation*] of the two movements,[41] the change in shape produces the movement, [there is an] internal flux of a kind of protoplasm within the rectangle.[42] Hence movement here = disclosure of being, [a] result of its internal configuration, and clearly something different than change of location.

Kinematic properties (speed) linked to being: [the] movement of an airplane on the horizon [is] different from that of a nearby insect but not through calculation: [there is a] different aggressive power, [a] hidden or concealed aggressive power.

4) INTERPRETATION: ORGANIZATION AND PERCEPTUAL LOGIC

Gestalt [theory] turns figural moments into objective conditions determining a third-person process of organization according to causal laws. E.g., Duncker studying induced movement[43] (two figures in the dark with subliminal movement of one of them and no visible figure-background relation = either *a* or *b* alone in movement, – or both, or both at rest. The distribution of [phenomenal] movement would occur in accordance with figural properties, i.e., 1) enclosing figure in movement 2) fixed figure [in movement] 3) when neither of these two conditions obtain, both move ('coordination') 4) [the] contributing effect [*intervention*] of the relation [between] figure [and] background 5) [the contributing effect] of the size of the figures 6) [the contributing effect] of intensity 7) [the contributing effect] of 'mutability' 8) [the contributing effect] of [the] *Haupterstrecktheit* [principal axis of extension] 9) [the contributing effect] of experience[44] – But in fact [Linschoten shows that there are only] statistical results with large gaps in the explanation – and in concrete perception, which doesn't occur in [the] *Bildwelt* [image world],

> /[*in left margin of the preceding paragraph, handwritten*]
> a) Gestalt [theory]: organization, configuration in the objective sense of an equilibration in itself – Critique [this]
> b) generalize the notion of configuration: it's exchange of means and end, [a] *Sinngebung* that's the work of the {elements} themselves
> c) hence reworking of the theory of perception: {reading}, field, constituent character of our corporeality, tracing [*traçage*], {inscribed} time, perceptual logic.
> c) ⟨*sic*⟩ all this to be shown better through [a] more concrete

analysis: abstract character of the Gestalt-theoretic analysis. Paliard's facts.[45] Pose the problem of perceptual logic here. Taximeter.[46] Passage to [the] study of [the] relation [between] corporeality [and] movement in psychopathology. Introduce it through [the] disturbance of movement in Schneider: sedimented symbolism and expression help him to conceal the {eclipse} of spontaneity. Homogeneity [of] perception [and] mind. Mind weighed down [*L'esprit alourdi*]/

/[71](VII7)/

we see the involvement of other motivations: e.g., if images = house and car, [then] the house at rest subordinates the car in movement, and everything doesn't reduce to a *Spiel der psychologischen Vektoren* [play of psychological vectors] (Linschoten *Ps Forschung* 1952),[47] or again the responses are mediated by [the] attitude of the subject depending on whether he sees the figures in a context of 'nothingness,' of 'real' space, or else in that of a 'screen' that is present but not visible. There is a *Situationserfassung* [grasping of the situation] that mediates the action of the objective figural conditions, and so the 'organization' is not a quasi-physical process, [not an] orientation toward an equilibrium of objective conditions. Struggle of factors of *Auffassung* [apprehension or construal] against objective figural conditions: if the small square is seen as the top of a truncated pyramid, [then] it doesn't count as [an] inscribed figure.

But apart from figural moments that are effectively abstract and which operate only in cases of labile formations that aren't very centered in our lives, from the fact that we reintroduce other moments, historical [moments], that define our situation not only as an experimental situation but as a moment of a certain personal drama, must we say that there is a *Sinngebung* through the *Wahrnehmungsakt* [perceptual act] (Linschoten [?][48] – This would leave aside what's most valuable in the phenomenal description of Gestalt [theory], for it is certainly true that all our perception gives us the impression of coming from the object, that movement in particular appears to us each time as coming from the appearance itself, that even if personal-historical factors are involved, they are only given to us as sedimented in the perceptual landscape, that therefore we don't have the elements of the perceptual calculus, but only the results, and that ultimately perception is not in this sense a mental [*spirituel*] act, the organization is not [a] *Sinngebung* by us as [a] thinking subject but as [an] incarnate total being /**[72](VII8)**/ endowed with a certain past – Who is it that perceives? Linschoten himself [said]: with regard to the *Bewegungsverteilung* [distribution of movement], the *Funktionsverteilung* [distribution of function] is neither effect nor cause, the apprehension of meaning and the apprehension of movement are the same thing[49] [—] *nennen wir die beide umfassende schöpferische Begegnung einen Entwurf* [we call the creative encounter that encompasses both a project][50] – Therein lies the miracle of perception: it makes us see meaning rather than seeing on the basis of meaning. Hence it is not the act of a *Subjekt* [[thinking] subject].

So who is [the] subject of the perception of movement? There is neither [the] composition of the whole based on abstract figural moments, nor [the] subordination of what is actually given to [an] almighty meaning, [rather] there is [a] change of what is given into meaning, and [an] incarnation of the meaning in vision. The organization is in neither the first nor third person. Like in [the] understanding of a sentence, [where] the end reacts on the beginning, [here too] meaning goes from the whole to the parts, but this whole is ultimately suggested by the parts. Compare perception to a reading. The 'signs' or what is given 'objectively' are recorded on [a] device, [they] are inscribed in a 'field' that is 'in charge' and which gives them situational value [—] all perception is [the] modulation of a situation, but whoever is situated is not an *I think*. [The] experiment of Zietz and Werner,[51] demonstrating the reinforcement of visible movement by sounds [—] e.g., the emphasizing of the arrow in the direction [*sens*] of its movement around a point [—] clearly shows our perceptual being as [a] network in tension with which external messages come into contact [*viennent toucher*].

Eighth Lecture

/[73](VIII1)/

EXPERIMENTS:

Movement ≠ [a] process defined by points of passage and their tracing [*leur tracé*], but [rather a] phenomenon to which the whole field contributes, and which is [a] part within its figural organization.

[Movement] develops figural possibilities or requirements (E.g., the point in [a] rectangle – Koffka's gutter).

Striking case: Michotte's auto-locomotion where local displacement results from variations of [the] internal articulation of the figure.

MICHOTTE

Description: preceding notes

Meaning: realization of an evental unity [*unité d'événement*] that extends across [*enjambe*] time

I. we move from the launching effect to [the] auto-locomotion effect depending on

(2) prior movement toward the left, i.e., influence of a preceding movement on the current movement, [a] change in the sense of the latter through its history that registers in the final phase: the preceding [phase] is 'preparation'

(1) closure of the figure: rectangle

i.e., it's the spatial and consequently [the] temporal delimitation that produces the specific effect. Thus 'swimming' = effect of [the] figural assembly [*dispositif*] in the broad sense of spatio-temporal figure. At each moment the spatial assembly becomes [the] manifestation of an evental unity that extends across the entire process.

II. [There is] already something analogous in the launching effect: the movement of the impacting body appears as 'preparation' for the impact. Element of imminence. The movement of the impacting [body] is not 'on its own account,' nor [is] that of the impacted [body]. In the case of triggering (increasing speed ratio), the movement of the impacted [body] is prepared not in [the movement] of the impacting [body], which is merely [the] occasion, but in the impacted [body] itself.

Thus: feedback [*rétroaction*] from the end of the process on the beginning. ('preparation')

encroachment [*empiétement*] of the beginning on the rest

encroachment of the change of place on the figural features and vice versa: movement [as the] becoming of a figure.

/**[74](VIII2)**/

III. This clarifies cases of movements [that are] simply local: they are inhabited by a power. [The] movement of an airplane on the horizon [is] different from that of an insect on the window. And not only through a calculation that would restore [the] greater 'real speed' by taking account of distance: the dark spot becomes [a] concealed aggressive power. Movement reveals being.*

/[*in margin*] *when I recognized an airplane, the movement didn't increase the speed, or rather this speed is not reckoned in terms of objective space: it's [a] relation to me, it's [a] radius of action, it's [a] threatening slowness, [a] concealed speed./

Even Wertheimer's stroboscopic movement [exhibits] this evental structure with its characteristic relations of imminence, of encroachment, of [the] preparation of forces in forms and vice versa, and its backward movement.

Projection of a point would make a point (possibly with autokinesis) – Projection of a second point reacts on the first, causes it to disappear as such and makes ϕ *ab*.[1] There was an event and not a journey [*parcours*] in the sense of [the] successive occupation of contiguous positions.

[The] innovation of Gestalt [theory is to] look closely at this organization of the field as [a] real process [and as a] sort of perceptual miracle.

Someone in the audience [i.e., at a previous lecture] was asking: why does the point inserted in two successively shifted rectangles appear in movement? Because it is enclosed? Is that it? – Yes – That's how it is, but this can only be understood on condition of bringing out the intuition of the perceptual field that stands behind it: we have to get used to recognizing the delimiting field as 'inherently at rest' due to the fact that it is what delimits, it is [the] 'ground' [*sol*].

It may be objected: – but it's because the delimiting rectangle reminds us of the earth [*la terre*], which is at rest, in its relation with the things that move on the earth

– but it's because the 'launchings' [and] 'triggerings' evoke prior experience

– but it's because Michotte's extended rectangles remind us of worms or frogs.[2]

Here [is the] originality of Gestalt [theory]: far from there being [an] evocation of prior experience here, [that experience] was only possible through the fact of organization and can only be recalled by it.

Why does the earth appear to us at rest and objects (birds) [appear to us] in movement, and not the other way around? When it is launched why does the arrow appear to us to be propelled by the bow? What are we calling 'worm,' 'caterpillar' or 'frog'? None of that is given physically, no more than [the] division of the field (trees [are] seen and not [the] spaces between them).

And besides, why are these prior experiences /**[75](VIII3)**/ evoked in present circumstances? They are evoked only if the phenomenon of the 'ground' [*sol*], of the 'triggering' or of the 'swimming' as internal organization are presently realized. Lewin and camouflage, showing that in order for one figure to be recognized in another, it's necessary that this other be organized appropriately, that the structure of the field allow for it.[3]

We are thus witnessing here the genesis of the signification 'ground' [*sol*], 'launching,' 'swimming' or 'crawling.' We shouldn't refer to these significations as given in prior experience (no more than the signification 'gutter' in Koffka's experiment): on the contrary, it's because there is a self-organization of the field that these experiences were possible.[4]

Clarify this notion to reach [an] overall interpretation
of [the] nature of movement
[of the] nature of the experience whereby we encounter it.

4) OVERALL INTERPRETATION: ORGANIZATION OF THE FIELD AND PERCEPTUAL LOGIC

a) What exactly are these 'figural moments' of which movement is a part? Gestalt [theory] has a narrow conception of it, to be enlarged. Duncker studying 'induced movement'[5] (2 figures in the dark with subliminal movement of one of them, with no relation to screen
either *a* solely in movement
or *b* solely in movement

or both at rest
or both in movement)

Gestalt [theory] tries to show that the distribution of the [phenomenal] movement depends upon figural moments that would be[6]

1) enclosing figure at rest[7]
2) fixed figure in movement
lacking these conditions: double movement and 'coordination'
3) relation [between] figure and background
4) relative size of the figures
5) luminous intensity
6) internal 'mutability' of the figure
7) its *Haupterstrecktheit* [principal axis of extension]
8) experience.

/[76](VIII4)/

In short, there would be distribution of movement as [an] effect of objectively given figural conditions.

In fact: (Linschoten, *Ps. Forschung* 1952)[8] [there are] just statistical results, [and] many discrepancies remain to be explained.

Incomplete determinism? Other factors? Yes. E.g., responses

— depend on the sense of the figures (house and car) 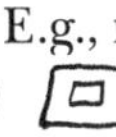 [e.g., is this an] inscribed figure or [a] truncated pyramid?

— depend on whether the subject – is positioned in [the] *Bildwelt* or in [the] 'real' world (in [the] *Bildwelt* [the] image of a house can move and [that] of a car [can] be at rest, [but] not in the real world)

– whether he [i.e., the subject] sees the figures in [the] context of 'nothingness,' of 'real space,' or finally in that of a 'screen,' not visible but present.

— depend therefore on the *Situationserfassung* [grasping of the situation], which itself pertains to [the] personality and history of the subject.

Therefore figural conditions don't operate inherently, like weight and shape in physical equilibration, but [rather] in accordance with their situational sense.

Therefore [the] organization of the field is not a process in itself.

But no more is it the apprehension of sense that governs the figural moments (classical theory of perception).

Linschoten (despite some equivocal formulations): the *Funktionsverteilung* [distribution of function] (or imposition of meaning) is neither effect nor cause of the *Bewegungsverteilung* [distribution of movement]. Apprehension of meaning and apprehension of movement are the same thing: *nennen wir die beide umfassende schöpferische*

Begegnung einen Entwurf [we call the creative encounter that encompasses both a project][9] – The miracle of perception: it makes us see the meaning of the spectacle rather than seeing according to a meaning [that is] posed arbitrarily. Taken up in a *Situationserfassung* that is motivated by it and which motivates how it looks, the 'objective' constellation becomes incarnate in it. No causality, [but rather] motivation, i.e., meaning preserves and goes beyond the objective conditions, [it] recognizes them as coming from it, but [it] only appears as their completion.

Therefore generalize but retain the idea of configuration.

Generalize it. It's not only a matter of adding other factors [i.e., to the above list of factors identified by Linschoten] but of going beyond the idea of factors. There is [an] infusion of meaning made[10] probable by the presence of a condition that is given as [a] 'symbol' (e.g., 'ground' [as a] symbol of rest)

Retain it. Symbols aren't signs, they convey /**[77](VIII5)**/ their meaning themselves, i.e., they have it, they don't get it from an absolute power of decision in the moment, [rather] they appeal to us to give it to them definitively, i.e., they speak to a power of signification already surrounded [*circonvenue*] by them, to a sort of prepersonal thought.

b) INTERPRETATION (BEYOND GESTALT [THEORY])[11]

(to be completed later)

1) EXCHANGE BETWEEN MEANING AND FIGURAL MOMENTS (movement or rest, figure and background, 2- or 3-dimensional space (cf. tunnel phenomenon in stroboscopic movement)), each being the means of the other, and that which appears being that which makes compossible the 2 series of 'conditions.' The [statement] 'it's an airplane on the horizon' (the meaning) [is] motivated by what is given [*la donnée*], while motivating an aspect of that. The [actual] airplane on the horizon is the crux [*noeud*] of the sense concerning the 'given' [airplane] [*le «donné»*], its aggressive and threatening manner of tracing movement is the display of the meaning 'airplane' which is [the] means of this end as much as [the] end of these means. 2) As a result: exchange of figural moments with one another: insect on the window = airplane on the horizon. Immediate equivalence, without going through the objective relation between apparent size and distance. Likewise equivalence [between]: [a] point in movement within [a] rectangle at rest, and [a] rectangle in movement around [a] point at rest. The equivalence is not laid out for myself: I don't see the point at rest at all. It is ~~observed~~ {self-evident} rather than known. What orients me toward it? The value of the rectangle as background, the value of the point as 'thing in motion,' I perceive in accordance with

this signification that I don't possess in virtue of a certain 'style' of the figures, a 'use value' [«*valeur d'emploi*»] that sets them up as equivalent. Hence [there is an] exchange of rest for movement and of movement for rest. Likewise [there is an] exchange between spatial and temporal articulation: apparent speed decreases in a brighter field, [and] increases in a dimmer field, when the spaces are maintained, because time flows faster in dark space than in bright space: time flows faster in smaller, darker, and nearer fields, and the more vertical, the less horizontal, the motion is (Koffka *Principles* p. 297)[12] – Thus time as well /**[78](VIII6)**/ [is] incorporated into configuration. [It's] not indifferent to content any more than space. And formulated in laws, these equivalences are lived by the perceiving subject as [the] style of a field: a bright, wide and distant field with horizontal movements has a peaceful style that entails slower time.

2) PERCEPTION AND SYMBOL. Hence [the] relation of the 'points' to the movement in Wertheimer or Duncker's experiment, [the relation] of [the] given to the constructed, is not [a] relation [between] sign [and] signification understood as relation [between] opaque fact [and] idea: for we don't understand intellectually why a greater distance from the movement in perception means [*veut dire*] [a] different physiognomy of the movement: a restructuring attracts this physiognomy and that's it. [It's] like the 'signs' are inscribed on [a] keyboard that assigns them a power [that is] out of proportion with their local value,* or on a screen where, swept up by an oblique or transversal power, they are translated according to the law of this power, [or] better: they act by appealing, i.e., by summoning from the background of the subject the arrangement that suits their interaction, by awakening a resonance or echo in it. Signs, if you like, but in the modern sense, not [in the sense] of a sum of givens, but [rather in the sense] of diverse realizations of a single power of phonetic variation, that are mutually distinct only through their opposition, that are in diacritical interaction. In this sense perception of movement = reading. Just as [the] perception of a sentence = *Deckung* [coincidence or overlapping] of the intentions carried by the beginning and of the conclusion, possibly with retroactive correction, the meaning being the cause and effect of the reading, likewise [with the] perception of movement.

> /[*in margin*] *why, in stroboscopic movement, [do] 2 points, in given conditions of succession and distance, form a movement? Or 2 offset rectangles [form] a single one at rest? That must be read in each of the points already, in the very impact of a rectangle on my looking [*regard*]: this impact is not, like that of a point, [the] presence of a figure, but of a background,

[not a] localized impact, but [the] scanning of an entire area by my looking./

3) THE PERCEIVING SUBJECT. Just as the speaking subject only understands and speaks as [a] possessor of [a] system of gesticulation defined by dimensions of variation, the subject that perceives /**[79](VIII7)**/ [*the remainder of this paragraph is crossed out by Merleau-Ponty*] movement can only do so inasmuch as he possesses the equivalences of a sort of natural language: that's what sensory fields are, given diacritical systems with use values [and] characteristic equivalences. But between these fields there are also equivalences, like a common language of these dialects.

Zietz and Werner: modification (or even creation) of visual stroboscopic movement by sonorous accompaniment:[13]

These two images don't give stroboscopic movement on their own – With [drum] beats we get movement of the arrow which tends to go around the point, especially with rhythmic beats: loud beat with [the] arrow, faint [beat] with [the] point → the arrow rotates around the point as [a] center. If it's the point that's accompanied by the louder beat, [then] the arrow [appears] stationary and [the] point moves. Visual emphasis: if the second beat is very faint, the point becomes nearly invisible. Higher-pitched sound acts like louder sound. Drumming = vibrational movement.[14] Clarity, expressive value, outlines [are] specified by these properties of the sound. The noise of the drum with rotation of the arrow [is] heard as the arrow scraping against [a] back wall.[15] What does sound and sonorous articulation mean [*veut dire*] for visible movement? It's not [a] contribution of intellectual meaning [or] explicit logic, [rather] it's [a] contribution of existential meaning [or] perceptual logic. Sound seems to release potentialities in the figure that depend on its articulation: 'a ball rolls,' 'an arrow flies,' and time and space become what is required by this configuration: time and space [are] "*eingehüllt in die besonderen Qualitäten des Bewegens, wie 'schweben', 'rollen', 'fließen', 'schießen'*" ["enveloped in the specific qualities of movement such as 'floating,' 'rolling,' 'flowing,' 'shooting'"][16] – It's that the figure is 'in charge' through its integration within [*insertion dans*] [the] 'visual field' and within [the] 'visual world.' And how does sound have triggering power? Through its rhythmic articulation, i.e., inasmuch as it too is the circuitry on a sort of auditory field where it can draw equivalent configurations. And sound means [*veut dire*] this visual equivalent ultimately because the 2 fields are set up on a single circuit, a single /**[80](VIII8)**/ existence that opens onto these different fields. Movement is not 'essentially something visible': it's "*eine dynamisch gerichtete Veränderung eines Gegenstands, die sich unter besonderen Umständen und Bedingungen in Form der optischen Bewegung entfaltet*" ["a dynamically oriented transformation of an object that unfolds in the form of visual movement under particular circumstances and conditions"][17] – Movement is [an] event, and not of a {*Sinnendings* [sensible thing]}, but of everything. Therefore the perceiving subject has [an] evental unity of movement (within one sense and from one sense to another) because he is geared into space as a system of the powers of his body.

Michotte's experiments = confirmation of an 'interior' of the figure as [the] occasion of a projection or an identification that is evinced by [an] apparent protoplasm, and [which] makes the relations [between] figure [and] movement equivalent [to] the relations [between] one's own body [*corps propre*] [and] objective movements.

[*The remainder of this page is crossed out.*]

Thus our analysis does not go from 'movement in consciousness' to 'consciousness of a movement' that would itself be 'not motor' but [instead] true. On the contrary, it reveals to us in [the] phenomenon of movement [the] entanglement of objective movement and [the] motor possibilities of one's own body. It's along these lines that we will have to continue the analysis.

4) PERCEIVED MOVEMENT

At this point, what have we learned about the perception of movement? What we call movement, with its mobility (Bergson), is a tracing. We have learned [the] possibility of an equivalence between trace [*trace*] and tracer [*traceur*], or conversely of an inscription or sedimentation of movement. Inscription of time and of a certain use that is made of it. 'Generalization' of the time of duration, that becomes tempo, and thereby inhabits movement itself. Cf. Piaget showing that in children time is first of all thought in the object, in the process, /**[81](VIII9)**/ [*the following lines, which continue a crossed-out paragraph, are not crossed out*] and that speed is first of all overtaking, [and that] movement [is] action (and not [the] definition of speed as *s*[*pace*]/*t*[*ime*] and [the] conception of movement as change of place).

Movement is to the trace what breath [*le souffle*] is to the sound, and is read in it just like breath [is read] in the sound.[18]

And meaning is read with movement (it is neither first nor second in relation to meaning). Cf. Epstein.[19]

Strangeness and questioning of meaning through [a] reversal of the sonorous trace (Jaubert) and through [a] change in time (slow motion [in] *Zéro de conduite*).[20]

Conclusion

[The] abstractness of Gestalt [theory]:[21] involve the body in free movement [i.e., outside the constraints of experimental situations] (cf. short note)[22] (Paliard)[23]

Transition to the study of the relation [between] objective movement [and] motricity proper (body schema, psychopathology)

Ninth Lecture

/[82](IX1)/

Clarify [the] idea of organization of the field, of which movement is a part.

Gestalt [theory]: it would depend on given figural moments: in given figural conditions we would have a certain Gestalt, laws of causality.

In fact: 'given' moments aren't decisive. *Situationserfassung* [grasping of the situation].

However: this [*Situationserfassung*] isn't another causality: [the] apprehension of meaning and [the] apprehension of movement are the same thing. Reciprocal motivation. E.g., figural moments operate inasmuch as they satisfy [*étanchent*] an apprehension of meaning, and [meaning] only appears as embodied in [the] figure.

Hence

1) Exchange between meaning and figural moments (particularly movement): each is for the other means and end: 'it's an airplane' = the meaning is [the] means of accounting for the style of [the] movement, but [it] precisely only appears in it: here the airplane is a style of movement. No representation of the airplane.

2) Equivalence, as a result, of figures (and of meanings) among themselves, which doesn't occur through subsumption under an idea: insect on the window = airplane on the horizon without going through the objective relation [between] apparent size [and] distance. So what is it that enables the passage from one organization to another? What is it that organizes?

Likewise equivalence of structure [between]: [a] stationary point in [a] moving rectangle, and [a] moving point in [a] stationary rectangle. Here we have merely the consequences of the equivalence, we don't see the stationary point. But even if retinal points have no absolutely fixed spatial value, there is nonetheless, until other factors are involved, a certain location assigned by [the] point of impact of the light ray. Cf. stroboscopic movement: there is nonetheless 1 point to begin with. Something therefore overcomes and displaces this local solicitation and substitutes an equivalent for it: there is a certain style of rectangles that makes them motionless in principle, [there is] a certain style of the point that makes it wandering, and [there is] a principle of exchange that saves the relation by changing the distribution of rest and movement. And this means that the movement of the point /**[83](IX2)**/ is held in a systematic distribution that respects a certain relation without knowing [what] it [is].

The scope of this distribution extends to the properties of the perceived that seem to come to it only from its relation to a consciousness. There is a tendency to derive them from [a] reference to [the] absolute time of consciousness. However, time itself is caught up in the configuration: exchange between [the] spatial articulation of the field and its temporal properties: apparent speed decreases in a brighter field, [and] increases in a dimmer field. Yet the spaces are preserved. Hence time flows faster in darker space than in bright space: time flows faster in smaller, darker, and nearer fields, and the more vertical, the less horizontal, the motion is (Koffka *Principles* p. 297)[1] There is a time that is the style of a certain field: a bright, wide, and distant field, with horizontal movements has a peaceful style that entails slower time. I'm not saying: there would be time without [a] subject, time [that would be] brought or given [to it]; but I do say: there is no time through the subject alone, there is a lateral relation between him and what he perceives, it doesn't just receive time from the subject, it gives it to him, it isn't only [an] object for the subject, he partakes of it.[2] The time of a field is an emanation of its total (spatial) structure, [it] isn't something different from its spatiality [—] according to an equivalence that is not thought, a bright field with rapid movement equals a dark field with slow movement, and this identification is only for whoever is sensitive to the configurations of these fields.

Thus space and movement [are] 'felt by the heart,' [they are] identical to [the] perceptual tissue itself:

Paulhan: Modern painting or the space felt by the heart:[3] "⟨I was thinking⟩ About the way the fields grow restless when the shadows of the clouds cross over them. About this young harvester of whom I'm unsure for a moment if she is big and far, or small and /**[84](IX3)**/ quite close. About this hotel room, where I wake up in the dark all disoriented: what side is the window on, and how did I get in? ([The room] just waits for my decision to rotate around me and recover its axis.) (. . .)

I don't want to mention just the mistakes. Space is also this smell of wet duck that the earth gives off when it rains; of lilacs and plowed land, women's hair. These distances that get narrower when the weather is about to change (and the distant noises, bells, car horns, suddenly come nearer). This flatness of the blood that sometimes heralds the snow; this cold down to the bones, the hail. But of course here everyone has their own personal spaces: there is one for the night, another for the day (where sight is challenged more than once). One for the ground and one for the water — and mixtures of ground and water also have their own. Ah! and this other space, so quick to shrink, but [also] to stretch to infinity, that separates us from a man. And thus from a woman. In short, these expanses, prior to reason, of which I initially feel (even more than I think) the invariable feature [or] the difference: it's that they have nothing in common with recognized space, the space of which we have the idea." (*Table Ronde* February 1948)[4]

Movement and meaning [are] inseparable [and] synonymous: [it's] not only [that] a certain meaning (house, car) demands a certain distribution of movement and rest, but it also depends on the realization of a certain tempo. Change of meaning through change in the cadence of the movement, accelerated or slowed down:

accelerated: plants becoming animals

slowed down: human movements changing meaning:

"during a slow-motion projection we observe, conversely, a degradation of forms (. . .) Thought vanishes in the [human] gaze, it goes numb and becomes illegible on the face. In gestures, awkwardness — a sign of will, the price of freedom — disappears, absorbed by the infallible grace of animal instinct. The whole man is nothing more than a being of smooth muscles swimming in a dense environment, where thick currents still carry and shape this clear descendant of ancient marine life and the maternal waters [*eaux-mères*]. The regression goes further and exceeds the animal stage. It rediscovers, in the movements of the torso and the neck [*nuque*], the active elasticity of the [plant] stem; in the undulations of the hair or the mane, stirred up by the wind, [it rediscovers] the /**[85](IX4)**/ swaying of the forest (. . .) Slowed down even more, every living substance returns to its fundamental viscosity [and] lets its basic colloidal nature rise to the surface." (Epstein, *L'intelligence d'une machine* p. 59)[5]

Thus the characteristic significations: gracefulness, clumsiness, instinct, will, life, matter, terrestrial life, marine life, nature, animality, humanity, are linked to a certain tempo of presentation, are modes of temporalization, are of a piece with the existence of a certain temporal field (it's the field that makes me unable, despite all my efforts, to see a movement [shown] in slow motion as the same movement at normal speed, even 'taking into account' the slow motion, the dilation of time). To be sure, the presence of intermediate phases that don't appear at all in 'normal' vision is involved (which is enough to prove that ['normal' vision] is by no means [the] successive occupation of 'all the points' of space). But above all [what's] involved [is] the impossibility of mastering the unity of a gesture, the merging [*fusion*] of its essence, its sense, [and] its intention, its characteristic curve, its project. And this is because we have a certain temporal field that does not permit us to *überschauen* [survey] just any multiplicity whatsoever.[6]

3 – [THE] NATURE OF PERCEPTUAL ORGANIZATION — THE LOGIC OF PERCEPTION

We don't understand why
2 successive points make stroboscopic movement
certain rhythms of movement make [the] above-mentioned significations (life, swimming, animality, etc.)
[a] certain distance from movement changes its physiognomy (airplane)
[a] certain relation [between a] point [and a] rectangle gives rise to [the] apparent movement of the stationary point
certain 'signs' are assigned to certain significations
They come to be inscribed on [a] keyboard that assigns them a new power, [or] on a screen scanned by a transversal energy
But it's their very arrangement on the keyboard or the screen that controls their organization, they act by soliciting from it the assembly [*l'assemblage*] that suits their interaction, a resonance or an echo, [they act] by making it similar to them, they address it from without and from within.

Signs, if you like, but in the sense that Saussure and /**[86](IX5)**/ phonology give to signs = diverse realizations of a single power of variation, whose existence is less separate than oppositional and diacritical — and which correspond less to significations than to differences between significations — and which consequently are less coordinated with signification than they articulate it based on a totality, such that signification is wholly immanent in the verbal chain (as its structure) and wholly transcendent (since [it's] beyond signs taken one at a time). In this sense perception is reading, comparable to reading a sentence where there is [a] *Deckung* [coincidence or overlapping] of the intentions carried by the beginning and by the end, and possibly retroactive correction, the meaning being cause and effect of the reading. That's what stroboscopic movement is. That's what sensory fields are: diacritical systems with these use values, systems of characteristic equivalence and substitution that no more rest on an explicit logic than language use [rests] on a scientific knowledge of language.

[The] nature of the oppositional and diacritical system. To see it best, let's not consider the case where the equivalences are internal to a field (e.g., visual), but [rather] cases of intersensory equivalence: common language of sensory dialects.

Cf. Zietz and Werner – and Michotte notes VIII7 and VIII8

It's ultimately through us and our mobility that movement spreads from one field to another.

Our mobility = simple observed fact that we move around like an object moves around.[7] Our mobility = bursting forth of a motor project in executed movements, immanence of the result in the initiative, magical joining of the hand to the goal, and not of the thought of the hand to the thought of the goal. Thus our mobility = can involve something other than [the] body, [it is] undefinable even without [making] reference to meta-corporeal space.

Therefore our analysis doesn't go from movement of consciousness to consciousness of a movement that itself wouldn't be movement but [rather the] truth of movement: the 'consciousness of movement' is [the] 'possibility of moving oneself,' bodily magic.

/[87](IX6)/

[THE] NATURE OF MOVEMENT

Bergson wondering about mobility and its nature. We either had, in the in-itself, [a] route [*trajectoire*] without [a] journey [*trajet*], or [else], in consciousness, undividedness of the movement, — which isn't movement.

All perceived movement is a tracing, i.e., [an] inscription or sedimentation of time in space, [the] taking shape [*figuration*] of the internal in the external, — or conversely [the] deciphering and taking up of this trace by my temporality — Monogram of a temporality — Cashing out of duration as such [*la durée*] as [a] certain tempo. Which explains why time (Piaget) is known first of all in things (generalized time), why speed is first of all [a] power of going beyond, [a] figure of action, and not [a] space/time relation. The 'fastest' movement is that which goes beyond. "Everything happens as if the conceptions of the path traversed [*chemin parcouru*], on the one hand, and of displacement [as] evaluated by its point of arrival (= displacement or change of location [*placement*]), on the other hand, were initially undifferentiated" (Piaget *Mouvement et vitesse chez l'enfant* p. 61).[8]

Perception has [a] system of equivalences among tracings because it is the work of an incarnate subject – The meaning of movement is the motor project – The project etches itself in the very texture of the movement and is read in it, like the breath [*le souffle*] of someone playing an instrument [is read] in the sound. Tacit reading, but real, as proven by the impression of strangeness and non-sense [*non-sens*] produced by the reversal of direction [*sens*] of recorded sounds. Jaubert: writes music, then transcribes it backward.[9] Has an orchestra play it that way. And plays the recording in reverse. Thus music in compositional order, but with sounds that begin with their end, and end with [the] force of the opening [*l'attaque*] (like movements in reverse. {Capra}[10]). Impression of irreality – Now specifically it's the music in the slow-motion scene of *Zéro de conduite*: impression of irreality. Like the reversed music, the slow motion breaks up the physiognomy or the dynamic of the movement inasmuch as [this is] tied to a certain perceptual tempo (image) and to a certain profile of intensity (sound). We thus perceive movement, its sense, its characteristic pace [*allure*], through motor possibilities of one's own body. The trace reveals movement just as sound [reveals] breath [*le souffle*], in its very grain.[11]

/[88](IX7)/

(as an aside, we see that there will be two impressions of irreality:

the first can be obtained through processes: dissociation of the harmony between my body and appearances (slow motion, Jaubert's process)

the other consists in the fact that (aural or visual) appearances come to be emblematic not only of motor possibilities that are known, common, [and] acquired, but of unique, individual or exceptional possibilities of praxis: it's the great work of visual art, painting or film.

surreal by	undersignifying	(plaster sugar cube)
		(automatic language)
	oversignifying	(creative language))

Tenth Lecture[1]

LECTURE X

GENERALIZATION

We have revealed corporeality in perceived movements ([the] magic of one's own body as [a] power to deploy intentions in space, [as a] power to trace [*tracer*]).
Our motricity as [the] ground of the mobility of objects.
The situations considered (stationary eye, stationary body) were abstract: only a possible corporeality or motricity could be involved there, not [an] actual [one]. In fact, corporeality as a whole (and not that of a single field) is involved in life. Abstract situations only give pre-movements (Duncker), or pre-movements ⟨*sic*⟩ (visual vertigo of the spiral [ganglion], labyrinthic vertigo), not yet 'real' movement with close dialogue between body and appearance. Perceptions of this kind, studied by Gestalt [theory], are to [the] perception of 'real' movement what poetry is to prose: [a] voice that says nothing, and only resonates in the other.
Nevertheless, these abstract situations had an advantage for us: they showed, better than perceptions of movement in fuller, more complex figural conditions, [the] pre-intellectual roots of perception – If we had considered more complex perception or illusions, we would have been tempted to bring in judgment.
On the contrary, we laid bare the perceptual logos as such – (the body)
It remains to show how we should understand [the] perception of more complex movements, in which 'perceptual thought' seems to be involved.

/[89](IX8 or X1)/
Example:

1) Ocular paralysis → movement of objects in the direction of [the] assumed movement of the looking [*regard*]

"Disimplication" [«*Désimplication*»] [—] I think I move my eyes; the appearance [*l'aspect*] of objects remaining the same on the retina, [I think that] the object must have moved

2) Illusion of lateral movement in [the] anaglyph[2] (Paliard) (*Pensée implicite et perception visuelle*)[3]
Paliard's analysis (ibid. p. 113 Attached notes)

Can we 'disimplicate' in this way, since I don't actually engage in this reasoning, and the result is intuitive? (especially in [the] first case)

Paliard admits that the first case can't be reduced to the second. But then he sees a vital implication there in which the results alone are given to us, and which is inscrutable, e.g., {thr[ough]} the illusion of better relief in [the] anaglyph [when viewed] further away (pp. 111–112, 114).*

/[*in margin*] *Cf. blue page IX8a/

But, if there are two types of synthesis, how are they connected? How could they be joined?

Actually Paliard sketches a way to get past this by designating "perception" as [an] original synthesis that occurs "on the world" (120)[4]*

/[*in margin*] *Cf. blue page IX8b/

/[90](IX8a)/

/[*in margin and at an angle*] PALIARD/

Relief in anaglyph [gets] better as one moves further away:[5]

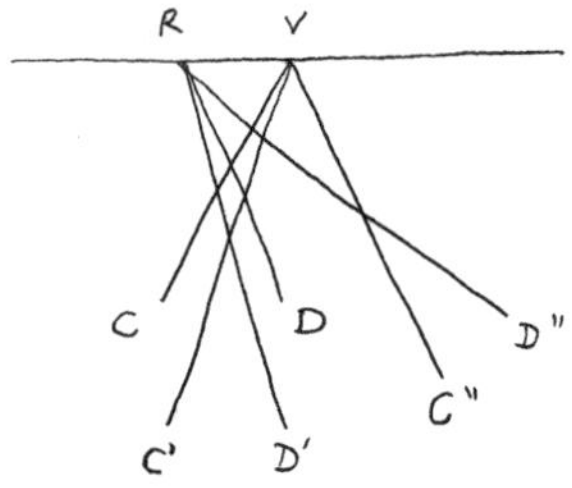

and the object in the foreground follows the observer in his lateral movement.

Paliard thinks that the diagram doesn't explain the enhancement of relief: [the enhancement] "resists every attempt at disimplication, because the ground of implication can only be the vital implication or biological synthesis that eludes every analysis from a psychological perspective. The fusion can't be rigorously explained (. . .) Therefore the geometric schema [*schéma géométrique*] that we gave expresses, but does not explain, binocular synthesis. It does not explain the birth of the phantom. It only explains how it varies with distantial position." (111–112)

"On the contrary, the door opens up [i.e., a possible new basis for explanation emerges] with the illusion of lateral movement. For at the same time as the same type of geometric expression is appropriate to it, it is also possible to refer the phantom no longer to just the distantial relation alone, as with the increase of artificial relief, but to the lateral perspective. Psychological analysis again **/[90]v(IX8a)/** finds a hold, and an explanation through explicitation becomes possible." (112)

/[91](IX8b)/

"Are nature and the understanding, thought and life, incommensurable?[6] Undoubtedly, but within the most powerful ongoing connection [*la plus puissante jonction persistante*]. (. . .) ⟨There are⟩[7] complicities as well as alliances. The most obscure synthesis, impenetrable to analysis and to our Euclidian modes of expression, accommodates and embodies knowledge within itself. (. . .) Nature prepared the pathways [*voies*], signification bursts out in the obliviously contemplative person [*le contemplative qui s'ignore*], we understand in the man who perceives. (. . .) this sensation-perception supplements our verifications while remaining implication, and it even goes beyond them: it verifies in the moment, not through modified points of view. It sketches out before our eyes the grasping and the outline of the volume, it unites, in a strange and beautiful way, the limit of envelopment in life and the limit of development through knowledge. (. . .) it expresses in objectivity the reflexive nature of human thought, for it makes [it] more than it symbolizes it, it realizes it. (. . .) the convergence (. . .) is indispensable for overcoming double vision in normal perception, or for creating from two images a phantom object in artificial perception, (. . .) it enables sensation to take in this way (. . .). It is an idea of distance that always adheres to distance. (. . .) original synthesis of two concurring reports, of two equal points of view into a single one that is true not because it distinguishes its two constituents by separating them, but because it unites them by mastering them. By mastering them? That is to say, by making of their small lateral difference* /[*in margin*] *DIACRITICAL SIGNS/ a sensitivity to distance. But it is impossible to witness this transposition, which would also be to see the subjective, (. . .) pass into the objective (. . .). We must only say that the synthesis is carried out on the object. (. . .) It is symbolic realization or reflexive projection." (120–122)

/[92](IX9 or X2)/

/[*in margin and at an angle*] INTERPRETATION OF PALIARD/

complicity [between] organism [and] thought = preordination of the organism to thought, incarnation, that is, realization of thought by the organism perception: contemplation unaware of itself [*contemplation qui s'ignore*]

Perception of relief, while remaining implication all the way down, implication without disimplication, does better than verifying thought: [a] single hold on a variety of points of view that are not made explicit, on [a] variety of senses [*sens*] (tactile just like visual), instantaneous synthesis, without analysis. [A] small lateral difference is transformed by the body into distance, but we can't witness the transformation, it is achieved through the emergence [*apparition*] of relief, and we don't see the subjective pass into the objective. Actually there is no transposition: the lateral differences belong to cognitive development, the implication [belongs] to vital envelopment. Perception is their common limit.

Perception "goes beyond" verifications, "it verifies in the moment, not through modified points of view" — It "realizes" the reflexive nature of human thought — Thus here we go beyond [the] opposition between "vital" implication and "psychological" implication that is susceptible to disimplication. Implication appears as a positive value.

Is it not necessary, therefore, even in the case where analysis seems possible, to be suspicious of [any] discursive translation of perception?

/[93](IX10 or X3)/

Let's return to the illusion of movement in [the] anaglyph

"Consciousness of our movement to the right makes us compensate unduly for a sensible variation that doesn't occur. And since, in virtue of the law of compensation, the motion [*mobilité*] of a sensible object to the left signifies its real motionlessness [*immobilité*], here the sensible motionlessness of the phantom signifies a movement to the right." (113)

Let's return to experience, with no conjectural reconstruction in terms of cognitive development.

1) Do we have "consciousness of our movement to the right" in the sense in which it is represented on [the] diagram, in the sense of movement [as] seen from above? No. We have consciousness of movement in the sense of [an] increase of tension toward what we leave and [a] decrease of tension toward what we approach.

2) Do we have consciousness of [a] stationary phantom as opposed to [a] "leftward motion [*mobilité*]" of the real objects? [And] this in the sense of identity in an objective point, or on the contrary [of the] successive occupation of several objective locations? But the "apparent movement" of the real objects is not at all the equivalent

of a genuine movement that would be "interpreted" according to an opposed "signification." It is their permanence.* [There is] no contradiction between [the] apparent movements of the horizon when I walk and its lived immovability [*immobilité*]. – Correlatively, in the case of the anaglyph, the phantom doesn't rest at all in the sense of objective rest that I have to translate, according to [a] law of compensation, into objective movement. It's its impact on my looking [*regard*] that remains the same, and this permanence is in turn movement. Cf. ocular paralysis. I don't deduce the movement of objects from their permanence on my eyes [that are] assumed [to be] in objective movement. I even notice [the] gearing together of my eyes — things in motion on them, — and that is immediately their movement. The error of disimplication

/[*in margin*] *There is a 'secret rest' of this apparent shift [*bougé*] like there is a 'secret blackness' of milk. The stability [*solidité*] of the tree lies in moving [*bouger*], i.e., in grazing the glance [*regard*] instead of sticking to it. The tractability of the anaglyphic image to [my] looking [*regard*] is immediately, if not 'movement' in the objective sense, [then] at least unrootedness, irreality.[1] It's [my] looking as [the] interrogation of things, and the precise or vague way that it is articulated over them, that gives them this or that value, and not thought in accordance with laws.
(1) The anaglyph always faces us but does not truly change objective orientation to do so: it follows us like the eyes of a portrait follow us: it would be better to say it is never lateral./

/[94](IX11 or X4)/
is to leave the point of view of the embodied and situated perceiving subject, to detach objective movement from my motricity as [a] reference from me to the world. Therefore movement ≠ one of the things we perceive; this objective movement is [a] projection of our motricity, of a motricity that links [the] subject to [the] space where he is situated; and this motor capacity is the light of perception.

Hence [the] possibility of an expression of movement that is not an imitation or reproduction of it, e.g., in still art (painting): a trace is given to the eyes, a text to read, and, taken up by my exploratory motricity, it means [*veut dire*]: movement.

of a universal expression, [an expression] of everything, through my motricity as my gearing into the world or my anchorage in it.

This is in no way to reduce perception to motricity in the sense of biological synthesis, since it's a matter of lived movement. It's not to reduce perception to non-thinking. It's to root perceptual thinking in the moving subject. Thought will then represent a higher order, but to be understood on that basis: there is perception of movement because between me (my body, my fields) and the spectacle there is an expressive relation, because each attitude is [the] power of a situation and each spectacle [is the] trace of an attitude – Now, expression initiated in this way starts a dialectic, [it] calls for developments and transformations, reversals: [the] attempt to recover the expressed, linguistic expression, sublimation of the body in language, cultural expression. Clarify this dialectic.

/[95](X5)/

ROLE OF THE FOLLOWING LECTURES

To be clarified (2 lectures):

nature of the notion that we have of our body (of our movement)

relation of this consciousness of the body with our perception of the world and of others

sublimation of the body, of movement, through passage to cultural expression

And specifically psychopathology teaches us a lot about

consciousness of the body (body schema)

[its] relation to consciousness of the world (agnosias and apraxias)

to symbolic consciousness

Supplementary proof (1 lecture): the expression of movement (painting)

universal expression through movement (cinema)

Conclusion (1 lecture) The notion of world (world and sense)

/[96]/

SCHILDER REFERENCES[8]

(1) PRELOGICAL UNITY

Autotopagnosia[9] as discrimination of a part of the body schema. Schilder p. 40

/[*in margin, to the right of the two preceding lines*] Schilder's experiment on the doubling of the tactile body by the visual body 106–107/

All visualization of a part of the body gives rise to a sort of phantom (Schilder p. 68)
allesthesia [*allo-esthésie*][10] – its relation with anosognosia[11] (28) (30) (35)

(2) BACKGROUND OF PRAXIS
that the body schema isn't a matter of intellectual synthesis, this is what the action of the labyrinth [i.e., the inner ear] proves.
body schema and [muscular] tonicity [*tonus*] – Idea of [a] privileged position or consciousness of effort 77, 78, 80, 81
Equivalences in the body schema: a position of the face translated into flattened face (83)
Apraxia resulting from right-left confusion
Heaviness of the hand resulting [from] ignorance of where it is
Schilder 41
Normal and pathological condition (Goldstein) of a motor possession of the body (27). Necessity of an optic thinking? (52)[12]
The body as [the] ground of movement, — and in particular of reflective movements (45)
The *Bewegungsentwurf* [motor project] (50)(53) — body image is movement (55: the Japanese illusion)

Apraxia, apraxia and agnosia: Schilder p. 45. Different apraxias p. 50.
The integration [*insertion*] of knowledge within [*dans*] praxia (58)
experimental apraxia: the Japanese illusion (55). Body schema is only clear when it is ready for movement.[13]
In principle praxia and gnosia are synonyms (58). But gnosia isn't praxis at the same level (59). Different levels of praxis: concrete action and expressive or volitional action,[14] pointing [*monstration*] (63) (cf. Goldstein)

(3) RELATION TO [THE] EXTERNAL WORLD
Aristotle's illusion (83)[15] — [Henry] Head: the feather and [the] annexation of instruments[16]
Analysis of concrete and abstract movement in Schneider (Goldstein) and of ext[ernal] movement *Zeigen et Greifen*[17]
Stratton's experiment: vision with the back of the head [*l'occiput*].[18]
Development of drawing and development of [the] body schema (106)
Hécaen p. 93 correlation [between] depersonalization of the body schema and of others cf. p. 103[19]
Constructional apraxia.[20]
Body schema and sleep.

(4) RELATION TO LANGUAGE AND TO THE THOUGHT OF OTHERS
equivalence [between] ego [and] other (83)
Pain asymbolia[21] (103)
Hécaen (113, 114): identification and relation [of] body schema – the world – others[22]
Body schema and phonemic system

/[97](X6)/

I. THE NOTION OF BODY SCHEMA

Our body ≠ an object (with distinctive 'characteristics' and 'gaps')
[—] something in front of [*devant*] us

1 its integration within [*insertion dans*] space is not that of an object
3 its unity is not that of a sum of parts (phantom limb)
2 its intersensory unity is not that of an object
4 it has [the] power to incorporate everything used for its action
it is dynamic (body schema and [muscular] tonicity [*tonus*])
5 body schema and external world (Schilder's experiment, Aristotle's illusion, and [the] Japanese [illusion])
Thus it's [a] schema in the sense of
1) [a] system of reference, absolute here, not [a] thing in space or [a] content
3) [a] totality that prescribes to its parts their sense
2) [a] system of immediate intersensory equivalences
4) [a] relation to an external space that forms a system with it, that it's in regular contact with [*qu'il fréquente*]

1) ITS INTEGRATION WITHIN [*INSERTION DANS*] SPACE

Quotation from Head based on Schilder[23]
it is that which, prior to the consciousness of this or that position, provides the spatial reference
it is therefore an absolute here — where I am — and not only a possible here.
This ground is absent in pathological case[s]: it is made up for by vision (subjects [who are] only able to move their body by looking at it) or by *Tastzuckungen* [exploratory twitchings] for 'finding' the body.[24]

3) ITS UNITY

The unity of its parts is not centripetal but centrifugal.

From which it follows that it can be realized over gaps (emphasized regions of the body: points of tension [between] skin [and] bone, points of contact with the world, points touched by clothing).

It is not static but dynamic: the body at rest is hardly felt – at rest, there is discordance between felt skin and bare skin (which is above), and the skin is not [a] surface. It only becomes one when the body is touched and especially [when it] touches.

The unity of the body persists despite local subtractions: the phantom limb. Head: [a] phantom leg resulting from an operation [is] suppressed by [a] cerebral lesion that also destroys /**[98](X7)**/ postural recognition.[25] Since Head, cases of peripheral dependence have been found: destruction of the phantom through cocainization of the stump and through peripheral interventions. In fact there is a double dependence. But the central dependence is undeniable ({psychogenic} {elements}: shrinkage of the phantom with the passing of time—absence of phantom in cases where there was no trauma and where the limb was lost gradually) – There is thus a central phenomenon of "organic regression," refusal of the impairment, cf. anosognosia.

The unity of the body persists independently of its objective state through reference to [a] privileged situation [or a] typology [*typique*]:[26] Ross's experiment, when [the] face is turned sideways [with] eyes closed, the body is represented with [the] face in [the] same direction as [the] body, but flattened.[27] Normality.

2) ITS INTERMODAL UNITY

Head: dissociation due to illness (and integration in normal cases) of the absolute notion of the point where the limbs are in space from the knowledge of these points transferred onto a diagram [*schéma*] or onto another person.

The first could be eliminated [with] the second remaining, [and] we will see that the converse is equally possible.

That implies: our (tactile kinesthetic) postural schema is normally in communication with a visual schema of the surface of our organism. The space of the existing body [is normally in communication] with a virtual or symbolic space of [a] visual nature.[28]

Normally [there is] visual-tactile translation of bodily space that is given ready-made (as in a taximeter[29] . . .) It's not a matter of judgment there either since judgment isn't involved in Head's pathological case.

Visualization of every point of our body that is touched or referred to. Imagination of the body.

Schilder [—] 'spiritual eye' that is not outside, but in [the] body [as] empty, and [which] sees the outside of our body from within. "It is like a psychic organ, which wanders round in the body and sees the outside of the body from the inside . . . This immaterial eye wanders according to the point of the surface that has to be observed" (*Image and Appearance* pp. 84–85).[30]

Therefore [the] relation [between the] tactile body [and the] visual body = not reference of a particular tactile aspect to a particular visual aspect by way of an idea of its objective structure, but [the] spontaneous translation from one language into the other. Cf. synesthetic perception.

/[99](X8)/

4) THE BODY IS [A] SCHEMA BECAUSE IT'S [A] MOTOR POWER

Quotation from Head (3) in Schilder.[31]

This shows that the body is less [an] object of perception than [a] means of action. It is the background against which [*le fond sur lequel*] our motor projects stand out.

In a general way, consciousness of our body depends closely upon what we do

Kohnstamm's phenomenon[32] and Schilder and Hoff's experiment[33]

Draw from this [an] overview [*tableau*] of the consciousness of our spatiality

The body schema as norm, as zero point of divergence, as privileged level or attitude – [There's a] return to these privileged positions as soon as our fingers aren't touching [one another] or we're not looking at them (Schilder p 81).[34]

/[**100**]/[35]

The integration or disintegration of the voice is the work of the body schema – The voice and the mouth as very important elements of the body schema – This isn't just a manner of speaking. In the body schema of normal people it highlights a certain way of assimilating the world, of identifying with it such as in their voices, a certain way of assimilating others and of identifying with them – Presence of others and presence to others in speaking, two-sided act: to speak is to speak to . . . , in order to be understood by . . . The whole set of facts of depersonalization, [which is] to be put in parallel with the facts of [the] disintegration of the body schema, acquires a concrete-intuitive character, at the same time, conversely, as our notion of [the] organic body is itself enriched because it appears as the locus of personalization – What we need to get a handle on, through an appropriate theory of consciousness and of the construction of cultural figures and backgrounds, is a crossroads [*un carrefour*] where there is communication between our being toward others, our being toward ourselves, and our nature. This crossroads is perception

Eleventh Lecture

/**[101](XI1)**/

BODY SCHEMA

Our analysis: Ext[ernal] movement → movement of one's own body.

But how is this different? Isn't the body just an ordinary object:
→ 1) it is perceived through intellectually coordinated sensations,
2) it is driven by mechanism.

Actually we see that it's not the same

1) It's not laid out in front of us like [an] object: it has gaps, – which indicate that we are with it, stuck to it, situated in it, – hence that its here is not [a] relation between objects but [the] contact of [a] self with the outside, – hence that its unity is not, like that of the cube, [the] participation of all its moments in a meaning or an idea, but [a] lived lateral unity of mutual implication.

2) It's not moved like an object, i.e., by another object: it's ultimately through it that I move instruments and its movement is not instrumental. It's [a] magical conveyance [*transport*] to the goal without knowledge of the means, with insight that doesn't wait for received messages in order to be regulated.[1]*

/[*in margin*] *experiments showing that in our movements there are very few representations of movement: regulation of movement [occurs] through messages that are inscribed in the field of tensions without giving rise to representations, [there is] not even representation of the movement prior to the movement/

Thus the body calls into question [the] distinction [between] consciousness or subject [and] object

perception (for itself) [and] movement (in space, in itself)
This is what the contemporary notion of body schema means [*veut dire*].

1) Schema = concrete [and] visible like a drawing, we don't have to think it, understanding it isn't hard, it's like a mnemonic map that doesn't even need interpretation

and yet schema ≠ opaque individual closed in on itself, our body is a system, the schema shows what's essential, it governs the details, it brings out the sense, it shows an order, an interior of the process.

It's thus like
- a 'natural' idea [*une idée – naturelle*]
- a thinking given to itself
- an implicit intellection
- a knowledge [*savoir*] that we have [solely] because we are[2]

2) And how is that possible?
Because the body schema is essentially attitude toward . . .
openness to goals . . .
background of a praxis

Clarify these two points:
knowledge without concept, totality without idea
background of a praxis,
before studying [the] relationship [between]
body schema [and] external world (3)
body schema [and] language, relations with others, [and] thought (4)

/[102](XI2)/

1) THE BODY AS NONIDEAL TOTALITY

TOTALITY OF ITS SENSES

a) Schilder's experiment: (*Image and Appearance* 106–107)

Key in right hand – double vision by staring into the distance – Finger of left hand touches key – after a while, [there is the] impression that these two keys are not only seen but also touched – [This] impression [is] emphasized through repetition of the contact – At this moment and at this moment alone the two visual givens are "vivid" and the two fingers are "living." Likewise doubling of the pin [*le poinçon*] or of the pricking [*la piqûre*]. – [The doubling] is clearer when I pay attention to the object and not to [my] sensations.[3]

[4](Sometimes: touch or pain [are] felt not in two fingers but between them, where the finger would be seen without [the] double vision. Then the visible fingers seem like "phantoms."[5]

Sometimes, too, one of the two visible fingers is [a] "phantom" – The "real" [finger] is that which is seen in connection with the body.[6]

If the hand is covered in a way that isolates the two visible fingers, one feels a single, living, invisible finger between the two visible fingers that seem like phantoms.

Meaning: 1) Relation of entailment [*entraînement*] [from the] visual body → [the] tactile body in pain (in other cases it's the opposite), lateral intermodal unity, what we touch [is] determined a priori by what we see (or conversely).

2) The passage to tactile duplication is at the same time [the] passage to 'reality': reality of visual phantoms, reality of the visual body. The fingers are indeed living fingers that explore.

3) It's through [their] integration within [*insertion dans*] [an] exploratory unity that the visual impressions [*données*] entail tactile impressions, and that tactile impressions yield 'reality.' Whatever is separate from the body is [a] phantom.

Thus [the] body = [an] intersensory system [that is] achieved not through judgment (we have to wait for that to 'take'), but through integration [*intégration*] in [a] unity that is my undivided body. Sensory impressions [*données*] belong to my body or not depending on whether or not they are integrated within this whole that isn't [the] sum of parts or of impressions. [Sensory impressions] reflect or express [my body] to varying degrees.

/**[103](XI3)**/

b) Head: a patient can indicate on a diagram or on the body of someone else the point on his body that is touched or pricked, without knowing the position in space of the limb involved or of the point that is touched.[7]

This dissociation reveals in normal cases [the] connection of [the] tactile body with [the] "model of the surface of the body" (visual model).[8]

The connection is not a matter of judgment. It lies deeper than judgment, in that which integrates [the] tactile body within [the] visual body.

c) Automatic visualization [*visualisation de principe*] of every part of our body to which we pay attention – Appearance [*apparition*] of a quasi-phantom – Imagination of the body – Schilder: spiritual eye of the empty body that sees its surface from within. "It is like a psychic organ, which wanders round in the body and sees the outside of the body from the inside . . . This immaterial eye wanders according to the point of the surface that has to be observed" (*Image and Appearance* pp. 84–85).[9]

Thus [there is an] automatic "translation" [*«traduction» de principe*] from the tactile to the visual[10] – The tactile is immediately translated into [the] visual for us "just as on a taximeter the distance is represented to us already transformed into shillings and pence" (Head).[11]

TOTALITY OF ITS LIMBS OR ORGANS

a) Autotopagnosia[12]

Pick's cases:[13] subjects with no visual or tactile disorders (and without hysteria): [one subject] looks for her ear on the table when she is told to touch it, [she] only finds it when the order is repeated. Doesn't find her left eye and says "I don't know, I must have lost it." Looks for her hands on the table when asked to show them and /**[104](XI4)**/ says: "Nowhere, for heaven's sake; I have lost them, but they must be somewhere." (Schilder p. 40)[14] = Deintegration [*désinsertion*] of body parts from the body schema.

Analogous subject of Pötzl[15] — which brings us into [the] very nature of the disturbance: [the] subject no longer knows where her right and left hands are. Afterward, when she recovers: "It came into her mind where the hand was, and that made the paralysis pass."[16] With right-left confusion there is heaviness in the hand, along with ignorance of where it is and its deintegration. Having a hand is thus the same thing as knowing where it is, [knowing] where to find it, [or] having it at your disposal. Character [*personnalité*] and integration within [*insertion dans*] [a] bodily situation, in [a] region of space that we inhabit, that is us or ours.[17]

b) Opposite case: phantom limb: Head: [a] phantom leg resulting from an operation [is] suppressed by [a] cerebral lesion that also destroys postural recognition.[18] Therefore [there is a] link between [a] phantom limb and [the] possession of a body situated in space. Phantom limb = the absent limb still counts in the schema, even though objectively it is removed, the whole without the parts. To be sure, there is suppression of the phantom through cocainization of the stump or through peripheral action: it never arises without paresthesia[19] or pain, but they don't explain it:

absence of phantom in the case where there was no trauma (accident or operation)

shrinkage of the phantom over time

the phantom is especially [the] active part (hand or foot) of the limb, that could be planted directly in the body, proof that it has something to do with activity. "Like Weir Mitchell's case of the rider whose left arm was amputated: wanting to whip his horse, he passed the reins to the absent left hand and for this reason let himself /**[105](XI5)**/ get thrown. Similarly, this patient of Van Bogaert whose left arm was amputated and who, at the moment he was hanging from a horizontal bar with his right arm, felt with surprise his absent hand close synkinetically around the bar." (Ombredane *Études de Ps. Médicale* II, 38–39).[20] "And if the extremities of the limbs, hand and foot, are more vivid in this illusion, it's probably because they occupy a privileged place, that of accountable leader, in these series of movements of organs in specifically arranged [*composé*] order, as [Hughlings] Jackson said, that constitute our voluntary gestures (. . .)" (39)

Hence [the] meaning of the illusion: continuation of the total activity, unawareness of the deficiency, "organic regression" (Schilder).[21]

Here, at the organic level, [we find a] phenomenon comparable to the one that we find at the psychic level in [the] unconsciousness of the repressed [*refoulé*]. Thus there is a sort of bodily self, with its defense mechanisms against sickness. And once again [the] relation [between] body schema [and] character, the body = a self-here-now.

c) Interpreted in terms of allesthesia [*allo-esthésie*]:[22]

[A] subject with localization disorders in half his body feels touching or pricking [occurring there] in the other [half].[23] As if one half of his body had been folded over onto the other: something is felt in the body not due to [a] local sign, but on the basis of [a] central distribution.[24]

And this distribution is [a] deep phenomenon, [a phenomenon] of existence: it is passage toward anosognosia. The dominance of the healthy side effects the transition. Schilder's subject does not transfer left to right, but [the] left leg [is] always crossed over the right in such a way that it's the right that acts when the left is examined. [He] hardly uses [his] left arm even though there's no paresis.[25] "Touches on the left side were called by him touches on the right side, /**[106](XI6)**/ though often he would point correctly to the point touched." (Schilder *Image* 35).[26] The left side is no longer "{appreciated}," [it] is "underestimated" or "inferiorized."[27]

[A] hemiplegic subject who is asked to act with his left hand makes the gesture with the right [hand] and says that he did it with the left. (Schilder)[28]

Thus [there is a] totality of the senses and of the segments of the body, – and [this is a] totality in relation to our integration within [*insertion dans*] the world and our being toward the world (the illusion of double contact in Schilder's experiment [is] stronger when one pays attention to the object)

2) THIS UNITY IS THAT OF A PRAXIS

Ever since the notion of body schema was first introduced.

Head (quote) defines the body schema first and foremost as [a] postural schema, i.e., [a] tracking of positions, of the point where we stand in a series of actions – the body schema is essentially

[the] background of a praxis, [a] pre-objective spatiality against the background of which the current objects of action take shape.

In this respect, the body schema is indistinct in immobility. Indistinct, but not inexistent.[29] The proof of this is provided by the patient of Goldstein who, with [his] body stationary and eyes closed, could not identify [a] point touched on his body, nor distinguish points of contact on his skin, nor make out letters written on his skin, nor recognize sizes and shapes, nor describe passive movements or [the] position of his limbs, nor initiate any voluntary movement. He does not know where his limbs are, he must first of all 'find' them. He finds them through increasingly {specific} automatic movements /**[107](XI7)**/ of the whole body (and in this way even figures out [a] point of contact and letters traced out mirrorwise, according to his movements).[30] This shows that in normal cases there is [a] spatial presence of the body even when it is stationary, and, for all instances of contact, [that there is a] projection of the touched points in a space beyond them, [a] tension of the whole body toward an external or visual spatiality that alone gives meaning to the stimulations. The body schema is imminent, although it becomes clearer through action: through [action], the seen skin sticks to the felt skin, the skin becomes [a] surface inasmuch as the body touches, or is not reduced to deducing from signs, as does Goldstein's patient, [the] horizontal position of the body through [the] pressure of the couch, or [the] shape of the stimulus from vaguely felt contact. Thus nascent movement or '*sensorische Bewegung*' ["sensory movement"].

That's what we have to clarify.

It can be done through [an] analysis of the role of [muscular] tonicity (and of the vestibulum, acting not as [a] sense but as [a] receptor)

1) the body schema and the body are situated not where they are objectively, but where we are preparing to put them

2) it follows that the body schema is always oriented toward privileged positions [or] norms, and that the consciousness that we have of it is above all that of a divergence with regard to these norms

Kohnstamm's phenomenon (Schilder *Image* p. 77)[31]

Hoff and Schilder's experiment (*ibid.* 77)[32]

Shifting [*déplacement*] of the body schema in cerebellar cases (*ibid.* 78)

Impossibility of maintaining non-'normal' position of the hands without visual control (p. 80)

Exclusion of the 'abnormal' and Aristotle's illusion[33]

Apraxia as supplementary proof: absence of this motor background, of these norms, of this project of a situation, of this presence of the world to our body

Twelfth Lecture

/[108](XII1)/

Hence unity of the body schema, — of its 'senses' and its 'segments,' — which is not that ~~of a~~ vertical ~~knowledge or of an object of~~ [vertical] ~~knowledge~~, through participation in an idea, but [an] open lateral unity of a coexistence.

That can only be understood as [the] unity of an action on the world, [as the unity] of a praxis.

2) UNITY OF PRAXIS

Praxis and action – I prefer praxis because

action (e.g., in Bergson's sense or [that] of pragmatism) = 1) adaptation to given aspects of the world → 2) functional [*utilitaire*] → 3) common to all living things: same problems for all even though different solutions 4) less dignified in contrast to knowledge of the truth (the 'demands of action' [are] always restrictive) 5) hence: incarnation [is] always conceived more or less as deprivation or loss [*déchéance*].

Praxis (= not only external production, but also the motives [*motifs*] = πρᾶξις [praxis]) = 1) not only adaptation to [the] given, but pre-adaptation, a priori of the organism (Bergson was not unaware of this, but restricted to biology: unsurpassable Nature) 2) not only functional, but projection of the whole man 3) the problems are not the same: milieu and world horizon 4) praxis even incorporates Theoria, involves a Theoria or gnosis that is its background, that it modifies and which modifies it in return.

The unity of the body schema is that of a praxis so construed, and the body schema is the background implied in [this praxis].

Already in Head: the body schema as [the] acquired standard on the basis of which we carry on. Quote Head.

Clarify this notion of practical background.

/[109](XII2)/

a) The background is not just [a] stage of vague perceptions [as the] context for subsequent perceptions – It's of a different order, that through which the world is present to our action – To be reduced to [an] object of 'reflected' perception is for it either [a] higher activity (which presupposes it in its pre-objective functioning), or else [a] result of disintegration.

Patients [*malades*] [i.e., individuals with certain pathologies] show us through [its] diminishment [*par différence*] what [the] practical presence of my body to myself is that makes its perceptual positing unnecessary for a normal person.[1]

Gelb and Goldstein: [with] body stationary and eyes closed [the patient] can't identify [a] point touched on the body, nor distinguish points of contact on his skin, nor make out letters written on his skin, nor recognize sizes and forms, nor describe passive movements or positions of his limbs, nor initiate voluntary movements. He doesn't know where his limbs are, he must first of all 'find' them – He finds them through gradually specified automatic movements of the whole body ([he] figures out in this way [the] point of contact and letters according to his movements, such that they must be written mirrorwise to be deciphered).

Goldstein blames visual agnosia: that would be the body when it's deprived of vision. – Debatable interpretation.

What's certain: this case shows us [an] *Ersatzleistung* [substitute or compensatory performance] for replacing [the] presence of the body to the subject that exists in normal cases. Through movement, [the patient] reactivates [the] body schema that is effectively dormant (cf. upon waking when, through [its] initial movements, the scattered body constitutes itself as an active totality face-to-face with a situation) – It always tends to doze off in immobility* /[*in margin*] *it's action that makes bare skin stick to felt skin, that [makes] the skin become a surface again inasmuch as the body 'touches' actively/. But [it's] never absent in waking consciousness: always imminent, although partially dissociated, it's mobilizable – And it's this presence to the world, this attentiveness [*vigilance*][2] that makes it such that in normal cases we don't need *Tastzuckungen* [exploratory twitchings] to feel [the] position of the body in space **/[110](XII3)/** (Goldstein's patient deduces [the] horizonality or verticality of the body from certain clues or signs: e.g., pressure of the couch on the body) or to feel [the] shape and signification of tactile stimuli — even if all of that is provided through vision and visual training of the tactile body, it remains that in normal cases this visualization is embodied in touch, the normal [person] does not have a separate touch, separate touch is a pathological formation and the disturbance must be understood not only as [a] subtraction of visual contents, but also as [a] change in the mode of coexistence of the 'senses' – So let's not say: the normal [person] adds [the] visual to the tactile, — but [rather] the tactile field of the normal [person] involves a presence of the body that is self-evident, that need not be expressly perceived, that makes it available, that opens it to a tactile perceptual horizon.[3]

The body is not only confused perception: it's what mediates a relation [between] here [and] over there.

b) The background is not only retrospective: it is prospective. Retrospective horizon and prospective horizon — But prospection is not [the] perception [of an] object, it's [a] project.

Kohnstamm's phenomenon: before [an] effort, the arm is 'at the disposal' of the subject in a certain position, after the effort it seems to him to be not where it [actually] is, but at a different point, situated in the direction of the effort.

Hoff and Schilder's experiment:[4] one arm raised and the other horizontal. With eyes closed, bring the two arms back to parallel. In fact, [the subject] brings the raised arm back a little higher than the other – It's not a matter of an error of judgment: if, with eyes open, he notices the discrepancy [*l'écart*], as soon as he closes his eyes again [he] puts the two arms back at different heights [*en écart*].* It's that he no longer knows the positions of the arm that worked as they [actually] are, it's that its positions were subjectively modified by his effort.[5]

/[*in margin*] *The repetition of the experiment changes nothing, even a knowledge of the result (repeated 12 times)/

Variation of the experiment: the arm that is too high is passively brought /**[111](XII4)**/ to the height of the other. The subject feels it "too low." The body schema was "pulled in the direction of [muscular] tonicity."[6]

In cerebellar cases, abnormal activation of [muscular] tonicity [*tonus*] (cf. that which is determined by vestibular hyperexcitation in normal cases) brings it about that the knee [on the] afflicted side appears to the subject less flexed than it is objectively, resulting in [a] tendency to hyperflexion, keeping the impaired knee above the healthy knee when it is relaxed.[7]

In normal cases: [it's] difficult to hold the hands and arms in [a] given position once the fingers are no longer touching and visual control no longer applies – At the moment the eyes are closed, the fingers move, there is abduction in particular of the little finger — Likewise [there is a] tendency to pronation: arms outstretched, hands horizontal and turned upward, as soon as the eyes are closed one tends to turn the thumbs upward.[8]

All that stems from the fact that muscular tensions involve [the] definition of a normal position of rest, [a] position where nothing would be felt as figure, where the body would return to its background, and in relation to which any other [position] is [an] expressly [*expressément*] perceived divergence or anomaly.

Thus the body schema is not perceived – It is [the] norm or privileged position in contrast to which the perceived body is defined. It is prior to explicit perception – It requires an overhaul of our notion of consciousness – Comparison of the body schema /**[112](XII5)**/ with language: language expresses not significations but differences of significations. Likewise [the] body ≠ perceived things, but [the] index of our pre-thetic relations with [the] space in which it establishes us.

Now, this shows us not only [the] mode of existence of the body but also of the world: the variations of [muscular] tonicity and of the body schema also bring about variations of perceived space (e.g., through irrigation of the labyrinth [i.e., inner ear])[9] — The reduction of the body schema to its norm in Aristotle's illusion involves a certain mode of emergence of external phenomena (two balls under the fingers) — Hence the body schema is also a certain structure of the perceived world, and the latter is rooted in it.

Apraxia as [a] verification of this idea of praxis and [as an] opportunity to clarify how [the] external world [and the] body are linked together [*l'articulation monde extérieur-corps*].

3) APRAXIA AND THE RELATIONS [BETWEEN] PRAXIA [AND] EXTERNAL PERCEPTION

Reality of this praxis

Apraxia = disturbance of this practical presence of the world to us, to our action, founded on [the] dissociation of praxis and the body schema.

Apraxia according to Schilder:[10] [the] subject knows what he should do, says it or at any rate shows that he knows it through [the] action of unimpaired parts of the body. Perceptual and gnosic integrity. But he can't do it with a certain part of the body. The "general plan" of the act can be formulated, but not transformed into action: disorder of specific actions in the overall plan: ideational apraxia[11] — Disintegration of certain specific actions = motor apraxia[12] — Purely executory disintegration of these specific actions = innervatory apraxia[13] — Root of the disturbance: intellectually defined tasks no longer call forth the praxical organization that would accomplish them – The normal subject, when he wants to move an arm, grasp an object, [or] light a match, does not know what part of his body will go to what part of the object "The plan for the movement is given as a germ, as undeveloped psychic knowledge . . . this germ of the plan to a movement finds its development only during the performance of the action, and the sensations provoked by the action will have a developing influence on the plan." (Schilder 51)[14]

/[113](XII6)/

This is indisputable and suffices to establish [the] reality of praxis.

But difficulties (that we can't get into [here]) begin when we have to situate these disturbances in relation to those of gnosia or even of phasia [*phasie*], and determine what is essential or primordial.* [And] this as a matter of principle: presented with a failure [i.e., by a patient on a diagnostic test], [the] difficulty of knowing whether its origin is 1) gnosic (no recognition of the object) 2) praxical: no practical presence of the object to us, although it is recognized 3) or even phasic [i.e., pertaining to speech]: non-verbalization. We could try to eliminate this last interpretation by giving silent tests to the subject. But if it's a matter of internal verbalization? E.g., Head saying that the inability to imitate movements in a mirror [is] due to [an] impairment of verbalization.[15]

> /[*in margin*] *Whether apraxia is an agnosia of use,[16] or conversely [whether] agnosia [is] an apraxia (gnosic disturbances in the apraxias), whether aphasia is an apraxia of language or [conversely] [whether] apraxia [is] an aphasia (Head), or finally whether aphasia is an agnosia or [whether] agnosia [is] an aphasia./

In truth, we mustn't draw a skeptical conclusion here: it could be that it makes no sense to speak of a disturbance that would have [a] gnosic or praxical or phasic cause. It could be that the three functions are not three things and that the equivocation is in man himself. Three "poles" (Ajuriaguerra and Hécaen):[17] corporeal pole (praxical), visual-tactile pole (gnosic) and even phasic pole, the same functions being at work at different levels in such a way that we could consider explanation by one of the poles, pure disturbances, or distinct faculties (action, knowledge, language).

Points that we agree upon

1) There are relatively independent [or] predominant disturbances.
2) A disturbance whose figure is praxical can result in gnosic disturbances at least to a certain level of gnosia: e.g.

Constructional apraxia and [the] apractognosia[18] that results from it (Lhermitte and Mouzon).[19] Subject with sound praxias (for [putting on] clothes, for lighting candle[s], for putting letters in envelopes), but unable to construct [a] figure with matchsticks, nor draw. This entails → no understanding of geometric symbols (cubes, triangles, circles), poor recognition of {?} (dancing couple, recognizes young man and young woman but not their comportment [*attitude*]).[20]

Other case (Paterson and Zangwill):[21] dressing apraxia,[22] disconnection [*mise hors circuit*] of left side and left hand, constructional inability, models imitated line for line, failure with puzzle, map of the room: objects in a single row.

/[114](XII7)/
All that → in the gnosic order: good recognition of colors and objects, distances, angles, directions, but no recognition of schematic drawings except through details, weak recognition of photos (photo of a heavily congested street: "It's quite confused, I see cars, it could be a road").[23]

Thus in certain cases a gnosic disturbance [is] rooted in somatognosia or praxia.

The Japanese illusion studied by Schilder shows how [a] partial disintegration of the body schema and of bodily space can have an impact on gnosia.[24] The positions of the Japanese illusion.[25] In position III we have 1) complete mixing up and depersonalization of the schema of the hand 2) errors each time that the finger to be moved is only pointed to by the experimenter, error by projection onto [the] corresponding finger on the other hand or those next to it 3) correct reactions when the finger to be moved is either touched or indicated verbally by the experimenter or through [an] internal [i.e., self-given on the part of the subject] order.

This example shows that the designative power [*la puissance de désignation*] of the experimenter's finger presupposes in the subject the practical presence of his body to himself, and outside this presence means nothing [*ne signifie rien*]. It's this [presence], i.e., the body schema, — that the subject tries to reconstitute, and he succeeds in moving the designated finger when this practical presence is reconstituted – a) in cases of remote designation [i.e., when the experimenter simply points], the point of the visible world to which the experimenter's gesture leads is without bodily existence, hence errors; b) in cases of [a] verbal order the subject applies a theoretical diagram of the hand by matching [the] thumb of the diagram with [the] felt thumb and deducing, — either by counting from the thumb with slight movements, — or else by analyzing [the] undifferentiated impression according to [the] predominance of one hand; c) in cases of contact, this contact entails [an] 'absolute localization,' i.e., we are capable of moving the touched finger, of 'finding' it. "We know the point in space which has been touched, but are not aware in what way this feeling and the represented space have to be brought in connection with the other part of the body. It seems to float in space. But still, there is a knowledge (. . .) that it belongs to one's own body and that one will be able to work out the exact relation." (Schilder *Image* p. 55).[26]

Absolute localization **/[115](XII8)/** [is] not to be taken literally: this would be an isolated "local sign" that means nothing [*ne veut rien dire*].[27]

In reality there is integration within [*insertion dans*] a body schema [that is] still vague. And it's this that must be contrasted with [the] visual non-presence of one's own body and especially [with the] visual non-presence of directions [that are] external to one's own body. In the normal [person] not only tactile sensations but all external impressions [*données*] are oriented in relation to the body, [they] have sense in relation to it. [The body] is thus our establishment [*installation*] in external space, and to have a body there is to be exposed to the world. The one is articulated with the other. And, through this articulation, [there is an] imperceptible transition from disorganization of the body schema to apraxia, and from apraxia to agnosia.

Conclusion – Distinguish "several levels of motility," otherwise all apraxia would be agnosia. "When there is apraxia present, a great part of motility of another level is preserved. Otherwise no perception of any value would be possible." (Schilder *Image* p. 59)[28]

Human praxis sediments in vision — The body schema is enriched by a visual schema (eliminated in the Japanese illusion), at the level of which the body becomes an object. This superstructure gains a relative independence with respect to praxical infrastructures, and [it] can conceal their collapse. Just as visual orientation conceals labyrinthic disturbances.

This independence is not absolute (the superstructures, deprived of the movement that gave life to them, can conceal the deficiency rather than make up for it. E.g., in Schneider, language and external verbal knowledge conceal [his] deficiency, but have lost their productivity. Likewise vision and visual recognition remain in constructional apraxia or apractognosia, even though the power of construction and projection have disappeared, as the manipulation of symbols shows.) The real integrity of the superstructures presupposes, if not that of the infrastructures, at least that of the power of construction.

Thus motility at several levels. I.e., 'elementary' motility is already [a] power of expression of the body /**[116](XII9)**/ in a world, and higher forms of expression ([the] manipulation and recognition of symbols) are still facts of praxis or of motility.

Therefore the joining of the sensible world and the world of expression comes about through movement.

Next time

Some clarifications concerning [the] relation [between] body schema, thought, others, [and] language (transition: Gerstmann's syndrome:[29] hand and thought)

Then: supplementary proof through: movement as universal mode of expression (cinema) and stationary expression of movement (painting)

4) THE BODY SCHEMA AND OTHERS
THE BODY SCHEMA AND LANGUAGE

Thirteenth Lecture

/[117](XIII1)/

/[*in margin*] Reread [the] Japanese illusion. Add apraxia ⇔ agnosia ⇔ aphasia]/

[The] presence of the body to us and, through it, [the presence] of the world
1) Supplementary proof: the Japanese illusion, which produces an impairment of [the] presence of the body and, to a certain extent, of the world:
[*argumentum*] *a contrario* [[argument] from the contrary]: the normal body, even visual:
not [an] object in space: what's produced by the illusion: external, alienated body.
Exteriority and dissociation [are] synonymous.
Thus belonging and unity are one and the same: [this is] not recognized point by point, nor even through [an] objective relation of points: that's [a] reconstruction of the body schema.
But [rather through its being a] totality of action: it's ours because its parts are in synergy.
Synergy for which actions? Not for any particular action on this or that singular object, but for types of action or gestures: taking the fingers [and] bending [them].
To 'find' or to recognize one's body is to know where these powers are located, to have [a] coincidence (*Deckung*) of a certain style with, on the one hand, certain aspects of the world (certain things to do) and [on the other hand] a certain background from which this initiative stems. The two relationships [are] interdependent.
In the Japanese illusion my tactile body is still at my disposal in this sense, but even on the basis of [a] verbal order that is abstract [*notionnelle*] [and] not actual [*inactuelle*], my visual body is no longer at my disposal in this sense: it no longer says anything to me, and the directions from the outside no longer say anything to it, [they] no longer emerge in relation to its internal directions [or] its pragmatic possibilities.

Normal body = a 'locality' (since in my initiative I have a presentiment of my integration with [*insertion dans*] things, and hence the possibility of 'reflective' πράξεις [praxes]: a touching, a seeing) that is not simply one place among others [i.e., among other places], singular like them, but [is] that from which the other [places] get their bearings,[1] [a] settled relation with them, *multorum in unum expressio* [the expression of many things into one] (Leibniz)[2] such that the outside can 'show' the body and the body [can 'show'] the outside, or that it can anticipate it through its style, i.e., divine it not through a knowledge but through a movement.

Therefore movement is not a category (in the third person) of relations between objects that would somehow have to be applied to a consciousness lacking [a] locality — There is an originary notion of movement as mine which is that of a situation of my own among things, the situation containing in its present appearance not only a determinate relation, but an infinitude of possible relations.

Hence [a] problem: relation of this praxis with knowledge [*connaissance*] or gnosia, with abstract [*notionnel*] [or] contemplative knowledge [*savoir*].

/**[118]**/

1) Originality of praxis
2) Certain gnosic disturbances result from apraxia
3) Nevertheless, apraxia is not [the] cause of all agnosia (as indeed agnosia is not always [the] cause of apraxia) — How to reconcile all that? Through the idea of levels of motility, of sedimentations, of [the] same basic function operating at different levels, with [the] possibility of superstructures concealing [the] weakening of infrastructure, but in the long run suffering from this weakening* /[*in margin*] *cf. Schneider/. This means: it's not because [we are] consciousness that we can move, nor [is it] because [we] can move that we are consciousness, in a causal sense. But [rather there is an] anticipation of the higher in the lower and [a] taking up of the lower with [a] change in sense – Thus movement and expression: [the] emergence in movement of a dialectic of expression: examples.
4) Gerstmann's syndrome, the hand according to Lange,[3] the surpassing of its purely praxical function in acalculia,[4] and yet the need for a praxical point of support even though the function goes beyond [it]. Surpassing that preserves: cf. language.
5) The body schema in sleeping and in waking, the total apraxia of deep sleep, the degrees of wakefulness corresponding to the degrees of articulation of the body schema, the aphasia of the dream, the

phonemic system and wakeful consciousness. Not: consciousness or motricity as [a] causal alternative, but mobility as means of articulation of a universe that extends far beyond 'motricity' as [a] function of local movement.

/[119](XIII1)/

Illustration of [a] supplementary proof of our presence to the body and to the world through motricity.

THE JAPANESE ILLUSION

Depersonalized hands, {?}, objects – fingers mixed up

– Eyes closed: subject correctly moves [the] finger [that is] touched or [the] finger [that is] verbally indicated by the observer or [the] finger that he verbally indicates himself

– Eyes open: errs with finger shown by the observer, — moves the same finger on the opposite hand or else fingers adjacent to that or adjacent to it [i.e., the finger pointed to]. Does not know praxically what he knows visually. The adjustment [of] external space [and] one's own space [*espace propre*].

Verbal order: success depends upon [a] roundabout means: it[5] enables [the subject] to count [the] exact position of the finger based on the thumb and the hand through [a] clue (that which {feels} most is the right, the fingers turned toward the left = left hand) — or else [it involves] making slight movements, — which {?} the visual aspect and "vivifies" the body schema.[6]

Contact: the subject moves the finger without knowing where it is (objectively) [—] 'absolute localization' = In fact around the touched spot we have [a] widened circle of contact that even overruns the whole hand – Thus even here [there are] processes of differentiation and integration[7]

The body is not [an] object

To say that it has [a] unity is to say that it is synergistic, that it is ours, our action, our expression

To 'have' the body, not to have to 'find' it, is to have at one's disposal localized powers, it's to live the relation between a certain style of action (aiming [at an] external configuration) and a certain seat of these actions. The relation [between] action [and] world and the relation [between] me [and] my body are one and the same: the body speaks to me because things speak to it [*le corps me dit parce que les choses lui disent*] – Its intentionality and my residing in it are synonymous

The 'locality' of my body [is] not simply one place among others [i.e., among other places], but [is] that from which all the others get their bearings,[8] in such a way that it 'shows' the other places and they 'show' it

Therefore movement is not [a] relation between objects that would have to be attributed to consciousness – Originary notion of movement as my gesture which is that of a situation of my own among things, [a] situation that contains multiple possibilities in its present appearance and 'understands' them.

Problem: relation of this praxis with knowledge [*connaissance*], gnosia, [or] abstract knowledge [*savoir notionnel*].

/[120](XIII2)/

Must we say that our mobility is grounded on our being as consciousness? Or that our being as consciousness is grounded on our mobility?

Examine this with the help of psychiatric materials, apraxia. Why?
It's not that we can't examine it through simple reflection, provided that it be reflection that is open [and] descriptive. We have in our experience enough to respond to this question: if we didn't have it there, [then] no 'scientific fact' would introduce it. Reflection and science are not heterogeneous: taken in its full sense, science forms a <u>part</u> of our experience. — The role of scientific facts is not to replace [*suppléer*] reflection (with risks of inconsistency and of building on provisional results), but to force it to really apply itself. We don't ask psychiatry to answer [the] question: mobility or consciousness, as if it were a matter of fact, — but to provide us with variants of our experience that awaken us to what it contains. Thus philosophy [and] science ≠ law and fact or essence and existence, but [the] consideration of facts calls essences into question, and in order not to be scholastic essences have to cover the facts.

Hence 1) [the] necessity of introducing facts: no philosophy is valid if it renders them inconceivable (no essences outside the existent), for the superstructure it's a matter of understanding its infrastructure, its history, [while] for gnosia [it's a matter] of understanding praxia.

2) [The] right to not push the consideration [of the facts] onto technical grounds, [the] right to not be a doctor (no blind determination of facts, without intuition)

It would be all or nothing here, total knowledge of the facts or none at all, if science were [the] correlation of purely established facts. Science would have total and exclusive jurisdiction over [the] relation [between] praxia [and] gnosia, if praxia and gnosia (and phasia) were three functions or three orders of external facts, whose relation could be known through induction.

But specifically [with] doctors: [the] impossibility of absolutely eliminating 2 factors in order to bring to light [the] causality of the 3rd* /[*in margin*] *[is] apraxia [an] agnosia of use? [is] aphasia [an] apraxia of speaking? is apraxia aphasia (Head)?/. Failure [i.e., by a patient on a diagnostic test] can depend on 1) praxia (manipulation, e.g., drawing) 2) gnosia (non-recognition) 3) and even phasia (no internal formulation – Head). This impossibility ≠ simply [an] imperfection of our science; it arises from the very being of man, to recognize it is a progressive step in [the] science of man, for it arises from the fact that human action as such is action of a being that knows and speaks. [There is] no sense in speaking of causality in the absolute sense. No pure disturbances, [no] distinct faculties, [no] absolute nosological entities (action, knowledge, language), but only three "poles" (corporeal-praxical, gnosic and phasic), the same functions being at work at different levels (Ajuriaguerra and Hécaen).[9]*

> /[*in margin*] *This recognition of a relation [of] 'acausality' or of a 'dialectical' psychiatry → end of the dilemma [between a] relation of meaning *or* [a] relation of fact, philosophical analysis *or* scientific analysis? – Even if the presence of two symptoms in a syndrome can be ascribed to <u>localization</u> (e.g., finger agnosia and acalculia), that <u>does not exclude</u> [a] relation of meaning since nowadays [the] local distribution of functions in the brain doesn't exclude their participation in a certain <u>level</u> of activity. And that therefore the proximity of cerebral instruments does not exclude [a] relation of meaning between the functions. That they are woven together is not simply due to [a] coincidence of cerebral geography./

Thus [the] rejection of empiricism and purely causal science shows that the question doesn't arise solely on [the] ground of facts, but on [the] ground of categorial construction to which philosophy can contribute without total knowledge.

What are the facts of which philosophy must, [and] can, avail itself?

/[121](XIII3)/

1) Originality of praxis, relative autonomy of the presence of the world to our mobility.

Schilder: in apraxia the subject knows what he should do* /[*in margin*] *perceptual and gnosic integrity — or in any case the gnosic disturbance doesn't come first/ (abstractly), says it, or shows it through the action of the unimpaired parts of his body. But [he] can't do it with a certain part of the body ({and} {us}: relative apraxia of the left hand). Apraxia: the general idea of the act can be defined in terms of knowledge, but not transformed into action. Schilder: [there are] different apraxias (ideational, motor, innervatory) depending on whether the incapacity concerns more the overall organization of the act or its detailed organization. In any case it's never a matter of the bare capacity to move the limb (which would be paralysis), nor of the capacity to conceive the task (which would be dementia [*démence*]). Apraxia is to movement what agnosia is to sensibility. Intellectually defined tasks no longer call forth the praxical organization that would accomplish them, no longer 'say' anything to the body or to some organ of the body, no longer exist for this organ. [A] disturbance that isn't [a] theoretical [*notionnel*] [one]: when he wants to move an arm, grasp an object, [or] light a match, the normal subject doesn't know which part of this body acts on which part of the object. "The plan for the movement is given as a germ, as undeveloped psychic knowledge (. . .) this germ of the plan to a movement finds its development only during the performance of the action, and the sensation provoked by the action will have a developing influence on the plan." (Schilder *Image* p. 51)[10]

Thus apraxia = disturbance of the gearing together [of the] body schema [and the] external world.

2) Praxical disturbances sometimes lead to gnosic disturbances: there is a gnosia founded on praxia, a practognosia.

Constructional apraxia and 'apractognosia' (Lhermitte and Mouzon)[11] [—] subjects having retained certain praxias (use of clothing, lighting candles, putting [a] letter in [an] envelope), but unable to construct [a] figure with matchsticks or small boards, nor draw. This leads to a lack of understanding of geometric symbols (cubes, triangles, circles), poor recognition of {?} (dancing couple: recognizes young man and young woman but not their comportment [*attitude*]).

Other case (Paterson and Zangwill) [—] dressing apraxia, disconnection [*mise hors circuit*] of left side and left hand, and constructional incapacity (models [are] imitated line for line, failure with puzzle, [when] trying /**[122](XIII4)**/ to draw the room, [the subject] draws all objects in a single row).[12] These praxical disturbances are accompanied by gnosic disturbances: while there is good recognition of colors, objects, distances, angles, directions, there is no recognition of simple drawings except for details, weak recognition of photos (photo of a heavily congested street: "It's quite confused, I see cars, it could be a road").[13]

Relation of the gnosic disturbance to the praxical disturbance: in the 2 cases [i.e., those described in the two preceding paragraphs], projection [and] the equivalence of a movement with a tracing or [an] external effect are elusive [*insaisissables*], the motor taking up of a form [*la reprise motrice d'une forme*] or the seeing [*vision*] of a form as embodying a motor project — Cf. Goldstein's subject who can't *nachzeichnen* [i.e., trace, or (literally) draw after], and [who] actually always draws spontaneously[14] — Or other subjects: phenomenon of closing in (Mayer-Gross): the patient sticks to the model, draws in or on the model when he wants to copy.[15] When he imitates the positions of the doctor's arms with his own he places them against those of the doctor.[16] Mayer-Gross "fear of empty space"[17] (cf. Goldstein's subject: can't start on a blank page, something has to pull him). For Wendell Muncie, it's rather [the] difficulty to symbolize, every copy always being abstract compared with [the] given existing model: the copy is abstract because it is necessary to let the structure of the model organize a movement that reproduces it, this structure must therefore emerge and be operative.[18] The letter and the spirit. Cf. sorting of color swatches [—] totalistic procedure and step-by-step procedure.[19] Thus the constitution of symbols (unlike relatively elementary givens such as distances or even directions) would require a praxis, the symbol being [a] non-natural object, [an] object of praxis, [the] trace of a human praxis. And it's this freedom of projection and incarnation that would represent praxis and which would be lacking in constructional apraxia. Cf. 2-year-old child, very attentive to images, going to look for a real lemon to put beside the image and saying "the real" and "just a picture."[20]

Must we conclude: gnosia [is] founded on praxia? Consciousness [is founded] on mobility?

/**[123](XIII5)**/
3) Relations between praxia and gnosia

The fact remains:	[there are] apraxias without significant agnosia [there are] agnosias without significant apraxia
The double fact of	[the] connection [*connexion*] [between] apraxia [and] agnosia [the] disjunction [between] apraxia [and] agnosia

can only be understood if gnosia and praxia are related while also being relatively autonomous.

Schilder: all agnosia involves [a] manipulative inability in relation to [the] structure of the object — all apraxia involves [the] erasure of a layer of signification, if not at the level of consciousness, then at least at the level of practical presence.

But 1) The 2 disturbances remain distinct because in the bipolar system [it is] sometimes the one (corporeal pole) [and] sometimes the other (visual-constructive pole) that is especially at issue. System in which the figure of the disturbance can be situated differently.

2) Nevertheless there is [a] fundamental relationship and [the] same function [is] at work in both cases: e.g., it's equally a praxis that made possible the distances and directions [that are] preserved in certain constructional apraxias. But a praxis of a simpler degree. [The] possibility in man of a sedimentation or historicity such that the results obtained at one level remain acquired even if the same function at other levels has disintegrated. Unimpaired infrastructures with damaged superstructures or even apparently unimpaired superstructures with damaged infrastructures. Cf. Goldstein's case of Schneider with visual agnosia, disturbances of symbolic consciousness and [yet] integrity of language. In fact, the integrity of language is only apparent: [he has] poor vocabulary and especially [a] lack of initiative and verbal improvisation. The deficiency is concealed and not truly compensated for. Deprived of the /**[124](XIII6)**/ movement that stimulated them, superstructures are *Ersatzleistung*[*en*] [substitute or compensatory performances] profoundly different from what they are normally. Schneider and "external verbal knowledge"[21] — True integrity of the superstructures presupposes that of the power of construction, and through this that of the infrastructures. But superstructures have their own kind of stability [*solidité*], understanding [*intelligence*] institutionalized in language. Cf. visual orientation concealing disorders of labyrinthic orientation. The construction of a visual body schema, the objectification of the body, the possibility of 'reflective' actions, of pointing gestures in the virtual [realm], [and] of symbolic gestures can sometimes conceal [the] deficiency of a more vital order (as with Goldstein's patient who can take motor initiatives on condition of having his eyes open). [This] does not preclude there being a relation, and that [the] same originary power is found across the entire structure [*est d'un bout à l'autre de l'édifice*], and that any impairment at one level has repercussions at other levels.

Thus praxis or motility [occurs at] at several levels, i.e., relation to [a] situation involves dialectic

otherwise 2) all apraxia would be agnosia. "When there is apraxia present, a great part of motility of another level is preserved. Otherwise no perception of any value would be possible." (Schilder *Image* p. 59)[22]
1) apraxia and agnosia would be absolutely separate.

Thus concerning [the] question: can [we] move because [we are] conscious or [are we] conscious because [we] can move? Impossible to answer in [a] causal sense: for mobility would only be the cause of consciousness by containing it already, and consciousness would only be the cause of mobility by containing it already (i.e., the situation). To be able to move [*être mobile*] in the human sense and to be conscious are the same thing. [There is] anticipation of the higher in the lower, but [a] taking up with [a] change in sense of the lower in the higher. Mobility in the sense in which it belongs to our body is /**[125](XIII7–XIV1)**/ already expression, but within this mobility [there is] also [the] emergence of a dialectic of expression that transforms it.

Body schema and opening to a world through motricity. But also relations with others, language, [and] thought. So at least sketch out this dialectic [of] movement – gesture – [and] language, in which movement becomes expression.

Fourteenth Lecture

4) BODY SCHEMA AND RELATIONS WITH OTHERS

a) All the transitions between dissociations of the body schema, strangeness of a body part, and [the] perception of others,* and [the] presence of an other: [a] patient saying not only that his arm does not belong to him, but that it's someone else's arm (between verbal autonomism and verbal hallucination). The total elucidation of the body schema shows not only the subject's relation to self but also his relation to others: my body schema already includes presentations of myself that are only obtained from the point of view of others (frontal view of my face): [the] advent of a vision of [the] self is [the] advent of others (mirror stage). There is an affective emphasizing of the body schema that is actually the establishment in me of a relation with others: e.g., predominance of some region of the body (oral) and [of some] type of behavior toward others (overestimation of speech – devouring, biting type, etc., oral type).** Libidinal structure of the body schema — And thereby opening to a social structure of the body schema: for once [it is] institutionalized, a corporeal-interhuman type (a pattern)[1] in turn determines its emphasis (cf. American advertisements with exaggerated oral type), — the body [is the] bearer of a whole symbolic system which shapes it in return. Thus not only relations between individuals, but socio-historical relations.

> /[*in margin*] *Stockert's patient who thought he had lost his left side saw the people he encountered as lacking their right side (Hécaen).[2] Hécaen's schizophrenic:[3] disturbance of body schema ("misshapen torso," distorted head especially from behind, legs too short, sometimes heavier, sometimes lighter than appropriate, soft arms [that] don't "take" with the rest of the body) → disturbance in relation with others [4](runs into people that look like him, but who are "more me than myself," [who] rob him [and] taunt him. They represent the ideal self of his youth. The weakness of his body schema is [the] predominance of others and of the past./

/[*in margin*] **Disturbances of body schema and paranormal forms of sexuality, i.e., of relations to others./

/[126](XIV2)/
That presupposes the body as [a] medium of intercorporeal significations that take hold of it, but [which] in turn adopt its mode of existence and can only be understood within this order of existence.

5) BODY SCHEMA AND THOUGHT, AND SPEECH

THE HAND
There is isolated finger agnosia. But *Gerstmann's* syndrome also shows [a] connection [*connexion*] [between]

1) finger agnosia [5] (2 hands – eyes open, difficulty recognizing, naming, showing, selecting fingers, identifying errors – (Corresponding errors moreover in the perception of the doctor's fingers) – Lack of freedom in individual {?} movements of the fingers – [The] hand [is] not knowable as [a] figure on [a] background.[6]
   Yet [the] fingers [are] unimpaired from the sensory and motor point of view.
2) right-left confusion
4) calculation [*calcul*]
3) constructional praxia.

In general finger agnosia [is] isolated or linked to disturbances [that are]

agnosic	(the hand of the doctor not specified)
apraxic	(constructional disturbances in the same hand)
	(disturbances of symbolic actions without [an] object)
aphasic	

This shows (as above in [the] problem [concerning] agnosia [and] apraxia)

[an] ambiguous relation between [the] hand and phasia, praxia, visual and constructive gnosia, [and] thought in general.* [The hand] acts as [a] point of support for calculation in the sense that it is [a] point of support for [the] direction of the calculation or even of complex numbers. *Richtungsstörung* [disturbance of direction]. But this interpretation is superficial: there are often undisturbed perceptual directions. The defect is linked to the hand and can't be defined in general as [a] defect of a function (Space of activity —

or *Gliederungsverlust* [loss of differentiated order] as Goldstein says)[7] — Lange has come to conceive the hand as [a] non-elective, but still indispensable, point of support for the superstructures, and to dismiss overly intellectualistic interpretation.

/[*in margin*] *Functionally, there is the hand as part of the body, – and the hand as integrated within complex and general circuits of behavior./

[8]*Fingeragnosie* [finger agnosia] whenever "it's not a question of the hand as [an] instrument to be put to work automatically /**[127](XIV3)**/ and when this instrument must be considered separately and {?} analyzed in its structure and its outline"[9] — The deficiency is found "in this focal point where the visual, the linguistic, the spatial, the praxical, and the constructive seem to converge. Everything happens as if in this point the articulated hand were laden with characteristics belonging to these different domains, in conditions such that at each moment the different types of load can be converted into one another"[10] — "The deficiency lies where one's own space and external space in Grünbaum's sense[11] interpenetrate most closely; the hand is dedifferentiated not as instrument but as object . . . not as instrument but as material for a spiritual activity . . . All our capacities, inasmuch as they concern the hand, manifest themselves only on condition that the articulated hand always becomes an object again, that it makes available to the organism the prior acquisitions as automatisms and thereby frees itself for other active acquisitions. With a lesion in this region it is not a matter of a loss of automatisms, but new acquisitions by means of the articulated hand are impossible or very difficult. What is lacking in finger agnosia is the capacity to change the hand as instrument at any moment into an object and by this means to transform it into a more complete instrument."[12]

/[*in margin*] Every disturbance simultaneously concerns [an] instrument and [the] totality (*Werkzeugsstörung* [disturbance (or malfunction) of a tool] and *Ganzheitsstörung* [disturbance (or disorder) of the totality])[13]/

This means [*veut dire*]: the hand is equivocal. The hand as [an] instrument of direct relations with the outside may be present, without the hand as [a] term of reflective actions, as [an] object, being [present], and this implies non-openness to other (symbolic) tasks that would require this objectification, that would make of [the] hand [an] instrument of [a] different power. — I.e., the hand carries an indefinite number of symbolic systems; it is not defined by its factual, physical presence (there are people missing arms who have no difficulty with what is 'handy' and with perception), but [rather] inasmuch as it incorporates such and such significations. It's in this sense that it /**[128](XIV4)**/ is necessary for thought: the hand gesture does not contain thought, it punctuates it, it sets it up in the world, it brings it into existence* /[*in margin*] *the 'mimicry of thought' of each [person]/. The hand as bone segments and chunk of flesh cloaks it with a different signification, makes it inhabit the world and history, exactly like the work sets up in a machine for thinking [*machine à penser*] (text)[14] a signification that is transcendent to the meaning of each of the words taken separately. Surpassing that enshrines [*Dépassement qui consacre*]. So we don't think with our hands, but we don't think without the transfigured body, [the] bearer of significations, that is the body schema.

LANGUAGE

[This applies] even more so [to] speech: even our presence to ourselves is mediated right away through internal monologue.
Language = the body opening itself to gesticulation according to [a] non-natural, non-gestural law of construction (language), i.e., ensuring radical transcendence of the signified with respect to the signifying: not only to sketch out a perspective, an articulation of the physical and social world, but also to reach [*rejoindre*] a truth. Something new emerges there that merits special study (next year).

Today just indicate [the] inclusion [*insertion*] of this order within [*sur*] its dialectical origin, [the inclusion] of language within the body schema.

And how the order of Λόγος [*Logos*] can be understood only as [a] sublimation of corporeality.

/**[129](XIV5)**/

Relationship [between the] body schema [and] language, deep relation [between] phasia [and] praxia, [the] same existential modality of speech and human motricity [is] evident in sleep.

Body schema in falling asleep: [it] loses its internal articulation and correlatively the world loses its; disappearance of the hands, of the oral-vocal tract, vague body mass, it seems an impossible effort to revive it; only open doors remain, but waking up appears very far — But there is also (Kraepelin)[15] disarticulation of language: sleep paraphasia[16] (which is only noticed after waking* /[*in margin*] *e.g., {?} by repetition of a word as an adjective/, and even a long time afterward, in the dream, we cling to these imperfect words with unconstrained satisfaction, knowing is not knowing that one knows) and this lack of exact articulation has as a consequence that the meaning does not adhere to the signs (the *Mitteilung* [message] of the dream occurs without an intermediary: the sense of the utterances [*paroles*] pervades us without it being carried by the words) and ultimately the nearly arbitrary character of the meaning ('obvious' and inexpressible upon waking). Thus phasia and praxia [are] parallel as [a] function of articulating a world that is consciousness as awakening.

The language of sleep clarified by F. Mayer:[17]

below waking consciousness there is paraphasia involving the layer of *Sprachbilder* [linguistic images]: articulated language remains but is no longer used in the same way: words function as images; leveling of the system of phonemic differentiations, which would account for clusters [*caillots*] of words that are only vaguely assonant (München [Munich], Münster de Fribourg [Freiburg Minster, cathedral in Freiburg im Breisgau], the city of Münster) (*Ente* [duck] – *England* [England] – *Ende* [end]) and [which] orient the dream.[18] Here 'association' is founded on the disintegration of an articulatory and diacritical power that is language.

Let's keep going: below the layer of *Sprachbilder*, gestural language would substitute for articulated language. Same characteristics [are found] in dream and gestural language.

The I [*Je*] and the You [*Tu*] [are] represented, [but] not the it or [the] he[19]

Construction, *Reihenbildung* [series formation],[20] and antitheses in the 2 cases [i.e., in the cases of dream and gestural language] (the assonances of which are special cases)

/[130](XIV6)/

Universal present, no tenses nor modalities
Spatial translation of all temporal relationships
No judgment, no comparison (we can't say with gestures: the 2 are good)[21]
No causality
Equivocation, anxiety ({us}[22] in a foreign country), and humor of the dream and of gestural language ("I have two legs" and "come see me at 2 o'clock")[23]
Thus the dream ≠ symbolism that dissembles, but [a] *Mitteilung* [message] in gestural language since articulated language is paralyzed — The dream [is] to be understood in the language of the dream and not in the language of waking life — Structural consideration of the dream.

— If we go down even lower: total apraxia and dreamless sleep: miss the train, be tied down on the rail in front of the engine and unable to call out or take action.[24] Experience of this apraxia in cases of sudden awakening: lack of muscular coordination, unable to act on an electric button.[25] Mouth sealed upon waking.

Thus system of speech = [a] particularly fragile superstructure of the body schema, subtleness of being in the world.

Relation [between] language [and] thought, world of expression = relation [between] body schema [and] sensible world.

Consciousness is always articulation, precise divergence, and thereby opening to . . . Not possession of representation. And without this articulation, [without] this power [*puissance*] to project and to incarnate, it is only [a] power [*pouvoir*] of divergence in general, consciousness of anything, which is to say, not consciousness.

Double movement: from signification descending into the world, which brings it into existence, the movement transforms into expression, — which it was already.

Man wakes up [*se lève*] and man speaks.

/[131](XIV7)/

To understand this double movement definitively it is necessary to study language which manifests it better than any expression — because it sublimates human movement more.

However, precisely for this reason and because it moves to another order, language conceals its own strangeness.

The conversion of movement into expression [is] to be studied through prelinguistic forms of expression.

That's why I'd like to study movement in painting and cinema — I can only make a sketch, we'll take this up in more detail next year.

1) PAINTING

"I cannot forget that one of the remarkable men of my time, [who was] a painter, [an] excellent prose-writer, [and] very skilled at discovering new geniuses, asked me what I meant when I spoke of movement in a line." (Berenson, *Esthétique et histoire des arts visuels*)[26]

How is there movement in something stationary?

([a] question that implies: what is movement?)

1) We might say: there are signs of movement.

Sign being understood as [a] substitute for movement that can't be represented by [a] criterion of movement = inexplicable fact without that [as a] clue [or] reference to movement [that is] absent.

But painting doesn't provide signs in that sense:

it provides actual expression of movement and not reference to absent movement. Rodin [—] sculpture produces movement as [a] transformation [*métamorphose*] of one position into another (like Daphne into [a] laurel tree and Procne into [a] swallow), how one position "slides" into another[27] — E.g., statue of Ney:[28] legs and left hand [are in the] position of Ney [when] drawing his sword, right arm and face [*figure*]: go toward the enemy [with] weapon raised.[29] Rodin's St. Jean-Baptiste:[30] left foot behind resting completely on the ground, — right leg pulls the /**[132](XIV8)**/ body forward, takes possession of the ground, left shoulder {?} helps body to pull the left leg forward.[31] The snapshot would not produce movement, but [rather] "petrified" man, because it would freeze the moment: "it's the artist who is truthful, while it's photo[graphy] that lies: for, in reality, time doesn't stop"[32] – Snapshots of galloping horses: when the front legs touch the ground, the back legs [are] already folded back under the belly (the horse looks like it's jumping on the spot). Géricault's races at Epsom:[33] horses flat-out [*ventre à terre*], appear to run[34] — action: it's lived movement.

Clarify what Rodin says: not just any mixture of successive moments produces movement (incoherence), and movement can be produced by [a] snapshot if the stance that is captured is suitably chosen (walking: photograph of walking is dynamic if the 2 feet are on the ground). Thus movement = [the] envelopment of a becoming in a stance [*attitude*], not [the] intellectual evocation of an absent movement, [but the] intuitive [or] perceptual production of movement [*réalisation intuition-perception du mouvement*] — Not [the] deciphering of signs by [an] understanding [*intelligence*] that would interpret them as indicating [a] change in location, but [the] intentionality of the horse's body, [the] immanent sense of the "transformation" [«*métamorphose*»],[35] gestural sense for a body that knows the syntax of gestures, synthesis without analysis. What we have called [the] trace of the movement.[36]

Thus not signs, but emblems of the movement, — and movement [as] founded on 'alteration' (against Descartes).

2) But if movement in the true sense enters into painting in the form of alteration in this way, [then] couldn't we generalize the notion of movement in painting: it "has nothing to do with change of place, or even with change of attitude or pose, and still less with transitive activity of any kind" (Berenson p. 87).[37] Movement is the energy that {naturally} inhabits a line like movements of water inhabit a whirlpool even though it outlines a constant shape . . . "I . . . beheld a world where every outline, every edge,

/[133](XIV9)/ and every surface was in a living relation to me and not, as hitherto, in a merely cognitive one" (88).[38]

Generalization of the notion of movement even beyond the movement of outlines, edges, surfaces: Wölfflin (*Principes fondamentaux de l'histoire de l'art*):[39] linear and painterly representation (see through patches not lines).[40] The first, [which is] less mobile, [and] the second, [which is] more mobile, define a sense of movement that is not the movement of masses in Baroque art in contrast to the tranquility of Renaissance art. Movement to the 3rd power that is present even in the Dutch [painter Gerard] ter Borch as painterly (Wölfflin pp. 12–13).[41] Movement [is] intrinsic to the painterly → tendency to open forms, the outline doesn't overlap with the form of the object, things [are] considered in their relations and not in themselves, hence "vibrations" of the whole painting, even when the details are not visible (32)[42] [—] architecture: ". . . a movement starts to blaze up, from a purely optical source, and takes hold of the totality of forms; the wall vibrates and the space trembles in every corner. [¶] We must be careful not to identify this fully painterly effect with the great movement of mass that is conveyed to us by certain Italian buildings. The pathos of convex or concave walls, and the power of aggregated columns, are only special cases."[43] – The movement of the painterly is a movement "of language," not of expression, in the sense of the most prominent movement of the Baroque.[44] "Forms breathe" (72).[45] They support each other, intertwine, fuse with one another.[46] Unambiguous privileged forms (frontal view of a face, circular view of the risen Christ's halo) are henceforth subordinated to non-canonical forms (Rembrandt: non-circular halo, – Rubens[:] non-frontal portraits) [—] "unstable equilibrium."[47] To the overall painting in itself, together with the edges of the frame, is opposed the painting as opening onto . . . a world that it carves up fortuitously. The appreciation of the linear in the 19th century (and even in the 20th) will not imply a return to before the painterly, but [an] attempt to identify absolutely all the elements of painting and drawing, / [134](XIV10)/ and to integrate the linear and the painterly, i.e., to move to an even more secretive form of movement (Juan Gris:[48] vibration of the painting): if color is truly drawing, then drawing is color (Cézanne).

Here movement = no longer displacement, nor even intuitive production of this displacement through messages that together denote transformation [*métamorphose*], (Rodin), [rather] movement = indirect presentation, reference of oblique, 'distorted,' partial appearance [*aspect*] to reality that is beyond, [reference] of color to form that is beyond, [reference] of signifying to signified that is elsewhere and only appears through [the signifying], presentation through divergences with respect to a norm that is itself never given. Presentation of the world through variations in modulations of our being toward the world.

The painterly and the linear are two diacritical systems of this sort.

2) CINEMA

/[*in margin*] Movement/

Is ostensibly [the] reproduction of movement.

In fact, it was invented for this purpose. — But what it found with movement was much more than movement [as] displacement. And that set off [a] dialectic in which movement is transformed.

Even as [a] representation of it, [cinema] isn't immediately movement: the mere recording of a man who jumps or a bird that flies does not, when projected, produce the impression of life: "grotesque array that no longer creates an illusion" – Lack of a certain rhythm.[49]

In reality, movement "is only perceived as a quality abstractly detached from more complex wholes":[50] e.g., movement must be represented for a certain duration, from this point to that point, it must occur in a certain context of behavior: tricks organized by the director and by the actors, "We read the cinematic gesture as much because we follow the momentum of the actors as because we correctly perceive the movements /**[135](XIV11)**/ of their limbs." (Francastel *Espace et illusion*)[51]

Thus movement = relationship of *Fundierung* [founding] with expression: [movement] certainly carries [expression], [movement] brings [expression] into existence, but [movement] is internally animated by [expression], local displacement is only seen across a network of signs whose meaning is ultra-spatial.[52] And how do they have this ultra-spatial meaning? Through their very arrangement, through the problem of organization that they present to our psycho-physical being.

Space: the representation of space ≠ conjuring [*illusionnisme*] [or] duplicating the thing itself. 2) I see a character at the end of a room, then [I see] the room from his point of view, then I see him walk. These points of view [are in] counterpoint, within my point of view. On the way out I don't recall these perspectives, I think I saw everyone living in a single space. But selection has operated at each moment and the beauty of it lies in the interaction of these perspectives.

1) Interaction of perspectives and interaction [of] things [and] subjects (through which [interaction] alone [perspectives] can be evoked). Extraordinarily intense presence of what is not made explicit here: glance toward . . . [a] {horrible} scene, that isn't seen — When it is presented, [it's through] its influence on facial expression — Thus soldering over the gaps, indirect presentation, i.e., indication of what is absent by what is present = gearing together of the one in the other, pregnance of the one in the other — Ultimately pregnance of the visual in sound and in speech (*The Man in the White Suit*,[53] the sound of the atomizer makes the asthma attack more present), or conversely [the] presence of noise in silent vision (passage to silence) – Error of {?} when he believed that sound and speech were realist elements: the true talking [film] speaks less and differently: the dialogue must be inscribed in the image: editing, cutting, audio-visual rhythm, etc.

/[136](XIV12)/

That's what makes the movement of a film, not the activity of the characters. (Cinema in the {1st} person or theatrical cinema are only modalities of this rhythm.)

Thus movement = questioning of my being toward the natural and {social} world through divergences.

Arriving at the cinema I bring sensory and cultural fields, i.e., a fully set up system of relationships between signs and significations. But the film is only a work of art if it plays this system through divergences with respect to it that realize emblems for significations that I did not {possess} in {this} {guise [*vêtement*]} [or] to this degree of presence. "networks of lines leading to a suggestive cutting up [*découpage*] of the screen"[54] – That isn't possible on the basis of just any gestural system, and in this way cinema isn't [a] plastic {Esperanto}. But at any rate, the given cultural system doesn't provide a sign-for-sign translation in cases of genuine works [of art].

We thus already find moments of language in [the] plastic arts 1) [a] system of signs [that is] institutional-cultural, not natural 2) [the] use of this system as [an] open whole that allows for [the] incorporation of unforeseen significations and [for the] recreation of signs. [With] the sensible world displaced by [the] world of expression that is established in it, we apply our eyes to invisible cultural things, we articulate the visible according to significations that transcend it, — but which were already at work within it.

This, which is tacit in the plastic arts (even when they make use of speech: cinema), [and] which is [the] art of engaging with certain gaps [*vides*] in the sensible world or in speech, — language claims to realize this completely, to take hold of the significations.

We must therefore analyze language to understand whether it's a special case of this unfounded upsurge [*surgissement*], and [whether] consciousness [is] articulation as opposed to absolute knowing, — or if on the contrary [language] reveals to us a logical necessity that would give life to it from within.

Working Notes

This section contains a selection of substantial working notes that Merleau-Ponty produced during the preparation of the course, and which can be a helpful resource for understanding it. Merleau-Ponty neither dated nor classified these notes. To facilitate their reading, the French editors organized them thematically in a way that closely follows the internal movement of the course itself. First, there are notes that present the course in summary fashion, conveying its general intentions or addressing one of its basic issues. Thereafter follow notes broadly devoted to the themes of movement, the body schema, language, diacritical perception, the imagination, and sleep. At the end, there are some notes that elude any straightforward classification. It should be borne in mind that since there is no intrinsic necessity to this ordering, the editors did not introduce any section headings that reflect it, and so readers should not feel constrained by it.

/[9]/

COURSE 1

1) With [the] philosophy of perception it isn't a matter of anti-intellectualism, but of a new type of analysis that applies to the understanding itself. Perceptual consciousness as expression, not signification. (Expression in a sense that isn't finalistic, Aristotelian, or pantheistic.) This means: polymorphism of consciousness, ambivalence, indirect or inverted consciousness: psychoanalysis, Marxism and the mystification of consciousness. Consciousness as divergence. The problem of the understanding is thus to understand how this polymorphism can be taken up in a way that transforms equivocation into signification, ambivalence into ambiguity.
This passage and this reversal [*renversement*] from the sensible world to the world of expression studied on the basis of movement.

2) Analysis of movement: movement as expression
— spatiality. Bring to light the notions of norm and variation of anchorage. (up and down – near and far) Between content and a priori form.
— movement – objective movement, [the] subject implicated in movement, – movement as phenomenon.
— Gestalt [theory]: movement as [a] figural moment. That is: movement as disclosive of being. Perception of causality. It's necessary to go beyond the Gestalt-theoretic conception of figural moments as causal conditions. But not in order to come back to an act of consciousness. Organization of the field and perceptual logic. Exchange between meaning and figural moments: perception as reading of symbols. Werner[1] — Movement 'felt by the heart'[2] – movement and meaning [are] indistinguishable: perceptual meaning is specified [*indiqué*] by [a] diacritical system. Jaubert, Epstein — Perceptual implication in more complex perceptions (Paliard).

Supplementary proof:
~~3)~~ The body in movement
Prelogical unity of the body. This unity is that of a praxis. Supplementary proof through the analysis of apraxia. Relationships [between] gnosia [and] praxia. Praxis at many levels.

/[9]v/
3) Expression through movement: dialectical passage from movement to expression. Sublimation of expression.

Body schema and thought, and speech. The 'hand' as [an] element of the body schema. Sleep as apraxia and aphasia. Body schema as [a] diacritical system.

Movement in painting: in what sense it is expressed: it is present there as alteration – generalization of the notion of movement.

Cinema or universal expression through movement as variation of the relationship [between] man [and] world.

Sublimation of expression at its highest point in language (next year).

/**[178]**/

COURSE I

Show [the] passage of physical movement to living or physiognomic [*physionomique*] movement.

Then come back to the analysis of physical movement in the light of this convergence, by showing that it is deciphering, reading by the body.

Go from there to perception of the movements of one's own body (or of rest).

Go from there to [the] study of the body schema and what it relies upon intentionally outside of us – Show reciprocity and *Einfühlung* ['feeling into' or empathy] of our body and physical movement, of our body and the body of the other.

From there: cultural and anthropological space.

Supplementary proof through painting and cinema.

/**[179]**/

CDF [COLLÈGE DE FRANCE] COURSE

At the beginning of my CDF [Collège de France] course analyze the world (sensible world)

Already at this point bring consciousness to light as that which does not touch insofar as it touches, [as that which] does not possess insofar as it seeks, [bring it to light] as ambiguity itself. That [is] implied in the simple definition of perception as perception of a figure on a background. Consciousness of background and consciousness of figure – Perceptual signification.

Bring this out further with regard to the universe of expression. Absolute falseness of our usual conception of consciousness as grasping an object. Consciousness always aims, not at being, but at gaps in being (glances, etc.) through which it grasps significations.

/[177]/
MY GOAL IN COURSE I:

Show that there are not 'the sensations' + a certain acquired experience of mnemonic connections or a timeless power of signification. Show that the coming to us of a sensory 'message' is only [the] vibrations or modulation of a 'schematic typology' [«*montage*»] or a 'field,' that it is therefore immediately significant, but where the signification is in principle not an object of consciousness. Here there is signification only as *Abweichung von* . . . [divergence from . . .] a certain level, only as relief against . . . a certain background.
Show that higher level consciousness, linguistic consciousness, must be understood in the same way: to understand a word [or] a sentence is to grasp it as [a] variation of an undivided power of speaking that is like the motor power of the body.
As a consequence, all consciousness is in principle something different than what it believes itself to be, it only thematizes something by leaving an entire remainder implicit. Self-evidence of words when we use them, – that ceases when we ask about their meaning.

/[172]/
SENSIBLE WORLD AND WORLD OF EXPRESSION COURSE

See authors cited by Piaget who introduce prolepsis into the perception concept of world (book of {?})
Produce [a] new analysis of perceptual consciousness as figure-background consciousness and consequently as ambiguous consciousness.
Produce [a] new analysis of perceptual consciousness (or of the consciousness of illusion) as essentially projective consciousness (in the Freudian sense): how we see on things what is obviously [an] expression of the subject. In this sense perceptual consciousness is essentially expression. Cf. Geneva talk on consciousness that knows insofar as it does not know, and does not know insofar as it knows.[3] Perceptual meaning as coherent deformation.
Analyze [the] perception of behavior [*des conduites*] [and] institutional perception.
Consider Helen Keller.[4]
Consider language learning in deaf-mute people
Ombredane on aphasia[5]
Panofsky – Francastel.[6]

——

Start with a lecture on philosophy and science.

———

Study the incursion of the imaginary into the perceived (it's the incursion of the symbolic). E.g., imaginary pain

———

/[180]/

COURSE (I)

Start course (I) with [the] analysis of perceptual intentionality inasmuch as it's not consciousness of . . . but [rather] being toward . . . — cf. Weizsäcker and the others.

To confirm this conception of intentionality, address the question of memory and of the retention of the past. (by discussing Bergson *Matter and Memory* II).

From there move to physiognomic [*physiognomique*] consciousness of things and introduce consciousness of expression as [a] particular case of *fungierende Intentionalität* [operative intentionality].

Analysis of emotional consciousness of the world.

Analysis of painting and of painterly [*picturale*] perception.

The institutional or cultural element of all perception.

Cinema.

Passage to linguistic expression.

/[174](1)/

PROBLEMS OF PERCEPTUAL CONSCIOUSNESS

ORIENTATION

Distance and obliqueness as divergences (in relation to levels). These divergences appear as such only inasmuch as each phenomenal oblique line rises like a pretension to verticality, [it] could be a vertical line, and each horizon [is] converted into nearby objects. Each level includes within itself the possibility of its internal destruction by elements whose orientation it nonetheless determines. Every situation encloses within itself its overcoming as [a] unique situation, the impending possibility of other situations: ambiguity of the spatial situation as of all the other [situations]: what it has in the way of limits is also [the] introduction to something other than itself. Distance doesn't move things away from us as much as it links them to us.[7] But ambiguity is ultimately only visible through haecceity [*l'eccéité*], and in order for the oblique [line] to pull on a vertical one, or [for] distance [to pull] on proximity, this vertical line and this proximity must be. Their being is first relative to that of the divergences. Where does this priority, this normality, this principle come from?

What do we mean in saying that the body or conversely the image in the mirror is 'inclined' in the Wertheimer experiment? [What do we mean] in saying that a thing is far or near?

In the Wertheimer experiment, inclined or straight are predicates that indicate, not [the] proximity of my body or of the spectacle, but [the] relationship between them, and that they form [a] system. It's their mutual gearing together that these words express. There are different signs of the body and the world (the one 'straight' [and] the other 'inclined') when I don't have the world 'at hand.' So to say that the spectacle is inclined and [that] I [am] straight, to say that it is only appearance relative to a real truth which I do have 'at hand,' [or] to say that my body is inclined and the spectacle [is] straight, is to say that my body is just an abnormal modality of that which /**[174]v(2)**/ has the spectacle 'at hand.'* When the two anomalies or divergences are at zero we have a straight body in a straight world. Hence 'straight' and 'inclined' properly belong neither to the body as given nor to the spectacle as given: nor therefore, it will be pointed out, can they emerge from [the] relationship [between body and spectacle], since they are unnecessary in each of them. So relative to what is the divergence of the one or the other established? or their coincidence? It is the same paradox here as with signs: signs are diacritical, i.e., each marks a significative difference and not a signification, and language ends up signifying by means of registering significative differences without ever bearing any that are positive. Likewise, neither the given facts [*les données*] of the body nor those of the spectacle give us the vertical. The whole experience of my body and [the whole experience] of the spectacle {diversifies} in relation to itself by oscillating around norms that are never truly given, but thereby {?} them in a univocal way. Cf. signification of silent gestures even before speech.

> /[*in margin*] *Ex[ample] of perceptual normalization: when I walk in the street, I don't see movement of the horizon every time my heel strikes the ground, — and likewise when I see someone walking with the street all around him and his feet

> on the ground. On the contrary, at the cinema, [a] shot of someone cut off near their feet or without [a] horizon: I see shaking from top to bottom, slightly ridiculous and frenetic. It's that [its] integration within [*insertion dans*] the horizon-of-walking [or] the motor project places the level within this horizon and assigns the body's shaking to the character of appearance. Which doesn't happen when the *Umweltintentionalität* [intentionality toward the environment or 'surrounding world'] of the body is broken.[8]/

Don't draw from Wertheimer's experiment, where one's own body is kept silent, the idea that orientation comes from the spectacle alone. In fact orientation comprises visual or {exteroceptive} givens + all the other givens. (Experiment showing that labyrinthic excitation provokes a shift in the apparent vertical.) The meaning of Wertheimer's experiment lies only in showing that orientation is not provided by a sense [*un sens*] like the labyrinth [i.e., the inner ear] nor by another elsewhere, nor finally by their sum: no [sense] possesses it alone,[9] all [senses] combined do not possess it, and yet they give it through their combination, all mark divergences relative to the vertical without being able to provide the vertical. We have a schematic typology [*montage*] {regarding} the vertical, we don't perceive it, since signification is always the background of a certain figure that is offered to us.

/[*in margin of the following paragraph*] Analysis of quality./

This leads to a complete transformation of what it could mean: to perceive space or to perceive things. A complementary analysis of quality would be useful, showing that it is not in us and not in objective space, neither *Tonempfindung* [sensation of sound] nor *Tonquale* [sound quale], not [an] event in my history /**[175](3)**/ nor [a] {constructum} or signification; against this dichotomy = the pre-spatial field = the thing is, not a quality or a sum of objective qualities, not a sum of *Empfindungen* [sensations], but the response to an interrogation, to a certain opening, a modalization of this opening. [10][Silence, understood as whistling (Valéry)[11] shows that, to have a sense is to never be entirely nothing, since the very absence of anything given shows itself, evinces itself, through something given: whistling. Cf. to not talk is to talk, to not choose is to choose, there is nothing without sense, we live in a field of sense.] It's in this language that we must understand the double reference 1) to a personal history 2) to an objective world that Husserl expresses through the dichotomy: *Rotempfindung–Rotquale* [sensation of red–red quale, or redness]. The key to the problem lies in an elucidation (in the terms of American psychologists) of the relationship [between] intelligence and personality. Show (cf. François Rostand)[12] that personal development carries the [development] of intelligence, that the personal constellation defines categorial power. [13][Not entirely however. What is the margin of freedom of categorial power? What is it within us that responds to affective situations that present themselves? Is it the same as what responds to linguistic situations that present themselves? the relationship is more complex: there are gaps in personal development that offer intelligence something to think about.] We must manage to imagine concretely the unity of the interpersonal dynamic and insight,[14] of interpersonal functioning and cultural functioning, of the capacity for taking [things] up vitally and for taking [things] up noetically [*la capacité de reprise vitale et de reprise noétique*]. To achieve this, it is obviously necessary to stop imagining the *Urerlebniss* [originary or primal experience] as *Urempfindung* [originary or primal sensation], for once it is defined as *Urempfindung*, the personal flow becomes an absolutely dense tissue where any distance or objectivity can no longer appear.

/[*In the lower left corner of the page, separate from the rest*] The notion of motivation that I used to account for the conditioning of consciousness (*Phenomenology of Perception*) is not satisfying in the sense that it's through a retrospective illusion that the meaning of the decision is projected into the motive, instead of it being the arrangement of my "machine for living" (Valéry)[15] that {assigns} to the retinal disparity the sense of 'depth' that [the disparity] will {take on [*revêtir*]} through our acts of [visual] fixation, such that here creation can't appear to me *ex nihilo*, and signification is not free: it appears to me as 'structure.' Relief is not a signification that can be exhausted by [statements of the form] I know that. Now, any historical or personal landscape offers structures of this sort: we see in them signs of the points at which there is something to do, etc. In such a way that, here again, the pregnance [*prégnance*] of the response in the question is not a retrospective illusion./

/[175]v(4)/

WHAT IS IT {TO PERCEIVE}?

This analysis of quality as structure (i.e., tacit, diacritical, non-thetic signification) would of course make possible a theory of the subject as incapable of being alienated or lost, and nevertheless living in objects. Conceive all our perspectives on the thing as so many slices taken from it, but which are still attached to it. Or alternatively conceive the thing as that which comes into contact within us with a preexisting schematic typology [*montage*] of our 'machine for living.'

(	thing	subject	perception
(	signification	language	speech
(	trace	being toward the world	taking up

This presupposes [a] relationship [of] proximity [and] distance between me and the world (instead of immediate presence which is Sartre's conception and objective distance which is [the] realist conception). I am completely at the thing in the sense that for me each perspective is only something emitted by . . . the thing itself, [in the sense] that I see it emerge from [the thing], that through it I reach the thing, in which I'm anchored.[16] And the thing is distant in the sense that it delivers these messages only on condition of remaining [an] inaccessible horizon [or] background, [a] style indicated by the convergence of the *Erscheinungen* [appearances]. The thing [is] accessible in the perspectives (diacritical signs) like the signification [is accessible] in the words. To speak is to sculpt, it's to prepare a cultural field, an audible configuration.

THE PROBLEM OF MOVEMENT
would justify even better than [the problem] of quality or [that] of space the reworking [of] the problem of perception and of the notion of the subject.

– Because movement, not being a thing, reveals even better the coexistence of the machine for living and what it lives than the thing which, at first sight, exists in itself. Being a variation of the thing, [movement] awakens its dormant motives, it recreates it.
– Because movement, being a mode of action of the thing [that] awakens its being (even if it's not spontaneous movement), shows it [i.e., the thing] to us in operation [*en activité*]. Hence we see two sorts of conceptions of movement:

1. Those that attempt to deal with it as an action of the thing.
2. Those that overlook this action and limit themselves to characterizing movement by its effect: var[iation] of relations with the outside (simple envelope of movement), which presupposes [an] absolute observer for whom movement is completely relative.

Or correlatively

1) Movement as event, something that happens, presupposing reference to a subject capable of movement.
2) Objective movement or movement in-itself, which is consequently no longer an event, no longer takes place here rather than there, is nowhere.

/[176](5)/

What Bergson demonstrated is that objective movement or movement in-itself is ultimately [the] negation of movement, [it is] relative movement that does not take place.[17] Change in the distance relationships themselves conceived as interobjective. The in-itself is instantaneous (*mens momentanea* [momentary or momentaneous mind]),[18] and without internal productivity in the sense of an instant, a Zenonian instant. Bergson overcomes Zeno by showing that time is not made of instants, nor space of spatial limits, and that's true. But the consequence remains to be clarified: which is that only an *erlebte Raum* [lived space] [and] an *erlebte Zeit* [lived time] are possible, that is, a space for a spatial project, [and] a time for a temporal project. Bergson only said that implicitly: he said it by saying: my movement is certain, I prove movement by walking or by stretching my arm. And he thought he was done with the problem. But my consciousness of my body could be consciousness of movement only if it is not consciousness of a unit, of an undividedness, of a bringing together of [the] beginning [and] end of the movement, but of such an undivided project that gets cashed out [*qui se monnaie*] in a journey [*trajet*], — and that presupposes reference of my body to [the] perceived world and [*] a common measure between them. The anti-Zeno, prespatial duration, is not yet movement. A theory of extension is required for there to be movement. Bergson: our body stretches as far as the stars. Very well. Nonetheless, in the movement of things I don't have [an] internal consciousness of the link between instant *t* and the instant *t'*, so it's necessary here to restore the idea of a sort of anthropological projection in things (comparable to the projection of my duration in [the] duration {of the universe}), which conversely presupposes a spatialization of the self and a theory of the perceiving body.

/[*inserted boxed paragraph*]* Question: what reality [are we] to recognize by this phantom that crosses the air and which in a moment, on a branch, will become a bird again? Must we say that it's merely appearance? Reflection? For itself, it's obviously a bird during the journey [*trajet*]. But it's not a bird at rest, it's something like what it seems to us. To affirm the reality of the bird's movement is to affirm the equivalent reality of this dynamic, of this physiology, and of the anatomical bird./

Thus Bergson [i.e., his argument] [is] valid against movement in itself. But his own thesis remains indecisive: whether mental tracing [*tracé spirituel*] or psychological immanence, in both cases it's insufficient. We have to work out a theory of movement [as] expression.

Actually [there are] 4 kinds of conception of movement:

1) relative movement, in itself = canceled
2) movement on the side of consciousness = psychologism of movement (B[ergson])
3) movement as [an] accident of a thing in motion which has no inherent kinship with movement: intellectualism, synthesis but not transitional. Movement [as] intellectual journey [*parcours intellectuel*]: it's a return of movement in itself
4) pure movement, or reality of the moving thing [*du mouvant*]. This is what, more or less confusedly, the Gestalt theorists glimpsed under the name of phenomenon *Phi*. Upon analysis that actually signifies [the] movement of a subject engaged in being through a body. Movement = expression

It's toward this thesis 4 that our preliminary considerations are leading us:
/[176]v(6)/

{Consider the} perception of a position of some object, of some object at rest here. There is movement when, the anchorage remaining the same, this element of the field varies its relations with the others. It's through me that my consciousness of the movement {passes}, i.e., through my body conceived as anchorage. Movement pulls on its anchors: proof: if too many elements of the field enter into it, [then there is] visual vertigo. Movement thus takes place in anthropological space and not elsewhere, as does indeed the entire sensible world.

Movement of things – movement of living things – gestures, languages, 'traces' – In all cases, movement is the trace of a 'behavior': the *Erscheinungen* [appearances] make a hollow appear for which this movement is and unfolds. Hence [the] indefinite expressive capacity of movement. Here expression [is] defined as [the] emergence [*apparition*] of an existence.

Even the movement of things is [a] transition from one Gestalt to another, [the] transposition of a physiognomy. Thus [movement] has meaning only in anthropological space.

Problem after all of that:

How do 'objective' [or] 'operational' (Piaget) conceptions of movement arise from that?

Through [the] elimination of everything that presupposes perspective: Piaget shows how movement is first of all [an] act of leaving or arriving (thus ambiguous notion of project), speed and first of all overtaking, — then how it is purified in becoming [an] operational concept. But this operational concept itself yields nothing that can be represented, it is [a] blind way to deal with movement, by definition there is no descending from these concepts to experience. This passage to objectivity has its validity. It is founded. But it is not passage to the truth since the objectivation itself [or] the formalization is still to be judged in comparison with [the] concrete appearance [*aspect*] of the world.

/[199]/
REDUCTIVE REFLECTION:

/[*in margin of the first two paragraphs*] 'Objective' conceptions of movement/

1) Movement is only change in relations. We avoid looking at movement to consider only consequences. Yet we can't [do this]: for change presupposes at the instant when it occurs that something happens somewhere and not everywhere.
2) So is movement the act of a thing in motion? [Is it] successive presence in different places? Movement as [an] attribute of a thing in motion: this presupposes movement [that is] always stopped. [An] intellectual journey is not a journey. This synthesis is still only the envelope of the movement.
   The *Etwas* [something] of the movement is not a thing identical to itself: and which moreover changes location while remaining the same. It is that which goes from one place to another, caught in the movement.
3) So is movement a matter of consciousness?
   Bergson: what he says amounts to saying that true time isn't made from [an] infinite sum of instants, true space [isn't made] from [an] infinite sum of spaces, true time is from consciousness, i.e., [true time] can be whole without parts, true space and true movement as well. Hence: if Zeno is right about space in itself, he is wrong about lived space. My movement is not in doubt.
   Clarify: for there also wouldn't be movement without reference to [the] objective world: that I reach the goal of the movement in advance, that its beginning and its end are internally connected, that is not enough: they must be connected across space, by a tracing. Bergson's time and space of envelopment are insufficient. There must [be a] wake [*sillage*].

MOVEMENT

I. Movement is a change in location: the fact that a thing is here at one moment and somewhere else at another moment with [an] indefinite series of intermediate positions.

This implies 1) [the] idea of a thing in motion of which movement is an extrinsic determination (Zeno's arguments: it is never in movement)

2) [the] unreality of movement that would be [a] simple change of relations with [a] reference point. [Movement] which therefore 1) would be reversible. 2) That is, [which] would never be, since it would be nowhere, neither in the thing in motion nor in its surroundings

3) would never be even as relation, since we will always have a value of space for a value of time, and since, even if we take them at the moment at which they emerge, we will only ever have the points of the tracing, and not the passage from one to the other.

So it must be that 1) the thing in motion is in movement

2) the movement is absolute, i.e., not only correspondence between [a] series of positions [and a] series of instants, but actual passage.

In other words, exclusion of the identical thing and of time and space in themselves: time, space, and things must be lived, [they must be] {of} consciousness.

II. Bergson: seems to have resolved Zeno's problem when he showed that movement is possible in space and time [that are] not [a] summation of elements, i.e., [the] "internal aspect" of the path of displacement [*trajet*] "for my consciousness" (*Matter and Memory* 210),[19] i.e., "undivided fact." The duration of the movement "is dense and undivided like it."[20]

/[199]v/

"a simple movement, like the journey taken [*trajet*] by my hand when it goes from A to B" (210)[21]

"immediately perceived movement is a very clear fact" (213)[22]

But this means that movement can be detached from its trajectory [*trajectoire*] and grasped in its purity and simplicity only if I think, not its duration, but my duration as undivided.

The obviousness of movement is more striking when it is a matter of the movement of my body because [this movement] is lived from the inside and thus because its inside, what's indivisible about it, is given, it's [a] "simple act."

But in reality it's not as movement that it's simple, it's as consciousness of the movement, [as] project, [as the] union through consciousness of [the] point of departure and [the] point of arrival.

Yet we only go from there to actual movement through a description of the movement in which the project {radiates} over space and extends across it. The problem is not resolved as long as this extension is not analyzed. If my body were for me [a] space like all the others, my duration could no more give unity to its moments than to any other. The privileged position of my body in the experience of movement implies that my duration is incarnated in the world in and through it [i.e., in and through movement]. [And] that conversely my body is like my machine for living, [and for] counting duration.

We have several conditions without which [there is] no movement:

1) no movement without identification,

2) no movement without undividedness

but that does not make conditions through which: for absolute identity and undividedness would not be movement.

III. MOVEMENT AS PHENOMENON

Description borrowed from the Gestalt theorists.

We can't conclude from stroboscopic movement, i.e., [movement] without [a] thing in motion and without physical continuity, that phenomenal movement is like that. We can't draw a conclusion from an appearance to something inconceivable: e.g., to a movement where there wouldn't be an identical *Etwas* [something].

But as always Gestalt [theory] affords access to the phenomenon, i.e., [the] suspension and reduction of prejudices concerning things and [the] rediscovery of the phenomena. I.e., things solely as they appear to us.

In this invaluable respect 1) [Gestalt theory] shows that there is no interposition of the thing in motion between initial and final position. The something that passes is movement without [a] thing, sensible {form [*formule*]} without matter

2) [Gestalt theory] shows that there is no consciousness of the object at extreme positions, [and] then at interpolated positions, that we can have movement without terminal points [*sans station*]

3) [Gestalt theory] shows that there is a temporal condition of the phenomenon, which shows that the synthesis is not of the logical order. Likewise *duale Bewegung* [dual motion]

/[*in margin of the preceding paragraph*] It's the phenomenon that makes its unity, the latter is not [a] unity of the significative order, [not a] unity of the order of the *I think*/

4) [Gestalt theory] shows that there is pure movement, with at most [a] marginal reference point, that can even destroy this reference point (visual vertigo, when the field is full of movement), [it shows] that there is a propagation [*contagion*] of space through movement, far from space always being the framework of movement. As [something] oblique, movement is one of these phenomena that threaten space from within.

/**[203]**/

MOVEMENT, SENSE OF MOVEMENT – EXPRESSION OF MOVEMENT AND MOVEMENT AS EXPRESSIVE

Movement [is] obtained in motionlessness, according to Rodin, because perceptual logic reads the positions of the different parts of the body as constituting a genetic series. There is a trace of movement in what is simultaneous here. The passage from stroboscopic movement to [a] phase of simultaneity and all the transitions (*duale Teilbewegung* [dual partial motion]) show how an expression of movement is established in what is simultaneous.[23] It's not a question here of really contracting movement into simultaneity, as Bergson does, through a continuity argument, but of showing the passage from actual movement to a sense of movement or to a movement as meaning.

/[*in margin of the following paragraph*] Movement as expression/

Show 1) that the perception of real movement is not [the] experiencing or thinking of a succession of positions, but [the] comprehensive grasp of a harmony on our spatial harp.

/[*in margin of the following paragraph*] Expression of movement/

2) that conversely there is [the] possibility for a simultaneous whole to present movement in virtue of its configuration (Rodin's statue – or, more simply, the arrow).

All that comes back to deepening the Gestalt-theoretic conception of vectors or dynamic phenomena, which in reality is a new conception of perceptual synthesis.

What's interesting is that in case (1) as in case (2) [see above] we have movement as being neither local displacement nor [the] thought of a local displacement, but as meaning (not signification) of the movement, i.e., institutionalized movement, [movement that has] become /**[203]v**/ [an] element of a symbolic system that is our spatial field. And time as well [has] become [a] component of a configuration. 'Generalized' time and movement, transformed into prelinguistic essences.

Study the same generalization of time in the very structure of sound (Köhler *Tonpsychologie*).[24]

/**[186]**/

IN COURSE (I)

Make use of the example of movement for determining the essence of expression.

Expression of movement is not at all {limitation} of one of the views that can be taken on it.

It's the constitution of a sign, — in relation to what language?

/**[181](1)**/

COURS I

Show that movement as change in location, according to its 'objective' definition, is only a very particular case of another kind of mobility which is expression.

E.g., Michotte's experiments[25] show that perception of a movement (of 'crawling') is integrally connected to an organization of the figure that makes it a whole that has an interior and where a beginning of 'behavior' is prepared — something analogous must exist in the inanimate movement of a 'thing in motion.' The basis is an anticipation or prolepsis of local displacement by the internal organization of the closed figure. — Ultimately, in Michotte's experiments, perceiving a movement is something completely different from perceiving the change in [the] relationship of the lines or [in the relationship between] figure and background. It's to perceive a sort of fictitious protoplasm that flows off toward the pseudopods, etc. And whoever perceives such a movement is not a surveying spectator [*spectateur géomètre*]. This movement does not take place in the sense that a point takes place in objective space. It speaks to me across anthropological space, it tempts my capacities of *Einfühlung* ['feeling into' or empathy], it's the movement of a certain 'interior,' which has anchoring relations toward its surroundings such as I have toward mine. It's the anchorage that understands anchorage, it's already an alter ego. And when the white surface circumscribed by Michotte's figure comes to be a 'quasi-protoplasm,' it's not the eye /**[181]v(1)**/ nor the thinking subject that sees that. The organization of the figure comes to interrogate the system of my relations with my spatial surroundings, and the *Sinngebung* that takes place is [a] response from my spatiality to something in the organization of the spectacle that {invites} it to *Einfühlung*.

———

/[*in margin of the following paragraph*] trace/

Movement as inscription of time. Movement as tracing, i.e., there is this miracle that temporality [and the] intention of movement are able to inscribe themselves in a trace, even though in principle nothing of them continues to exist in this trace, which is only in space. It's the passage from actual movement or time to their stored meaning. It's the beginning of sedimentation. In this regard consider in Piaget's book on time everything he says to rehabilitate a perception of time in things. Study that and look for the extent to which the perception of a trace as trace presupposes the taking up of the inscribed movement by my body. — But what is this taking up that is obviously not an actual taking up? Don't I make movements like Schneider? What is virtual movement? *Bewegungsentwurf* [motor project] or prolepsis? It's the correlate of perceptual meaning as such, of structure. My body not only as [an] actual body but as [a] possible body, as [a] 'machine for living,'[26] /**[182](2)**/ as [a] machine for making time. Study the relationship of time and rhythms or tempos. Is it true that universal homogeneous time is presupposed by tempos? Or else on the contrary is it necessary, as with space, to admit that universal and formless time is a sublimation of temporalities?

———

Finally [the] relationship between [the] movement of one's own body and objective movement.

/**[201]**/

TIME

Perception as [a] 'machine for living.' In particular [as a] 'machine for living' time. We always assume that our notion of time is drawn from an absolute contact with an absolute time that is us. This would be the *Empfindungszeit* [time of sensation],[27] an ultimate flux [or] absolute plenitude that would give us the meaning of time. But, like all meaning, that of time is given to us first of all in a configuration, and [is] cultural (cf. Halbwachs social frameworks of memory).[28] It is perceived. (Cf. Piaget and [his account of] children learning time in the world, despite the philosophical analyses that show with Cassirer that there is time only for a consciousness).[29] My body is not only a device for producing anchorages in space. It is also [a] device for producing anchorages in time. Time forms part of the total organization of the field. A certain field requires and induces a certain kind of temporality. We are (Claudel)[30] clocks, machines for marking time. And not only for marking it: for founding it. This relationship between self and temporal symbols can't be a pure relationship of centrifugal *Sinngebung*, because the self that gives meaning to the social symbols is itself integrated by perception into a field of which institutional temporality forms [a] part. It's true that I still have the power to /**[201]v**/ question the institution and the symbols. But this power is only applied through the constitution of new symbols. It's true that the symbols are inseparable from the new overall arrangements [*ensembles*] that give them a new sense. But that itself is prompted by movement of the symbolism within which I am integrated. Bergsonian time is cultural reality.

/**[183]**/

COURS I

SHORT NOTE

Interpretation of the preceding facts

Show that it's a matter of a sort of reading by my spatiality. Reading in the sense of an exchange between means and end. Diacritical 'signs' [are] taken as elements of a situation (of launching, of transport, of triggering, etc.)

In particular: Michotte: the interior of the figure as source of movement. reference to my spatiality

Thus phenomenon of movement (as opposed to objective movement) = a trace induces something that traces, or conversely a thing in motion leaves a trace. The inscription of time, tempo, generality of tempo. Cf. Piaget *Movement* and Piaget *Time*[31]

> /[*in margin of the preceding paragraph, and continuing into the margin of the following paragraphs*] Compare the trace as disclosive of movement to sound as disclosive of breathing [*le souffle*] (Jaubert) ({without their knowing}, slow motion disclosing the colloidal in man Epstein and Jaubert's reversed sound are homogeneous experiences)[32]
> Definition of a ready-made, mechanical surreal (the one that is abstracted through these processes) (or conversely through acceleration of plant growth), and of an oversignifying that is expressive movement.
> [THE] ABSTRACTNESS OF Gestalt [theory]/[33]

But these facts are abstract

1) Zietz and Werner:[34] intermodal deciphering. The something in common to the arrow and the [drum] beat is only their nature as event. We must explore [the] intermodal field
2) In particular, [the] artificiality of an analysis of movement based on experiments with [a] stationary eye and [a] stationary body. It's corporeality as a whole that's involved and not just that of a field. The movements studied thus far are actually pre-movements: like vertigo (visual vertigo of the spiral, – labyrinthic vertigo). That doesn't produce 'real' movement yet. It's to the latter what poetry is to prose: [the] trial run [*essai*] of a voice that says nothing and only 'resonates' in the other. At once [a] pathological mode and [a] higher mode of behavior, not [a] perceptual mode.[35] We'll return later on (movement as '*Bild*' ["image"]) to the higher mode, but we know now that it's not the basis on which we have to generate the 'originary' phenomenon of movement.

Thus passage 1) to {free} perception of movement in non-experimental situations
2) to perception of one's own movement as [the] source of the 'understanding' of the movement of things.

/[183]v/

Interpretation of Michotte's facts:

[*Merleau-Ponty's writing breaks off here*]

/[198]/

Thus[36] 1) The thing in motion [*le mobile*] {or} {rather} the moving thing [*le mouvant*] = an *Etwas* [something], an indeterminate not-just-anything: not just anything because it is defined by its style of movement. For it, to move is an act that is inscribed in its visible structure, which issues from [that structure] no less than from local displacement, and which gives the local displacement its hint of prolepsis. {?} of the movement is that of a behavior. For there are behaviors of things. Michotte's experiment shows that the perception of spontaneous movement is tied to a structure that gives the object an 'interior.'

2) For the same reason it's the thing in motion that goes forward and makes its own synthesis itself.

3) That being the case, what is the subject of the perception of movement? Ternus's experiment showing the simultaneity of the identification and the movement, or even that the identification results from the movement: the cross {shows itself} [as] identical while moving.[37] Movement is the internal vibration of a form extended to two positions, it's the 'figure' in transit — Movement [as] field phenomenon:

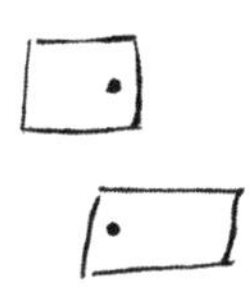

it's the function
of the detail in the set [*ensemble*]
which indicates [the set] as
being 'at rest' or 'in movement.' Variant movement within a situation. The movement of the spiral shows that it's the configuration of the object that controls the kind of movement seen. Thus movement and configuration or structure are two aspects of the same phenomenon.
Cf. 
And that which sees the structure is also what sees the movement.
Movement = that which enables structure to be kept constant for the most part = not local displacement but {modeling} of my apprehension of the structure. Shows itself as structure, and if time appears {a} {?} Koffka's experiment showing that time is also [an] element of [the] configuration. Configuration in the broad sense: not only visual (stroboscopic movement from one sense into another). Thus movement = variation of the field of existence. A movement shows itself in the way a thing or {an} {emblem} is recognized, as a physiognomy. It's a sort of successive {ambiguity}. [It's]

the way to say that the thing stayed the same in a certain action [that is] more or less characteristic of its 'interior.'

Consequence: movement = expression, = different *Erscheinungsweise* [manners or modes of appearance] or *Abschattungen* [adumbrations] of the same term.

What is called the animism of children = this anthropological perception that is {ultimately} founded on {coupling} [{accouplement}].

Supplementary proof that will provide justification: movement is able to produce all expressions.

/[184]/

Continuity of the phenomenon of movement with the phenomena of succession and simultaneity, or [continuity] of optimal movement with the *Teilbewegungen* [partial movements or motions], shows in movement [a] special case of the organization of the field, motivation of the movement by the content, solicitation of this perception. But that, which excludes both realism and idealism of the movement, does not on its own give a solution, and in particular does not substantiate the Gestalt-theoretic solution.

Facts revealed by Jacques Paliard:

Ternus: movement merges with identification which is itself not ~~intellectual synthesis~~ real identity (nor identity for the understanding) but physiognomic [*physionomique*] identity, resulting from the movement as much as it conditions it.

The movement of an object is not the sum of the movements of its points. Consequently, the movement of the object, like the object [itself], = encroachment of the points on each other, [a] totality without parts. Experience of the apparent movement of a stationary point because its framework moved.

For the subject who perceives, so-called real movement can only be [the] limit case of a stroboscopic movement, i.e., [an] overall phenomenon: Rubin's experiment: we see real movement because the edges of the object {induce it}. All the rest of the object here has only stroboscopic movement, and thus the identification of its points from one position to another, their movement, depends on the structure [of] figure and background: the movement is [the] property of a figure on a background, thus figural.

The form of the movement also depends on the field: cycloidal movement of a point on a wheel split up into circular movement and translational movement on account of [the] strong linkage [between] wheel [and] background. Likewise the apparent form of the movement of a spiral depends on the structure of the spiral.

Thus movement [is the] expression of a figural arrangement.

/[184]v/

Thus movement is local displacement only in a secondary way: it is only [local displacement] through the intermediary of the dynamic of the figures.

Hence [the] possibility of an expression of movement through [a] figural arrangement [that is] stationary in principle, and of an expression through the movement of any dynamic of the figures.

Movement of an object = extension [*prolongement*] of its figural properties. [It is the] disclosure of a possibility of the figure, of an internal possibility. Cf. ~~Michotte's~~ experiments showing that movement is [a] transformation [*métamorphose*] of an interior of the object or of [the] properties of the field.

zigzags

converted into 

movement of a ball in [a] gutter.

Linke: it's experience[38]

But it works just as well with [the] figure turned upside down

The curved line becomes [a] 'pathway' [«*chemin*»][39]

Cf. Michotte's experiments:

[*Merleau-Ponty left a blank space here*]

Cf. Zietz and Werner:

Visible local movement as [the] development in certain cases of an internal dynamic of the object: 'rolling,' 'flying,' 'floating' = modalities of movement prescribed a priori by the object (the arrow). From this it follows that phenomenal movement can be created through [the] action of another sense that contributes nothing visually but [which] triggers these possible [modalities of movement]

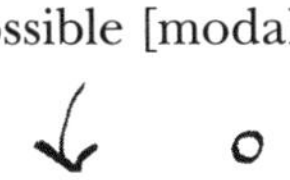

With louder [drum] beat at the same time as [the] arrow we have movement of the arrow around the point

"The figure: as something in dynamic movement prescribed by its form based on the total movement; likewise the form of the movement turns out to be a sensible image of the dynamic of the figure. By emphasizing **/[185]/** the arrow the partial rotation is completed for certain subjects, i.e., the completeness of the movement is as it were the spatial expression of a larger dynamic intensity" (Zietz and Werner)[40]

Arrow with drum: scraping of the arrow on the wall, and completed movement. A perceptual logic finds a solicitation in the circumstances and responds to it.

Perception of movement = like a sort of reading in which the signs have only diacritical value for an intention that is not visible separately, and which runs across them [and] drives them. Perceptual field and linguistic field. Movement affects motor-expressive possibilities in us. And conversely our possibilities (e.g., time) are incarnated in it.

Our duration does not impose its tempo but becomes [a] simple sensitivity to a general duration, the tempo of which is prescribed by the situation: time flows faster in a dark space than [in a] bright [space], apparent speed decreases in a brighter field.

/[*in margin of the preceding paragraph, written at an angle*]
perceptual logic
Head's taximeter/

/**[189]**/

Reading – field – language
(to be clarified)
with regard to {sensible} movement:
the perceptual meaning in [movement] is not intellectual but existential signification (Zietz and Werner)

not passage of movement in itself
to consciousness of movement which
would not be a movement.

Exchange: reciprocal means-end relationship between movement and meaning (e.g., of the movement of the airplane) = equivalence of the meaning and the figural moments, and of the latter among themselves (time too as [a] figural moment) – movement and rest

Therefore not [a] relationship [between] signs [and] significations, the 'signs' ({illuminated} points in Wertheimer's experiment, figural moments, etc.) (or whatever figural element, e.g., depth and outline [*plan*]) have sense inasmuch as they come to play on a keyboard or solicit an echo [*résonance*] or inscribe themselves in a field, i.e., not one by one but, inasmuch as they mutually alter one another, [they have meaning inasmuch as they] form parts of a system that sets up dimensions of differentiation.

Natural language, natural knowledge, i.e., we have it solely because we are, without cultural relation, solely because we have a body, i.e., a system of equivalent fields. Perceptual meaning as coexistence: Zietz and Werner.

Sound signifies {thr[ough]} visible movement on the basis of its internal 'resonance.' Michotte's experiments show that the appearance [*apparition*] of a closed figure gives rise to [the] identification of my body with it and *Einfühlung* ['feeling into' or empathy] of its relationship with the outside.

/[*in the margin, perpendicular to the above*] The movement of objects as [a] tracing in which we {recover} a something just as sound is disclosive of breath. Tracing understood not only in the spatial sense but [also] in the temporal sense: [there is] inscription of time as such in the speed of the movement, [and] the change in speed, like the change in spatial scale, is synonymous with change in being. Epstein. Jaubert/

/[189]v/

Don't go from movement in itself to consciousness of movement that 'would not be a movement'

/[193]/

{Here} {stepping-stones}

The end of the sentence determining the beginning.

From the whole to the parts (or exchange?)

All movement is stroboscopic.

Experience of the square and the point:

Is there identification? That would mean: a thought that generates the εἶδος [*eidos*], that goes from the 'real' to the ideal-objective. It's not in this sense that the square is identical. The square is identical because it is this square, that's all.

The mode of identity of the point is deduced from this mode of identity of the square, of which it is the complement, the counterpart according to the logic of perception: it's not [the] identity of the point with itself on its own, it's [the] identity of the function of the point here and there: to be surrounded by a square. The perception of a movement is part of an overall arrangement [*ensemble*], motivated by a configuration. Thus it's never [the] simple reflection of a real movement. (Besides, there is no

real movement on the retina. All movement there is stroboscopic. I.e., phenomenon of reading in which the end retrospectively determines the beginning. The structure [of] movement [is a] special case of the structure [of] succession.)
So what is the nature of the apprehension of /**[193]v**/ this phenomenon? The same nature as that of a figure on a background, of an outline [or] a signification, i.e., presupposing my spatiality (the screen effect).

Cf. Michotte [—] movement as disclosive of the figure.

> /[*in margin, written perpendicularly*] Previously: study of [the] perception of movement through sound and of [the] structure of the sonorous world (by analogy with [the] structure of the world of colors or of touch). So as to bring to light the passage from quality to configuration through [its] integration within [*insertion dans*] existence and {?} the problem of the symbol./

Critique of Linschoten: the figural facts don't determine the *Bewegungsverteilung* [distribution of movement] on their own, but only by motivating a *Funktionsverteilung* [distribution of function]. Very well, but the latter, according to the author himself, is only 'justified' by the movement, [it] is the same thing as [the movement]. Here, therefore, there is neither {*Vervollständigung* [completion]} nor *Sinngebung*, but exchange of means and end. The given facts [*les données*] come to play on a perceptual device, [they] trace the outlines of a 'message' there, and the deciphering comes from the field. What characterizes perceptual deciphering is that the meaning doesn't appear to come from that which deciphers: it's a situational meaning. Signs are taken as elements of a situation ({possibly} defined by the historical intellectual field as a whole [*le champ mental historique tout entier*] and not only as [a] perceptual situation in the laboratory).

Thus, change of place is [a] special case of configuration in becoming, configuration understood as [a] meeting of stimulus and situation.

The clearest way to prove it is to observe intermodal influences: Zietz and Werner. For here configuration, being intersensory, is clearly distinguished from objective visual givens. It's the solicitation enacted by what is given on my machine for perceiving [*machine à percevoir*].

The machine for perceiving and body schema. Shillings and pence. Movement is what shows on the meter, hence [a] product of my perceptual logic. Cf. Paulhan.[41]

Thus movement = able to be seen [*capable de s'inscrire*] within a tracing with [this] tracing able to express movement. Perception of movement = symbolic [and] situational consciousness.
Clarify: [the] relationship between praxia, somatognosia and gnosia, [and the] nature of the perceiving subject.

/[194]/

PRAXIS AND GNOSIA

The existence of agnosias without apraxia and vice versa, of sensory aphasia without aphasia of expression and vice versa, demonstrates that there is no immediate identity of praxis and theoria — nor any possible reduction from theoria to praxis.

I don't wish to make any such reduction.

The idea is to make use of the praxical reference (this paper as 'for writing' or 'for wrapping') as something disclosive of the relationship of true intentionality or of being toward . . . of which theoria is also a modality.

There is [a] storing of practical intentionality when we move to theoria: the relationship of orientation toward the thing becomes something that can be seen, its trace in a visible world substitutes for it, with the result that disturbances are possible at each of these levels that don't affect the other. In gnosia there is sedimentation or cumulative history.

/[188]/
BODY SCHEMA — COURSE I

Consider [the] role and signification of movement in the Rorschach [test].

Perception of movement conditioned by the vestibular system (Christian)[42] [—] that is to say, by the body schema.

Portray the introduction of the body schema (as conditioning [the] orientation of objects, rest and movement, etc.) as [the] disclosure of an existential layer of perception beyond the physiological mechanisms studied up to now.

/[**205**]/

BODY SCHEMA AND MOVEMENT
(Ajuriaguerra and Hécaen, Méconnaissances
et H corporelles, Paris, 1952)[43]

Head's remark about the taximeter suggests the idea of a perception of somatic and external space that synthesizes and summarizes an unfolding of duration in a temporal 'relief.' Cf. the facts that demonstrate that the perception of movement in painting is linked to the portrayal of a privileged moment of this movement that has the value of [a] trace.

("in the same way as the distance traveled in a taxi presents itself to us transformed into shillings and pence" (344–345))[44]

To study the relationship between [the] movement of things and [the] movement of the body, the nature of our 'hold' on movement, — this is to study the body schema as mediation between the absolute here and the world.
To study the relationships between expression at the sensible level and at the specifically symbolic level is again to study the relationship [between] apraxia, agnosia [and] aphasia, and hence the relationship between the different symbolic stratifications.
Idea of a body schema in time (Ajuriaguerra and Hécaen, p. 345)[45]

/[**214**]/

THE HAND

None of the disturbances of *Fingeragnosie* [finger agnosia], of acalculia, and of {?} necessarily appear in subjects who no longer have their hand.[46]
The hand that is important for orienting oneself in space is thus not the hand part, the empirical hand, the chunk of flesh and bone. It's the hand only inasmuch as it forms part of the active body and appears in the body schema. It's the hand laden with human signification.
The question is to clarify the relation of the one hand to the other.
What we have just said is not 'spiritualism.' For if the hand can be preserved in the body schema while being removed from the empirical body, it's only capable of exploration when it is incarnated in the empirical body, and if amputees don't lose the notion of orientation, it's to the extent that they retain the true relation of orientation with the world

through some other organ, the other hand or vision. But visual functioning itself presupposes a specific incarnation. Therefore 1) [there is the] possibility of a sedimentation that places the subject above empirical deficiencies or failures 2) however this sedimentation only remains living through /**[214]v**/ the contribution of some other means of incarnation. Incarnation may be reduced, but not abolished.

Describe in the same way the relationship [between] language [and] thought: there is more in thought than in language, but language (and gesticulation) bring rhythmic patterns [*scansions*] [and] make possible the implantations [*implantations*] without which everything would become unarticulated. This power of packing more into the gesture or the words than is there, this is the very power that we find in every successful expression.

/**[187]**/
COURSE I

study perceptual signification as silent signification
and the advent through it of [the] 'voices of silence'
and the emergence of language as [a] special case of this inarticulate signification

/**[192]**/

What is the scope of a linguistic analysis of space, time, etc.? Does it really reveal to us the architectonic of lived time through speaking subjects? Can it move us toward an intuition of time more comprehensive than our own, which would be but a moment in the development of [a] universal symbolics? What is the relation between the lived and the spoken? What is the sense in ourselves of the lived?

/**[190]**/
Why the thing said is immediately different from the lived thing. It passes to the imagination. It's innocent when it's a matter of what we live, [but] it's dreadful [when] put into words (e.g., the {page} from Vigny *Pour lire au lit* stained with semen).[47] It's absolutely necessary to distinguish a knowledge [*connaissance*] of what we live, [which is] barely knowledge, resting on something self-evident, inarticulate, unqualified [*inqualifiée*], — from a knowledge put into significations, [a] morally qualified [*qualifiée*] knowledge of the imagination.

/**[195]**/
Consider aphasia as an apraxia of language.
Highlight in exactly that way the distinction between praxis and language, since these two disturbances (apraxia and aphasia) don't always go together.
Difference between manipulation of language and of other symbols, – and yet aphasia is definitely an apraxia, our relation with words is definitely analogous to our relation with symbols ({musical}-physiognomic [*physiognomique*] character of the disturbances in agrammatism[48]). Language is a symbolism that succeeds in concealing its own destruction.

/**[196]**/
Depersonalization = *Es* [Id] = splitting apart of the phonemic system and the body schema = autonomization of speech.
All pathological manifestations of speech (verbal hallucinations, etc.) imply, as their condition of possibility, a relationship of incarnation between personality and speech in normal cases.

All beliefs concerning the taboos of language, verbal magic, etc. are expressions of a true relationship of man with his speech. And in this respect the scientific attitude, the attitude of *Aufklärung* [Enlightenment], is itself a certain structuration of speech.

/**[209]**/
To distinguish linguistic-creative expression from expression that is not speech: analyze the psychoanalytic explanations of Hamlet and show the remainder that they leave: the remainder is precisely language as creation. Do the same work for Marxist explanations. Read Lukács and discuss him. Thus portray history as creative expression, and the implicit rationality [*rationalité en filigrane*] that it generates.

/**[210]**/

DIACRITICAL CONCEPTION OF THE PERCEPTUAL SIGN

It's the idea that we can perceive differences without terms, divergences in relation to a level that is itself not [an] object, — [the] only way of producing a consciousness of perception that would be faithful to it and not transform the perceived into [an] ob-ject, into what it signifies in the isolating or reflective attitude.

It's the mediation of the in-itself and the for-itself. [It's] the only way to distinguish what I said concerning perception from a finalism (critique of Lachièze-Rey) or an organicism. To be sure, we still need to differentiate the diacritical sign at the 'natural' level from that at the 'cultural' level, and until that's done one could always think that we're reintroducing nature into consciousness.

/**[211]**/

DIACRITICAL PERCEPTION

To perceive a physiognomy, an expression, just like making an expressive gesticulation with one's body, is always to use diacritical signs. Here each sign has no other value than to differentiate itself from the others, and differences appear for the spectator or are used by the speaking subject that are not defined by the terms between which they occur, but which on the contrary define them. To have a body capable of expressive gesticulation or action is the same thing as having a phonemic system as [the] capacity to construct signs. Body schema and phonemic system.

Like the phonemic system, the body schema is [a] power to vary a certain principle without explicit knowledge of this principle. What I was able to say of the body in this respect, brought together with the phonemic system in this way, makes no compromise at all with finality or naturalism: so understood, it's not nature that makes the body, any more than it makes phonemic systems. Nor is it an unconscious that's at work here, since on the contrary this playing with a principle that's not possessed is consciousness itself. Consciousness is, if you like, synonymous with imperception. Consciousness of [a] figure is /**[211]v**/ consciousness without knowledge of the background.

Describe birth as waking up or awakening: what begins or begins again stands out against a shapeless background. And it certainly doesn't derive from this background. The act through which it comes together and links up with the world doesn't arise from this background. And nonetheless there is an attentiveness [*vigilance*] of the body that makes it capable of generating or reviving the total being.[49]

The advent of a visual perception and its guiding role represent something analogous to what will be the advent of a cultural world and its displacement of the natural world.

The process of distribution that the Gestalt theorists talk about, or the cybernetic power of the organism, — these are indirect, abstract (and hypothetical) translations of the art of perceiving.

/[204]/

MOVEMENT – LANGUAGE

The perception of movement [is] comparable to the understanding of a sentence. We only understand the beginning of the sentence through the end [*fin*]. We only see movement by starting with its conclusion [*terme*]. Perception does not follow it from place to place. The sentence is a wave that travels over the linguistic field, a fold in the tissue of language. Movement (real as well as stroboscopic) is not the conveying [*transport*] of a solid thing from one objective point to another, but [the] successive activation of different points of the space on which I'm in circulation [*sur lequel je suis en circuit*]. Like signs in language, the points crossed in movement have only [a] diacritical value, they don't function each for their own sake by signaling a place, but only by indicating a passage, just as the words in the sentence are the trace of an intention that is merely reflected through [them]. Language is [the] opening of a reorganized field, with different contours [and] different coordinates than those of the 'natural' perceptual field.

As a result: perception, like language, /**[204]v**/ is not [the] confrontation of an ob-ject. The ob-ject only speaks to me laterally, i.e., it doesn't affect me frontally, but from the side by awakening complicity in me, its presence is obsessive because it is exogenous and endogenous. I.e., it "solicits" me (Valéry).[50] It always appears to me as [a] fragment of a world to reconstruct, just as in literary creation a sentence presents itself to me as part of a work to be made. This is due to a kind of postural impregnation [*imprégnation*] whereby I crystallized an entire order of nascent significations on this twig.[51] In this way language is built on itself, circularly, on a piece of itself, —just as the perceived world is built on a perspective appearing as a piece of . . . this world.

The conception of the body schema is a theory of lateral, indirect symbolism (sexual, for example)

/[191]/
The indirect as constitutive of expression (and moreover of natural perception at its level)
[The indirect] as constitutive of consciousness

/[197]/

Theory of indirect language: the mode of expression even in cinema. Editing [*montage*] [and] cutting express by creating figures on backgrounds.

All that is in Valéry's {saying} that the expressive power of a work comes solely from the fact that different minds don't have the same gaps [*lacunes*] (and private universes have the strange property of being polarizable by other significations than those that already reside within them). What he calls 'gaps' is the fact that what is figure for one [mind] is background for another.[52]

Conceptualize even sensation, sensing, as action of a figure on a background, modulation. E.g., noise [as] modulation of silence. Color [as] modulation of an open space that it varies.

Every sign is diacritical: it's the above idea of Valéry.

"lyricism of the black and white" (Focillon)[53]

/[213]/

[THE] IMAGINARY AND LANGUAGE –
[THE] PERCEIVED AND LANGUAGE

What Sartre says of the image, — that it presents us with an object across gaps, not in the firm tissue of the perceived, that the object is not observable in it, — all that applies even more so to language (and not only to literary language, but even to the language of 'witnessing,' to ordinary language in extreme situations). That expresses the transcendence of the signified relative to the signifier. Here there is expression through [the] modulation of the verbal chain, through flashes, signification through divergences.

In truth, it's no different with the perceived itself since, as Sartre observed, we don't need to make certain of the continuity of the tissue to believe, — and to distinguish the perceived from the imaginary. So it must be that the distinction is of such an order that it doesn't take away the transcendence of perception. It must be that the natural language of perception also remains a language, — which we usually express by opposing the sensible and the non-sensible, the emptiness of culture and the fullness [or] fundamental solidity [*solidité*] of nature.

/**[202]**/

[THE] IMAGINARY

Sartre defines the imaginary as unobservable, etc. And yet it is embodied in an analogue. Hence [the] difficulty for Sartre of maintaining the absolute distance between the imaginary and the real.

This distance exists. But perhaps it isn't that between the unobservable and the observable, or perhaps at least this distinction exists within the perceived world itself.

Cf. Linschoten ("Experimentelle Untersuchung der sog. Induzierten Bewegung" – *Ps. Forschung* Bd 24, 1952)[54] describing, within the perceived, the world of psychological experiments as having a *Bildcharakter* [image character], as making room for a freedom and an ambiguity that don't exist in the world of *Alltäglichkeit* [everydayness]. We would have [the] imaginary whenever we simply live in the *Bild* [image], [whenever we] settle into the reduced life of the spectator, whether it is in the cinema, with the determination to live in this little {drama} of shadows and light that happens over there in a greatly reduced space, — or else in the psychological experiment. The characteristic feature of the imaginary is in the transition [*passage*] to seeing, [to] only seeing.

For Linschoten, it would be abstract to /**[202]v**/ involve only the *figurale Geschehnisse* [figural events] in perception. This would be to reduce the perceived to the *Bildhaft* [pictorial].

The expression 'it's a {scraper [*grattoir*]}' conceals that the subject doesn't give a moment's thought to placing himself in the 'real,' and here takes the perceived only as [a] symbol (it concerns a drawing).[55]

/**[206]**/

SITUATION [THE] PAST [THE] IMAGINARY

Apply the concept of situation ('situation of movement,' for example, to express the supposed perceptual *Sinngebung* in ambiguous cases), not only to the elucidation of perceptual meaning as such, of the meaning of the present, — but also to the elucidation of the meaning of the past and the meaning of the imaginary — The imaginary and the past [are] too easily reduced by Sartre to signification, to the unobservable. These are facts of expression, i.e., of [the] constitution of myths. The phantom limb, the body schema, and everything it implies can only be understood by reference to an expressive function that admits of degrees.

/**[138]**/

COURSE I

Study sleep and especially awakening as reconstitution of perceptual consciousness.

Correlative variation, with sleep, of the body schema and the phonemic system

This (the transformation of the phonemic system that accounts for the logic of sleeping consciousness) would enable the clarification of my idea that all consciousness is [the] constitution of an architecture of signs, that the unconscious is the ambivalence of this architecture, that all consciousness is of the type of linguistic structuration. Nonetheless there remains, beneath the architecture of signs, and as its condition of possibility (or that of the body schema), a 'consciousness in general' — What is it?

Study the distinction [between] right [and] left

/**[207]**/

SLEEP

The problem of sleep: our being toward the world, regained upon waking, what sort of permanence does it have? What sort of break [is it] between sleep and wakefulness? Even if we show that {we} are always thinking, that there is a consciousness of sleep, etc., the problem remains unresolved since this consciousness is only for itself and not immediately for wakeful consciousness. Every attempt to avoid the problem in the name of the transcendental consciousness that 'is' consciousness of the past and therefore doesn't need to account for its gaps or irregularities, meets up with it again in the form of a difficulty that is no less [problematic]: that of understanding how this transcendental consciousness could be participated in to a greater or lesser extent by our empirical being.

Sketch of a solution by Husserl with regard to memory: [the] idea of an essential envelopment [*un enveloppement de principe*] of time by time, but which retains all the gaps of the present as it was lived, and which therefore does not assume a total consciousness. That's fine, it just means [*veut dire*] that the explication of memory is guided at once by something given and [yet] entirely /**[207]v**/ attributable to the one who carries it out. This disagreement or this contradiction is inevitable as long as perception (and memory) are conceived as acts of consciousness, and [as long as] a solution doesn't have to be sought in terms of the totality of consciousness (just as the problem of some particular emotion [or] of a certain grief isn't solved by saying that they result from a series of involvements of which I am not unconscious because I made them: for they surprise me as much as the ether surprises me by bogging me down in artificial sleep. There are infrastructures [and] standpoints [*prises de position*] that are not acts but institutions, and which carry my life). The solution would be to look in the idea that we carry with ourselves, by way of horizon, a set of private institutions (our past, our involvements, our 'thought,' etc.), a system of *imagines* [images or 'imaginings'] or of symbols for soliloquy, which lets itself condense as much as we like and reduce to a single 'situation.' The productivity of this system is not automatic (it's not a warehouse of traces), it needs to be taken up by the present self, but this present self is of the same sort as these 'traces,' since according to Head my present movement is related to the movements that I have made previously. The permanence of memories and of habitus is of the same kind as that of the body, that is, not actual permanence, in the 3rd person, but [the] permanence of an expressive system.[56] Sleep is the simultaneous disintegration of the body schema and the phonemic system, and of 'consciousness' insofar as it needs these articulations in order to be [a] specific consciousness. There remains the pure power of being toward . . . X that plays with certain *analoga* [analogues].[57] The problem of the reconstitution of the personality upon waking is of the same order as that of the reconstitution of the body, of the reappearing of a system of articulated powers on the basis of the {present}.

/**[212]**/

FIELD AND TIME

Describe a field time (e.g., time goes faster in [a] field structured in such and such a way). Such a time, in order to have [a] temporal sense, clearly must be accessible to a duration (cf. Bergson). But what's important is that it defines an *Erleben* [lived experience] in general, that it bears a mode of existence, and that absolute time or duration would not be consciousness of time without such institutional traces of time. The whole problem of the sensible therefore reappears here.

/[**200**]/

FIGURE AND BACKGROUND – NOTION OF CONSCIOUSNESS – OTHERS

Relations of sense and contiguity. Elucidate the action of one part of the field on adjacent parts, and how sense here depends on distance, [how] common sense [*le sens commun*] only asserts itself up close, – this would be to understand perceptual consciousness, this thinking [that is] linked to areas or to localities.*

> /[*in margin*] *{?}'s experiment ({?}'s gaze upon child playing, {coffin}, etc. and change in expression) is an important case of contiguity with transfer of signification.[58] Here the phenomenon appears linked to our body's understanding of the relationship [between] spectator [and] spectacle. The whole associative phenomenon would be linked to corporeality./

Figure and background and [the] experience of others. The world of others would be against [the] background [that is] always presupposed by the figures of [my world]. Not an opaque lived experience, [not] a tissue of sensations forever private, topped off with an ideal identity, but a sampling taken from . . . the intersubjective world, a fold of my world, a figure that will only ever be background for me, but which all the same {takes shape} in the behavior of the other, in the way in which he deals with certain aspects of the world and brings them into existence for his body.

/[**208**]/

PSYCHOLOGY – PHILOSOPHY

Use the facts of psychology while showing that I am indifferent to inductive {debates} (e.g., to the question of knowing whether the body schema is predominantly postural, as Head thinks, or visual, as Schilder thinks), and that consequently what I say about [these facts] is not subject to refutation. They only help me by disclosing the milieu where, in any case [*en toute hypothèse*] [i.e., regardless of how those debates may turn out], they are situated, i.e., the existing body. It's not science, it's philosophy, but a philosophy that doesn't construct.

/[139]/

D. EFRON[59]

Under the pretense of [a] {mimetic} method, this whole construction of types of conduct (further defined geographically or racially) in conformity with prejudices, and which justifies them, is part of a certain social perception rather than a true unbiased experience of others – That is closely related to the tendency to define others through tests, or through a destiny inscribed in writing or in the structure of the body – The {mimetic} method of *Einfühlung* is not in question: it's that of Goldstein, but there is a danger of applying it unrigorously. Induction is not sufficient, but it is always necessary. Tests [and the] study of cultural pattern[60] (e.g., of the conditions of {enculturation} during childhood) must not be used as means of thaumaturgy, of [the] divination and imposition of a destiny, — but as [a] supplementary means of reading individual or historico-collective behavior [*conduites*]. It is absolutely necessary to free the notion of {physiognomy} from any conception of destiny – Establish the difference between the idea of a total spontaneity that encompasses all gestures, and that of a blind causality that controls all life as the simple result of an archetype or of a mode of parental care.[61]

The inclination for psychoanalysis and {physiognomics [*physiognomonie*]} may be suspect.

Also flag the psychopathic interest in gestures [*l'intérêt des psychopathes pour les gestes*].

Translator's Notes

First Lecture

1. Cf. *Inédit* 43/7, where Merleau-Ponty says of this idea of "a concrete theory of mind" that it "will show it [the mind] in a relationship of exchange with the instruments that it provides itself with, but which return to it what they received from it, and more."

2. Here Merleau-Ponty is referring to the exchange that he had with Jean Hyppolite in November 1946 at the Société française de philosophie. See PrP 98–102/39–41.

3. Here Merleau-Ponty may be alluding to Eugen Fink's *VI. Cartesianische Meditation*, in which, in exploring the methodological assumptions of transcendental phenomenology, Fink presented a speculative reinterpretation of the project as an absolute science; see *VI. Cartesianische Meditation: Teil 1, Die Idee einer transzendentalen Methodenlehre*, ed. Hans Ebeling, Jann Holl, and Guy van Kerckhoven (Dordrecht: Kluwer, 1998); *Sixth Cartesian Meditation: The Idea of a Transcendental Theory of Method*, trans. Ronald Bruzina (Bloomington: Indiana University Press, 1995). But see also Eugen Fink, "L'analyse intentionnelle et le problème de la pensée spéculative/Die intentionale Analyse und das Problem des spekulativen Denkens," in *Problèmes actuels de la phénoménologie*, ed. H. L. Van Breda, 53–87 (Paris: Desclée de Brouwer, 1952); reprinted in *Proximité et distance: Essais et conférences phénoménologiques*, trans. Jean Kessler, 113–27 (Grenoble, Fr.: Jérôme Millon, 1994). On Merleau-Ponty's relation to Fink, see Ronald Bruzina, "Eugen Fink and Maurice Merleau-Ponty: The Philosophical Lineage in Phenomenology," in *Merleau-Ponty's Reading of Husserl*, ed. Lester Embree and Ted Toadvine (Dordrecht: Kluwer, 2002); but with regard to Fink's *Sixth Cartesian Meditation* in particular, cf. Bryan Smyth, "The Meontic and the Militant: On Merleau-Ponty's Relation to Fink," *International Journal of Philosophical Studies* 19 (2011): 669–99.

4. Here Merleau-Ponty may be referring to §10 of *Sein und Zeit* (45–50), "Die Abgrenzung der Daseinsanalytik gegen Biologie, Psychologie und Anthropologie" ("How the Analytic of Dasein Is to Be Distinguished from Anthropology, Psychology, and Biology"). See Martin Heidegger, *Sein und Zeit*, 8th ed. (1927; repr., Tübingen: Max Niemeyer, 1957); *Being and Time*, trans. John Macquarrie and Edward Robinson (Oxford: Blackwell, 1962).

5. The idea of "absolute survey" (*survol absolu*) is drawn from Raymond Ruyer, and I am following Alyosha Edlebi's translation of the term (rather than rendering it as, e.g., "absolute overview"). Introduced by Ruyer in his *Éléments de*

psycho-biologie (Paris: Presses Universitaires de France, 1946), the idea is developed in his major work, *Néo-finalisme* (Paris: Presses Universitaires de France, 1952); *Neofinalism*, trans. Alyosha Edlebi (Minneapolis: University of Minnesota Press, 2016), especially chapter 9, "'Absolute Surfaces' and Absolute Domains of Survey" (90–103), where Ruyer writes, "The notion of absolute survey, of nondimensional survey, is the key not only to the problem of consciousness but also to the problem of life," for it shows that "there is at bottom only a single mode of consciousness: primary consciousness, form-in-itself of every organism and at one with life" (*Neofinalism*, 94, 98). Concerning the idea of "absolute surfaces," see Raymond Ruyer, *La conscience et le corps* (Paris: Presses Universitaires de France, 1937), 56–58.

6. Merleau-Ponty may be alluding here to §§85 and 97 of Husserl's *Ideen zu einer reinen Phänomenologie und phänomenologischen Philosophie. Erstes Buch: Allgemeine Einführung in die reine Phänomenologie*, originally published in *Jahrbuch für Philosophie und phänomenologische Forschung* (Halle: Max Niemeyer, 1913), 1–323; *Ideas Pertaining to a Pure Phenomenology and to a Phenomenological Philosophy: First Book, General Introduction to a Pure Phenomenology*, trans. Fred Kersten (1913; repr., Dordrecht: Kluwer, 1982). More specifically, he was likely referring to Paul Ricœur's French translation, *Idées directrices pour une phénoménologie et une philosophie phénoménologique pures. Tome premier: Introduction générale à la phénoménologie pure* (Paris: Gallimard, 1950)—which was, it is worth noting, the first volume to appear in Gallimard's Bibliothèque de Philosophie series coedited by Merleau-Ponty and Sartre. In a note to §85 ("Sensuous *hyle*, Intentive *morphe*"), Ricœur remarked critically that "the study of *hyle* pertains to the constitution of objects in consciousness to the extent that intentionality animates it. The 'hyletics' corresponds to the 'noetics' as matter does to form. But in a more profound sense, *hyle* connects with the constitution of time and the *Urkonstitution* of the Ego . . . : the flux of the 'adumbrations' gives its immanent duration to the intention of an object. As E[ugen] Fink has emphasized, if we do not proceed to the constitution of the *hyle*, (and thus time and the pure Ego), the constitution of the thing itself cannot assume its radical sense, that is, as creative. The beginning of §85 declares that, because it will not 'descend into the obscure profundities of ultimate consciousness which constitutes all temporality of what is experienced,' the analysis of *Ideas I* will deal only with transcendent intentionality" (*A Key to Husserl's* Ideas I, ed. P. Vandevelde, trans. Bond Harris and Jacqueline Bouchard Spurlock [Milwaukee, Wis.: Marquette University Press, 1996], 129–30). Later, in §97, Ricœur noted that "the object is not included in the noesis as is the *hyle* and the *hyle* commands, in some way, the object although the noesis 'constitutes' it. But the noesis constitutes it 'through' the *hyle* whose changes govern the appearance of the object. This role of the *hyle* recalls the idea which was glimpsed several times before: the constitution of the Ego as temporality and *hyle* is more radical than the constitution of objectivity 'in' what is experienced" (*A Key to Husserl's* Ideas I, 142). Along with the first note, this points back to Husserl's overly optimistic statement in §81 of *Ideas I* that "we can leave out of account the enigma of consciousness of time in our preliminary analyses without endangering their rigor." Here Ricœur commented that the "reduction of transcendences, or limited reduction (§32), can only lead to a 'closed' sphere of problems of constitu-

tion," and that the enigma in question stems from the fact that consciousness of time "impinges upon the *Urkonstitution* of the Ego itself . . . which is in a sense an auto-constitution, [and which] is the subject of an important group of unpublished materials" (*A Key to Husserl's* Ideas I, 127–28; cf. 59n34).

7. Concerning "typical," see note 8 in lecture 4 and note 26 in lecture 10.

8. Here, as well as at [29](II5) and [33](III1), phrases to the effect that "consciousness is cross-eyed" are translating Merleau-Ponty's claim that "la conscience louche." While in many ordinary contexts the verb *loucher* means "to squint," that would be misleading here, inasmuch as Merleau-Ponty is using it metaphorically in the sense of having strabismus, or "crossed eyes," a family of visual conditions in which the eyes are misaligned such that when one focuses on an object, the other cannot, in some cases leading to double vision. A more technical translation would thus say that "consciousness is strabismic," but "cross-eyed" seems to better capture Merleau-Ponty's tone, and it renders more conspicuous the link to the adjectival use of *louche* at [58](VI1) as "weird or dubious."

9. Merleau-Ponty may be alluding to the work of Viktor von Weizsäcker or Alfred Prinz von Auersperg, where the notion of prolepsis plays a fundamental role in the temporality proper to living things. See, e.g., Viktor von Weizsäcker, *Der Gestaltkreis: Theorie der Einheit von Wahrnehmen und Bewegen* (Leipzig: Georg Thieme, 1940); reprinted as vol. 4 of Weizsäcker's *Gesammelte Schriften*, ed. Dieter Janz, Wilhelm Rimpau, and Walter Schindler, with the collaboration of Peter Achilles und Mechthilde Kütemeyer (Frankfurt am Main: Suhrkamp, 1997), 256–58; Alfred Prinz von Auersperg and Harry C. Buhrmester, "Experimenteller Beitrag zur Frage des Bewegtsehens," *Zeitschrift für die Sinnesphysiologie* 66 (1936): 274–309; cf. Jean Piaget and Marc Lambercier, with the collaboration of B. Bergert-Demetriades, H. Aebli, and M. Gantenbein, "La perception d'un carré animé d'un mouvement de circumduction (effet Auersperg et Buhrmester)," *Archives de psychologie* 33, no. 130 (1951): 131–95. See also Martin Sack, *Von der Neuropathologie zur Phänomenologie: Alfred Prinz von Auersperg und die Geschichte der Heidelberger Schule* (Würzburg: Königshausen & Neumann, 2005), 67–72.

10. Concerning Bergson's notion of action, see [108](XIII1).

Second Lecture

1. See Pierre Lachièze-Rey, *Le moi, le monde et dieu* (Paris: Boivin, 1935), in particular chapters 5–7.

2. See note 5 in lecture 1.

3. Reading *Wesen* for *wesen*.

4. Jean-Paul Sartre, "La transcendance de l'ego: Esquisse d'une description phénoménologique," *Recherches philosophiques* 6 (1936–37): 85–124; *Transcendence of the Ego: An Existentialist Theory of Consciousness*, trans. Forrest Williams and Robert Kirkpatrick (New York: Noonday Press, 1962).

5. See Max Wertheimer, "Experimentelle Studien über das Sehen von Bewegung," *Zeitschrift für Psychologie* 61, no. 1 (1912): 161–265; "Experimental Stud-

ies on Seeing Motion," trans. Michael Wertheimer and K. W. Watkins, in Max Wertheimer, *On Perceived Motion and Figural Organization*, ed. Lothar Spillmann (Cambridge, Mass.: MIT Press, 2012), 1–91. See [44](III11). Merleau-Ponty had previously commented on Wertheimer's work in PhP 287–89/259–61.

6. On the notion of *Umweltintentionalität*, see PhP 269n1/241, 538n63. There Merleau-Ponty referred to Helmuth Plessner and Frederik Buytendijk, "Die Deutung des mimischen Ausdrucks: Ein Beitrag zur Lehre vom Bewußtsein des anderen Ichs," *Philosophischer Anzeiger* 1, no. 1 (1925): 72–126 (Merleau-Ponty's reference was to page 81); reprinted in Helmuth Plessner, *Gesammelte Schriften in zehn Bänden. VII: Ausdruck und menschliche Natur*, ed. Günter Dux, Odo Marquand, and Elisabeth Ströker (Frankfurt am Main: Suhrkamp, 2003), 65–129 (the passage Merleau-Ponty referred to is on page 79; cf. 122). On the notion of *Umwelt*, see Jakob von Uexküll, *Streifzüge durch die Umwelten von Tieren und Menschen: Ein Bilderbuch unsichtbarer Welten* (Berlin: Springer, 1934), and Jakob von Uexküll, *Bedeutungslehre* (Leipzig: J. A. Barth, 1940); *A Foray into the Worlds of Animals and Humans, with* A Theory of Meaning, trans. Joseph D. O'Neil (Minneapolis: University of Minnesota Press, 2010).

7. The relevant text from Freud dealing with jealousy is "Über einige neurotische Mechanismen bei Eifersucht, Paranoia und Homosexualität," *Internationale Zeitschrift für Psychoanalyse* 8, no. 3 (1922): 249–58; "Some Neurotic Mechanisms in Jealousy, Paranoia and Homosexuality," in *The Standard Edition of the Complete Psychological Works of Sigmund Freud, Volume 18: Beyond the Pleasure Principle, Group Psychology and Other Works, 1920–1922*, ed. James Strachey (in collaboration with Anna Freud, assisted by Alix Strachey and Alan Tyson), 221–35 (New York: Vintage, 1999). The same argument concerning the relation between homosexuality and heterosexuality can be found in Merleau-Ponty's notes from his 1954–55 course on institution, but there in connection with Proust's *À la recherche du temps perdu*, specifically the narrator's relation with Albertine; see *L'institution. La passivité: Notes de cours au Collège de France, 1954–1955*, ed. Dominique Darmaillacq and Stéphanie Ménasé (Paris: Belin, 2003), 75–77; *Institution and Passivity: Course Notes from the Collège de France, 1954–1955*, trans. Leonard Lawlor and Heath Massey (Evanston, Ill.: Northwestern University Press, 2010), 38–40.

8. An allusion to Alfred de Vigny's affair with the actress Marie Dorval, recounted by Armand Parviel in *Le roman douloureux d'Alfred de Vigny* (Paris: Les éditions de France, 1934). See also Dorval's *Lettres à Alfred de Vigny*, ed. Charles Gaudier (Paris: Gallimard, 1942), and Alfred de Vigny and Marie Dorval, *Lettres pour lire au lit. Correspondance amoreuse d'Alfred de Vigny et Marie Dorval, 1831–1838*, ed. Ariane Charton (Paris: Mercure de France, 2009).

9. The end of page [30] along with pages [31] and [32] are crossed out by Merleau-Ponty and are not included here.

Third Lecture

1. As is not uncommon in French academic writing, among other contexts, Merleau-Ponty sometimes engages in the practice of nosism—i.e., referring to himself in the first-person plural.

2. In addition to certain works by Marx himself, Merleau-Ponty undoubtedly had in mind here Norbert Guterman and Henri Lefebvre's important Marxist work on ideology, *La conscience mystifiée* (Paris: Gallimard, 1936).

3. Most of these terms are drawn from the beginning of Marx's "Contribution to the Critique of Hegel's Philosophy of Law. Introduction." See Karl Marx and Frederick Engels, *Collected Works*, vol. 3 (Moscow: Progress Publishers, 1975), 175–87. Thanks to Jérôme Melançon for making this observation.

4. The distinction that Merleau-Ponty is invoking here is not perfectly clear, but it is not without precedent. See, for example, the following in "Le métaphysique dans l'homme": "Religious experience always occurs in an actual or virtual collectivity, . . . it implies an idea of interpersonal relations, and . . . it always expresses, directly or indirectly, as reflection or compensation [*à titre de reflet ou de contrepartie*], the actual human relationships in a given civilization" (SNS 156/89). And the following in "Marxisme et philosophie": "The 'spirit' of a society is already implied in its mode of production, because the latter is already a certain mode of human coexistence of which scientific, philosophical, and religious concepts are either the simple development, or for which they are the fantastic compensation [*ou le simple développement ou la contrepartie fantastique*]" (SNS 231/131, translation modified). The contrast is thus between an imaginary compensatory ideology and ideology understood as a simple, direct (hence passive) reflection of the status quo.

5. This parenthesis does not close.

6. Reading *saisis* for *saisi*.

7. In this and the preceding sentence, "impersonal" is obviously not a literal translation of the French pronoun *on*. But inasmuch as Merleau-Ponty is using *on* as an adjective here, it seems to convey the sense well enough without the need for additional terms that would alter the structure of the sentence.

8. Merleau-Ponty is probably referring to passages such as the following in Trần Đức Thảo's important work, *Phénoménologie et matérialisme dialectique* (Paris: Minh-Tân, 1951), 97: "La réalité de la *Dinglichkeit* ne peut être reconnue que dans un naturalisme d'un genre nouveau"; *Phenomenology and Dialectical Materialism*, trans. Daniel J. Herman and Donald V. Morano (Dordrecht: D. Reidel, 1986), 50: "The reality of *Dinglichkeit* can only be recognized in a new kind of naturalism." See also Jocelyn Benoist, "Une première naturalisation de la phénoménologie?," in *L'itinéraire de Tran Duc Thao: Phénoménologie et transfert culturel*, ed. Jocelyn Benoist and Michel Espagne (Paris: Armand Colin, 2013), 25–46.

9. See Léon Brunschvicg, *Le progrès de la conscience dans la philosophie occidentale* (Paris: Félix Alcan, 1927), in particular the final chapter, "La conscience religieuse" (741–98).

10. Cf. *Inédit* 44/8, where Merleau-Ponty refers to a book in progress with the title *L'origine de la vérité*.

11. Here Merleau-Ponty is probably alluding to Ernst Cassirer's use of the notion of *Darstellungsfunktion* in his *Philosophie der symbolischen Formen. Dritter Teil: Phänomenologie der Erkenntnis* (Berlin: Bruno Cassirer, 1929), as standing between the "expressive function" (*Ausdrucksfunktion*) and the "significative function" (*Bedeutungsfunktion*) of thought. But bear in mind Cassirer's note in the third volume, where he credits the term to Karl Bühler: "I use the term 'representative function' (*Darstellungsfunktion*) in the same sense as Karl Bühler, whose works were not known to me when I treated the problem from the standpoint of the philosophy of language in the first volume [of *Philosophie der symbolischen Formen*] . . . This is all the more reason to mention here the fundamental agreement between the findings of a general analysis from the standpoint of the philosophy and history of language and of Bühler's investigations, which are essentially oriented toward psychology and biology." See *The Philosophy of Symbolic Forms, Volume Three: The Phenomenology of Knowledge*, trans. Ralph Manheim (New Haven, Conn.: Yale University Press, 1957), 110n4. Among other articles, Cassirer specifically refers to Bühler's "Über den Begriff der sprachlichen Darstellung," *Psychologischen Forschung* 3 (1923): 282–94; but see also his later work, *Sprachtheorie: Die Darstellungsfunktion der Sprache* (Jena: Gustav Fischer, 1934).

12. With the expression "symbolic thinking"—which he wrote in English—Merleau-Ponty is probably alluding to Henry Head's work on aphasia that focused on disturbances of symbolic meaning and categorical representation rather than of capacities for speaking, writing, and reading. See, e.g., Head's "Aphasia and Kindred Disorders of Speech," *Brain* 43, no. 2 (1920): 87–165; "Disorders of Symbolic Thinking and Expression," *British Journal of Psychology* 11, no. 2 (1921): 179–93; and *Aphasia and Kindred Disorders of Speech*, 2 vols. (Cambridge: Cambridge University Press, 1926). Cassirer also made reference to Head's work, and just as with Bühler (see preceding note), he drew attention to his agreement with it despite a belated awareness: "I myself became acquainted with Head's investigations only after the phenomenological analyses of perception in the first two volumes of [*Philosophie der symbolischen Formen*] were largely completed. This made me attach all the greater importance to the indirect confirmation of my conclusions by Head's observations and the general theoretical view which he developed solely on the basis of clinical experience" (*The Philosophy of Symbolic Forms, Volume Three*, 209n5).

13. Concerning Bergson's notion of action, see also [108](XII1).

14. In laying out a Gestalt-theoretic approach to thinking, Wertheimer proposed a "structural" conception of truth—see *Productive Thinking* (New York: Harper and Row, 1945), 235, 259. This volume expanded on some ideas that Wertheimer had originally published in *Über Schlussprozesse im produktiven Denken* (Berlin: De Gruyter, 1920), which was reprinted as part of *Drei Abhandlungen zur Gestalttheorie* (Erlangen: Verlag der Philosophischen Akademie, 1925), and to which Merleau-Ponty made reference in PhP (e.g., 440/404). But *Productive Thinking* also made explicit reference to Wertheimer's (English-language) article "On Truth," *Social Research* 1, no. 2 (1934): 135–46. Along with the general Gestalt-theoretic idea of "structuration," Merleau-Ponty discussed *Productive Thinking* in his Sorbonne lectures, *Psychologie et pedagogie de l'enfant: Cours de Sorbonne, 1949–*

52, ed. Jacques Prunair (Lagrasse, Fr.: Verdier, 2001), 262–75; *Child Psychology and Pedagogy: The Sorbonne Lectures, 1949–1952*, trans. Talia Welsh (Evanston, Ill.: Northwestern University Press, 2010), 208–19, where he summed up by saying, "In short, Wertheimer says that truth itself must be given a 'structural' conception" (*Psychologie et pedagogie de l'enfant*, 275; *Child Psychology and Pedagogy*, 219). See also *L'institution. La passivité*, where Merleau-Ponty wrote, "ce qu'il y a à chaque moment, [c'est] 'vérité structurale', liée à perspective, à centration, à structuration" (91; cf. 95); *Institution and Passivity*, "What there is at each moment [is] 'structural truth,' connected to perspective, to centering, to structuration" (52; translation modified. Cf. 55). See also *La prose du monde*, ed. Claude Lefort (Paris: Gallimard, 1969), 167; *The Prose of the World*, trans. John O'Neill (Evanston, Ill.: Northwestern University Press, 1973), 119.

15. Merleau-Ponty discusses this idea in *L'œil et l'esprit* (Paris: Gallimard, 1964), 72–73; "Eye and Mind," trans. Carleton Dallery, in *The Primacy of Perception*, 182–83. There the locution "flexuous line" (*ligne flexueuse*) occurs within a quotation as follows: "Puisque Vinci dans le *Traité de la peinture* parlait de 'decouvrir dans chaque objet [. . .] la manière particulière dont se dirige à travers toute son étendue [. . .] une certaine ligne flexueuse qui est comme son axe générateur.'" Merleau-Ponty was quoting from Bergson's discussion of Félix Ravaisson in *La pensée et le mouvant* (Paris: Félix Alcan, 1934), where the complete sentence is situated as follows (264): "Il y a, dans le *Traité de* [*la*] *peinture* de Léonard de Vinci, une page que M. Ravaisson aimait à citer. C'est celle où il est dit que l'être vivant se caractérise par la ligne onduleuse ou serpentine, que chaque être a sa manière propre de serpenter, et que l'objet de l'art est de rendre ce serpentement individuel. 'Le secret de l'art de dessiner est de découvrir dans chaque objet la manière particulière dont se dirige à travers toute son étendue, telle qu'une vague centrale qui se déploie en vagues superficielles, une certaine ligne flexueuse qui est comme son axe générateur.'" ("There is, in Leonardo da Vinci's *Treatise on Painting*, a page that Ravaisson loved to quote. It is the one where the author says that the living being is characterized by the undulous or serpentine line, that each being has its own way of undulating, and that the object of art is to render this undulation distinctive. 'The secret of the art of drawing is to discover in each object the particular way in which a certain flexuous line which is, so to speak, its generating axis, is directed through its whole extent, like one main wave which spreads out in little surface waves'" [*The Creative Mind*, trans. Mabelle L. Andison (New York: Philosophical Library, 1946), 272]). (Note that Dallery's translation of "Eye and Mind" followed Andison's rendering but added back into the quoted sentence some parts of it that Merleau-Ponty himself had omitted.) For his part, Bergson was quoting from Ravaisson's entry on "Dessin," in the *Dictionnaire de pédagogie et d'instruction primaire*, part 1, vol. 1, ed. Ferdinand Buisson (Paris: Hachette, 1887), 680: "La forme, disait Michel-Ange, doit être 'serpentine' [*serpentinata*]; et Léonard de Vinci: 'Observe, pour dessiner, la manière de serpenter de chaque chose [*il modo di* [*sic*] *serpeggiare*]'. Autrement dit, le secret de l'art de dessiner est de découvrir en chaque objet la manière particulière dont se dirige à travers toute son étendue, telle qu'une vague centrale qui se déploie en vagues superficielles, [une] certaine ligne flexueuse qui est comme

son axe générateur.'" It may have been the following passage from da Vinci that Ravaisson had in mind here: "Siano con somma diligenza considerati i termini di qualunque corpo, ed il modo del lor serpeggiare" (*Trattato della pittura di Lionardo da Vinci, tratto da un codice della Biblioteca Vaticana e dedicato alla maestà di Luigi 18. re di Francia e di Navarra*, ed. Guglielmo Manzi [Rome: Nella stamperia De Romanis, 1817], 89), which may be thus rendered in French: "Que l'on considère avec un soin extrême les contours d'un corps, la manière dont ils serpentent" (*Traité de la peinture, traduit intégralement pour la première fois en français sur le codex vaticanus (urbinas) 1270, complété par de nombreux fragments tirés des manuscrits du maître . . .*, ed. Joseph-Aimé Péladan [Paris: Delagrave, 1910], 100), and in English: "The contours of any object should be considered with the most careful attention, observing how they twist like a serpent" (*Treatise on Painting, Volume 1: Translation*, trans. Amos Philip McMahon [Princeton, N.J.: Princeton University Press, 1956], 64). In any case, given that there is a slight ambiguity concerning who said what in Bergson's quotation from Ravaisson's entry in the *Dictionnaire*, and that this ambiguity is greatly heightened in Merleau-Ponty's selective requotation of it, and that this situation has led to some confusion—given all this, it is worth noting that the passage in question, including the locution "flexuous line," is *Ravaisson's own gloss* on da Vinci's (and possibly also Michelangelo's) views on drawing, rather than a quotation from da Vinci's *Trattato della pittura* itself.

16. See note 14 above.

17. See Immanuel Kant, *Critique of Pure Reason*, ed. and trans. Paul Guyer and Allen W. Wood (Cambridge: Cambridge University Press, 1998): "Thus if, e.g., I make the empirical intuition of a house into perception through apprehension of its manifold, my ground is the necessary unity of space and of outer sensible intuition in general, and I as it were draw its shape in agreement with this synthetic unity of the manifold in space" (B 162). See also Helge Svare, *Body and Practice in Kant* (Dordrecht: Springer, 2006), 177–212.

18. An antiessentialist opposition to what he called "the method of the 'that without which'" is an important theme in Merleau-Ponty's phenomenology, which he presented conversely as aiming to disclose the "that through which" (see PhP iv, 118, 334, 506/lxxiii, 103, 302, 468).

19. The "goggles" (*lunettes*) mentioned here and in the next paragraph refer to the "optical contrivance" employed in experiments conducted by George Malcolm Stratton (see note 21).

20. This is a difficult passage that brings together several senses of the term *sens*: "Si c'est l'âme qui voit, elle devrait voir dans tous les sens la même chose. L'idée même d'un sens où il faut les prendre atteste que le sens du perçu n'est pas la pure signification spirituelle." Rendered more literally, the second sentence would read as "The very idea of a sense in which [directions] must be taken . . . ," but that seems awkward. In altering the structure somewhat as I have, the key point—that *directions* have *senses* that are not yet *meaning*s—seems to come across more clearly.

21. Merleau-Ponty is referring to the well-known experiments concerning visual perception and spatial orientation conducted by American psychologist George Malcolm Stratton using specially designed goggles (or "optical contriv-

ance") that substituted an upright retinal image for the normal (inverted) one. See his "Some Preliminary Experiments on Vision Without Inversion of the Retinal Image," *Psychological Review* 3, no. 6 (1896): 611–17; "Vision Without Inversion of the Retinal Image," *Psychological Review* 4 (1897): 341–60, 463–81; and "The Spatial Harmony of Touch and Sight," *Mind*, 8 (1899): 492–505. Merleau-Ponty had previously commented on these three texts in PhP 282–87/254–59.

22. Reading *pâlir* for *pâtir* (see PhP 284/256), and I have removed the curly braces found in the French edition. Merleau-Ponty is alluding to Stratton, "Vision Without Inversion," 351, and "Some Preliminary Experiments," 617.

23. See note 5 in lecture 2.

Fourth Lecture

1. On the term *lekton*, see Alain de Libera and Irène Rosier-Catach's entry under "Dictum" in *Vocabulaire européen des philosophies: Dictionnaire des intraduisibles*, ed. Barbara Cassin (Paris: Le Seuil / Le Robert, 2004); Barbara Cassin, ed., *Dictionary of Untranslatables: A Philosophical Lexicon*, trans. Steven Rendall, Christian Hubert, Jeffrey Mehlman, Nathanael Stein, and Michael Syrotinski (Princeton, N.J.: Princeton University Press, 2014). I have followed Émile Bréhier's rendering of the term as *exprimable* (expressible) at the very beginning of his work, *La théorie des incorporels dans l'ancien stoïcisme* (Paris: A. Picard, 1907), as it seems likely that such is what Merleau-Ponty would have had in mind.

2. Wertheimer, "Experimentelle Studien," 258–59; "Experimental Studies," 84–85.

3. An allusion to Bergson's observation near the beginning of *L'évolution créatrice* concerning the sugar cube: "Si je veux me préparer un verre d'eau sucrée, j'ai beau faire, je dois attendre que le sucre fonde. Ce petit fait est gros d'enseignements. Car le temps que j'ai à attendre n'est plus ce temps mathématique qui s'appliquerait aussi bien le long de l'histoire entière du monde matériel, lors même qu'elle serait étalée tout d'un coup dans l'espace. Il coïncide avec mon impatience, c'est-à-dire avec une certaine portion de ma durée à moi, qui n'est pas allongeable ni rétrécissable à volonté. Ce n'est plus du pensé, c'est du vécu. Ce n'est plus une relation, c'est de l'absolu" (*L'évolution créatrice* [Paris: Félix Alcan, 1908], 10) ("If I want to make a glass of sugar water, then like it or not I have to wait for the sugar to melt. This little fact teaches us a lot. For the time that I have to wait is no longer that mathematical time that would apply equally well to the entire history of the material world, even if that history were spread out instantaneously in space. It coincides with my impatience, that is to say, with a certain portion of my own duration, which cannot be extended or contracted at will. It is no longer something thought, it is something lived. It is no longer a relation, it is an absolute" [*Creative Evolution*, trans. Arthur Mitchell (New York: Holt, 1911), 9–10; translation modified]).

4. Reading *ce* for *de*.

5. "Mais on n'a pas l'impression qu'elles fassent l'expérience de profon-

deur"—the pronominal subject here (*elles*) could refer back to "these explanations," which would fit best with the overall sentence structure, given the parentheses, or else to "these perspectives," as the immediately subsequent reference to perspective might suggest. (Grammatically, it could also refer to "other experiments," but semantically that seems quite improbable.) In the first case, the idea would seem to be that while the putative explanations in question are *possible* in virtue of an internal coherence, they are not *actual* explanations because they are inadequate with regard to depth as the experiential explanandum. In the second case, the idea would seem to be that the perspectives invoked in those explanations do not themselves generate experienced depth. The two possibilities are closely related, but given the verb (*fassent*), the latter seems more likely. In general, the expression *faire l'expérience de* simply means to experience something, or else, less commonly, to conduct an experiment. Both these senses happen to be relevant in this case, but given the possible subjects ("explanations" or "perspectives"), neither is exactly appropriate. Rather, given the emphasis that he places upon it, Merleau-Ponty seems to be using *fassent* in the more basic sense of "making," for which reason it is likelier that *elles* refers to "ces perspectives," rather than to "ces explications." Translating "fassent" in this instance as "[actually] yield" thus seemed to be a reasonable way to capture the sense of perspectives giving rise to the experience of depth, while also allowing for the reading according to which Merleau-Ponty's point was to deny the adequacy of the corresponding explanations.

6. See Paul Valéry, *Degas, Danse, Dessin* (Paris: Gallimard, 1938), 138; reprinted in *Œuvres, tome II*, ed. Jean Hytier (Paris: Gallimard, 1960), 1221. Merleau-Ponty cites the same passage at [56](V2).

7. Here, and in the next sentence, Merleau-Ponty uses the hyphenated Anglicism "feed-back" (underscored). The term is also used on [55](V1).

8. Outside contexts concerning cinema, where it standardly denotes "editing" in the sense of the creative process of selecting, arranging, and assembling separate takes of camera footage and elements of recorded sound into a complete sequence with a certain continuity (or the more specific eponymous editing technique in which shots are juxtaposed or superimposed usually in short rapid sequence), the translation of Merleau-Ponty's use here of the substantive *montage* presents difficulties. Stemming from the verb *monter*, the general denotation of the term is the action of carrying something to a higher point, or of assembling or arranging something from its parts, or else the resulting assembly or arrangement itself (hence the cinematic senses). But that does not address the translation question concerning *montage* in the present context. For this we should turn back to *Phénoménologie de la perception*. Consider the following passages (with *montage* left untranslated, a term that Don Landes usually renders as "arrangement," although sometimes as "structure"): "Il y a une logique du monde que mon corps tout entier épouse et par laquelle des choses intersensorielles deviennent possibles pour nous. Mon corps en tant qu'il est capable de synergie sait ce que signifie pour l'ensemble de mon expérience telle couleur en plus ou en moins, il en saisit d'emblée l'incidence sur la présentation et le sens de l'objet. Avoir des sens, par exemple avoir la vision, c'est posséder ce montage général,

cette typique des relations visuelles possibles à l'aide de laquelle nous sommes capables d'assumer toute constellation visuelle donnée. Avoir un corps, c'est posséder un montage universel, une typique de tous les développements perceptifs et de toutes les correspondances intersensorielles par-delà le segment du monde que nous percevons effectivement" (377) ("There is a logic of the world that my entire body merges with and through which intersensory things become possible. My body, insofar as it is capable of synergy, knows what more or less of some color signifies for the totality of my experience; and my body immediately grasps the effect of the change in the presentation and in the sense of the object. To have senses such as vision is to possess this general *montage*, this typology [*typique*] of possible visual relations with the help of which we are capable of taking up every given visual constellation. To have a body is to possess a universal *montage*, a typology [*typique*] of all perceptual developments and of all intersensory correspondences beyond the segment of the world that we are actually perceiving" [341; translation modified]). Alongside this, recall the following: "La signification motrice des couleurs ne se comprend que si elles cessent d'être des états fermés sur eux-mêmes ou des qualités indescriptibles offertes à la constatation d'un sujet pensant, si elles atteignent en moi un certain montage général par lequel je suis adapté au monde, si elles m'invitent à une nouvelle manière de l'évaluer (243) ("The motor signification of colors can only be understood if colors cease to be self-enclosed states or indescribable qualities offered to the observation of a thinking subject, if they reach in me a certain general *montage* by which I am adapted to the world, if they entice me toward a new manner of evaluating it [the world]" [217–18; translation modified]); "Le champ est un montage que j'ai pour un certain type d'expériences, et qui, une fois établi, ne peut être annulé (379) ("The field is a *montage* that I have for a certain type of experiences, and which, once established, cannot be rescinded" [343; translation modified]); and finally, "Quand je comprends une chose, par exemple un tableau, je n'en opère pas actuellement la synthèse, je viens au-devant d'elle avec mes champs sensoriels, mon champ perceptif, et finalement avec une typique de tout l'être possible, un montage universel à l'égard du monde (490) ("When I understand a thing, such as a painting, I do not at that moment perform the synthesis of it; rather, I come before it with my sensory fields, my perceptual field, and finally with a typology [*typique*] of every possible being, or a universal *montage* with regard to the world" [453; translation modified]). In these passages Merleau-Ponty is saying that the prereflective synthesis of perceptual experience occurs on the schematic basis of a pregiven "typology" (*typique*), a *general* one within each sensory modality, and a *universal* one at the intersensory level of the perceiving body. As a rendering of the German *Typik*, this term *typique* seems to provide the key to clarifying what Merleau-Ponty means by *montage* in the present context.

Here we may just further note two relevant points of reference. First, there is Husserl's understanding of empirical typicality—"types" as distinguished from essences strictly speaking (see, e.g., *Erfahrung und Urteil: Untersuchungen zur Genealogie der Logik*, ed. Ludwig Landgrebe [Hamburg: Felix Meiner, 1997]; *Experience and Judgment: Investigations in a Genealogy of Logic*, trans. James S. Churchill and Karl Ameriks [Evanston, Ill.: Northwestern University Press, 1973], part 3, chapter 1, §§81–85)—and his corresponding use of the term *Typik*, translated in various ways, including as "set of types," "typicality," "typification," or "typology," as a structural feature of prescientific experience (see Dorion Cairns, *Guide for Translating Husserl* [The Hague: Martinus Nijhoff, 1973]). Without getting into a detailed discussion, it is worth recalling Husserl's frequent use of the term *Typik* in the *Crisis* texts in connection with the lifeworld (*Lebenswelt*)—e.g., in claiming in §51 that despite whatever changes that may be encountered within a lifeworld, or the differences that may be encountered between lifeworlds, *the* lifeworld as such involves a certain invariant structure: "The world of life [*die Welt des Lebens*] holds to its essentially lawful set of types [*wesensgeseztliche Typik*], to which all life, and thus all science, of which it is the 'ground,' remain bound" (see *Die Krisis der europäischen Wissenschaften und die transzendentale Phänomenologie: Eine Einleitung in die phänomenologische Philosophie*, ed. Walter Biemel [The Hague: Martinus Nijhoff, 1962], 176; *The Crisis of European Sciences and Transcendental Phenomenology: An Introduction to Phenomenological Philosophy*, trans. David Carr [Evanston, Ill.: Northwestern University Press, 1970], 173). It is "part of the lifeworld's formal typology [*lebensweltliche Formtypik*] that bodies have typical ways of being together, in coexistence (above all in a given perceptual field) and in succession—i.e., a constant universal spatiotemporal set of types [*eine beständige universale raumzeitliche Typik*]" (§62, *Krisis*, 221n; *Crisis*, 218n); the lifeworld itself, "as existing prescientifically for us (originally) purely through experience, furnishes us in advance, through its invariant set of essential types [*ihrer invarianten Wesenstypik*], with all possible scientific topics . . . Things have their concrete set of types [*ihre konkrete Typik*] . . . But all particular sets of types [*Sondertypik*] come under the most general of all, the set of 'regional' types [*der „regionale" Typik*]" (§66, *Krisis*, 229–30; *Crisis*, 226–27). It is also worth recalling Alfred Schütz's claim—which certainly resonates with the general sense of Merleau-Ponty's existential interpretation of Husserl—that with these (and other) later formulations, the crisp distinction that Husserl wanted to draw between empirical type (*Typus*) and pure essence (*reine Wesen* or *eidos*), or between empirical and eidetic universality, ultimately breaks down—see "Type and Eidos in Husserl's Late Philosophy," *Philosophy and Phenomenological Research* 20, no. 2 (1959): 147–65; cf. Colin Pritchard, "Type and Eidos—Schutz and Husserl," *Journal of the British Society for Phenomenology* 15, no. 3 (1984): 307–11. From this it would follow that experience in general, hence even ostensibly theoretical experience, is conditioned or predelineated by some kind of *practical interest.*

Second, in this connection, Kant's use of the term *Typik* also merits mention, specifically the section of the *Critique of Practical Reason* titled "On the Typic of the Pure Practical Faculty of Judgment" ("Von der Typik der reinen praktischen Urteilskraft," *Akad.*, 5:67–71), where Kant addresses the problem of the sensible presentation or "hypotyposis" (see *Critique of the Power of Judgment*, §59) of moral ideals. (Note that in the *Vocabulaire technique et critique de la philosophie*, ed. André Lalande, vol. 2, 4th ed. [Paris: Félix Alcan, 1932], "Typique" referred to this section in Kant, glossing it as the "theory of the process whereby concrete acts can be subsumed under the ideas of good and evil" [*Théorie du procédé par lequel les actes concrets peuvent être subsumés sous les idées de bien et de mal* (914)].) This is analogous to the schematism (or schematic hypotyposis) of concepts dealt with in the first *Critique*, but crucially different in that in the moral sphere it is a matter of the sensible presentation of supersensible ideas of reason. Kant addresses the problem that the moral law cannot be applied directly to concrete actions by turning to a certain form of symbolism (or symbolic hypotyposis) in which the law of natural causality, purely qua law, serves the power of judgment as the "type" (*Typus*) or formal analogue of the moral law. Kant strongly contrasts the *symbolic* nature of this *Typik* of pure practical judgment with schematism, although it may be argued that it has more to do with the theoretical notion of "symbolic anthropomorphism" that Kant discusses in the *Prolegomena* than with the aesthetic notion of "symbolic hypotyposis" dealt with in the aesthetic part of the third *Critique* (see Adam Westra, *The Typic in Kant's* Critique of Practical Reason*: Moral Judgment and Symbolic Representation* [Berlin: De Gruyter, 2016]). At any rate, Merleau-Ponty's reading of Kant's theoretical philosophy is filtered largely through the third *Critique* (see Diana Coole, "The Aesthetic Realm and the Lifeworld: Kant and Merleau-Ponty," *History of Political Thought* 5, no. 3 [1984]: 503–26), such that in either case there may be a significant resonance with his discussion of "le corps comme symbolique générale du monde" (PhP 274/245) in the "Sensing" chapter of *Phénoménologie de la perception*, and this in a way that need not conflict with the idea of the body playing, in a looser and more practical sense, a schematic role in perceptual experience.

Thus, as for Merleau-Ponty's use here of the term *montage*, what is meant thereby is a set of corporeally sedimented empirical typicalities that predelineate perceptual experience structurally, or, pace Kant, that schematize it symbolically. So rather than in any more literal fashion, all viable possibilities for which (e.g., arrangement, composition, assembly, or assemblage) would be inadequate and ultimately unhelpful, I have chosen to render the term directly in terms of its immediate philosophical meaning for Merleau-Ponty as "schematic typology."

9. Reading *qui* for *que*.

10. These square brackets are in the original.

Fifth Lecture

1. Pages [55] to [72] were typewritten by Merleau-Ponty.

2. Again, Merleau-Ponty used the Anglicism "feed-back." Note that in the French edition, the term is italicized in this instance.

3. Cf. Merleau-Ponty's reference in *Recherches sur l'usage littéraire du langage*, in a discussion of Valéry, to "fixation oculaire qui a quelque chose de 'génial'" (132) ("ocular focusing about which there's something 'amazing'"). In a note there, Benedetta Zaccarello commented as follows: "L'image de l'ajustement du cristallin est très présente dans l'œuvre de Valéry, aussi bien dans des considérations à caractère psychologique (où elle vient essentiellement représenter le fonctionnement de l'attention), que dans des développements à visée esthétique, où elle renvoie notamment à la capacité de regard que Valéry reconnaît au peintre,

ou à l'artiste en général" (The image of the adjustment of the lens has a significant presence in Valéry's work, as much in his considerations of a psychological character (where it essentially comes to represent the operation of attention [as in, e.g., his *Mémoire sur l'attention*]), as in specifically aesthetic discussions, [such as, most notably, his *Introduction à la méthode de Léonard de Vinci*], where it refers especially to the capacity of looking that Valéry recognized in the painter or the artist in general).

4. Valéry, *Degas, Danse, Dessin,* 138 (see note 6 in lecture 4).

5. See Henri Piéron, *Psychologie expérimentale* (Paris: Armand Colin, 1927), 125–26; *Principles of Experimental Psychology,* trans. James Burt Miner (London: Routledge, 1999), 106, with the accompanying figure on 107: "When objects are at a short distance, and one which may be perceived by the degree of convergence of the eyes, we appreciate the size of the object as of the dimension which corresponds to the angular size of the retinal image projected to the distance of the plane on which the eyes are fixed through their convergence (Law of Giraud-Teulon). This estimation is such that, if the ocular convergence is artificially increased or diminished, this is enough to change the apparent size of the objects and to produce experimentally a micropia or macropia. In a similar way, people in a drawing take on the size which corresponds to their apparent distance."

6. The sentence starting with "Lateral interdependence . . ." was added by hand.

Sixth Lecture

1. Henri Bergson, *Matière et mémoire* (Paris: Félix Alcan, 1896), 210; *Matter and Memory,* trans. Nancy Margaret Paul and William Scott Palmer (London: Allen and Unwin; New York: Macmillan, 1911), 249; (repr., New York: Zone Books, 1991), 190.

2. Bergson, *Matière et mémoire,* 212, 210; *Matter and Memory* (1911), 251, 249; (1991), 192, 190. (Note that Paul and Palmer rendered *compacte* as "whole.")

3. Bergson, *Matière et mémoire,* 213 ("le mouvement immédiatement perçu est un fait très clair"); *Matter and Memory* (1911), 253; (1991), 192–93.

4. Bergson, *Matière et mémoire,* 210 ("un mouvement simple, comme le trajet de ma main quand elle se déplace de A en B"); *Matter and Memory* (1911), 249; (1991), 190.

5. Concerning the expression "machine for living," Merleau-Ponty almost certainly had Paul Valéry in mind—see, e.g., Valéry's Sir Basil Zaharoff lecture (Oxford, March 1, 1939), "Poésie et pensée abstraite," published by the Clarendon Press in 1939, reprinted in *Variété V* (Paris: Gallimard, 1944) and then in

Œuvres, tome I, ed. J. Hytier (Paris: Gallimard, 1957), to which Merleau-Ponty referred explicitly in the companion course from the same year (*Recherches sur l'usage littéraire du langage*, 123): "J'étais sorti de chez moi pour me délasser, par la marche et les regards variés qu'elle entraîne, de quelque besogne ennuyeuse. Comme je suivais la rue que j'habite, je fus tout à coup *saisi* par un rythme qui s'imposait à moi, et qui me donna bientôt l'impression d'un fonctionnement étranger. Comme si quelqu'un se servait de ma *machine à vivre*. Un autre rythme vint alors doubler le premier et se combiner avec lui; et il s'établit je ne sais quelles relations *transversales* entre ces deux lois . . . Ceci combinait le mouvement de mes jambes marchantes et je ne sais quel chant que je murmurais, ou plutôt qui se murmurait au *moyen de moi*" (*Œuvres, tome I*, 1322) ("I had left my house to relax from some tedious piece of work by walking and by a consequent change of scene. As I went along the street where I live, I was suddenly *gripped* by a rhythm which took possession of me and soon gave me the impression of some force outside myself. It was as though someone else were making use of my *machine for living*. Then another rhythm overtook and combined with the first, and certain strange *transversal* relations were set up between these two principles . . . They combined the movement of my walking legs and some kind of song I was murmuring, or rather which was being murmured *through me*" ["Poetry and Abstract Thought," in *The Art of Poetry*, trans. Denise Folliot (Princeton, N.J.: Princeton University Press, 1958), 61; translation modified]). In the same text (*Œuvres, tome I*, 1337) Valéry also claimed that a poem is "une sorte de machine à produire l'état poétique au moyen des mots" (a kind of machine for producing the poetic state of mind by means of words), a point that echoed an earlier claim made in his 1926 text "Les deux vertus d'un livre" (*Œuvres, tome II*, 1249), that a book is ideally "*a reading machine*" ("un beau livre est sur toute chose une parfaite *machine à lire*"). Valéry also used the expression *machine à vivre* in "La politique de l'esprit: Notre soverain bien" (*Œuvres, tome I*, 1027), and in "Philosophie de la danse" (*Œuvres, tome I*, 1392).

With his many machinic references, Valéry may well have been echoing Charles-Édouard Jeanneret (Le Corbusier), in particular his well-known claim that "une maison est une machine à habiter" (a house is a machine for living in)—see, e.g., *Vers une architecture* (Paris: Georges Crès, 1923); *Toward an Architecture*, trans. John Goodman (Los Angeles: Getty Research Institute, 2007), 87, 160. It is interesting to note that in discussing in some detail the relations between Valéry and Le Corbusier, especially the influence of Valéry's philosophical-architectural dialogue *Eupalinos* (1923) on Le Corbusier, Niklas Maak reported that in acknowledging reception of a copy of *Vers une architecture*, Valéry wrote to Le Corbusier that "I have often dreamt of a house in which the structure and all the qualities are those of a modern machine" (*Le Corbusier: The Architect on the Beach* [Munich: Hirmer, 2011], 128).

But the expression "machine for living" may have other sources as well. Tolstoy, e.g., used it in a well-known passage from *War and Peace*, the key parts of which were, it is worth noting, *written in French in the original* (underlined here): "Rapp répondit qu'il avait pris lui-même les mesures nécessaires à cet effet, mais Napoléon secoua la tête d'un air mécontent: il semblait douter que ce dernier ordre eût été exécuté. Un valet de chambre apporta du punch, Napoléon en fit donner un verre à son aide de camp; tout en le dégustant à petites gorgées. 'Je n'ai ni goût ni odorat,' dit-il; 'ce rhume est insupportable, et l'on me vante la médecine et les médecins, lorsqu'ils ne peuvent pas même me guérir d'un rhume! Corvisart m'a donné ces pastilles, et elles ne me font aucun bien! Ils ne savent rien traiter et ne le sauront jamais. Notre corps est une machine à vivre. Il est organisé pour cela, c'est sa nature; laissez-y la vie à son aise, qu'elle s'y défende elle-même: elle fera plus que si vous la paralysez en l'encombrant de remèdes. Notre corps est comme une montre parfaite, qui doit aller un certain temps: l'horloger n'a pas la faculté de l'ouvrir; il ne peut la manier qu'à tâtons et les yeux bandés. Notre corps est une machine à vivre, voilà tout!'" (*La guerre et la paix, traduit avec l'autorisation de l'auteur par une Russe*, vol. 3 [Paris: Hachette, 1885], 38–39) ("Rapp answered that he had given the Emperor's orders about the rice; but Napoleon shook his head with a dissatisfied air, as though he doubted whether his command had been carried out. A servant came in with punch. Napoleon ordered another glass for Rapp, and took a few sips from his own in silence. 'I have neither taste nor smell,' he said, sniffing at the glass. 'I am sick of this cold. They talk about medicine. What is medicine, when they can't cure a cold? Corvisart gave me these lozenges, but they do no good. What can they cure? They can't cure anything. Our body is a machine for living. It is organized for that, it is its nature; leave life to it unhindered, let life defend itself in it; it will do more than if you paralyze it, encumbering it with remedies. Our body is a perfect watch, meant to go for a certain time; the watchmaker does not have the ability to open it, he can only handle it in a fumbling and blindfolded way. Our body is a machine for living, that's all'" [Leo Tolstoy, *War and Peace*, trans. Constance Garnett (New York: Modern Library, 1931), 735; translation from French modified]).

6. The reference is of course to Gelb and Goldstein's case of Schn. (Schneider), originally discussed in their work "Psychologische Analysen hirnpathologischer Fälle auf Grund von Untersuchungen Hirnverletzer," *Zeitschrift für die gesamte Neurologie und Psychiatrie* 41 (1918): 1–142; see also PhP 159/138, and *La structure du comportement*, 78 (*The Structure of Behavior*, 71). This patient was the subject of numerous follow-up studies, by Gelb and Goldstein, as well as by other collaborators. The idea of *das Simultan-Überschauen* stems from Wilhelm Benary's study of the case in "Studien zur Untersuchung der Intelligenz bei einem Fall von Seelenblindheit," *Psychologische Forschung* 2 (1922): 209–97: "Wo im Denken das Simultan-Überschauen einer gegliederten Struktur unbedingt erforderlich wird, da scheint das Denken geschädigt; nur wo durch schrittweises Vorwärtsschreiten von einem Denkschritt zum nächsten die Aufgabe lösbar ist, kommt der Patient zu adäquater Leistung, und hier sehr wohl von dem bei solchen Operationen *sinnvoll* Möglichen" (293) (Thought appears impaired where the simultaneous survey of an articulated structure becomes absolutely necessary; the patient can perform adequately only where the task can be solved by progressing stepwise from one thought to the next, and this most definitely with what is *meaningfully* possible for such operations). Note that the term *überschauen* also has the sense of "command" and that in *Phénoménologie de la perception*, e.g., Merleau-Ponty typically translated its verbal form as *dominer*.

7. See Wertheimer, "Experimentelle Studien" ("Experimental Studies"), §§9, 7, respectively.

8. Here Merleau-Ponty later added a line in the margin, in black ink, with the note "(1956)."

9. Here too Merleau-Ponty later added a line in the margin, in black ink, with the note "(1956)."

10. The French editors did not include the transcription of the remainder of this page or of the following page, which give a preliminary presentation of some experiments conducted by, respectively, Max Wertheimer and Joseph Ternus. Merleau-Ponty clearly abandoned this discussion (it breaks off midsentence) but took it up again more fully between pages [66] and [69] of the seventh lecture.

Seventh Lecture

1. On some of the historical nuances of the term *eidôla*, see Gerard Simon's entry under "eidolon" in *Vocabulaire européen des philosophies* (*Dictionary of Untranslatables*). The term can also carry the sense of an idolic or phantasmic apparition.

2. Reading *à* for *a*.

3. See Edgar Rubin, "Visuell wahrgenommene wirkliche Bewegung," *Zeitschrift für Psychologie* 103 (1927): 384–92. This was a talk given at the Kongreß für experimentelle Psychologie (Bonn, April 1927) in which Rubin discussed primarily the perception of the motion of wheels as involving translational, rotational, and cycloidal movements, depending upon points of reference. Koffka referred to this discussion in his *Principles of Gestalt Psychology*, (New York: Harcourt, Brace, 1935), 283–84, and this may have been how Merleau-Ponty learned of this source. But Koffka did not refer to the "experiment" to which Merleau-Ponty alludes here, which in any case Rubin introduced more as a preliminary thought experiment: "Man denke sich, daß man einen großen weißen Schirm mit einem kleinen Loch in der Mitte vor sich habe, und daß dahinter sich ein Stück schwarzen Kartons befindet. Wird nun das Kartonstück etwas hin und her bewegt, dann sieht man in dem Loch keine Bewegung. Die vorbeipassierenden Punkte des schwarzen Kartons geben ganz gleiche Reize, und diese Reize geben absolut keinen Anlaß eine Bewegung zu erleben. Wird nun der Schirm fortgenommen, dann sieht man—selbstverständlich—daß der ganze Karton eine einheitliche Bewegung hin und her ausführt, also auch die mittleren Teile von denen keine Bewegungsreize ausgehen. Wir haben was diese mittleren Teile betrifft ein Beispiel der Sachlage, daß die erlebte Bewegung nicht reizbedingt sondern ganzheitbedingt ist. Diese Sachlage, die in dem Figur-Grundkomplex hineingehört, hat, glaube ich, in verschiedener Hinsicht große theoretische Bedeutung" (385–86) (Imagine that in front of you there is a large white screen with a small hole in the middle, and that behind it there is a piece of black cardboard. If the piece of cardboard starts to move back and forth, then no movement is seen in the hole. The stimuli yielded by the passing points of the black cardboard are completely

the same, and they offer absolutely no occasion to experience movement. Now, if the screen is removed, then one sees—self-evidently—that the whole piece of cardboard carries out a single movement back and forth, hence also the middle parts from which no movement-stimuli emanate. These middle parts exemplify the fact that experienced movement is conditioned, not by stimuli, but by the totality. I believe that this fact, which belongs to the figure-ground complex, has in several respects major theoretical significance). Following this, there is no explicit mention of any "screen" (*Schirm*), nor did Rubin discuss a "screen effect" here. In *La perception de la causalité* (Louvain: Éditions de l'Institut Supérieur de Philosophie; Paris: Vrin, 1946), however, Albert Michotte presented a similar experiment that, along with nonspecific reference to Rubin's work (among that of others) on the figure-background structure of perception (Rubin's principal work was *Visuell wahrgenommene Figuren: Studien in psychologischer Analyse* [Berlin: Boghandel, 1921]), he discussed in these terms: "The Screen Effect is a phenomenal datum *sui generis* . . . and its simplest form is clearly that which occurs when we distinguish between figure and ground in such a way that the figure is seen to be situated in front of the ground and seems to cover it. The experimental conditions in the Screen Effect give rise to the formation of a structural organisation in the third dimension, in the sense that the screen appears to be placed in front of the background against which it stands out, or in front of the object over which it slides, or which slides behind it" (*The Perception of Causality*, trans. Tim R. Miles and Elaine Miles [London: Methuen, 1963], 301; see also 290–92). Although he had no published text devoted specifically to the "screen effect," it may be noted as indicative that at the annual Congress of the British Psychological Society in April 1947, "Michotte a fait une conférence très remarquée, avec plusieurs séries de démonstrations, sur l'Effet Ecran et sur la perception de la causalité" ("Michotte gave a high-profile talk, with many series of demonstrations, on the Screen Effect and the perception of causality")—see the (unsigned) "Chronique générale" in *Revue philosophique de Louvain* 45, no. 6 (1947): 293.

4. Here Merleau-Ponty will refer to Wertheimer's "Experimentelle Studien" ("Experimental Studies"), in particular Wertheimer's central claim to have discovered the phi phenomenon; i.e., the phenomenon of "pure movement" or apparent movement without an object. The main idea of the experimentation was as follows (but note that Wertheimer varied the experimental conditions in numerous ways): Using a tachistoscope, Wertheimer presented subjects successively with two displaced visual projections (*a* and *b*) of a simple figure or line, and he varied the time interval (or switching speed) between them. With a longer time interval (i.e., lower switching speed), the experience was of the succession (or successivity) of *a* and *b*, with a shorter interval (i.e., higher switching speed) the experience was of the simultaneity of *a* and *b*, while with intermediate intervals or switching speeds subjects experienced movement—merely *apparent* movement, though, in the sense that no visual stimulus actually moved. At a certain interval or switching speed subjects reported the experience of *a single object* (i.e., *a* and *b* are identified) moving from the initial to the second position, which Wertheimer termed "optimal," or beta, movement, and which resembles real movement (but

it is of course merely apparent). At other intervals or switching speeds there was the experience of "dual" or "partial" movement, where *a* and *b* remained distinct and each was seen to move partially, while with much shorter intervals (i.e., at switching speeds much closer to simultaneity than to those producing optimal movement) subjects reported the experience of *a* and *b* as distinct and stationary (but typically flickering), *and yet there also being some sort of movement in the space between them*—this is what Wertheimer called "pure," or phi, movement. As he put it (§16): "Diese Fälle zeigten sich so, daß auch nicht etwa der Gedanke vorhanden war: ein Objekt habe sich hinüberbewegt; was von Objekten vorhanden war, war in den zwei Lagen gegeben; nicht eines oder eines von ihnen oder ein ähnliches betraf die Bewegung; sondern zwischen ihnen war Bewegung gegeben; nicht eine Objektbewegung. Auch nicht: das Objekt bewegt sich hinüber, ich sehe es nur nicht. Sondern es war einfach Bewegung da; nicht auf ein Objekt bezüglich" (223) ("In these cases there was not even a thought that an object had moved across the field. Whatever of the objects was there was seen in the two extreme positions only. Neither one nor the other nor anything else had anything to do with the motion. Rather, motion was given between them—but not motion of an object. It was not even that the object moves across, only I don't see it. Rather, only motion was there, unrelated to any object" [54]).

5. Note that Merleau-Ponty omitted the word *nicht* (not) from this quotation, although it does not appear to involve a misunderstanding. The original line reads as follows: "Die eventuelle Statuierung, es sei in *b* das Identische gegeben, fließt nicht direkt aus dem Erlebnis" ("Experimentelle Studien," 187) ("The eventual conclusion that *a* and *b* are identical does not flow directly from perceptual experience" ["Experimental Studies," 24]).

6. Merleau-Ponty is referring to Wertheimer's discussion ("Experimentelle Studien," 224; "Experimental Studies," 54–55) of an experimental setup in which *a* and *b* are white "strips" that exhibit optimal rotational movement across a ninety-degree angle, and where *c* is a shorter white strip positioned, as shown in the diagram, in such a way as to study the experience of the intermediate positions of the movement; e.g., whether *c* is "completed" by the rotational passage of the longer strip from *a* to *b*, even by a momentary "shimmer" between *c* and the vertex—as Merleau-Ponty notes, Wertheimer answered negatively, claiming there is just a pure "passage across" (*'Hinüber'*).

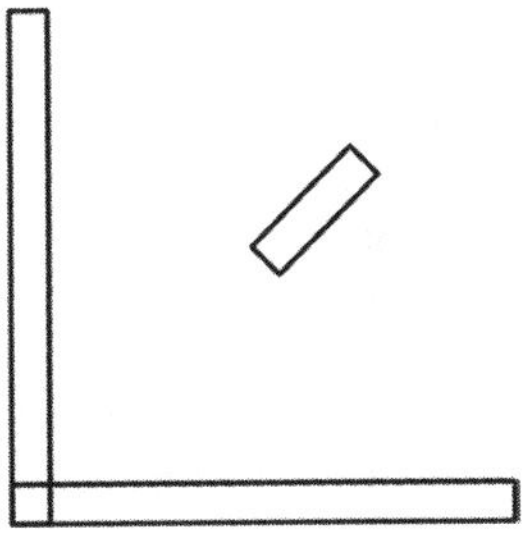

7. I.e., as if the apparent movement passed behind the object and came out the other side (see "Experimentelle Studien," 224–25; "Experimental Studies," 55).

8. See Wertheimer: "Man kann ähnliches in einem einfachen Experiment beobachten: auf einem Blatt Papier, auf das Buchstaben (einer oder mehrere) gedruckt sind, wird ein (vertikal liegender) Bleistift horizontal von einer Stelle links nach einer rechts bewegt; über einen mittleren Buchstaben hinweg z. B. 10 cm

(in bequemer Sehweite) weit; einmal, mehrmals; oder hin und her; man fixiert den Buchstaben in der Mitte. Wird der Bleistift rasch hinüber (oder hinüber und herüber) bewegt, so sieht man nichts von Zwischenlagen; über dem fixierten Buchstaben wird er nicht gesehen, er geht als solcher nicht über ihn weg, auch sonst, zwischen Anfangs- und Endlage, ist der Bleistift und seine Farbe nicht dagewesen, d. h. nicht im geringsten gesehen worden trotzdem ist nicht bloß die Sukzession der gesehenen Anfangsund der gesehenen Endlage da, sondern die Bewegung . . . bei langsamer Bewegung tritt aber oft das Charakteristische ein: war es so, daß man ihn wirklich in allen Lagen im kontinuierlichen Nacheinander gesehen zu haben glaubt, dann ist der charakteristische Eindruck der *Bewegung selbst* oft weg—das Paradoxe tritt ein, daß, sofern das Raumzeitfolgende der Zwischenlagen psychisch wirklich da ist, die Bewegung selbst sehr oft nur als bloß Erschlossenes, als bloßes Wissen hinzutritt" ("Experimentelle Studien," 228–29) ("One can make similar observations in a simple experiment: at a comfortable distance, hold a pencil vertically to one or more letters printed on a sheet of paper, and move the pencil 10 cm horizontally across a centrally located letter, once, several times, or back and forth, while fixating on the letter in the middle. If the pencil goes across (or back and forth) quickly, one sees nothing of intermediate positions. The pencil is not seen above the fixated letter; it does not go over it as such. Indeed, between the initial and final positions, the pencil and its color are not there, that is, are not seen in the slightest. Nevertheless, it is not only the succession of the seen initial and final positions that is there, but also the motion . . . But if the motion is slow enough that one believes that one has seen the pencil in all the intermediate positions in continuous succession, then the characteristic impression of *the motion itself* is often gone. So long as the spatiotemporally successive intermediate positions are psychologically really there, then, paradoxically, motion itself is often no more than a mere inference, a mere awareness" ["Experimental Studies," 58–59]).

9. This parenthesis does not close.

10. See Wertheimer: "Man könnte auch den apriorischen Satz heranziehen, Bewegung sei nicht denkbar, ohne daß sich ein Gegenstand, Objekt, Sehding bewegt" ("Experimentelle Studien," 221) ("One could also invoke the a priori proposition that motion is inconceivable without a thing, an object, [or] a visual item that moves" ["Experimental Studies," 52; translation modified]).

11. See Wertheimer: "Es sind psychische Phänomene [which in a footnote at this point Wertheimer glossed as "spezifischen, beobachtbar Gegebenen" (specific observable givens)], die in solcher Weise wie gegebene sinnliche Form-, Farbeninhalte gegenständlich gerichtet sind, objektivisch, nicht subjektivisch erscheinen; im Gegensatze zu anderen psychischen Gegebenheiten sind sie nicht statischer, sondern dynamischer Natur; in dem spezifisch charakterisierten „Hinüber" usw. haben sie ihr psychologisches Fleisch und Blut, nicht zusammensetzbar aus dem der üblichen optischen Inhalte" ("Experimentelle Studien," 227); "Es ist kein innerer Grund dafür vorhanden, psychologisch „dynamisches" a priori auf „statisches" zurückführen zu müssen" (245) ("These psychological phenomena are specific, observable givens. They appear to be inherent: not subjective, but just as objective as sensations of form and color. However, by contrast

with other psychological givens, their nature is not static, but dynamic. Their psychological reality, their flesh and blood, as it were, lies in the 'passage across' specifically described above, which cannot be built up out of the ordinary optical properties" ["Experimental Studies," 57–58]; "There is no fundamental reason a priori to assume that the psychologically 'dynamic' arises from the 'static'" [73]).

12. Josef Ternus, "Experimentelle Untersuchungen über phänomenale Identität," *Psychologische Forschung* 7 (1926): 81–136; translated in abridged form as "The Problem of Phenomenal Identity," in *A Sourcebook of Gestalt Psychology*, ed. Willis D. Ellis (New York: Harcourt, Brace, 1939), 149–60. The specific experiment Merleau-Ponty considers here is discussed by Ternus on page 93 of "Experimentelle Untersuchungen" ("The Problem of Phenomenal Identity," 152, but the specific arrangement is omitted), and he may also have referred to Koffka's commentary on it in *Principles of Gestalt Psychology*, 299–300. For Ternus, the point of this and other stroboscopic experiments was to corroborate the following thesis: "Phänomenale Identität bestimmt sich . . . in Hinsicht auf Gestaltidentität, auf phänomenale Identitätsverbundenheit gestalthomologer Teile; phänomenale Identiät bestimmt sich vorzugsweise vom Ganzen her, nicht von stückhaften Verhältnissen" ("Experimentelle Untersuchungen," 101) ("Phenomenal identity is a function of Gestalt-identity, of the phenomenal binding [or 'fusion'] of Gestalt-homologous parts; phenomenal identity is primarily determined by wholes, not by piecewise relationships" ["The Problem of Phenomenal Identity," 154; translation modified]). It does this by illustrating differences with regard to the "retention" and "exchange" of the identity (*Identitätserhaltung* and *Identitätsvertauschung*) of the points that are exposed successively in two sets of six (first the six on the left, then the six on the right—the middle three points are thus always visible) when their configuration is slightly altered. In B, where the nine point locations form a smooth arc, one sees the visible six points as a curved line moving back and forth (hence identity exchange occurs between the middle three points and the other sets of three), while in A, where the nine point locations form three straight segments at supplementary angles, one sees a stationary bar (the middle three points, hence identity retention) with an angled arm jumping from one side to the other (hence identity exchange but now oriented differently, in that the leftmost point exchanges with the rightmost, rather than the leftmost, and similarly the second (and third) from the left with the second (and third) from the right. Note that Ternus presented the case of the smooth arc first (followed by a variety of variations), and Koffka, who considered only this single variation, did likewise (*Principles of Gestalt Psychology*, 300), labeling the smooth arc A and the segmented case B (Merleau-Ponty reversed this labeling), and note that Koffka also labeled the individual points (something Ternus did not do).

13. I.e., the binding together of the sliding arc—first from these six points, then from those six points—as a "Gestalt-homologous part," and the fact that the always visible middle three points do not themselves form such a part. Note the term "fusion" (*fusion*) is likely drawn from Koffka's discussion of the experiment.

14. I.e., in this case the always visible middle three points do "fuse" to form a "Gestalt-homologous part."

15. Merleau-Ponty is presumably referring to a similar experimental setup

using a cross (specifically a quincunx) figure (see Ternus, "Experimentelle Untersuchungen," 88).

16. This reference is to Karl Duncker, "Über induzierte Bewegung: Ein Beitrag zur Theorie optisch wahrgenommener Bewegung," *Psychologische Forschung* 12 (1929): 180–259; translated in abridged form as "Induced Motion," in Ellis, *A Sourcebook of Gestalt Psychology*, 161–72. The stroboscopic experiment that Merleau-Ponty discusses here (see "Über induzierte Bewegung," 224–25; "Induced Motion," 167) was one among many experiments that supported Duncker's claim ("Induced Motion," 170) that "phenomenal motion is displacement in a natural frame of reference" ("phänomenale Bewegung ist Verschiebung im natürlichen Bezugssystem" ["Über induzierte Bewegung," 246]). Merleau-Ponty probably referred to Koffka's discussion of the experiment (*Principles of Gestalt Psychology*, 287–88), the upshot of which Koffka glossed as follows: "Under special conditions an enclosing object in stroboscopic displacement may appear practically stationary while the enclosed one, successively exposed in the same place, carries the entire motion" (287), and which was taken by Koffka as "a demonstration that real and stroboscopic motion are essentially alike" (288). To be clear, though, according to Duncker what is typically perceived in cases like this is that the rectangle does move stroboscopically, *but that the objectively stationary point also appears to move*: "Der fixierte Punkt und das Rechteck bewegen sich nach entgegengesetzten Seiten" (The stationary point and the rectangle move in opposite directions ["Über induzierte Bewegung," 225; cf. "Induced Motion," 167]). Note that Merleau-Ponty's first illustration (on the left) directly resembles Koffka's (whereas Duncker's illustration overlaid the two rectangles) but that Merleau-Ponty's second illustration (on the right) would appear to be his own.

17. Reading *à* for *a* (*à raison des propriétés structurales*).

18. These outer square brackets were added (by hand) by Merleau-Ponty.

19. It is not perfectly clear what illusion Merleau-Ponty is referring to here. He may simply be referring to the optical illusion that he is about to illustrate—note that in the quote drawn from Koffka (see below), Merleau-Ponty's "these figures" (*ces figures*) glosses Koffka's "Figuren wie die Kreisringsektoren" (figures such as the circular ring segments), which could thus be the referent of Merleau-Ponty's "rings" (*anneaux*). But there are other conceivable answers to the question—e.g., an experiment designed by Adhémar Gelb and discussed by Koffka (*Principles of Gestalt Psychology*, 205) (see Adhémar Gelb, "Grundfragen der Wahrnehmungspsychologie," in *Bericht über den VII. Kongreß für experimentelle Psychologie*, ed. Karl Bühler [Jena: Gustav Fischer, 1921], 114–26), or the much more well-known case of the illusion variously known as the Wertheimer-Koffka Ring, the Koffka-Benussi Ring, or the Wertheimer-Benussi Ring, which Koffka also discussed in his *Principles of Gestalt Psychology* (134–36), as well as in earlier work. Neither of these, however, seem to have a direct bearing on the immediate point concerning figural field modification. Most likely, then, Merleau-Ponty's reference is to the optical illusion generally known as the Jastrow illusion (see Joseph Jastrow, "Studies from the Laboratory of Experimental Psychology of the University of Wisconsin.—II," *American Journal of Psychology* 4, no. 3 [1892]: 381–428), and which was subsequently (and separately) discussed by Franz Carl

Müller-Lyer and Wilhelm Wundt (see Franz Carl Müller-Lyer, "Optische Urteilstäuschungen," *Archiv für Physiologie* [1889 suppl.]: 263–70; Wilhelm Wundt, *Die geometrisch-optischen Täuschungen* [Leipzig: B. G. Teubner, 1898]), in which adjacent equal circular segments appear to be of different sizes (see Jastrow, "Studies from the Laboratory," 397–98). Jastrow did not name the figures, while Müller-Lyer (270) called them *Kreissegmente* or *Kreisschnitte*, and Wundt also called them *Kreissegmente* (153–54). This illusion was also discussed by Koffka (*Principles of Gestalt Psychology*, 32–33), and specifically with regard to figural field modification (and in relation to experiments conducted by Géza Révész involving, interestingly enough, the behavioral environment of chickens). Here Koffka's English rendering of his term *Kreisringsektoren* would be "segments of a circle," for which Merleau-Ponty's *anneaux* would be somewhat inapt. But in a later discussion emphasizing the field modification theme, Koffka did refer to this illusion as involving "*ring* sectors" (346; italics added). And note that he had expressly described it as "the *well-known* illusion called the Jastrow illusion" (32; italics added).

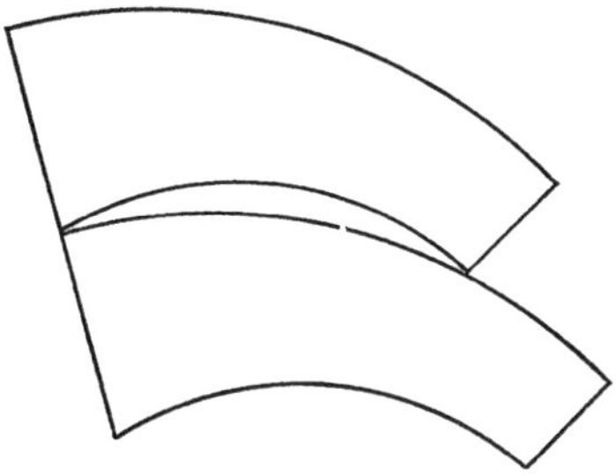

20. Merleau-Ponty is quoting from Kurt Koffka, "Die Wahrnehmung von Bewegung," in *Receptionsorgane II*, vol. 12/2 of *Handbuch der normalen und pathologischen Physiologie, mit Berücksichtigung der experimentellen Pharmakologie*, ed. Albrecht Bethe, Gustav von Bergmann, Gustav Embden, and Alexander Ellinger (Berlin: Springer, 1931), 1182: "Figuren wie die Kreisringsektoren beeinflussen das sie umgebende Feld in einer Weise, die sich dynamisch in der bestimmten Form der Bewegung, statisch in der Form der optischen Täuschung offenbart." Note that Koffka used the term *Form* in both cases, whereas Merleau-Ponty used *forme* and then *allure.*

21. Discussed by Koffka in "Die Wahrnehmung von Bewegung," 1182, with reference to Friedrich Kenkel, "Untersuchungen über den Zusammenhang zwischen Erscheinungsgrösse und Erscheinungsbewegung bei einer sogenannten optischen Täuschungen," *Zeitschrift für Psychologie* 67 (1913): 358–449, although Koffka disagreed with Kenkel's interpretation.

22. A stroboscopic experiment originally designed by Paul Ferdinand Linke in which a point is shown successively in four positions, first in the upper left, then in the lower middle, then in the upper right, and finally again in the lower middle. With no other figure visible, the point is perceived to jump between successive positions in a straight zigzag movement. If, however, a semicircle with its concave side facing upward is presented around each of the points, then the path of the movement is distinctly perceived to follow the perimeter of the semicircle like a ball rolling in a gutter, something Linke accounted for in terms of prior experience; see "Die stroboskopischen Täuschungen und das Problem des Sehens von Bewegungen," *Psychologische Studien* 3, no. 5/6 (1907): 393–545 (the setup is described on page 524).

23. A modification by Koffka of Linke's experiment in which the semi-

circles are inverted so that their concave sides are facing downward. Koffka found that the movement still tended to follow the perimeter, even though this "contradicts all experience" ("Auch jetzt folgte die Bewegung dem Bogen, was aber aller Erfahrung widerspricht"). With regard to the perception of movement, then, contra Linke this affirmed the greater relative importance of the structure of the perceptual field over past experience; see Koffka, "Die Wahrnehmung von Bewegung," 1185–87.

24. An allusion to Michotte, *La perception de la causalité*. Translations of the specific terms of art concerning the perception of causality that Merleau-Ponty borrows from Michotte are drawn from the Miles and Miles translation (*The Perception of Causality*).

25. Michotte's "déclenchement" or "l'effet déclenchement" (the triggering effect): "The impression that one object has 'touched off' the movement of another, the second object then appearing to move of its own accord" (*The Perception of Causality*, xvii). For Michotte, this is a variation on "launching" or "the launching effect" (see note 26): "The essential difference between the two lies in the fact that in the case of launching there is an impression that the first movement *produces* the second, while in the case of triggering there is the impression that one movement, which is otherwise clearly autonomous, *depends on* the appearance of a separate event which is its antecedent" (*The Perception of Causality*, 57–58n6). For a summary view of launching and its contrast with triggering, see pages 128–47. Note that Merleau-Ponty sometimes wrote "décl*a*nchement."

26. Michotte's "lancement" or "l'effet lancement" (the launching effect): "The impression of one object 'bumping into' another and setting it in motion" (*The Perception of Causality*, xvi; see also 20–21). This, along with "entraining" or "the entraining effect" (see note 32), are the two basic forms of perceived causality and are discussed in parts 1 and 2, respectively, of *The Perception of Causality*.

27. See *The Perception of Causality*, 58–67, for a discussion of "the approach and withdrawal effects" and how in the launching effect proper, "it is object A which completely holds the initiative" (65).

28. This effect "involves the approach of A to a static object (the 'tunnel') and then its withdrawal on the other side" (*The Perception of Causality*, 377; see also 48, 68–69).

29. See *The Perception of Causality*, 56.

30. See *The Perception of Causality*, 60: "When the movements are very slow, we see induced movements of the stationary object; it appears to go to meet the moving object or withdraw from it."

31. Michotte's "lancement au vol" (but note that Merleau-Ponty had "lancement *en* vol"): "The impression which occurs when two objects are in motion and when the first comes up and sets the second in motion once again" (*The Perception of Causality*, xvi; see also 69–72).

32. Michotte's "entraînement" or "l'effet entraînement": "The impression of one object joining another and carrying or pushing it along" (*The Perception of Causality*, xv; see also 21). Here Merleau-Ponty alludes to the "very interesting fact" that when the difference in speeds passes below a certain threshold, "the

Launching Effect gives way to the Entraining Effect . . . object A seems to *carry off* object B" (72; some italics removed).

33. Michotte described the significance of the triggering effect as being "un lancement larvé" (*La perception de la causalité,* 139), which the Miles and Miles translation renders by "a weakened form of the Launching Effect" (*The Perception of Causality,* 146), but I have modified this translation.

34. See *The Perception of Causality,* 175: "The participation by the arrow in the 'movement' of the bowstring must take place at each moment, as a result of stages which are qualitatively different; it must thus be continually renewed as the metamorphosis of the active object progresses" (italics removed). On "propulsion" and the "propulsion effect," see *The Perception of Causality,* 172–82, 385–86; see also 129n1, where Michotte says the following: "I use the term 'metamorphosis' rather than 'transformation' because the second of these has already been used in psychology with a technical meaning and might lead to misunderstandings."

35. On "launching by expulsion," see *The Perception of Causality,* 165–71.

36. On the "traction effect," which is a special case of entraining involving "the impression that one object 'pulls' another or 'tows' it behind," see *The Perception of Causality,* 160–61.

37. "The Transport Effect occurs whenever we see an object transported by any sort of vehicle . . . The movement *belongs* to the vehicle, while the transported object remains intrinsically *motionless* and seems simply to *share* in the movement of the vehicle" (134); on this, see *The Perception of Causality,* 150–58.

38. See *The Perception of Causality,* 128–32, where Michotte considers and answers in the affirmative the question as to whether the launching effect can be conceived in terms of metamorphosis understood as "change of shape" (e.g., windblown clouds), "a metamorphosis of process rather than of things." Noting a strong prima facie analogy, Michotte poses the objection that there is nothing permanent that endures through the metamorphosis. In reply to this, he raises the example of a sound: "When we sound a note of a certain pitch and gradually change it, there is the impression that it is the heard note which changes pitch." In fact, however, "the permanence, the maintenance of the identity of the note-object, does not lie in the permanence of matter in the ordinary sense of the words, but in the continuity of impression and the permanence of some characteristics common to the successive notes." Similarly, in the launching effect, "the approach-impact and withdrawal–pushing away follow one after the other without interruption, and although they differ qualitatively they have certain common [spatiotemporal] properties . . . This is what constitutes their permanent 'matter', and it is this that [Karl] Duncker and [Wolfgang] Metzger, using a term introduced by [Hermann] Minkowski, have called the common *Weltlinie* of events." Cf. *The Perception of Causality,* 16–17; Wolfgang Metzger, *Psychologie: Die Entwicklung ihrer Grundannahmen seit der Einführung des Experiments* (Leipzig: Steinkopff, 1941), 120–21: concerning cases of perceived causality, "while there is *discontinuity* as regards the individuality of the two entities, the 'Weltlinie' of their respective qualities of states, as they transfer from one bearer to the other, remain continuous." Cf. also Karl Duncker, "On Problem-Solving," trans. Lynne S. Lees,

Psychological Monographs 58, no. 5 (1945): 67: "We generally perceive as 'cause' of an event, of a singularity, another singularity which coincides spatially and above all temporally with the first. This in its turn results as 'intersection' of two uniform developments or 'world lines.'"

39. See *The Perception of Causality*, 183–200. The "caterpillar" experiment is described on pages 184–86.

40. "It is the tail in effect which provides the movement while the head seems inert; the head is pushed forward by the tail and does not actively take part in the forward movement" (*The Perception of Causality*, 187)—unlike the case of crawling, in which "the locomotor function seems to be located in the region of the 'head'; it is the head which *advances* when the animal expands, while the contraction which follows seems to consist of a simple pulling in of the tail, which merely moves nearer to the head and does not seem to be taking any part in the forwards movement" (185–86).

41. Here Merleau-Ponty picks up Michotte's fundamentally important but effectively neologistic use of the term *ampliation*, or "ampliation of movement" (*ampliation du mouvement*), which Michotte defined as follows as a way to express the underlying common basis of causal "launching" and "entraining": "un processus qui consiste en ce que le mouvement dominant de l'agent paraît s'étendre au patient, tout en demeurant distinct du changement de position que celui-ci subit de ce chef" (*La perception de la causalité*, 208); "a process which consists in the dominant movement, that of the active object, appearing to extend itself on to the passive object, while remaining distinct from the change in position which the latter undergoes in its own right" (*The Perception of Causality*, 217; cf. xv, 143, 217–28). And Michotte applied the concept of ampliation—"and indeed of *continuous ampliation*"—to auto-locomotion (194–95; italics added).

42. On the idea of an "internal flux," see *The Perception of Causality*, 197–99. Merleau-Ponty's reference to "protoplasm" may reflect Michotte's statement that the experience of auto-locomotion occurs "as though the object were made up of an infinite number of particles simultaneously performing a movement [*exécutant simultanément un mouvement*]" (197; translation modified).

43. The reference is again to Duncker, "Über induzierte Bewegung" (see note 16).

44. This list is adapted from Johannes Linschoten's discussion of Duncker's experiment in "Experimentelle Untersuchung der sog. induzierten Bewegung," *Psychologische Forschung* 24 (1952): 36–38. Note that Linschoten distinguished more clearly the different distributions of phenomenal movement (1–3) from the other conditioning factors that follow thereafter.

45. An allusion to Jacques Paliard, *Pensée implicite et perception visuelle: Ébauche d'une optique psychologique* (Paris: Presses Universitaires de France, 1949). Merleau-Ponty comments on Paliard's work at [89]–[94].

46. A reference to an illustrative analogy originally evoked by Henry Head—see note 29 in lecture 10.

47. Linschoten ("Experimentelle Untersuchung," 71) quotes the italicized phrase ("play of psychological vectors") from Wolfgang Köhler, *Gestalt Psychology: An Introduction to New Concepts in Modern Psychology* (New York: Liveright, 1947),

301. Merleau-Ponty is also referring to the "House-Car experiment" (*Haus-Auto-Versuch*) discussed by Linschoten ("Experimentelle Untersuchung," 38) bearing upon the distribution of movement (*Bewegungsverteilung*) between projected images of a house and a car, and which Linschoten analyzed in terms of "subordination," where the relation of subordination (*Subordinationsverhältnis*) could be seen as a special case of the relation between figure and background.

48. See Linschoten, "Experimentelle Untersuchung," 90.

49. See Linschoten, "Experimentelle Untersuchung," 89: "Als Prinzip beider kann die *Funktion* der Figuren im ganzen gelten, in der Lokalisation und Bewegungsverteilung zugleich und indifferenziert bestehen. In der Funktionsverteilung ist der Sinn konkretisiert, und wir erkennen ihn aus dieser Verteilung. Was also für Lokalisation und Bewegungsverteilung gilt, gilt auch für Funktionsverteilung und Sinn: sie sind zugleich gegeben im sich entwickelnden Geschehen. Keiner geht dem anderen voraus. Keiner kann Ursache des anderen sein; sie sind eben dasselbe."

50. Linschoten, "Experimentelle Untersuchung," 90. Merleau-Ponty is quoting from the following sentence: "Wenn sich nun erwiesen hat, daß das Subjekt am Zustandekommen der Bewegungsverteilung—als 'Inhalt' des Wahrnehmungsaktes—mindestens beteiligt ist, und wir durch die Abweisung der Voraussetzung einer Subjekt-Objekttrennung im Cartesianischen Sinne nicht bestimmen können, 'wo (oder wann) der trennende Schnitt zwischen beiden zu liegen kommt' [quoting Viktor von Weizsäcker, *Der Gestaltkreis*, 121], nennen wir die beide umfassende schöpferische Begegnung einen *Entwurf*" (If it has been shown that the subject is at least involved in establishing the distribution of movement as the "content" of the act of perception, and if by rejecting the presupposition of a subject-object separation in the Cartesian sense we are unable to determine "where (or when) the line of separation between the two comes to rest," we call the creative encounter that encompasses both a *project*).

51. The reference is to Karl Zietz and Heinz Werner, "Über die dynamische Struktur der Bewegung," *Zeitschrift für Psychologie* 105 (1927): 226–49. In the experiment in question, Zietz and Werner show that if perception alternates between a point and an arrow that circles around it, and if this alternation is accompanied by sounds, then the visual perception of the arrow is changed—it is seen to go farther along its path than if the perception took place in silence.

Eighth Lecture

1. On Wertheimer's phi phenomenon, see note 4 in lecture 7.

2. In addition to caterpillars and worms, Michotte also referred to frogs (see *The Perception of Causality*, 188).

3. This is probably an allusion to Kurt Lewin, but it is not perfectly clear. Merleau-Ponty is presumably alluding to Lewin's critique of perceptual associationism as based upon his research into affective and motivational factors as functions of what he termed field forces (*Feldkräfte*). This is consistent with

Merleau-Ponty's reference in *Phenomenology of Perception* (25/18, 501n6) to Lewin's "Untersuchungen zur Handlungs- und Affekt-Psychologie. I: Vorbemerkungen über die psychischen Kräfte und Energien und über die Struktur der Seele," *Psychologische Forschung* 7 (1926): 294–329 (translated in abridged form in "Will and Needs," in *A Sourcebook of Gestalt Psychology*, 283–99), although as far as Lewin is concerned, what Merleau-Ponty was actually discussing there had more to do with Lewin's "Das Problem der Willensmessung und das Grundgesetz der Assoziation. I," *Psychologische Forschung* 1 (1922): 191–302 (see Don Landes's observations in *Phenomenology of Perception*, 501n6). More important, however, that discussion in *Phenomenology of Perception* turned (26/20, 501n8) to the work of Kurt Gottschaldt (cf. Wolfgang Köhler, *Gestalt Psychology: An Introduction to New Concepts in Modern Psychology* [New York: Liveright, 1947], 189–91), in particular his two-part article "Über den Einfluss der Erfahrung auf die Wahrnehmung von Figuren, I: Die Wirkung gehäufter Einprägung von Figuren auf ihre Sichtbarkeit in umfassenden Konfigurationen," *Psychologische Forschung* 8, no. 1 (1926): 261–317, and "Über den Einfluss der Erfahrung auf die Wahrnehmung von Figuren, II: Vergleichende Untersuchungen über die Wirkung figuraler Einprägung und den Einfluss spezifischer Geschehensverläufe auf die Auffassung optischer Komplexe," *Psychologische Forschung* 12, no. 1 (1929): 1–87 (translated in abridged form as "Gestalt Factors and Repetition," in *A Sourcebook of Gestalt Psychology*, 109–22 and 123–35, respectively). And it is more precisely here, in connection with experimental figures drawn from Gottschaldt (see PhP 26/19), rather than in direct connection with Lewin, that Merleau-Ponty made the following comment: "If we wanted to introduce association through resemblance rather than simple contiguity, we would again see that in order to evoke a previous image that in fact resembles the present perception, this perception must be *patterned* [*mise en forme*] in such a way that it becomes capable of bearing this resemblance. A subject will recognize Figure 1 nearly as readily in Figure 2, where it is 'camouflaged' [«*camouflée*»], whether he has seen it 5 times or 540 times, and moreover he will never recognize it there consistently" (PhP 26/19f); see Gottschaldt's 1926 article (276) and 1929 article (72), and the former (296) for the figures, although Merleau-Ponty's second figure is somewhat simplified (cf. Köhler, *Gestalt Psychology*, 189–90, where the same figures from Gottschaldt are reproduced). At any rate, this bears directly upon the remark above, and there is clearly some degree of similarity between Figure 2 in *Phenomenology of Perception* and the above figure in Merleau-Ponty's notes, with regard to which he made no clarificatory comment. And we may note further that in the conclusion to his 1929 article (83–84) Gottschaldt did refer to Lewin's own conclusion in "Das Problem der Willensmessung und das Grundgesetz der Assoziation. II," *Psychologische Forschung* 2 (1922): 65–140: "Eine Assoziation *stellt keine bewegende Kraft* dar, die beim Eintreten des einen Erlebnisses auf die Reproduktion des andern gewöhnlich gefolgten Erlebnisses hindrängt . . . Vielmehr muß eine—z.B. auf einem Trieb oder einem willensmäßigen Akt beruhende—Tätigkeitsbereitschaft hinzukommen, wenn eine Reproduktionstendenz einsetzen soll" (138; Gottschaldt altered Lewin's italics) (An association *exhibits no motive power* that, with the occurrence of some experience, presses toward the reproduction of another experience that typically follows . . . Rather, if a reproductive tendency is to occur, a preparedness for activity must be added, e.g., one based on a drive or a will-like act). And we might also note that Ruyer, although generally critical of Gestalt approaches, alluded (without specific reference) to Lewin in discussing biological camouflage, noting that in certain fish (*Pomacanthus imperatur*) there are no false eyes or deflective marks, but rather "an arrangement of curved lines that form . . . a field oriented toward the caudal region" (see *Neofinalism*, 30).

Beyond this, Merleau-Ponty may also have had in mind Lewin's short but relatively well-known article "Kriegslandschaft," *Zeitschrift für angewandte Psychologie* 12 (1917), 440–447 ("The Landscape of War," trans. Jonathan Blower, *Art in Translation* 1, no. 2 [2009]: 199–209), where Lewin develops the idea of "the directed landscape" (*die gerichtete Landschaft*) or "the directedness of the landscape" (*das Gerichtetsein der Landschaft*) in connection with his experience serving in the German artillery. Merleau-Ponty may also have had in mind Koffka's reference to this article in *Principles of Gestalt Psychology* (43–44). (Although without direct reference to Lewin, Koffka does touch on questions of camouflage [*Principles of Gestalt Psychology*, 77, 375–76], as does, e.g., Köhler [*Gestalt Psychology*, 157–88, 186], along with several other Gestalt theorists interested in visual perception.) Note, however, that in his 1917 article Lewin does not use the term "camouflage" (*Camouflage, Tarnung*), and he draws no direct connection with camouflage in the usual narrow sense of concealment, either in artificial (military or otherwise) or natural (i.e., biological) terms but rather is concerned with the nature of and distinction between behavioral and geographical fields, and how in a war zone, e.g., objects transform from "peacetime things" to "combat things." Nevertheless, the article is often cited as being specifically concerned with camouflage. A probable early source of this misleading view is George Wilfried Hartmann's remark that even while Lewin's academic career was interrupted by his military service in World War I, he still "maintained sufficient composure to prepare a unique article on the figure ground phenomena present in the camouflaged scenery of trench warfare" (*Gestalt Psychology: A Survey of Facts and Principles* [New York: Ronald Press, 1935], 202), although Hartmann does not explicitly reference the 1917 article. Hartmann's remark is cited in later work, such as Roy R. Behrens, "Camouflage, Art and Gestalt," *North American Review* 265, no. 4 (1980): 13, while more recent work tends more accurately to recognize that the relevance to camouflage of Lewin's article lies merely in how it prefigures the later development of his field theory (see, e.g., Greer Crawley, "Strategic Scenography: Staging the Landscape of War" [PhD diss., University of Vienna, 2011], 84–85).

4. Scare quotes have been added to the terms "crawling" (*reptation*) and "gutter" (*gouttière*).

5. The reference is again to Duncker, "Über induzierte Bewegung" (see note 16 in lecture 7).

6. As above, the following list is adapted from Linschoten, "Experimentelle Untersuchung," 36–38. See note 44 in lecture 7.

7. It is not clear why Merleau-Ponty wrote "at rest" (*en repos*) here, as opposed to "in movement" (*en mouvement*), as he had written earlier at [70](VII6) and which would make better sense inasmuch as these first two points are sup-

posed to describe, respectively, the situation in which the enclosing figure, which objectively does move, is in fact seen to move, and that in which the objectively fixed point, rather than the enclosing figure, is seen to move (so-called induced movement). As it is here, both points 1 and 2 would effectively describe the latter situation.

8. Linschoten, "Experimentelle Untersuchung."

9. See note 50 in lecture 7.

10. Reading *rendue* for *rendu.*

11. Reading "Gestalt" for "gestalt."

12. Koffka, *Principles of Gestalt Psychology,* 297 (the underlined sentence is quoted in English).

13. See note 51 in lecture 7.

14. See Zietz and Werner, "Über die dynamische Struktur der Bewegung," 237 ("*Schwingbewegung*").

15. See Zietz and Werner, "Über die dynamische Struktur der Bewegung," 243: "In einem Falle wird das Trommelzeichen bei der Rotation des Pfeiles als ein „Kratzgeräusch" desselben an der hinteren Wand gehört . . . Das Trommeln vor seinem Auftauchen wurde empfunden als ein Entlangkratzen des Pfeiles an einer hinteren Wand" (In one case, the signal from the drum during the rotation of the arrow was heard as a "scraping noise" of the latter against the back wall . . . Prior to its emergence, the drumming came to be felt as a scraping of the arrow along a back wall).

16. Zietz and Werner, "Über die dynamische Struktur der Bewegung," 227.

17. Zietz and Werner, "Über die dynamische Struktur der Bewegung," 228.

18. Note that "le souffle" could be translated in a more general way as, e.g., "the displacement of air." But Merleau-Ponty seems to have the relatively specific case of wind (musical) instruments in mind (here and later at [87](IX6) and [183]). As he wrote in the course summary (*Résumés* 15/6), "Le son d'un instrument à vent porte dans sa qualité la marque du souffle qui l'engendre et du rythme organique de ce souffle, comme le prouve l'impression d'étrangeté que l'on obtient en émettant à l'envers des sons normalement enregistrés" ("The quality of the sound from a wind instrument bears the mark and the organic rhythm of the breath that produces it, as is shown by the feeling of strangeness we get when sound recorded normally is played backwards"). As a claim about wind instruments, this point may be connected in a nontrivial way to Merleau-Ponty's references to Maurice Jaubert's music in the Jean Vigo film *Zéro de conduite*—see the parenthetical comment concerning this in note 9 in lecture 9.

19. The reference is to Jean Epstein, *L'intelligence d'une machine* (Paris: Jacques Melot, 1946)—see [84](IX3)–[85](IX4).

20. The reference is to *Zéro de conduite,* a 1933 film directed by Jean Vigo (1905–1934), with a score by Maurice Jaubert (1900–1940). The film (which runs forty-four minutes with approximately sixteen minutes of music) is about a student revolt at a repressive boarding school. Shortly after its initial screening in April 1933 it was banned by the French Board of Film Control, ostensibly on the grounds of its "dénigrement de l'instruction publique" (defamation of state education) (cited in Michael Temple, *Jean Vigo* [Manchester: Manchester University

Press, 2005], 58). It was not shown publicly again in France until November 1945. Merleau-Ponty was particularly interested in a rebellious scene set in the dormitory near the end of the film, a scene that Vigo shot in slow motion, and for which Jaubert recorded music backward. Merleau-Ponty will refer to this more explicitly at [87](IX6).

21. "Abstraction de la *Gestalt*"—it is tempting to hear in this phrase, which also occurs in the note that Merleau-Ponty refers to at [183], the idiomatic expression *faire abstraction de* . . . , which generally means "to ignore" or "to disregard," and which could be rendered here as "Set Gestalt [theory] aside." Although in the sense of moving beyond Gestalt theory this is exactly what Merleau-Ponty is doing, there are a number of textual reasons to resist this temptation and to read this phrase simply as a critical observation of the how the experimental basis of Gestalt theory effectively abstracts away from the role of the body as a whole. In any case, it may be kept in mind that the reason why Merleau-Ponty is moving beyond Gestalt theory—i.e., why he would *faire abstraction* from it—is precisely because of this abstractness.

22. See [183] (147–48 in working notes).

23. Another reference to Paliard, *Pensée implicite et perception visuelle*—see [89]–[94].

Ninth Lecture

1. As earlier at [77](VIII5), this is quoted from Koffka in English.

2. There is considerable pronominal ambiguity in the latter part of this sentence: "Il n'y a pas temps par le sujet seul, il y a entre ce qu'il perçoit et lui un rapport latéral, il ne reçoit pas seulement le temps du sujet, il le lui rend, il n'est pas seulement objet pour le sujet, il participe de lui"—especially beginning with the phrase "il le lui rend," "il," "le," and "lui" could refer to "le sujet" (the subject), "ce qu'il perçoit" (what he [the subject] perceives), or "le temps" (time). It probably makes best sense when read as follows: "There is no time through the subject alone, there is a lateral relation between him and what he perceives, it [i.e., what the subject perceives] doesn't just receive time from the subject, it [i.e., what the subject perceives] gives it [i.e., time] to him [i.e., the subject], it [i.e., time] isn't just [an] object for the subject, he [i.e., the subject] partakes of it [i.e., time]." But other grammatically correct readings are possible.

3. The reference is to Jean Paulhan, "La peinture moderne ou l'espace sensible au cœur," *La table ronde* 2 (February 1948): 267–80, from which Merleau-Ponty will draw the following extended quotation.

4. Paulhan, "La peinture moderne," 277–78.

5. Epstein, *L'intelligence d'une machine*, 59; *The Intelligence of a Machine*, trans. Christophe Wall-Romana (Minneapolis: Univocal Publishing, 2014), 29; translation modified. Concerning Merleau-Ponty and Epstein, see Ken Slock, *Corps et machine: Cinéma et philosophie chez Jean Epstein et Maurice Merleau-Ponty* (Sesto San Giovanni, It.: Éditions Mimésis, 2016).

6. Note again (see note 6 in lecture 6) that the term *überschauen* also has the sense of "command," and that in *Phénoménologie de la perception*, e.g., Merleau-Ponty typically translated its verbal form as *dominer* (which is what "mastering" in the previous sentence here translates).

7. Merleau-Ponty's use of the equal sign in these notes never necessarily expresses any sort of equivalence, and that is particularly clear in this case.

8. Jean Piaget, *Les notions de mouvement et de vitesse chez l'enfant* (Paris: Presses Universitaires de France, 1946), 61; *The Child's Conception of Movement and Speed*, trans. G. E. T. Holloway and M. J. Mackenzie (New York: Basic Books, 1970), 64; translation modified.

9. The reference is to the music Maurice Jaubert produced for the slow-motion "dormitory revolt" scene near of the end of Jean Vigo's 1933 film *Zéro de conduite*. Reprising a phrase from an earlier part of the soundtrack as melody, Jaubert experimented as follows: he first recorded his orchestra playing the melody, then rerecorded it backward, transcribed *that* version and recorded the orchestra playing *it*, and then finally reversed that recording for the film itself (see François Porcile, *Maurice Jaubert: Musicien populaire ou maudit?* [Paris: Les Éditeurs Français Réunis, 1971], 206n; Claudia Gorbman, "Vigo/Jaubert," *Cine-Tracts* 1, no. 2 [1977]: 77; Claudia Gorbman, *Unheard Melodies: Narrative Film Music* [Bloomington: Indiana University Press, 1987], 138; Hannah Lewis, "'The Music Has Something to Say': The Musical Revisions of *L'Atalante* (1934)," *Journal of the American Musicological Society* 68, no. 3 [2015]: 568). As Gorbman put it, then, "the music thus underwent two electronic reversals, so that we may hear the melody make musical sense forwards. At the same time, we hear all the instrumental articulations backwards—i.e., a note's resonance will be heard *before* its attack—producing the otherworldly effect that matches the [slow-motion] visuals so well" (*Unheard Melodies*, 138). And Lewis: "The resulting melody plays from beginning to end, but with an eerie fade-in of each note instead of a precise attack" (568), a surreal quality that contributed to altering the perception of the slowed-down movements. (And it may be noteworthy that because of concrete limitations of musical recording and reproduction technology at the time, Jaubert used a reduced orchestra that featured woodwinds and brass, i.e., wind instruments [see Gorbman, "Vigo/Jaubert," 72; *Unheard Melodies*, 131; Lewis, "'The Music Has Something to Say,'" 568n36].) In illustrating his realization that playing a soundtrack backward results in "a sound that is truly 'unheard of' [*une sonorité proprement «inouïe»*], the opening [*l'attaque*] of a sound becoming its ending [*terminaison*] and vice versa," Jaubert himself discussed the same example, and this was likely Merleau-Ponty's source: "Dans *Zéro de conduite* de Jean Vigo, le compositeur [i.e., Jaubert himself] avait à accompagner un défilé nocturne d'enfants en révolte (assez fantômatique à la vérité et d'ailleurs tourné au ralenti). Désirant utiliser cette sonorité irréelle, une fois la musique nécessaire achevée il la transcrivit à reculons, la dernière mesure devenant la première et, dans cette mesure, la dernière note devenant la première. On enregistra le morceau sous cette forme qui ne rappelait que de très loin la musique initiale. En «retournant» dans le film la pellicule ainsi obtenue, on retrouvait le contour de la mélodie primitive, mais

l'«émission» en était alors intégralement inversée et empruntait tout son mystère à cette simple opération mécanique" ("La cinéma: La musique," *Esprit* 43 [1936]: 118–19) (In Jean Vigo's *Zéro de conduite,* the composer [i.e., Jaubert himself] had to accompany a nighttime procession of rebellious children (quite ghostly actually and moreover shot in slow motion). Wanting to make use of this irreal sound, once the necessary music was completed he transcribed it backward, the last bar becoming the first, and within this bar, the last note becoming the first. The piece was recorded in this form, which was only remotely reminiscent of the original music. By "reversing" the resulting recording in the film, the outline of the basic melody was recovered, but its "output" was completely turned around, and derived its entire mystery from this simple mechanical operation). It should be noted that the (unreferenced) citation of this passage in the entry on *Zéro de conduite* in Peter Morris's translation of Georges Sadoul's *Dictionnaire des films* (Paris: Seuil, 1965) (*Dictionary of Films* [Berkeley: University of California Press, 1972], 430) very misleadingly omits Jaubert's reference to the final postproduction rereversal of the recording (Morris evidently did not catch Jaubert's play on the word *retournant*)—many commentaries follow this account, thus effectively making the same error and as a result missing a crucial point, as expressed in Gorbman's astute comment as to how Jaubert's score in this scene epitomizes the film's overall message of subversive creativity: "To record a piece backwards makes chaotic non-sense of it: but to return it to its normal state via a second transformation restores it to a new order, creatively different from the original" (*Unheard Melodies,* 139). Cf. Merleau-Ponty's other references to Jaubert in "Le cinéma et la nouvelle psychologie" (SNS 101/56). Concerning the history and versions of that article, see François Albera, "Maurice Merleau-Ponty et le cinéma," *1895: Revue d'histoire du cinéma* 70 (2013): 121–53.

10. If this uncertain reading is correct, then it is presumably an allusion to Italian American film director Frank Capra (1897–1991).

11. See note 18 in lecture 8.

Tenth Lecture

1. Merleau-Ponty explicitly began lecture 10 on page [88], and then paginated pages [89] to [94] as potentially being either the last pages of the ninth lecture or the first pages of the tenth.

2. A stereoscopic photograph with the two images superimposed and printed in complementary colors, usually red and green, producing a three-dimensional effect when viewed through correspondingly colored filters over each eye.

3. Paliard, *Pensée implicite et perception visuelle.* Quotations on pages [89]–[93] are drawn from this work.

4. Here Merleau-Ponty cited the phrase "sur le monde," but this phrase does not occur on page 120 of *Pensée implicite et perception visuelle.* Merleau-Ponty

is probably referring to pages 121–22, where Paliard wrote that *la synthèse se fait sur l'objet* (122)—*the synthesis occurs on the object* (original italics)—as in the longer quotation below.

5. Albeit with slightly different (and fewer) notations, the diagram drawn here by Merleau-Ponty basically reproduces that of Paliard, *Pensée implicite et perception visuelle*, 110. Note that the *R* designates the red (*rouge*) image and the *V* designates the green (*vert*) image, while the other letters, *G* and *D*, as well as *G'* and *D'*, and *G"* and *D"*, designate the left (*gauche*) eye and the right (*droite*) eye, respectively, and track their repositioning as the observer moves further away and laterally (note that Merleau-Ponty's *G*s look like *C*s, but it is likelier that they are simply unusually drawn *Gs*). Key to the diagram are the points at which the lines *GV* and *DR*, *G'V* and *D'R*, and *G"V* and *D"R*, respectively, intersect—these are the positions where the red and green images fuse, yielding the illusion of relief, and these were labeled by Paliard *F* (*F'*, *F"*) for phantom (*fantôme*), but Merleau-Ponty did not include that notation in his diagram.

6. Paliard wrote, "Incommensurables la nature et l'entendement, la pensée et la vie?," but Merleau-Ponty wrote, "Incommensurables, la nature de l'entendement, la pensée et la vie?" I have translated the correct passage from Paliard.

7. Reading the French editors' addition of "il y a" as "Il y a," as this does begin a new sentence in Paliard's text. Note that the ellipsis here replaces the following: "Et comme il y a des servitudes, il y a aussi des triomphes; des complicités, et aussi des alliances" (And just as there are constraints, there are also accomplishments; complicities as well as alliances). For his part, Paliard may have been suggesting a greater contrast between "complicities" and "alliances" than comes across in Merleau-Ponty's excerption.

8. As noted above (see "Translator's Introduction," note 87), the pagination given by Merleau-Ponty corresponds to the 1950 edition of Schilder's *The Image and Appearance of the Human Body*.

9. "Disturbance of body schema involving the loss of ability to localize, recognize, or identify the specific parts of one's body" (John E. Mendoza, "Autotopagnosia," in *Encyclopedia of Clinical Neuropsychology*, ed. Jeffrey S. Kreutzer, John DeLuca, and Bruce Caplan (New York: Springer, 2011).

10. "Misperception of the location of a stimulus. Although it can occur in other modalities, it is most commonly elicited by tactile stimulation and is often seen in the presence of other symptoms of unilateral asomatognosia.† If a tactual stimulus is applied to the side of the body contralateral to a hemispheric lesion, the allesthetic patient may perceive the nature of the stimulus correctly but identify it as being applied to the comparable area on the opposite (unaffected) side of the body. In some instances the stimulus may be perceived as being on the same side of the body to which it was applied, but displaced significantly from the point of the actual stimulation (usually toward the midline). When present, this phenomenon likely results from post-rolandic (parietal) lesions of the right rather than the left hemisphere. More rarely it has been associated with brainstem lesions" (John E. Mendoza, "Allesthesia," in *Encyclopedia of Clinical Neuropsy-*

chology). Also referred to as alloaesthesia, alloesthesia, or allochiria. Here and at [105](XI5) Merleau-Ponty wrote it as "allo-esthésie." Cf. Schilder, IAHB 24–26.

†Asomatognosia: "Disturbance in the normal awareness of one's own body, typically characterized by one or more of the following symptoms: (1) a tendency to ignore or neglect one side of the body, (2) a failure to recognize or difficulty in identifying a specific part of the body (usually a limb or part of a limb), (3) difficulty in differentiating the right from the left side of the body, or (4) recognizing an impairment in a part of the body (anosognosia)" (John E. Mendoza, "Asomatognosia," in *Encyclopedia of Clinical Neuropsychology*).

11. Type of asomatognosia (see previous note) "characterized by denial of illness or lack of awareness of disability" (Kenneth M. Heilman, "Anosognosia," in *Encyclopedia of Clinical Neuropsychology*).

12. "Optic thinking" is Schilder's term that Merleau-Ponty translated as "pensée visuelle."

13. See Schilder, IAHB 23–24: "When, as in the so-called Japanese illusion, hands and fingers are doubly crossed and intertwined, the optic impression of hands and fingers becomes so complicated that the optic gnosia is not sufficient to disentangle the picture. We are dealing then with a relative optic agnosia concerning one's own body. Tactile and kinaesthetic helps are then necessary to start the movement of a specific finger."

14. Schilder used the term *volitional*, which Merleau-Ponty rendered as *pour la plaisir.*

15. See Schilder, IAHB 81–83.

16. See note 29.

17. The reference is to Kurt Goldstein, "Über Zeigen und Greifen," *Nervenartzt* 4 (1931): 453–66; reprinted in Goldstein, *Selected Papers/Ausgewählte Schriften*, 263–81.

18. This is probably an allusion to part of Stratton's description of the third day of his experiment ("Vision Without Inversion of the Retinal Image," 350): "It is difficult to describe my attitude of mind toward the inverted scene. Little more can be said than that there was clearly an abnormal relation between the general localization of my body and the position of the scene as a whole; but, as when looking at the landscape the day before, it was not clear which of the terms was standard and normal and which was thereby condemned. I had, however, a distinct consciousness that the feelings connected with certain positions in the visual field were by no means what they had been in the normal experience. What had been the old 'upper' position in the field was beginning to have much of the feeling formerly connected with the old 'lower' position, and vice versa. Once as I stood before the fire-place, watching the fire, an odd sensation came over me, as if I were looking at the fire out of the back of my head."

19. The references are to Henry Hécaen, "La notion de schéma corporel et ses applications en psychiatrie," *L'évolution psychiatrique* 2 (1948): 75–122.

20. "An inability to reproduce patterns or join component parts into a whole. This condition is assessed through observation of a patient completing activities such as drawing, copying, or building three-dimensional objects . . .

Impairments in processing spatial forms observed in constructional apraxia can occur in the absence of apraxia of singular motor movements" (Amy K. Byerley and Andrew S. Davis, "Constructional Apraxia," in *Encyclopedia of Clinical Neuropsychology*).

21. "A condition in which pain is perceived, but with an absence of the suffering that is normally associated with the pain experience. Individuals with pain asymbolia still identify the stimulus as painful but do not display the behavioral or affective reactions that usually accompany pain; no sense of threat and/or danger is precipitated by pain" (Stephen T. Wegener and Mathew Jacobs, "Pain Asymbolia," in *Encyclopedia of Clinical Neuropsychology*).

22. See Hécaen, "La notion de schéma corporel."

23. It is not perfectly clear what Merleau-Ponty is referring to here. Schilder cites Head's work frequently throughout IAHB, although typically without direct quotation. But he did build his introduction (11–16) around a series of quotations from Head concerning his notion of body schema, and it is likely that Merleau-Ponty's attention was directed there. See also note 29.

24. *Tastzuckungen*, or "exploratory twitchings," denotes the compensatory movements that enabled Gelb and Goldstein's patient Schn., e.g., to locate a touched point on his body with his eyes closed; cf. Schilder, IAHB 22; Goldstein, "Zeigen und Griefen," 265.

25. Schilder, IAHB 12: "One of our patients had lost his left leg some time before the appearance of the cerebral lesion which destroyed the power of recognising posture. After the amputation, as in so many similar cases, he experienced movements in a phantom foot and leg. But these ceased immediately on the occurrence of the cerebral lesion; the stroke which abolished all recognition of posture destroyed at the same time the phantom limb" (citing Henry Head and Gordon Holmes, "Sensory Disturbances from Cerebral Lesions," *Brain* 34, no. 2/3 [1911]: 187; reprinted in Henry Head, *Studies in Neurology*, 2 vols. [Oxford: Oxford University Press, 1920], 2:606). But cf. Schilder, IAHB 66: "Head reports that in one case after a cerebral operation the phantom disappeared. So far as I am aware no detailed report of this case has been given."

26. ". . . par référence à situation privilégiée, typique." A more straightforward translation of this phrase would be "through reference to [a] privileged [or] typical situation." But the standard connotation of "typical" contrasts with "privileged" and would not seem to be what Merleau-Ponty had in mind here. Rather, here *typique* is a substantive term that echoes the Kantian and Husserlian notion of *Typik*—see note 8 in lecture 4.

27. See IAHB 83, where Schilder refers to Nathaniel Ross, "The Postural Model of the Head and Face in Various Positions (Experiments on Normals)," *Journal of General Psychology* 7, no. 1 (1932): 144–62.

28. Reading *espace* for *Espace* in the initial instance.

29. See IAHB 12, where Schilder refers to Henry Head's analogy concerning the recognition of postural change: "In both cases the image, whether it be visual or motor, is not the fundamental standard against which all postural changes are to be measured. Every recognisable change enters consciousness already charged with its relation to something that has gone before, just as on

a taximeter the distance is presented to us already transformed into shillings and pence. So the final product of the tests for the appreciation of posture or passive movement rises into consciousness as a measured postural change. ¶ For this combined standard, against which all subsequent changes of posture are measured before they enter consciousness, we propose the word 'schema'" (Head and Holmes, "Sensory Disturbances from Cerebral Lesions," 187); see also Henry Head, "Sensation and the Cerebral Cortex," *Brain* 41, no. 2 (1918): 157; these passages are also found in Head's *Studies in Neurology*, 2:605 and 723, respectively. Cf. Head, *Aphasia and Kindred Disorders*, 2:488. Note, however, that Schilder wrote that with the taximeter the distance is "represented" in shillings and pence, whereas Head (and Holmes) wrote that it "presented" in that way.

30. Merleau-Ponty translated this "C'est comme un organe psychique qui se déplace dans notre corps et en voit le dehors de l'intérieur . . . Cet œil immatériel se déplace selon le point de la surface qu'il y a à observer," but I have just provided Schilder's original English.

31. As earlier (see note 23), it is not clear what, if any, particular quotation Merleau-Ponty is referring to here—note that the "(3)" would not seem to be a page reference (page 3 in Schilder's book is front matter); it may just refer to Merleau-Ponty's own previous subsection. In any case, he is likely referring in general to the series of quotations concerning Head's notion of body schema that are found in Schilder's introduction (perhaps Merleau-Ponty numbered them in his copy), where the "taximeter" reference is also found. And specifically he may be referring to the same quoted passage as the earlier allusion to "the feather and [the] annexation of instruments" (see [96]), which is on page 13 of IAHB: "It is to the existence of these 'schemata' that we owe the power of projecting our recognition of posture, movement and locality beyond the limits of our own bodies to the end of some instrument held in the hand. Without them we could not probe with a stick, nor use a spoon unless our eyes were fixed upon the plate. Anything which participates in the conscious movement of our bodies is added to the model of ourselves and becomes part of these schemata; a woman's power of localization may extend to the feather in her hat" (Head and Holmes, "Sensory Disturbances from Cerebral Lesions," 188; Head, *Studies in Neurology*, 2:606). Note that here Merleau-Ponty wrote "in Schilder," perhaps inadvertently using the English word *in* because he was reading in English, rather than, as earlier, "d'après Schilder" [97](X6).

32. See IAHB 76n1, where Schilder describes "the so-called Kohnstamm phenomenon" as follows: "When one innervates one arm against an immovable resistance and the resistance is removed suddenly, the arm starts to move in the direction of the effort, although the subject has no intention of moving the arm in this way. The arm seems to rise by itself and becomes at the same time lighter, when the hand is pushed against the resistance which is upwards to the arm. When the arm was pressing downwards against a resistance below the arm, the arm continues with a movement downwards. It does not matter in which posture the arm has been. When the arm was in the lower quadrant and is pushed against an obstacle, it will rise in the same way as when the arm was pushed against an ob-

stacle in the upper quadrant." For the original account, see Oskar Kohnstamm, "Demonstration einer katatonieartigen Erscheinung beim Gesunden (Katatonusversuch)," *Neurologisches Zentralblatt* 34 (1915): 290–91.

33. Merleau-Ponty is no doubt referring to the experiment (and a slight variation on it) that Schilder describes in IAHB 75–77, and which stems from his collaborative work with Hans Hoff on "postural persistence" (*Lagebeharrung*): "We order a subject to stretch his hands forward, so that one arm is parallel to the other. One arm is now raised in an angle of about 45 degrees above the horizontal. (One may also bring the arm 45 degrees below the horizontal plane.) Bring the arm of the subject passively to the inclined position or let the subject take this position in an active way. Either support the resting arm (R. arm) and the raised (or lowered) mobile arm (M. arm) or let the subject keep the position actively. The subject may have his eyes open or closed. After 25 seconds, the subject is ordered to close his eyes (if they were open) and to bring his M. arm into the same position as the R. arm. When the M. arm is raised, the subject does not bring his arm into the same plane as the R. arm, but the M. arm remains several centimetres higher than the R. arm. When the M. arm is lowered, the M. arm is not brought back to the horizontal line but remains several centimetres lower than the R. arm. The subject does not know that he has made a mistake and is of the opinion that both arms are at the same height. After a few seconds, the M. arm returns into the same position as the R. arm. The subjects generally do not know that they have changed the position. A registration with the kymograph shows that the disappearance of the difference does not decrease steadily but by jerks that bring the arm back into the position of the R. arm . . . [¶] The theoretical meaning of this phenomenon is that the normal position of the M. arm, after the tone has influenced it, is the position into which the tone pull would bring the arm; or the tone of the postural persistence influences the body image in the sense that it is pulled into the direction of tone. The limb, therefore, is felt in a position that is opposite to the direction of the muscular pull. Or, in a more general formulation, the postural model of the body is dependent on the pull of the tone. This formulation has considerable general importance. The phenomenon of postural persistence is a phenomenon all over the body. It is also present for every single posture of the body. We are dealing therefore with a phenomenon of general significance." See Paul Schilder and Hans Hoff, "Über Lagebeharrung," *Monatsschrift für Psychiatrie und Neurologie* 58 (1925): 257–64; "Lagebeharrung und Körperschema," *Monatsschrift für Psychiatrie und Neurologie* 61 (1926): 109–13; and "Der Verlauf der Lagebeharrung," *Monatsschrift für Psychiatrie und Neurologie* 66 (1927): 356–59.

34. Schilder, IAHB 81: "It is comparatively easy to keep the hand and fingers in any position, so long as the fingers touch each other. When the fingers do not touch and we look at our hand, there is generally some difficulty in keeping the fingers unmoved. The very moment we close our eyes we are unable to maintain the position of our fingers and abduction takes place, which is especially marked in the little finger."

35. This page forms a separate short note, written on a page torn in two, on the back of which there is a draft of a letter.

Eleventh Lecture

1. Merleau-Ponty used the word "insight" in English.

2. The French edition has the following: "un savoir que nous avons parce [*sic*] que nous sommes." If, as the editorial insertion suggests, we discount the *parce*, then the statement would simply be, "a knowledge that we have *that* we are" (italics added). However, I have disregarded the insertion and translated the transcribed words directly (with an addition for clarity): "a knowledge that we have [solely] because we are"—cf. the comment concerning "natural knowledge" at [189] (153 in working notes).

3. Schilder, IAHB 106–7: "I have before me a key which I hold in a vertical position. I produce a double vision by staring into the distance. I then touch the end of the key from above with the finger of my other hand so that I have a clear double vision of the finger. I now clearly see two fingers, both of which touch the key. After a while, the impression is imperative that these two keys are not only seen, but also touched. This impression is more vivid when the finger is removed several times and put on the key again. When the tactile impression is doubled, both optic impressions are vivid, and every finger seen is a living finger. The same doubling occurs when I inflict pain by pin-pricks to the double vision of the finger. Two pin-pricks are felt. The doubling is clearer when my interest is directed towards the object and not to my sensation."

4. This parenthesis does not close.

5. Schilder, IAHB 107: "In some subjects, touch or pain is often felt, not on one or both of the fingers seen, but at a point which lies between the two fingers. The finger would be seen at this point, if one had not produced a double vision, but had fixated the finger. The optic picture of the fingers then makes a rather unreal and ghostlike impression."

6. But note the possible ambiguity in Schilder: "One generally feels as the real finger that finger which one brings in connection with the *other* body. The finger which is connected with the body is the real and living finger" (IAHB 107; italics added).

7. Schilder, IAHB 12: "In the same way, recognition of the locality of the stimulated spot demands the reference to another 'schema'. For a patient may be able to name correctly, and indicate on a diagram or on another person's hand, the exact position of the spot touched or pricked, and yet be ignorant of the position in space of the limb upon which it lies" (quoting Head and Holmes, "Sensory Disturbances from Cerebral Lesions," 187; in Head, *Studies in Neurology*, 2:606).

8. Schilder, IAHB 12: "This faculty of localisation is evidently associated with the existence of another schema or model of the surface of our bodies" (quoting Head and Holmes, "Sensory Disturbances from Cerebral Lesions," 187; in Head, *Studies in Neurology*, 2:606). Cf. IAHB 85–87.

9. This is the same quotation as at [98](X7).

10. See Schilder, IAHB 112, in discussing Stratton's experiments: "The tactile sensations were translated into another optic world . . . The experiment I mentioned above concerning the doubling of tactile impressions when we produce a double vision and the experiments of Stratton and his successors definitively prove the influence of optic impressions on the body-image."

11. Quoting Schilder's reference (IAHB 12) to Head and Holmes's analogy. Note again (see note 29 in lecture 10) that Head and Holmes had written "presented," not "represented."

12. See note 9 in lecture 10.

13. See IAHB 40, where Schilder refers to a case of autotopagnosia discussed by Arnold Pick near the beginning of *Über Störungen der Orientierung am eigenen Körper: Arbeiten aus der deutschen psychiatrischen Universitätsklinik in Prag* (Berlin: Karger, 1908). Pick discussed similar cases in "Störung der Orientierung am eigenen Körper: Beitrag zur Lehre vom Bewußtsein des eigenen Körpers," *Psychologische Forschung* 1 (1922): 303–18.

14. Pick's account reads as follows: "Schon bei der ersten Untersuchung fällt eine eigentümliche Orientierungsstörung auf, die vorwiegend den Kopf und die Teile desselben, aber nicht selten in der gleichen Weise auch die andern Körperteile betrifft; aufgefordert, mit dem Finger das rechte Ohr zu zeigen, tut sie das sofort; als sie dasselbe bezüglich des linken Ohres tun soll, denkt sie nach, sucht auf dem Tische herum, und erst nach mehrfachen Aufforderungen fährt sie nach dem linken Ohr. Als der gleiche Versuch beim linken Auge zunächst mehrfach mangelhaft bleibt, sagt sie: 'Ich weiss nicht, ich muss es verloren haben'; nach wiederholten Aufforderungen findet sie das Auge dann sofort. Als sie die Beine zeigen soll, denkt sie eine Weile nach, dann beginnt sie, sichtlich erfreut, mit den Beinen zu zappeln und sagt: 'Da sind sie.' Aufgefordert die Hände zu zeigen, sucht sie auf dem Tisch und sagt: 'Nirgends! Um Gottes willen, ich habe sie verloren, sie müssen aber doch da sein'" (*Über Störungen der Orientierung am eigenen Körper*, 3) (With the first examination a peculiar disturbance of orientation stands out, one that pertains predominantly to the head and its parts but that also not infrequently pertains similarly to other parts of the body. Asked to point to the right ear with her finger, she did it right away; when she is supposed to do the same with regard to the left ear, she thinks, looks around on the table, and only after multiple requests does she go to the left ear. When the same attempt with the left eye initially fails several times, she says, 'I don't know, I must have lost it.' After continued requests, she finds the eye right away. When she is supposed to point to her leg, she thinks for a while, then, visibly delighted, she starts to fidget with her legs and says, 'There they are.' Asked to show her hands, she looks for them on the table and says, 'Nowhere! For heaven's sake, I've lost them, but they must be here somewhere.'). Note that Merleau-Ponty quotes the subject's statements (from Schilder) in English.

15. See IAHB 40f, where Schilder refers to a case discussed by Otto Pötzl in "Über die Herderscheinungen bei Läsion des linken unteren Scheitellappens," *Medizinische Klinik* 19 (1923): 7–11.

16. See IAHB 41. Note that Merleau-Ponty quoted Schilder's own English rendering of the passage from Pötzl, although in this case (unlike the previous) he did translate it into French. This may be because Schilder's rendering is awkward in that, in the middle of an extended direct quotation, he includes what looks like a first-person statement from the patient, but it is expressed in the third person: "But later on she performed the movements she was asked to do with the left or right hand and said, 'It came into her mind where the hand was, and that

made the paralysis pass.'" Merleau-Ponty presumably tried to fix this by translating the statement into an explicitly first-person form: "Je me suis rappelé où était ma main et cela a fait passer la paralysie" (I remembered where my hand was and that made the paralysis pass). But Pötzl's own account was entirely in the third person and did not include any sort of quoted statement at all: "Später aber führte sie die geforderten Bewegungen mit der linken oder mit der rechten Hand aus und erklärte, es sei ihr später eingefallen, wo die betreffende Hand sei, und damit sei die Lähmung von ihr gewichen" (Later, however, she carried out the requested movements with her left or right hand and stated that it had occurred to her where the relevant hand was, and with that the paralysis vanished). In fact, this is how Schilder himself cited the passage in *Das Körperschema*, 32 (it was also cited by Johannes Lange in "Agnosien und Apraxien," in *Handbuch der Neurologie*, vol. 6, ed. Oswald Bumke and Otfrid Foerster [Berlin: Springer, 1936], 867). I have thus retained Schilder's rendering of the cited phrase.

17. In connection with the previous, this sentence might be read as follows: "Character [is thus the same thing as] integration within [a] bodily situation, in [a] region of space that we inhabit, that is us or ours."

18. See [97](X6)–[98](X7), including note 25 in lecture 10.

19. "Paresthesia is a tingling or prickling sensation, often compounded by numbness, perceived in the skin or mucosa. It is described variably as pins and needles, skin crawling, electricity or a limb going dead and is familiar to most people who have sat too long with their legs crossed or fallen asleep with their arm crooked under their head. In healthy people paresthesias are usually transient, disappear quickly when the cause has been removed and cause limited discomfort. In diseases affecting the nervous system, the symptoms usually persist and may become very annoying" (Turo Nurmikko, "Paresthesia," in *Encyclopedia of Pain*, ed. Gerald F. Gebhart and Robert F. Schmidt (Berlin: Springer, 2013).

20. André Ombredane, *Études de psychologie médicale, tome II: Geste et action* (Rio de Janeiro: Atlantica Editora, 1944), 38–39. Ombredane alludes to American physician and author Silas Weir Mitchell (1829–1914), whose experience during the American Civil War led to important early work on phantom limbs (a term he is often credited with coining); see, e.g., "Phantom Limbs," *Lippincott's Magazine of Popular Literature and Science* 8 (1871): 563–69, although in this regard he is perhaps best known for his fictional account in "The Case of George Dedlow," *Atlantic Monthly* 18, no. 105 (1866): 1–11. In the passage cited here by Merleau-Ponty, Ombredane seems to be referring to an observation in Mitchell's *Injuries of Nerves and Their Consequences* (Philadelphia: Lippincott, 1872), 350: "One of my cases attempted, when riding, to pick up his bridle with the lost hand, while he struck his horse with the other, and was reminded of his mistake by being thrown" ("Un de mes clients, qui montait à cheval, s'imaginant tenir fermement la bride avec sa main amputée, se mit à frapper l'animal de la cravache qu'il tenait dans l'autre main: il fut précipité à bas et s'aperçut ainsi de son erreur" (*Des lésions des nerfs et de leurs conséquences*, trans. Albert Dastre [Paris: G. Masson, 1874], 383). Ombredane also alludes to Belgian neuropathologist Ludo van Bogaert (1897–1989)—this is a reference to van Bogaert's article "Sur la pathologie de l'image de soi (Études anatomo-cliniques)," *Annales médico-psychologiques* 92

(1934): 519–55, 744–59, to which Merleau-Ponty also referred in *Phenomenology of Perception* (173/150, 526n4). Here, Ombredane is referring to a case described by van Bogaert on pages 523–24 in which the patient, whose left arm had been amputated (leaving a stump measuring eight centimeters from the axillary fold, i.e., his armpit), was experiencing terrible phantom pain, to which the bar in question offered a sort of therapeutic solution: "Il dit avoir la sensation qu'on écrase la main et le poignet gauche, avec des lancements violents à la pointe de l'omoplate et au niveau du creux sus-claviculaire. La main-fantôme est étendue sur l'avant-bras, les doigts étendus, le pouce écarté, l'avant-bras souffre, mais cette souffrance ne peut se comparer à celle de la main, surtout au bord interne de celle-ci. Malgré nos efforts, nous ne parvenons pas à obtenir du patient qu'il plie la main-fantôme sur le poignet, et qu'il plie les doigts dans la main et appuie le pouce sur ceux-ci dans le geste de fermer le poing. On le voit tendre violemment le moignon, l'épaule, mais, dit-il, sans résultat. Nous lui demandons alors de se suspendre par le main droite à une barre fixe; des deux bras, il exécute ce mouvement, et nous dit avec étonnement qu'il sent sa main absente se fermer, les doigts plier comme s'il tenait également la barre" (He claims to have the sensation that his hand and left wrist are being crushed, with stabbing pain at the tip of the scapula and throughout the supraclavicular cavity. The phantom hand is stretched over the forearm, with fingers extended and thumb pushed aside. The forearm hurts, but this pain is nothing compared with that in the hand, especially its inner side. Despite our efforts, we cannot manage to get the patient to bend the phantom hand across his wrist and to fold his fingers into his hand and support the thumb on them in the gesture of making a fist. We see him forcibly extend the stump and support it, but, he says, to no avail. We then ask him to hang by his right arm from a horizontal bar. He carries out this movement with both arms and says to us with surprise that he feels his absent hand close and the fingers flex as if it were holding the bar as well).

21. Note that whereas here, as well as earlier at [98](X7), Merleau-Ponty wrote "*régression* organique," Schilder had used the expression "organic *repression*" (IAHB 32–33; cf. 36, 74, 292), and that in *Phenomenology of Perception* Merleau-Ponty had likewise invoked the idea in terms of *répression* or *refoulement* (PhP 92/80; cf. 98–100/85–87), with imprecise reference to Schilder's *Das Körperschema* (Berlin: Springer, 1923), along with Erich Menninger-Lerchenthal's *Das Truggebilde der eigenen Gestalt: Heautoskopie, Doppelgänger* (Berlin: Karger, 1935), and Jean Lhermitte's *L'image de notre corps* (Paris: Editions de la Nouvelle revue critique, 1939). For his part, Schilder claimed (IAHB 32n1) that together with Heinz Hartmann he had introduced the term 'organic repression', subsequent to the publication of *Das Körperschema*, in their co-authored article, "Zur Psychologie Schadelverletzter," *Archiv für Psychiatrie und Nervenkrankheiten* 75, no. 1 (1925): 287–300. If so, then the term he had in mind was most likely "*organische Hemmung*" [organic inhibition] (295), although they did link this closely to the theme of *Verdrängung*, which is how Merleau-Ponty's reference to the notion of repression in *Phenomenology of Perception* is often interpreted. The expression "organische Verdrängung" itself long predates *Das Körperschema*, and at least in a Freudian sense the term Merleau-Ponty uses here—*régression*—would seem to point more in the direction

of *Unterdrückung* (suppression)—on this, see Thamy Ayouch, "Lived Body and Fantasmatic Body: The Debate between Phenomenology and Psychoanalysis," *Journal of Theoretical and Philosophical Psychology* 28, no. 2 (2009), 341.

22. See note 10 in lecture 10.

23. See Schilder, IAHB 312–19.

24. See note 27 in lecture 12.

25. "A state of incomplete paralysis in which the patient may be able to execute part of a motor response independently" (Maryellen Romero, "Paresis," in *Encyclopedia of Clinical Neuropsychology*).

26. Schilder, IAHB 35, quoted by Merleau-Ponty in English.

27. See Schilder, IAHB: "His alloaesthesia therefore was not based upon a real transfer of sensations, but upon the loss of the appreciation of the left side, which was turned away by motor impulses over to the right side" (35). And: "There is somehow a physiological tendency in everybody to neglect the left side of the body . . . The focal non-perception of the left side of the body is therefore the exaggeration of an attitude which we normally have towards the left side of the body" (38; cf. 36).

28. Schilder, IAHB 315. This is the same subject as above.

29. Reading *inexistant* for *existant.*

30. Reading *par* for *pas* (*par mouvements automatiques*).

31. See Schilder, IAHB 76n, and note 32 in lecture 10.

32. See Schilder, IAHB 75–77.

33. See Schilder, IAHB 81–83.

Twelfth Lecture

1. There is a distinct subtractive sense to the expression *par différence* that Merleau-Ponty uses here—as in, e.g., the method of "weighing by difference"—such that it's not simply a question of there being a contrastive difference but more specifically an observable decrease or reduction.

2. It may be noted that "vigilance" was a fundamental concept for Henry Head, who used the term to refer to a certain sense of "physiological efficiency" as distinct from straightforward "excitability"—see especially *Aphasia and Kindred Disorders*, 1:479–97. "If we say that some part of the nervous system is in a state of raised excitability, we mean that it responds in the same manner to a stimulus of diminished strength. The excitability of a tissue is measured by the ease with which it can be provoked to activity by a suitable external stimulus and is therefore inversely proportional to the strength of the excitation needed to produce any recognizable sign of activity, in fact to its threshold value. But, in the phenomena [associated with vigilance], the main factor is not the diminution or increase in the strength of the stimulus which is required to evoke a reaction, but the fundamentally divergent nature of the response according to whether the [subject] is in a high or low state of vitality. At one time it is not only more prepared to receive and react to external impressions than at another, but an identical stimulus pro-

duces a different result and, during a high state of vitality, tends to evoke more or less high-grade adapted movements . . . vigilance is expressed in heightened extensor postural tone and acutely differentiated responses. This high state of physiological efficiency differs from a pure condition of raised excitability; for although the threshold value of the stimulus is not of necessity lowered, it is associated not only with an increased reaction but with highly adapted responses. These may vary profoundly according to circumstances, which are not inherent in the nature of the stimulus" (1:485–86).

3. These last clauses read as follows: "Mais le champ tactile du normal comporte une présence du corps qui va de soi, qui n'a pas à être expressivement perçue, qui la rend disponible, et qui l'ouvre à un horizon perceptif tactile." Here I am reading *le* for *la* as the direct object (it) in the penultimate clause, as the only feminine noun (*une présence*) is clearly the subject (*qui*), and presuming that the contracted direct object in the final clause has the same referent. This object is nevertheless still ambiguous, since in grammatical terms it could refer to "the tactile field," "the normal [person]," or "the body." As for the term *expressivement*, this is clearly synonymous with *expressément* (cf. [111](XII4)).

4. See Schilder, IAHB 75–76.

5. Or possibly "by its effort."

6. Quoting Schilder, IAHB 76–77. Note that Merleau-Ponty rendered this last phrase as "poussé dans la direction du tonus" (pushed into the direction of [muscular] tonicity). I have retained Schilder's "pulled" but have changed his "into" to "to."

7. See Schilder, IAHB 78.

8. See Schilder, IAHB 81.

9. See Schilder, IAHB 97.

10. See Schilder, IAHB 45–52. Much of Schilder's discussion of apraxia is drawn from or related to the work of Hugo Karl Liepmann, including *Drei Aufsätze aus dem Apraxiegebiet* (Berlin: Karger, 1908), and "Apraxie," *Ergebnisse der gesamten Medizin* 1 (1920): 516–43. This includes the threefold taxonomy that Merleau-Ponty notes. Then as now, however, these categorial distinctions are disputed and there is no consensus view. At any rate, Schilder's (possibly exaggerated) remark that "the greatest progress that has been made so far in the understanding of a human action is due to Liepmann's investigations" (50) is noteworthy. Concerning Liepmann's contributions, see Georg Goldenberg, "Apraxia and Beyond: Life and Work of Hugo Liepmann," *Cortex* 39 (2003): 509–24, and his *Apraxia: The Cognitive Side of Motor Control* (Oxford: Oxford University Press, 2013); see also J. M. S. Pearce, "Hugo Karl Liepmann and Apraxia," *Clinical Medicine: Journal of the Royal College of Physicians* 9, no. 5 (2009): 466–70.

11. A form of apraxia (sometimes called ideatory apraxia, which is how Schilder [IAHB 50] referred to it) principally characterized by "an impairment in carrying out sequences of actions requiring the use of various objects in the correct order necessary to achieve an intended purpose" (Klaus Poeck, "Ideational Apraxia," *Journal of Neurology* 230, no. 1 [1983]: 1–5). On Liepmann's conception, see Goldenberg, "Apraxia and Beyond," 518–19; *Apraxia*, 35–36; Pearce, "Hugo Karl Liepmann and Apraxia," 467–69). See also the following note.

12. Note that Schilder wrote nonspecifically "an apraxia of the motor type." Liepmann had originally called the form of apraxia in question motor apraxia but later proposed the designation "ideo-kinetic apraxia": "The kinematics of the extremities are preserved but separated, dissociated from the ideational general scheme of the movement" (*Drei Aufsätze aus dem Apraxiegebiet*, 80, cited in Goldenberg, "Apraxia and Beyond," 518). Today this is often termed ideo-motor apraxia, a label that stems from Arnold Pick. But see Goldenberg's discussion ("Apraxia and Beyond," 519–20) concerning the differences between Leipmann's and Pick's respective conceptions, and the misunderstandings that arose, in particular in the French context. Citing Joseph Morlass (*Contribution à l'étude de l'apraxie* [Paris: Amédée Legrand, 1928], 17–19): "Apraxia . . . is the incapacity to perform the gesture which the patient wants to perform. Thus (Liepmann) calls it 'motor apraxia' . . . (Pick) insisted on deficits of attention in co-ordinated actions: each of the elements of the gesture being correct, it is only their succession which is impaired. Pick called this variant of apraxia 'ideo-motor' to emphasize the role of attention. There thus emerged an important distinction between motor and ideo-motor apraxia. A number of authors, particularly [Pierre] Marie, [Henri] Claude, [Charles] Foix, [Rudolf] Brun retain this separation as the basis for their classification . . . However, in these authors' and our classification, motor apraxia becomes ideo-motor, ideo-motor apraxia becomes ideational." To be clear, then, in Liepmann's own account, "'ideational' and 'ideo-motor' were synonymous and he opposed them to 'ideo-kinetic' apraxia which was synonymous with motor apraxia'" (Goldenberg, "Apraxia and Beyond," 520). On motor apraxia, cf. also Kurt Goldstein, "Zur Lehre der motorischen Apraxie," *Journal für Psychologie und Neurologie* 11 (1908): 169–87, 270–83.

13. Liepmann called this limb-kinetic (or melokinetic) apraxia, and the term "innervatory" stems from Karl Kleist, "Kortikale (innervatorische) Apraxie," *Jahrbuch fur Psychiatrie and Neurologie* 28 (1907): 46–112; cf. Karl Kleist, *Gehirnpathologie* (Leipzig: Ambrosius Barth, 1934). This form of apraxia "is confined to the limbs . . . , mainly affects skilled actions, no matter how well-practised they are, and gives rise to clumsy, fragmented, and 'inexpert' movements . . . However, the general form of the roughly executed movement is always recognisable by the examiner as if it were a bad copy of the model movement that the patient has to imitate . . . Patients often appear to perform movements as if they were in the course of learning them for the first time" (Ennio De Renzi and Pietro Faglioni, "Apraxia," and Hans Spinnler, "Alzheimer's Disease," in *Handbook of Clinical and Experimental Neuropsychology*, ed. Gianfranco Denes and Luigi Pizzamiglio (Hove, U.K.: Psychology Press, 1999), 434 and 727, respectively). See also Gianfranco Denes, Maria Christina Mantovan, Alessandra Gallana, and Jee Yun Cappelletti, "Limb-Kinetic Apraxia," *Movement Disorders* 13 (1998): 468–76.

14. Schilder, IAHB 51, quoted in English.

15. See Head, "Aphasia and Kindred Disorders," 113–15, 121–27; cf. Schilder, IAHB 49.

16. The term *agnosie d'utilisation* stems from Morlass, *Contribution à l'étude de l'apraxie*, 54, 85.

17. It is not clear what specific work by Ajuriaguerra and Hécaen, let alone

what specific passage, if any, Merleau-Ponty is referring to here (and [120](XIII2) with regard to the same point). Nonetheless, the following passages—which are drawn from a discussion of apractognosia resulting from damage to the right parieto-occipital region—are relevant, and it is possible that Merleau-Ponty had them in mind, although he is clearly not simply relating ideas presented by the authors: "Les difficultés visuo-constructives, l'apraxie de l'habillage, l'agnosie spatiale unilatérale, bien que pouvant se manifester de manière plus ou moins isolée, ne sauraient être considerées comme des syndromes absolument indépendants. Ils sont souvent intriqués et nous paraissent représenter des aspects de la désorganisation fonctionnelle due aux lésions de la région pariéto-occipitale droite. Chacun d'entre eux peut, par son intensité, constituter un pôle symptomatique, mais très habituellement certains des éléments des deux autres syndromes peuvent être décelés dans le tableau clinique où de prime abord le premier aspect apparaissent presque pur" (*Méconnaissances et hallucinations corporelles: Intégration et désintégration de la somatognosie* [Paris: Masson, 1952], 250–51) (Although they can manifest in more or less isolated ways, visioconstructive problems, dressing apraxia, and unilateral spatial agnosia cannot be considered as absolutely independent syndromes. They are often entangled and to us seem to represent aspects of the functional disorganization that results from lesions to the right parieto-occipital region. Each of them can, by means of its intensity, form a symptomatic pole, but typically certain elements of the other two syndromes can be recognized in the clinical history where the first aspect initially appears nearly pure). And continuing along similar lines, "Aussi, continuellement oscillons-nous au cours de ces différents syndromes cliniques d'une 'figure' kinesthétique à une 'figure' visuo-spatiale, l'une et l'autre sous-tendue par la désorganisation du schema corporel, désorganisation quasi constamment présente, tantôt de manière évidente, tantôt devant être devinée sous d'autres aspects, tantôt même ne se révélant que dans un second temps. Troubles de l'espace corporeal et troubles de l'espace extérieur paraissent parfois s'opposer, parfois au contraire s'interpénétrer étroitement. Ceci ne peut être compris, croyons-nous, que si on n'envisage les données optiques et les données kinesthétiques que comme deux pôles fonctionnels. On ne saurait, comme le souligne fortement [Ludwig] Binswanger, concevoir une function spécifique de l'espace. Dans l'espace orienté, dit ce auteur, le corps constitue 'l'ici absolu' autour duquel s'organise le 'là-bas', espace extérieur . . . On ne peut qu'être d'accord avec Binswanger quand il affirme que dans l'unité structurale fonctionnelle, espace du corps-espace entourant, tout est en rapport avec tout, et que les troubles partiels amènent donc des perturbations générales; néanmoins dans le syndromes apractognosiques ici étudiés, les conduits pathologiques se concentrent de manière prévalente autour de l'un ou l'autre des pôles fonctionnels de cet espace orienté. Mais cet aspect 'prégnant' ne doit pas faire négliger le fond de désorganisation globale de l'unité fonctionnelle évoquée par Binswanger. Appréhension de l'espace, conscience du corps, ne sont pas alors des fonctions isolées, abstraites et juxtaposes, elles sont ouvertes l'une et l'autre, elles représentent des possibilités d'action pour nous-mêmes, des moyens de connaissance du monde: la dynamique du corps agissant ne pouvant s'accomplir que dans l'espace, l'espace n'étant rien pour nous sans le corps qui agit" (*Méconnaissances et hallucinations corporelles*, 251–52) (Further, over the course of these different clinical syndromes we continually oscillate between a kinesthetic 'figure' and a visiospatial 'figure,' both of which are subtended by the disorganization of the body schema—a disorganization that is practically always present, sometimes in an obvious way, sometimes needing to be figured out through other aspects, sometimes being revealed only at a later stage. Disturbances of bodily space and disturbances of external space sometimes appear to be opposed, sometimes on the contrary they appear to interpenetrate closely. This can be understood, we think, only if the optical givens and the kinesthetic givens are considered as merely two functional poles. As [Ludwig] Binswanger emphasized, a distinct spatial function is inconceivable. In oriented space, according to Binswanger, the body constitutes 'the absolute here' around which external space, the 'over there,' is organized . . . We can only agree with Binswanger when he affirms that in the functional structural unity of bodily space and surrounding space, everything is connected to everything else, and that partial problems thus lead to general disturbances. Nonetheless, in the apractognosic syndromes studied here, the pathological behaviors are predominantly concentrated around one or the other of the functional poles of this oriented space. This 'pregnant' aspect must not, however, make us overlook the ground of global disorganization of the functional unity brought up by Binswanger. Apprehension of space and consciousness of the body are therefore not isolated, abstract, juxtaposed functions, they are open to one another, they represent possibilities of action for ourselves and means of knowledge of the world: the dynamic of the acting body can be achieved only in space, and space is nothing for us without the body that acts). And, finally, in criticizing an interpretation offered by McFie, Piercy, and Zangwill of a case involving right-left confusion with regard to external space but not the patient's own body (see John McFie, Malcolm Piercy, and Oliver Zangwill, "Visual-Spatial Agnosia Associated with Lesions of the Right Cerebral Hemisphere," *Brain* 73, no. 2 [1950], 167–90, specifically Case 4): "Sur le corps, la kinesthésie joue un rôle prééminent dans cette orientation, dans l'espace extérieur les données optiques interviennent. Isoler les unes des autres, données optiques et données kinesthésiques, est impossible, elles doivent être considérées comme deux pôles fonctionnels" (*Méconnaissances et hallucinations corporelles*, 253) (On the body, kinesthesia plays a preeminent role in this [lateral] orientation, while optical givens operate in external space. It is impossible to isolate optical and kinesthetic givens from each other; they have to be considered as two functional poles).

18. "Impaired ability to organize movements in space, to remember such movements, or to analyze spatial relationships" (Ray Corsini, *The Dictionary of Psychology* [New York: Routledge, 2016], 62). See Henry Hécaen, Wilder Penfield, Claude Bertrand, and Robert Malmo, "The Syndrome of Apractognosia Due to Lesions of the Minor Cerebral Hemisphere," *Archives of Neurology and Psychiatry* 75, no. 4 (1956): 419: "The apractognosic syndrome of the minor (nondominant) hemisphere includes (1) disturbances of body scheme (anosognosia or related

phenomena); (2) apraxia for dressing; (3) visuoconstructive disabilities, and (4) unilateral spatial agnosia, disturbances of topographical relationship, and, more questionably, loss of topographical memory." On constructional apraxia, see note 20 in lecture 10.

19. Merleau-Ponty is most likely referring to Jean Lhermitte and Jean Mouzon, "Sur l'apractognosie géométrique et l'apraxie constructive consécutives aux lésions du lobe occipital," *Revue neurologique* 73 (1941), 415–31. Cf. Ajuriaguerra and Hécaen, *Méconnaissances et hallucinations corporelles*, 226–27.

20. See Lhermitte and Mouzon, "Sur l'apractognosie géométrique": "Si la malade reconnaît certains dessins, elle ne peut saisir la signification d'un ensemble. Ainsi, lorsque nous lui présentons un couple dansant, la malade reconnaît bien le jeune homme et la jeune fille, mais elle ne saisit pas leur attitude ni leur comportement" (419) (Although the patient recognizes certain drawings, she cannot grasp the signification of a whole. Thus, when we present her with a dancing couple, she certainly recognizes the young man and the young woman, but she does not grasp their stance nor their behavior).

21. Merleau-Ponty is most likely referring to Andrew Paterson and Oliver Zangwill, "Disorders of Visual Space Perception Associated with Lesions of the Right Cerebral Hemisphere," *Brain* 67, no. 4 (1944): 331–58; see also McFie, Piercy, and Zangwill, "Visual-Spatial Agnosia." But the specific case that Merleau-Ponty refers to here would not seem to correspond in all respects to either of the two cases discussed by Paterson and Zangwill and may instead refer to one studied and described by Ajuriaguerra and Hécaen (*Méconnaissances et hallucinations corporelles*, 228–35) and presented in connection with this related research by others (to which they allude on page 227).

22. "Closely related to the phenomenon of constructional apraxia, [dressing apraxia, or 'apraxia for dressing'] refers to confusion in the orientation of clothing during dressing . . . Dressing apraxia may be considered a special type of constructional apraxia associated with right-hemisphere damage that disrupts the proper assembly and orientation of one's clothing" (Daniel Hier, Philip Gorelick, and Andrea Gellin Shindler, *Topics in Behavioral Neurology and Neuropsychology: With Key References* [Stoneman, Mass.: Butterworths, 2013], 167). Cf. McFie, Piercy, and Zangwill, "Visual-Spatial Agnosia," 180: "These difficulties appeared to be due to confusions regarding top and bottom, back and front, and right and left with reference to the garments." See also W. Russell Brain, "Visual Disorientation with Special Reference to Lesions of the Right Cerebral Hemisphere," *Brain* 64 (1941): 244–72, and Henry Hécaen and Julien de Ajuriaguerra, "L'apraxie de l'habillage: Ses rapports avec la planotopokinésie et les troubles de la somatognosie," *Encéphale* 35 (1942): 113–44.

23. See Ajuriaguerra and Hécaen, *Méconnaissances et hallucinations corporelles*, 231 (Merleau-Ponty's emphasis).

24. In addition to the discussion of this illusion in IAHB, see also Elmer Klein and Paul Schilder, "The Japanese Illusion and the Postural Model of the Body," *Journal of Nervous and Mental Disease* 70, no. 3 (1929), 241–63.

25. See Klein and Schilder, "Japanese Illusion," 244–48, for an illustrated discussion of what they termed Positions I, II, and III (the last, which is the posi-

tion of the Japanese illusion itself—"arms flexed, wrists twisted, fingers dovetailed"—is illustrated on page 248).

26. Schilder, IAHB 55 (quoted in English).

27. The term *signe local* here is presumably a translation of the German term *Localzeichen*, which, following Schilder, might be better translated as "sign of localization" (IAHB 20). Cf. IAHB 21–24, where Schilder's discussion of tactile localization, including reference to Gelb and Goldstein's work, invokes this notion: "Everything points to the conclusion that the 'Localzeichen' . . . is not given with the sensation itself but is added to it . . . the 'Localzeichen' is indeed dependent on a process which correlates the single impression with the whole of the impressions of the body-image."

28. Schilder, IAHB 59 (quoted in English).

29. "A collection of symptoms which includes finger agnosia, right-left disorientation, dyscalculia [or acalculia], and agraphia [or dysgraphia]" (John E. Mendoza, "Gerstmann's Syndrome," in *Encyclopedia of Clinical Neuropsychology*. Cf. Robert Wilkins and Irwin Brody, "Gerstmann's Syndrome," *Archives of Neurology* 24, no. 5 [1971]: 475). See Josef Gerstmann, "Fingeragnosie und isolierte Agraphie—ein neues Syndrom," *Zeitschrift für die gesamte Neurologie* 108 (1927): 152–77; "Syndrome of Finger Agnosia, Disorientation for Right and Left, Agraphia and Acalculia: Local Diagnostic Value," *Archives of Neurology and Psychiatry* 44, no. 2 (1940): 398–408. On acalculia, see note 4 in lecture 13.

Thirteenth Lecture

1. The phrase here is "mais relèvement des autres," and it could admit of several different readings. The term *relèvement* most commonly means "raising," "recovery," or "rehabilitation," but nothing like that would seem to make sense in this context. However, the word also means "bearing"—or the taking of a bearing—in the navigational and cartographical sense, and in an even broader topological sense, "the action of determining and recording the position, configuration, and layout of something," or, metonymically, the result of such action (see http://www.cnrtl.fr/definition/relèvement). This sense would seem to fit better with what Merleau-Ponty had in mind here, that the body is that "locality" from which other places get their bearings as in a topographical projection, although the rendering given does alter the structure of the phrase slightly.

2. Here Merleau-Ponty was likely quoting from memory (and using the accusative rather than the ablative) a well-known passage from a letter that Leibniz wrote to Jesuit theologian Bartholomew Des Bosses (dated July 11, 1706): "Cum perceptio nihil aliud sit, quam multorum in uno expressio" (Since perception is nothing but the expression of many things in one)—see Gottfried Wilhelm Leibniz and Bartholomew Des Bosses, *The Leibniz-Des Bosses Correspondence*, trans. and ed. Brandon C. Look and Donald Rutherford (New Haven, Conn.: Yale University Press, 2007), 44–45. Leibniz similarly characterizes perception as the expression of "the many in the one" elsewhere, e.g., in the text *Specimen inventorum de admi-*

randis naturae generalis arcanis, in *Die philosophischen schriften von Gottfried Wilhelm Leibniz*, vol. 7, ed. Carl Immanuel Gerhardt (Berlin: Weidmann, 1890), 317: "Patet etiam quid perceptio sit, quae omnibus formis competit, nempe expressio multorum in uno, quae longe differt ab expressione in speculo, vel in organo corporeo, quod vere unum non est."

3. See [126](XIV2)–[128](XIV4).

4. Acalculia, or dyscalculia, "is the inability to perform mathematical tasks. These difficulties can stem from other deficits or can exist independently. Acalculia deficits can be global or selective and manifest in a wide variety of number processing and calculation abilities" (Natalie Wahmhoff and Elaine Clark, "Acalculia," in *Encyclopedia of Clinical Neuropsychology*).

5. Reading *il* for *elle* (all the nouns in the preceding phrase are masculine, but "it" most likely refers to "roundabout means" [*détour*]).

6. The illegible word here may be along the lines of "disentangles"—see Klein and Schilder, "Japanese Illusion," 259: "It is remarkable that movement of one of the fingers gives immediately a very definite clearness to the whole situation; disentangles the visual structure and brings it into a close relation to the postural model . . . There is no doubt that every movement vivifies the postural model of the body and that with this primitive motor activity the postural model of the body becomes much clearer."

7. Cf. Klein and Schilder, "Japanese Illusion," 259–61.

8. See note 1 above.

9. See note 17 in lecture 12.

10. Schilder, IAHB 51 (same quotation as earlier at [112](XII5), again quoted in English).

11. See [113](XII6).

12. Reading *dessine* for *dessinent.*

13. See [113](XII6)–[114](XII7). In this last quotation it is again Merleau-Ponty's emphasis.

14. Cf. PhP 153–54/134.

15. See Wilhelm Mayer-Gross, "Some Observations on Apraxia," *Proceedings of the Royal Society of Medicine* 28 (1935), 1211. In attempting to "specify the space disturbance in constructive [i.e., constructional] apraxia," Mayer-Gross noted that "the disturbance is present preponderantly *in the small realm of hands and fingers* and in all performances dependent on these. Here all functions concerned with positions, movements and notions have become uncertain." And he went on to propose what he called the symptom of "closing-in" as based upon a certain "fear of empty space" as follows: "During any manual performance the hand pushes away from loneliness, as it were, it tries to find company in anything that fills up the space. In rhythmic movements the hands tend towards one another. I have observed the same thing in gymnastic exercises. One patient was bending forward towards the doctor, who was showing her how to do the exercise, apparently in order to get closer to his hands. I recall the behaviour in writing, drawing, in imitating finger postures, in copying mosaics—always the hand tends to go out of the empty towards the filled space. As frightened chickens flock together, so do the active hands go closer to the pattern or anything else that fills the space.

The tendency gets stronger and more manifest in proportion as the spatial task appears more difficult. The spontaneity and promptness of this symptom gives one the impression of *a primary biological protective mechanism*, like perseveration. To give a preliminary name, may I propose to call it the '*closing-in*'-*symptom*?" Cf. Julien de Ajuriaguerra and Henry Hécaen, *Le cortex cérébral: Étude neuro-psycho-pathologique* (Paris: Masson, 1949), 234; *Méconnaissances et hallucinations corporelles*, 224. Like Ajuriaguerra and Hécaen, Merleau-Ponty uses the expression "closing in" in English.

16. Merleau-Ponty's specific formulations in this and the previous sentence seem clearly to echo a passage from Wendell Muncie, "Concrete Model and Abstract Copy: A Psychobiological Interpretation of the 'Closing-in' Symptom of Mayer-Gross," *Journal of Nervous and Mental Disease* 88 (1938): 1: "A most interesting observation was stressed by Mayer-Gross: namely, the tendency of the patient in performing constructive tasks to 'close-in' on the model. For example, the patient would draw over, or into the model when attempting a copy; when imitating arm postures (as in setting-up exercises) he would bring the hands close to those of the examiner, etc."

17. See Mayer-Gross, "Some Observations on Apraxia," 1211; cf. Muncie, "Concrete Model and Abstract Copy," 2. Cf. also Ajuriaguerra and Hécaen, *Le cortex cérébral*, 234, and *Méconnaissances et hallucinations corporelles*, 224. Note that whereas Merleau-Ponty wrote "crainte de l'espace vide," Ajuriaguerra and Hécaen had translated the expression as "peur de l'espace vide."

18. Merleau-Ponty appears to be relating but also elaborating on Muncie's view of the closing-in symptom: "An attempt will be made to show that the closing-in symptom is only one manifestation of a larger disturbance best interpreted as a difficulty in making through symbolization an abstract copy from a concrete model; that the same difficulty operates through the influence of widely different factors, producing superficially different symptoms, but genetically and psychologically closely related . . . The material presented appears to give a sound basis for a generalization of the closing-in symptom as an overt demonstration of disturbance in the ability to make an abstract copy from a concrete model. This disturbance has special presenting characteristics depending on the nature of the disturbing factor and the personality function so damaged . . . This explanation seems more reasonable than the fear of empty space postulated by Mayer-Gross and offers that biological significance which he hinted at as its final likely meaning" ("Concrete Model and Abstract Copy," 2, 11). Cf. Ajuriaguerra and Hécaen, *Le cortex cérébral*, 234, and *Méconnaissances et hallucinations corporelles*, 224. (Note that in both works Ajuriaguerra and Hécaen referred to Muncie as *Wundell* Muncie.)

19. Muncie refers briefly to the poor performance of subjects in color-matching tests, but Merleau-Ponty is likely making another allusion to Goldstein, in this case to Kurt Goldstein and Adhémar Gelb, "Über Farbennamenamnesie: Nebst Bemerkungen über das Wesen der amnestischen Aphasie überhaupt und die Beziehung zwischen Sprache und dem Verhalten zur Umwelt," *Psychologische Forschung* 6 (1924): 127–86; cf. PhP 204–5, 222–23/180–81, 197.

20. This example is drawn from Muncie (Case 1): "Since the age of 2 years,

or a little before, the child has shown a marked tendency to differentiate objects by stating the new one is not an old familiar one. For example, looking at a small Russian peasant doll's tousled yellow hair, she said: 'Not a dandelion!' The likeness is implied, the unlikeness stressed. This tendency was occasionally carried to laughable limits. At the same time she became aware of the difference between the concrete physical object and the pictured object, which soon became classified respectively as 'the real' and 'just a picture.' This distinction, whose basis can only be guessed at as probably the result of three dimensional vs. two dimensional spatial perception, exerts a positive fascination for the child, and now for over a year events like the following are common: [¶] The child will be seated on top of the bed upstairs thumbing the pages of a current magazine. She comes delightedly on a picture in color of SunKist lemons. She names all the objects in the picture, then without saying anything to anyone scrambles down from the bed, trudges downstairs to the kitchen, opens the refrigerator door, picks out a lemon, and comes back upstairs, climbs onto the bed, lays the lemon down carefully alongside or directly over the pictured lemon, and smiles to herself in what, without any great stretch of the imagination, may be called self-satisfaction. There is obvious gratification as she gazes first at one, then the other" ("Concrete Model and Abstract Copy," 3). Note that Merleau-Ponty quotes the expressions "the real" and "just a picture" in English.

21. The expression "external verbal knowledge" (*savoir verbal extérieur*) is drawn from Ajuriaguerra and Hécaen's discussion of Goldstein's view of language use: "Lorsque le mot a perdu sa valeur de signe, un savoir verbal extérieur peut, chez quelques individus particulièrement doués au point de vue de la parole, compenser en partie la perte du langage représentatif" (*Le cortex cerebral*, 199).

22. Schilder, IAHB 59 (same quotation as earlier at [115](XII8), quoted in English).

Fourteenth Lecture

1. Merleau-Ponty wrote the word "pattern" (underscored) in English.

2. The reference is to Hécaen, "La notion de schéma corporel et ses applications en psychiatrie," 113, whom Merleau-Ponty (who wrote "Malade de Stockert qui pensait avoir perdu son côté gauche voyait les personnes qui lui faisaient face privées de leur côté droit") effectively cited verbatim: "Un malade de Stockert (atteint de tumeur thalamo-pariétale) qui pensait avoir perdu son côté gauche voyait les personnes qui lui faisaient face privées de leur côté droit, et lorsqu'il se regardait dans la glace, il se voyait privé aussi du côté droit" [A patient of Stockert (suffering from a thalamic-parietal tumor) who thought he had lost his left side saw the people he encountered as lacking their right side, and when he looked at himself in the mirror, he saw himself as also lacking his right side]. The account is drawn from Franz Günther von Stockert, "Lokalisation und klinische Differenzierung des Symptoms der Nichtwahrnehmung einer Körperhälfte," *Deutsche Zeitschrift für Nervenheilkunde* 134 (1934): 1–13. The same case is also discussed in

Ajuriaguerra and Hécaen, *Méconnaissances et hallucinations corporelles*, 172, but it may be noted that with regard to the observation concerning the mirror, there we read the following: "Enfin il présente des épisodes brefs pendant lesquels il a le sentiment que la moitié gauche du corps lui manque, s'il se regarde dans une glace c'est avec surprise mais aussi avec une espèce de joie qu'il voit que la moitié gauche est absente" (Finally he exhibits brief episodes during which he has the feeling that he is missing the left half of his body, and if he looks at himself in a mirror it is with surprise but also a sort of joy that he sees that the left half is absent).

3. The reference here is also to Hécaen, "La notion de schéma corporel," 113–14: "De même un des nos malades dont toutes les activités ne sont plus centrées que sur la recherche du moi ideal qu'il possedait dans ses jeunes années croise sans cesse des gens qui lui ressemblent et ceux-ci ont 'plus de moi que moi-même'; ils me volent et ils me narguent. Ce schizophrène qui 'se raccroche désespérément à ce moi qu'(il) était avant' a l'impression d'être complètement changé, 'mon corps et mon esprit': son torse est déformé, sa tête a changé de forme, derriére surtout, ses jambes sont trop courtes, il est tantôt plus lourd tantôt plus léger, ses bras sont mous, ne 'prennent' pas avec le reste de son corps" (Likewise one of my patients, all of whose activities are focused exclusively on the search for the ideal self that he had in his youth, constantly runs into people who look like him and who are "more me than myself"; they steal from me and they taunt me. This schizophrenic who "clings desperately to this self that [he] once was" has the impression of being completely changed, "my body and my mind": his torso is misshapen, his head has changed shape, especially in the back, his legs are too short, he is sometimes heavier, sometimes lighter, his arms are soft and don't "take" with the rest of his body). This case is also discussed in Ajuriaguerra and Hécaen, *Méconnaissances et hallucinations corporelles*, 283–85.

4. This parenthesis does not close.

5. This parenthesis does not close.

6. The curly braces in the French edition contain the word *patients* (which would yield "individual {patient} movements"). But this adjective would seem to be extraneous to Gertsmann's account. In "Fingeragnosie und isolierte Agraphie—ein neues Syndrom," Gerstmann had written, "Dieser Störung . . . zeigte auch konsequent eine gewisse Unfreiheit der Einzelbewegungen ihrer motorisch wie sensibel sonst vollig intakten Finger . . . und eine gewisse Erschwerung der gesonderten Verwertung derselben im Handeln" (cited in Johannes Lange, "Probleme der Fingeragnosie," *Zeitschrift für die gesamte Neurologie und Psychiatrie* 147, no. 1 [1933]: 594) (This disturbance . . . consequently also exhibits a certain lack of freedom in the individual movements of the fingers that are fully intact in motor and sensory terms . . . and a certain impediment to their separate use in action). Gerstmann put it thus in "Syndrome of Finger Agnosia, Disorientation for Right and Left, Agraphia and Acalculia: Local Diagnostic Value," 400: "The phenomenon of finger agnosia, representing a primary disturbance of recognition and orientation confined to the fingers of both hands, may also, according to the degree of its development, be accompanied secondarily by a certain lack of freedom in the individual actions of the fingers and by difficulty in their sepa-

rate practic realization." So while with this unfreedom in movement it is indeed the *patient's* fingers that are directly in question, the movements themselves are not necessarily *patient*. Given this, and given that the transcription is in any case uncertain, I have replaced it with a question mark.

7. Concerning the preceding lines, see Lange, "Probleme der Fingeragnosie," 608.

8. The following quoted passages are from Lange, "Probleme der Fingeragnosie," 601, 607–8 (note that Merleau-Ponty altered the original emphases).

9. The original passage from "Probleme der Fingeragnosie" (601) that Merleau-Ponty is roughly (and somewhat misleadingly) translating reads, "wenn die Hand nicht als automatisch in Betrieb zu setzendes Werkzeug in Frage kommt, sondern wenn dieses Werkzeug auseinandergenommen, gewissermaßen in seinem Bauplan analysiert werden muß" (when the hand is not available as a tool to be automatically set to use, but rather when this tool must be taken apart and, as it were, analyzed in its blueprint). The illegible word would thus presumably correspond to *gewissermaßen* (as it were).

10. Lange: ". . . in jenem Brennpunkt . . . an dem Optisches und Sprachliches, Raumliches, Praktisches und Konstruktives zu konvergieren scheinen. Es ist, als würde an jener Stelle die gegliederte Hand zugleich beladen mit Merkmalen aus allen diesen Gebieten, und zwar so, daß in jedem Augenblick die Beladungsformen miteinander vertauscht werden können" ("Probleme der Fingeragnosie," 607).

11. Lange's reference is to Abraham Anton Grünbaum, "Aphasie und Motorik," *Zeitschrift für die gesamte Neurologie und Psychiatrie* 130 (1930): 385–412.

12. Lange: "Die Störung liegt dort, wo im Sinne von *Grünbaum* Eigen- und Fremdraum am innigsten sich durchdringen; die Hand ist nicht als Werkzeug, sondern als Gegenstand entdifferenziert, . . . nicht als Werkzeug, sondern als Material geistiger Aktivität . . . alle unsere Fertigkeiten, soweit sie die Hand betreffen, erst dadurch zustande kommen, daß die gegliederte Hand immer erneut zum Gegenstand wird, daß sie den so gewonnenen Erwerb dem Organismus als Automatismen zur Verfügung stellt und sich dadurch zu neuem aktiven Erwerb freimacht. Bei einer Schädigung der Region kommt es nicht zum Verlust der Automatismen, wohl aber wird Neuerwerb auf dem Wege über die gegliederte Hand unmöglich oder sehr ersehwert sein. Es entfällt mit der Fingeragnosie *die Fähigkeit, das Werkzeug Hand jederzeit in einen Gegenstand und auf diesem Wege stetig in ein vervollkommnetes Werkzeug zu verwandeln*" ("Probleme der Fingeragnosie," 608).

13. Lange's own discussion continued as follows: "Bei dieser Auffassung erhebt sich endlich die Frage, die in den Veröffentlichungen zur Fingeragnosie seit meiner Analyse immer erneut erörtert worden ist, nämlich ob wir es hierbei mit einer Ganzheits- oder mit einer Werkzeugstörung zu tun haben" ("Probleme der Fingeragnosie," 608) (This interpretation ultimately poses the question that, since my analysis, has been repeatedly discussed in the literature on finger agnosia; to wit, whether in this connection we are dealing with a disturbance of the totality or with a disturbance of a tool).

14. The parenthesized word "(text)" is written between the lines, under the word "machine."

15. The allusion is of course to German psychiatrist Emil Kraepelin (1856–1926). Merleau-Ponty likely had in mind Kraepelin's work on *Traumsprache* (dream speech) in his work *Über Sprachstörungen im Traume* (Leipzig: Wilhelm Engelmann, 1906).

16. "Paraphasia is the production of unintended phonemes, syllables, or words during the effort to speak or to name in the absence of effortful or poor articulation of speech sounds. Production errors may take several forms including substitution of a semantically related word (*chair* for *table*), a word that is phonemically related (*takle* for *table*), an unrelated word (*flower* for *table*), or a nonsense word (*spodle* for *table*). Paraphasia is frequently an associated symptom in aphasia and in some forms of dementia" (Linda Meyer, "Paraphasia," in *Encyclopedia of Clinical Neuropsychology*).

17. The reference is to Felix Mayer, "Die Struktur des Traumes," *Acta Psychologica* 3, no. 1 (1937): 81–136.

18. See Mayer, "Die Struktur des Traumes," 96. Note that Mayer had italicized the "Mün-" beginning of *Mün*chen, das Freiburger *Mün*ster, and die Stadt *Mün*ster.

19. See Mayer: "Darstellbarkeit des Ich und Du, des Wir und Ihr und der besitzanzeigenden Fürwörter, dagegen U[n]möglichkeit das abwesende Neutrum oder das abwesende Er darzustellen, oder nur durch Reihenbildung" ("Die Struktur des Traumes," 93; cf. 87).

20. Here this term specifically denotes the formation of a series of like-structured compound words from the same constituent elements.

21. Reading *on ne peut dire* for *on ne veut dire*. See Mayer: "'Schokolade schmeckt gut, Apfelsine schmeckt gut' kann in der Gebärdensprache mitgeteilt werden, dagegen nicht: 'beide schmecken gleich gut'. Denn zum Vergleichen gehört die Isolierung eines Merkmals, also eine urteilsmäßige Abstraktion, die in der Gebärdensprache nicht möglich ist. Darzustellen ist ein Vergleich jedoch, wenn die Vergleichsobjekte sinnlich in ein schon durch Anschauung erklärbares Beisammensein gebracht werden können, also z.B. 'dieser Stuhl ist so groß wie jener'" ("Chocolate tastes good, oranges taste good" can be communicated in gestural language, but not "both taste equally good." For comparison involves the isolation of an attribute, and thus a judgment-like abstraction, that is not possible in gestural language. A comparison may be presented, however, when the objects to be compared can be meaningfully brought into an already intuitively explicable togetherness; for example, "this chair is as big as that one") ("Die Struktur des Traumes," 87; cf. 91).

22. The uncertain transcription is "ns," a possible abbreviation for *nous* (us).

23. Mayer: "Aussagesätze, die Konkretes betreffen, bieten schon wegen ihrer Mehrdeutigkeit, ob ein allgemeiner Inhalt gemeint ist, oder ob die Person des Versuchsleiters als Subjekt der Mitteilung betont werden soll, beträchtliche Schwierigkeiten. Der einfache Satz: 'Ich habe zwei Beine', gebärdlich ausgedrückt durch Zeigen des Versuchsleiters auf sich, hindeuten auf die eigenen Beine und emporstrecken von zwei Fingern nach oben, wurde zwar von der überwiegenden Mehrzahl der Versuchspersonen richtig verstanden, aber eine Versuchsperson

meinte zu verstehen: 'Herr Witte braucht neue Strümpfe' oder 'er will sich ausziehen'. Eine Versuchsperson entnahm sogar der Gebärde die Wunschäußerung: 'Kommen Sie um 2 Uhr zu mir'" (If only because of their ambiguity, concrete declarative sentences present considerable difficulties, whether the intended content is general, or whether the investigator himself is to be emphasized as the subject of the message. The simple sentence, "I have two legs," expressed gesturally by the investigator by pointing at himself, pointing to his own legs and extending two fingers upward, was certainly correctly understood by the overwhelming majority of subjects. But one subject understood this as "Mr. Witte needs new socks" or 'he wants to get undressed." One subject even took from the gesture the expression of a request: "Come see me at 2 o'clock") ("Die Struktur des Traumes," 85).

24. In discussing total apraxia in dreamless sleep, and raising the idea of missing a train (*das Nichterreichen des abfahrenden Zuges*), Mayer quoted (without citation) what he thought was a good illustration from the *War Memoirs* of British politician David Lloyd George (1863–1945): "Manchmal träumt man, daß man an Händen und Füßen gefesselt und in ein Netz vieler Hindernisse verstrickt ist und mit weit aufgerissenen Augen irgendein Unglück herannahen sieht, während die erstickte Kehle keinen Protest und keinen Hilferuf hervorzubringen vermag" (One sometimes dreams that with hands and feet tied one is entangled in a web of many obstacles and sees with eyes wide open some disaster approaching, while the stifled throat is unable to produce any protest or call for help) ("Die Struktur des Traumes," 100–101).

25. See Mayer, "Die Struktur des Traumes," 106.

26. Bernard Berenson, *Esthétique et histoire des arts visuels*, trans. Jean Alazard (Paris: Albin Michel, 1953), 91 ("Je ne peux pas oublier qu'un des hommes remarquables de mon temps, peintre, excellent prosateur, très habile à découvrir les nouveaux génies, m'ait demandé ce que je voulais dire quand je parlais de mouvement dans une ligne"). The original line is from Bernard Berenson, *Aesthetics and History in the Visual Arts* (New York: Pantheon, 1948), 75: "I cannot forget that one of the most admired authorities of my time, himself a painter, a stylist in prose, and a pioneer in discovering ever new genius, asked me what I could mean by movement in a line."

27. See Auguste Rodin, *L'art: Entretiens réunis par Paul Gsell* (Paris: Grasset, 1911), 76–77.

28. The reference is to François Rude's statue of Marshal of the Empire Michel Ney (1853), located at the Carrefour de l'Observatoire in Paris.

29. See Rodin, *L'art*, 77–78: "Les jambes du maréchal et la main qui tient le fourreau du sabre sont placées dans l'attitude qu'elles avaient quand il a dégainé: la jambe gauche s'est effacée afin que l'arme s'offrît plus facilement à la main droite qui venait la tirer et, quant à la main gauche, elle est restée un peu en l'air comme si elle présentait encore le fourreau. [¶] Maintenant considérez le torse. Il devait être légèrement incliné vers la gauche au moment où s'exécutait le geste que je viens de décrire; mais le voilà qui se redresse, voilà que la poitrine se bombe, voilà que la tête se tournant vers les soldats rugit l'ordre d'attaquer, voilà qu'enfin le bras droit se lève et brandit le sabre" (The marshal's legs and

the hand that's holding the sheath of the sword are placed in the position they were in when he drew; the left leg is pulled aside so that the weapon would be more readily accessible to the right hand that was coming to draw it, while the left hand remains slightly raised as if it were still presenting the sheath. [¶] Now consider the torso. It should lean slightly toward the left at the moment when the gesture I just described was performed; but there it is straightening up, there's the chest thrown out, there's the head, turning toward the soldiers, bellowing out the order to attack, and then finally the right arm rises and brandishes the sword) (see Auguste Rodin, *Art: Conversations with Paul Gsell,* trans. Jacques de Caso and Patricia B. Sanders [Berkeley: University of California Press, 1984], 29; translation modified). See also the epigraph, attributed to Rodin but without reference, to chapter 8 in Jean Paulhan's *Les fleurs de Tarbes* (Paris: Gallimard, 1941): "Il est aisé de remarquer que la statue du maréchal Ney unit deux attitudes: la main gauche et les jambes sont placées comme elles étaient au moment où le maréchal tirait son sabre; le torse, qui devrait être incliné, se redresse au contraire en même temps que le bras droit élève l'arme en signe de commandement. De cette dualité résulte la vie de la figure" ("It is easy to see that the statue of Marshall Ney combines two poses: His left hand and his legs are placed where they were at the moment the marshall drew his sword; his upper body, which should be bent forward, is instead straightened up at the same time as his right arm is raising his weapon as a command signal. The lifelike quality of the statue results from this duality" [*The Flowers of Tarbes; or, Terror in Literature,* trans. Michael Syrotinski (Urbana-Champaign: University of Illinois Press, 2006), 66]).

30. The reference is to *Saint John the Baptist,* a sculpture by Rodin (1880).

31. See Gsells's account in Rodin, *L'art,* 79–84, especially: "Le personnage appuyé d'abord sur le pied gauche qui pousse le sol de toute sa force, semble se balancer à mesure que le regard se porte vers la droite. On voit alors tout le corps s'incliner dans cette direction, puis la jambe droite avance et le pied s'empare puissamment de la terre. En même temps, l'épaule gauche qui s'élève semble vouloir ramener le poids du torse de son côté pour aider la jambe restée en arrière à revenir en avant" (83) ("The figure, which first rests on its left foot that pushes with all its force against the ground, seems to swing as the glance turns to the right. We can see the whole body leaning in this direction, then the right leg advances, and the foot powerfully lays claim to the ground. At the same time, the left shoulder is raised as if to bring the weight of the torso back to its side to help the back leg come forward" [Rodin, *Art,* 30; translation modified]). The illegible word in Merleau-Ponty's notes thus likely corresponds to "raised."

32. Rodin, *L'art,* 85–86. Merleau-Ponty also refers to the latter passage in *L'œil et l'esprit,* 80 ("Eye and Mind," 185–86).

33. The reference is to *Le derby de 1821 à Epsom* (or *Le derby d'Epsom*), a painting by Théodore Géricault (1821).

34. See Rodin, *L'art,* 87–88.

35. See Rodin, *L'art,* 76, 78.

36. Concerning Merleau-Ponty's notions of *trace* and *tracé,* here it might just be noted that in the case of a stationary object (like a painting or a statue) that expresses movement without there being any actual tracing (or passage) on its

part, it does so by presenting an emblematic trace that can be taken up or "read" in the projective tracing effected by an appropriate perceiving body.

37. Berenson, *Aesthetics and History in the Visual Arts*, 71. Merleau-Ponty quoted the Alazard translation: "il n'a rien à voir avec le changement de place ou même avec le changement d'attitude ou de pose, et encore moins avec l'activité transitive sous toutes ses formes" (*Esthétique et histoire des arts visuels*, 87).

38. Berenson, *Aesthetics and History in the Visual Arts*, 72. Merleau-Ponty quoted the Alazard translation: "J'aperçus un monde où toute forme, tout angle, toute surface avait avec moi un rapport vivant et non, comme jusqu'alors, fondé sur la pure connaissance" (*Esthétique et histoire des arts visuels*, 88).

39. Heinrich Wölfflin, *Kunstgeschichtliche Grundbegriffe: Das Problem der Stilentwicklung in der neueren Kunst* (1915; repr., Munich: Hugo Bruckmann, 1921); references in the notes will be to the 1921 edition. The original English translation is *Principles of Art History: The Problem of the Development of Style in Later Art*, trans. Marie Donald Mackie Hottinger (New York: Dover, 1932), but I refer to the more recent translation, *Principles of Art History: The Problem of the Development of Style in Early Modern Art*, trans. Jonathan Blower (Los Angeles: Getty Publications, 2015). Merleau-Ponty's own citations were drawn from (and his page references refer to) *Principes fondamentaux de l'histoire de l'art: Le problème de l'évolution du style dans l'art moderne*, trans. Claire Raymond and Marcel Raymond (Paris: Plon, 1952).

40. Note that Merleau-Ponty followed the Raymond translation of Wölfflin's key term *malerisch* (painterly) as "pictural." While this is an adequate French translation of Wölfflin's term, it would be misleading to go from there to the English "pictural" or "pictorial," for this would fail to capture the stylistic contrast in question. Here I follow the standard English translation of *malerisch* as "painterly."

41. Wölfflin, *Kunstgeschichtliche Grundbegriffe*, 12 (*Principles of Art History*, 93). Merleau-Ponty's phrase "movement to the 3rd power" (*mouvement à la 3e puissance*) may be alluding to the following point that Wölfflin made in this immediate context: "Allein mit einer Analyse auf Qualität und auf Ausdruck hin ist der Tatbestand überhaupt noch nicht erschöpft. Es kommt ein drittes hinzu—und damit sind wir zu dem springenden Punkt dieser Untersuchung gelangt—: die Darstellungsart als solche. Jeder Künstler findet bestimmte 'optische' Möglichkeiten vor, an die er gebunden ist. Nicht alles ist zu allen Zeiten möglich. Das Sehen an sich hat seine Geschichte, und die Aufdeckung dieser 'optischen Schichten' muß als die elementarste Aufgabe der Kunstgeschichte betrachtet werden" (*Kunstgeschichtliche Grundbegriffe*, 11–12) ("An analysis that considers only quality and expression is still far from exhausting the whole state of affairs. There is a third factor ['Un troisième élément entre en jeu' (*Principes fondamentaux de l'histoire de l'art*, 12)], which brings us to the crucial point of our investigation: the mode of representation as such. Every artist finds certain preexisting 'optical' possibilities, to which he is bound. Not everything is possible at all times. Seeing as such has its own history, and uncovering these 'optical strata' has to be considered the most elementary task of art history" [*Principles of Art History*, 93]).

42. Cf. Wölfflin: "Der Bewegungsbegriff gehört . . . zum Wesen des malerischen Sehens: das malerische Auge faßt alles als ein Vibrierendes auf und

läßt nichts in bestimmten Linien und Flächen sich verfestigen" (*Kunstgeschichtliche Grundbegriffe*, 29) ("The concept of movement is . . . an essential part of painterly seeing: the painterly eye perceives everything in vibration and lets nothing solidify into definite lines and planes" [*Principles of Art History*, 108]); "Was Rembrandt von Dürer wesentlich unterscheidet, ist das Vibrieren des Bildes im ganzen, das sich auch dann behauptet, wenn die Formzeichen dem Auge nicht mehr im einzelnen erkennbar sein sollten" (*Kunstgeschichtliche Grundbegriffe*, 32) ("What essentially distinguishes Rembrandt from Dürer is the vibration of the picture as a whole, and this still asserts itself even when the eye can no longer make out the individual marks that constitute the form" [*Principles of Art History*, 110]); "Das malerische Auge ist auf die Wahrnehmung der Gesamterscheinung eingestellt, in der das einzelne Objekt als Gegenstand keine wesentliche Bedeutung mehr hat. Es geht unter im Ganzen, und das Vibrieren aller Linien befördert den Prozeß der Verflechtung zu einer gleichartigen Masse" (*Kunstgeschichtliche Grundbegriffe*, 44) ("The painterly eye is set up to perceive the overall appearance, in which the individual object no longer has any essential significance as a thing. It is subsumed by the whole and the vibration of the lines drives the process of entwining into an undifferentiated mass" [*Principles of Art History*, 122]).

43. This is a rendering of Merleau-Ponty's quotation of the Raymond translation of Wölfflin, which reads as follows: "Un mouvement se met à flamboyer, de source purement optique, et s'empare de la totalité des formes; la paroi vibre et l'espace tressaille en tous ses angles. [¶] Il faut se garder d'identifier cet effet tout pictural avec le grand mouvement de masse qui nous est transmis par certaines constructions italiennes. Le pathos des murs convexes ou concaves, et la puissance des colonnes accumulées, ne constituent que des cas particuliers" (*Principes fondamentaux de l'histoire de l'art*, 72). But this translation is somewhat imprecise—cf. Wölfflin, *Kunstgeschichtliche Grundbegriffe*, 71: "Es entzündet sich, unabhängig von der besonderen Ansicht, eine (rein-optische) Bewegung über die Gesamtheit der Formen hin. Die Wand vibriert, der Raum zuckt in allen Winkeln. [¶] Ausdrucklich soll hier davor gewarnt werden, diesen malerischen Bewegungseffekt mit der großen Massenbewegung gewisser italienischer Bauwerke gleichzusetzen. Das Pathos geschwungener Mauern und gewaltiger Säulenhaufen ist nur ein Sonderfall" ["A (purely optical) movement flares up over the totality of forms. The wall vibrates, every corner of the space twitches. [¶] Here we should explicitly warn against equating the painterly effect of movement with the grand movement of mass in certain Italian buildings. The pathos of curving walls and of formidable groups of columns is merely a special case" (*Principles of Art History*, 147; translation modified)].

44. It's unclear what Merleau-Ponty may be referring to here, but some possibly relevant passages are as follows: "Diese Analyse ist gewiß nicht erschöpfend, aber sie kann genügen, um zu zeigen, in welcher Weise Stile Zeitausdruck sind. Es ist deutlich ein neues Lebensideal, das aus der Kunst des italienischen Barock spricht, und wenn wir die Architektur vorangestellt haben, weil sie die eindrücklichste Verkörperung dieses Ideals gibt, so sagen die zeitgenössischen Maler und Bildhauer in ihrer Sprache doch desselbe" (*Kunstgeschichtliche Grundbegriffe*, 10) ("This analysis is certainly not exhaustive, but it may suffice to show that

styles are the expression of their age. There is clearly a new ideal that speaks from the art of the Italian baroque, and though we have given precedence to architecture as the most impressive embodiment of this ideal, the contemporary painters and sculptors nevertheless say the thing in their own language" [*Principles of Art History*, 92]) ("Cette analyse, sans être exhaustive, suffit à montrer comment un style est l'expression d'une époque. Il y a là, visiblement, un nouvel idéal de vie qui émane de l'art baroque italien; si nous avons consideré en premier lieu l'architecture, c'est qu'elle offer une réalisation plus frappante de cet idéal, mais les peintres et les sculpteurs contemporains dissent la même chose dans la langue qui leur est proper" [*Principes fondamentaux de l'histoire de l'art*, 11]); "Größere oder geringere Bewegtheit sind Ausdrucksmomente, die mit einheitlichen Maßstab gemessen werden können: malerisch und linear aber sind wie zwei verscheidene Sprachen, in denen man alles mögliche sagen kann, wenn auch jede nach einer gewissen Seite hin ihre Stärke haben und aus einer besonderen Orientierung zur Sichtbarkeit hervorgegangen sein mag" (*Kunstgeschichtliche Grundbegriffe*, 12) ("Greater and lesser degrees of movement are expressive values that can be measured on the same scale, whereas the painterly and linear styles are like two different languages in which one can say virtually anything, even if each has strengths in a certain area and each may have emerged from a particular approach to the visible" [*Principles of Art History*, 93]) ("Des mouvements plus ou moins accentués ne sont que des éléments expressifs réductibles à une même mesure; ce qui est 'pictural' et ce qui est linéaire, en revanche, constituent deux langages différents capables de tout exprimer, alors même que chacun d'eux possède des vertus particulières et a dû naître d'une orientation spéciale de la vision" [*Principes fondamentaux de l'histoire de l'art*, 13]); "Es kommen schiefe Urteile in die Kunstgeschichte hinein, wenn man von dem Eindruck ausgeht, den Bilder verschiedener Epochen, nebeneinander gesehen, auf uns machen. Man darf ihre verschiedene Ausdrucksweise nicht rein stimmungsmäßig interpretieren. Sie sprechen verschiedene Sprache" (*Kunstgeschichtliche Grundbegriffe*, 245) ("Skewed judgments find their way into art history if one proceeds from the impression that paintings from different epochs make on us when laid side by side. Their various modes of expression should not be interpreted purely in terms of mood. They speak different languages" [*Principles of Art History*, 307]) ("Il s'introduit dans l'histoire de l'art des jugements erronés si on part de l'impression que font sur nous des tableaux d'époque différente, placés l'un à côté de l'autre. Il faut se garder de réduire simplement à leur contenu sentimental les divers modes d'expression. En fait, ils ne parlent pas le même langage" [*Principes fondamentaux de l'histoire de l'art*, 261]). See also the passage cited in the following note.

45. Wölfflin, *Kunstgeschichtliche Grundbegriffe*, 71—but note the modality: "Auch in der tektonischen Kunst soll sich nichts mehr verfestigen in tastbaren Linien und Flächen, auch in der tektonischen Kunst soll der Eindruck des Bleibenden aufgehoben werden durch den Eindruck des Sich-Verändernden, auch in der tektonischen Kunst *soll die Form atmen.* Das ist, abgesehen von allen Ausdrucksverschiedenheiten, die Grundidee des Barock" (italics added) ("In the tectonic arts as with the other arts, there should no longer be anything that solidifies into tangible lines and planes; as with the other arts, the impression

of permanence should be superseded by the impression of transformation; as with the other arts, *form should breathe.* That, if we ignore the various modes of expression, is the basic idea of the baroque" [*Principles of Art History*, 147; italics added]) ("Dans l'art tectonique aussi, plus rien ne doit se fixer en lignes et en surfaces palpables; à l'impression de la stabilité doit se substituer celle d'une réalité en voie de metamorphose; en bref, *il faut que* dans l'architecture également les forms respirent. Voilà l'idée centrale du baroque, abstraction faite de toutes les différences d'ordre expressif" [*Principes fondamentaux de l'histoire de l'art*, 72; italics added]).

46. Cf. Wölfflin, *Kunstgeschichtliche Grundbegriffe*, 72: "Der Todfeind des Malerischen ist die Isolierung der einzelnen Form. Damit die Bewegungsillusion zustande kommt, müssen die Formen zusammenrücken, sich verflechten, ineinander verschmelzen" ("The archenemy of the painterly is the isolation of individual form. In order to create the illusion of movement the forms have to come together, interlace, and fuse with one another" [*Principles of Art History*, 148]) ("L'ennemi mortel de l'effet pictural, c'est l'isolement de la forme. Pour susciter l'illusion du movement, il faut que les forms s'épaulent les uns les autres, s'entrelacent, se confondent" [*Principes fondamentaux de l'histoire de l'art*, 73]).

47. The expression is "équilibre en suspens" and it appears in the Raymond translation on pages 145 ("un . . .") and 146 ("l' . . ."), although the original terms do differ: in the first instance, it is "ein schwebendes Gleichgewicht," and in the second it is "das aufgehobene Gleichgewicht" (*Kunstgeschichtliche Grundbegriffe*, 140). The Blower translation also renders both expressions as "suspended equilibrium" (*Principles of Art History*, 209–10).

48. José Victoriano Carmelo Carlos González-Pérez (1887–1927), better known as Juan Gris, was a Spanish artist associated with Cubism who worked primarily in France.

49. Merleau-Ponty is citing Pierre Francastel, "Espace et illusion," *Revue internationale de filmologie* 2, no. 5 (1949): 65: "Faute d'un certain rythme les formes se superposent en un monstrueux éventail qui n'a plus rien d'illusionniste ou, si l'on veut, de réel."

50. Francastel, "Espace et illusion," 65.

51. Francastel, "Espace et illusion," 70.

52. With this expression, Merleau-Ponty may have in mind Henri Wallon's child-psychological notion of "ultra-things" (*ultra-choses*) as denoting those beings "that exist for children but [which] are not within their reach, . . . that in a word they are not able to *observe* . . . Ultra-things are horizons of reality that the child does not doubt, but toward which he cannot take an objective or objectifying attitude . . . The presence of these 'ultra-things' in children's experience implies or presupposes in them the presence of a preobjective time and space which is not yet dominated and measured by their thought, and which adheres in some way to the subject who lives [this preobjective time and space]" (*Psychologie et pedagogie de l'enfant*, 242–43, 512–13; cf. 304, 478–79; *Child Psychology and Pedagogy*, 192–93, 412–13; translation modified; cf. 241, 384). Cf. Henri Wallon, *Les origines de la pensée chez l'enfant* (Paris: Presses Universitaires de France, 1945). See also Emmanuel de Saint Aubert, "Au croisement du réel et de l'imaginaire: Les

'ultra-choses' chez Merleau-Ponty," in *Est-ce réel? Phénoménologies de l'imaginaire*, ed. Annabelle Dufourcq (Leiden: Brill, 2016), 240–58.

53. A popular 1951 British satirical comedy, adapted from a play by Roger MacDougall, and directed by Alexander Mackendrick. Alec Guinness starred as a young chemist (Sidney Stratton) who invents an artificial fiber that is dirt repellent and indestructible, and Ernest Thesiger played an asthmatic industrial baron (Sir John Kierlaw) who at one point (48:22), with his breathing audible but without his being directly seen, has an attack and requests his atomizer ("No, no, the asthma atomizer!"). Merleau-Ponty referred to the film by its French title, *L'homme au complet blanc.*

54. Francastel, "Espace et illusion," 70. The immediate context from which this phrase is drawn reads as follows: "Ce n'est pas parce que la caméra nous offre le spectacle d'images successives et non plus d'images condensées que le rôle de la mémoire est apparu dans la vision plastique et que celui de l'imagination a été réduit. Tout signe, pour être lu, exige un effort de reconnaissance. L'imagination seule rend vivant un tableau ou un film. Qu'il soit couvert d'images arretées ou successives, sur l'écran plastique, ce n'est jamais le réel qui apparait. Avec ses champs variés mais tout de même limités, avec ses sautes et ses reprises, la caméra monoculaire est un système d'enregistrement tout aussi artificiel que les autres. Les objets filmiques ne sont pas plus ni moins vrais que les objets dessinés. Les uns et les autres sont des signes au sens plein du terme, c'est à dire des réseaux de lignes aboutissant à un découpage allusif de l'écran" (It is not because the [movie] camera offers us the spectacle of successive rather than condensed images that memory now plays a role in the visual arts while the role of the imagination has been reduced. In order to be read, every sign demands an effort of recognition. The imagination alone brings life to a painting or a film. It is never the real that appears on the artistic screen, whether it is covered in images that are still or moving. With its diverse but nonetheless limited fields, with its shifts and retakes, the monocular [movie] camera is a system of recording that is just as artificial as the others. Cinematic objects are no more nor less true than drawn objects. Both are signs in the full sense of the term; that is, networks of lines leading to a suggestive cutting up of the screen). Note that *découpage* is a typical term for editorial cutting in the cinematic sense.

Working Notes

1. Presumably an allusion to Heinz Werner, but note that every other reference to him is made in connection with Karl Zietz.

2. The idea of movement (and space) as "felt by the heart" is drawn from Jean Paulhan—see [83](IX2).

3. Here Merleau-Ponty is alluding to "L'homme et l'adversité" ("Man and Adversity"), a talk he gave at the Rencontres internationales de Genève (September 10, 1951), which was published in *La connaissance de l'homme au XXe siècle* (Neuchâtel: La Baconnière, 1952), 51–75, and reprinted in *Signes* (Paris:

Gallimard, 1960), 284–308 (*Signs*, trans. Richard C. McCleary [Evanston, Ill.: Northwestern University Press, 1964], 224–46). The following passage is directly relevant: "Dans un langage approximatif, Freud est ici sur le point de découvrir ce que d'autres ont mieux nommé *perception ambiguë*. C'est en travaillant dans ce sens qu'on trouvera un état civil pour cette conscience qui frôle ses objets, les élude au moment où elle va les poser, en tient compte, comme l'aveugle des obstacles, plutôt qu'elle ne les reconnaît, qui ne veut pas les savoir, les ignore en tant qu'elle les sait, les sait en tant qu'elle les ignore, et qui sous-tend nos actes et nos connaissances exprès" (*Signes*, 291) ("In an approximate language, Freud is on the point of discovering what others have more appropriately termed *ambiguous perception*. It is by working in this direction that we shall find a civil status for this consciousness which brushes against its objects, that shies away from them just when it's going to posit them, that takes account of them, like the blind person takes account of obstacles, rather than recognizing them, that does not want to know them, that does not know them inasmuch as it knows them, that knows them inasmuch as it does not know them, and that subtends our explicit actions and knowledge" [*Signs*, 229–30; translation modified]).

4. See Helen Keller, *The Story of My Life* (New York: Doubleday, 1903); Merleau-Ponty would have been referring to *Sourde, muette, aveugle: Histoire de ma vie*, trans. Antoinette Huzard (Paris: Payot, 1915). Recall that with regard to linguistic understanding Cassirer had made an important reference to Keller in the third volume of *The Philosophy of Symbolic Forms* (112).

5. The reference is to André Ombredane, to whose *Études de psychologie médicale, tome II*, Merleau-Ponty briefly referred at [104](XI4)–[105](XI5). Neither that work nor the first volume (subtitled *Perception et langage*) deals much with aphasia, however, so here Merleau-Ponty may have had in mind Ombredane's subsequent work, *L'aphasie et l'élaboration de la pensée explicite* (Paris: Presses Universitaires de France, 1951).

6. Presumably a reference to art historians Erwin Panofsky (1892–1968) and Pierre Francastel (1900–1970), the latter of whom is referred to at [134](XIV10)–[135](XIV11). Concerning the former, Merleau-Ponty likely had in mind Panofsky's key text, "Perspektive als 'symbolische Form,'" in *Vorträge der Bibliothek Warburg 1924/1925*, ed. Fritz Saxl (Leipzig: B. G. Teubner, 1927), 258–330 (*Perspective as Symbolic Form*, trans. Christopher S. Wood [New York: Zone Books, 1991]). Concerning this, see Denis Courville, "La naissance de l'espace moderne: Merleau-Ponty et Panofsky sur la perspective linéaire," *Ithaque: Revue de philosophie de l'Université de Montréal* 7 (2010): 21–46.

7. Reading *elle* for *elles*.

8. See note 6 in lecture 2.

9. Reading *aucun* for *aucune*.

10. These square brackets are in Merleau-Ponty's notes.

11. "Entends ce bruit fin qui est continu, et qui est le silence. Écoute ce qu'on entend lorsque rien ne se fait entendre. [¶] Il couvre tout, ce sable du silence. [¶] Je considère toute mon histoire, mes volontés et mes amours comme une ville d'autrefois, par la cendre ou le desert, ensevelie et efface. [¶] Mais entends ce sifflement si pur, si seul, si loin, créateur d'espace, comme au plus

profond, comme existant solitaire par soi-même. [¶][¶] Plus rien. Ce rien est immense aux oreilles. [¶] Sifflet encore. Sifflet sinistre, simple, éternel, égal à lui-même; filet éternel du temps, qui se perd dans l'univers de l'ouïe, consubstantiel à l'espace, coulant dans le sens de l'attente infinie, emplissant la sphère croissante" (Paul Valéry, "Poésie perdue," in *Œuvres, tome II,* 656–57) ("Listen to this delicate endless susurration which is silence. Hear what is heard when nothing is heard. [¶] All is gone under the sand of silence. [¶] The story of all my delights and desires is a dead city, erased and enlaced in desert cinder. [¶] But hear this lone far pure whistling, creating space, as if alone it existed, of itself, to its depth. [¶] Now nothing. But this nothing is huge in the ears. [¶] Still whistling. Sinister whistling; regular, endless, unchanging monotone whistling; unwinding thread of time losing itself in the universe of the heard, consubstantial with space, running toward eternal expectation, filling the swelling sphere with the desire to hear it" [*Collected Works of Paul Valéry, Volume 2: Poems in the Rough,* trans. Hilary Corke (Princeton, N.J.: Princeton University Press, 2015), 166]). This passage is quoted by Merleau-Ponty in the companion (Monday) course from the same year, *Recherches sur l'usage littéraire du langage* at [36](III4).

12. Merleau-Ponty is most likely alluding to François Rostand, "Grammaire et affectivité," *Revue française de psychanalyse* 14 (1950): 299–310. See also Merleau-Ponty, *Child Psychology and Pedagogy,* 244–45.

13. These square brackets are in Merleau-Ponty's notes.

14. Merleau-Ponty used the English word "insight."

15. See note 5 in lecture 6.

16. For "something emitted by" (*une émission de*), reading *émission* for *émision.*

17. Cf. the discussion of Bergson and Zeno at [59](VI2)–[61](VI4).

18. A term introduced by Leibniz in his *Theoria motus abstracti* (Theory of abstract motion): "*No motive momentum (conatus) without motion exceeds the moment except with the minds.* For what is the motive momentum at one moment is the motion of a body in a time series. At this point, every person who wants to proceed has the door of the true distinction—which no one has explained so far—between body and mind open to him. For every body is a momentaneous mind (mens momentanea), that is to say, a mind without *memory.* For it does not hold on to its own, and at the same time to its alien, contrary motive momentum longer than the moment (as both action and counter-action, that is to say, equation and thus *harmony* are necessary for any sort of *sensory sensation,* and without this no sensation exists, neither *pleasure* nor pain); [the mere body] therefore has no memory; it has no sensation of its actions and passions; it has no consideration" (cited in Hubertus Busche, "Mind and Body in the Young Leibniz," in *Individuals, Minds and Bodies: Themes from Leibniz,* ed. Massimiliano Carrara, Antonio-Maria Nunziante, and Gabriele Tomasi [Stuttgart: Franz Steiner, 2004], 151).

19. Bergson, *Matière et mémoire,* 210; *Matter and Memory* (1911), 249; (1991), 190. Cf. [59](VI2).

20. *Matière et mémoire,* 212, 210; *Matter and Memory* (1911), 251, 249; (1991), 192, 190.

21. *Matière et mémoire,* 210; *Matter and Memory* (1911), 249; (1991), 190.

22. *Matière et mémoire,* 213; *Matter and Memory* (1911), 253; (1991), 192–93.

23. Reading *montrent* for *montre.*

24. The reference is presumably to Wolfgang Köhler, "Tonpsychologie," in *Handbuch der Neurologie des Ohres,* vol. 1, ed. Gustav Alexander and Otto Marburg (Vienna: Urban & Schwarzenberg, 1924), 419–64.

25. Here Merleau-Ponty is particularly interested in Michotte's work concerning "auto-locomotion"—see *The Perception of Causality,* 183–200; see also [69](VII5)–[70](VII6), [73](VIII1)–[74](VIII2), and [80](VIII8).

26. See note 5 in lecture 6.

27. It's not clear what exactly Merleau-Ponty had in mind here. Although the term is occasionally (albeit infrequently) found in discussions of Husserl, e.g., as denoting a kind of phenomenologically "felt" time, a more common usage to which Merleau-Ponty may have been at least indirectly referring here stemmed from Friedrich Fröhlich's empirical research into the temporal lag between the application of a stimulus and the conscious registration of sensation—see "Über die Messung der Empfindungszeit," *Zeitschrift für Sinnesphysiologie* 54 (1923): 58–78, and *Die Empfindungszeit: Ein Beitrag zur Lehre von der Zeit-, Raum- und Bewegungsempfindung* (Jena: Gustav Fischer, 1929). Relevant to the critical point that Merleau-Ponty is about to make, Edgar Rubin had argued that such test results vary with changes in the stimulus setting—see "Kritisches und Experimentelles zur 'Empfindungszeit' Fröhlichs," *Psychologische Forschung* 13, no. 1 (1930): 101–12.

28. Merleau-Ponty is presumably alluding to Maurice Halbwachs, *Les cadres sociaux de la mémoire* (Paris: Félix Alcan, 1925); *On Collective Memory,* ed. and trans. Lewis Coser (Chicago: University of Chicago Press, 1992).

29. As at [181]v(1), Merleau-Ponty is presumably alluding to Jean Piaget and his book *Le développement de la notion de temps chez l'enfant* (Paris: Presses Universitaires de France, 1946); *The Child's Conception of Time,* trans. Arnold Julius Pomerans (New York: Routledge, 1969).

30. Merleau-Ponty is presumably alluding to French writer Paul Claudel (1868–1955), and he may have had the following passages in mind: "L'univers est une machine à marquer le temps. Comparaison avec les horloges humaines . . . Je dis que tout l'univers n'est qu'une machine à marquer le temps. [¶] Dans cette vue, considérons les instruments humains qui ne sont que la copie, sans savoir, de l'horloge totale, et l'inclusion dans une boite au moyen d'ancres et de pignons de cette même force qui fait rouler les grands chars de la Lune et des autres dieux" (*Art poétique* [Paris: Mercure de France, 1913], 10, 30) ("The universe is a machine for marking time. Comparison with human clocks . . . I am saying that the universe is nothing but a machine for marking time. [¶] In this light, let us consider the human instruments that are merely the unwitting copies of the total clock, and the boxing up using anchors and gears of this same force that drives the great chariots of the Moon and of the other gods" [*Poetic Art,* trans. Renée Spodheim (New York: Philosophical Library, 1948), 3, 20; translation modified]).

31. Merleau-Ponty is presumably alluding to Piaget, *Les notions de mouvement et de vitesse chez l'enfant* (see note 8 in lecture 9), and *Le développement de la notion de temps chez l'enfant* (see note 29).

32. See [81](VIII9).

33. Reading "Gestalt" for "gestalt."

34. See note 51 in lecture 7.

35. The portion of this paragraph starting with "The movements studied" and ending with "not [a] perceptual mode" is highlighted by two lines in the margin.

36. The French editors were unable to determine with certainty the page or pages, if they still exist, of which this note is the continuation.

37. See [67](VII3), including note 12 in lecture 7.

38. Concerning this experiment by Linke, see [69](VII5), including note 22 in lecture 7.

39. Concerning this modification of Linke's experiment by Koffka, see [69] (VII5), including note 23 in lecture 7.

40. I have translated Merleau-Ponty's slightly imprecise French rendering of the following passage from Zietz and Werner, "Über die dynamische Struktur der Bewegung," 242: "So wie die Figur als dynamisch bewegtes Etwas in ihrer Form die Funktion der Gesamtbewegung anzeigt, so erweist sich auch die *Gesamtform der Bewegung* selbst als *Sinnbild des Dynamischen.* Bei Betonung des Pfeiles wird beispielsweise bei einer Versuchsperson die teilweise Rotation vervollständigt, d.h. die Vollkommenheit der Bewegung ist geissermaßen der *räumliche Ausdruck* einer *dynamischen Intensivierung*" (italics in the original) (Just as the figure as a dynamically moving something indicates in its form the function of the total movement, so too does the *total form of the movement* itself turn out to be a *sensible image of what is dynamic.* By placing emphasis on the arrow the partial rotation is completed for some subjects; that is, the completeness of the movement is as it were the *spatial expression* of a *dynamic intensification*).

41. See the reference to Jean Paulhan at [83](IX2)–[84](IX3); see also Paulhan's allusion to Rodin's view of François Rude's statue of Michel Ney at [131](XIV7).

42. Paul Christian, "Wirklichkeit und Erscheinung in der Wahrnehmung von Bewegung," *Zeitschrift für Sinnesphysiologie* 68 (1940): 151–84. From Christian's conclusion: "Die vorliegende Arbeit hat Probleme des Bewegungssehens zum Gegenstand. An Hand von Versuchen wird . . . erfahren, daß die Sinnesschwelle des Auges unmittelbar und erheblich von unterschwelligen und daher unbewußten Erregungen des Vestibularorgans beeinflußt wird" (184) (The present work deals with problems concerning the seeing of movement. On the basis of experiments we have learned . . . that the sensory threshold of the eyes is directly and significantly influenced by subliminal and therefore subconscious excitations of the vestibular organs).

43. This refers to Ajuriaguerra and Hécaen, *Méconnaissances et hallucinations corporelles* (see note 17 in lecture 12).

44. The reference is to Ajuriaguerra and Hécaen's citation of the Head taximeter analogy in *Méconnaissances et hallucinations corporelles,* 344–45. Note that unlike Schilder's English in IAHB, their French rendering of the verb (*se présente*) was accurate. Concerning the original reference, see note 29 in lecture 10.

45. The reference is to Ajuriaguerra and Hécaen, *Méconnaissances et hallucinations corporelles,* 345.

46. See [127](XIV3)–[128](XIV4).

47. Merleau-Ponty is referring to an explicitly erotic letter from Alfred de Vigny to his mistress, Marie Dorval, dated January 7, 1833—see *Lettres pour lire au lit*, 11–14, 40–41.

48. "Agrammatism [or agrammatic aphasia] refers to language production that is lacking in grammatical structures. The basic signs of agrammatism are short phrase length, simplified syntax, errors and omissions of main verbs, and omission or substitution of grammatical morphemes . . . There may also be errors in tense, number, and gender, and difficulty in producing sentences with movement of grammatical elements . . . Spoken and written production typically shows similar error patterns. Typically, individuals with agrammatic aphasia also show impaired comprehension of grammatical structures" (Lyn Turkstra and Cynthia Thompson, "Agrammatism," in *Encyclopedia of Clinical Neuropsychology*).

49. Concerning *vigilance*, see note 2 in lecture 12.

50. See Paul Valéry, *L'idée fixe, ou deux hommes à la mer* (Paris: Les Laboratoires Martinet, 1932), in *Œuvres, tome II*, 233: "Un homme n'est rien tant que rien ne tire de lui des effets ou des productions qui le surprennent . . . en bien, ou en mal. Un homme, à l'état non sollicité est à l'état néant . . ." (A man is nothing as long as nothing draws from him effects or products that take him by surprise . . . for good or for ill. A man unsolicited is nothing . . .). The phrase "Un homme, à l'état non sollicité est à l'état néant" is cited by Merleau-Ponty in *Recherches sur l'usage littéraire du langage* at [69](VI7).

51. This is an allusion to Stendhal's metaphor of crystallization—see Stendhal [Marie-Henri Beyle], *De l'amour* (Paris: Pierre Mongie, 1822), 5: "Aux mines de sel de Saltzbourg, on jette dans les profondeurs abandonnées de la mine un rameau d'arbre effeuillé par l'hiver; deux ou trois mois après, on le retire couvert de cristallisations brillantes: les plus petites branches, celles qui ne sont pas plus grosses que la patte d'une mésange, sont garnies d'une infinité de diamants mobiles et éblouissants; on ne peut plus reconnaître le rameau primitif. [¶] Ce que j'appelle cristallisation, c'est l'opération de l'esprit, qui tire de tout ce qui se présente la découverte que l'objet aimé a de nouvelles perfections" (At the salt mines of Salzburg, a twig that has been stripped of its leaves by winter is thrown into the abandoned depths of the mine. Taken out two or three months later, it is covered with brilliant crystals. The smallest branches, those no larger than the leg of a sparrow, are coated with an infinity of shimmering, dazzling diamonds, and it is impossible to recognize the original branch. [¶] I call crystallization the operation of the mind that, from everything that is presented to it, draws the revelation that the object of its love has new perfections).

52. See Merleau-Ponty's discussion of Valéry in *Recherches sur l'usage littéraire du langage* at [51](IV5): "Tout langage nous trompe parce qu'il nous fait croire en autrui à des pleins là où il y a des vides ou des lacunes" (All language deceives us because it makes us believe there is fullness in others where there is actually emptiness or gaps); "Ce que l'auteur montre correspondant chez moi à lacune ou vide me fait croire à plénitude totale chez lui: 'Le génie quelquefois est une apparence due à ce fait—que le *plus facile*, le *chemin* le *plus favorable* n'est pas le même pour tous les hommes' [citing Valéry, *Tel quel I*, in *Œuvres*, II, 518] [¶] Davantage: c'est quelquefois justement par manque qu'autrui comprend [¶] C'est

quelquefois pour l'esprit un bien de manquer de ceci ou cela, il ne construit que dans l'absence. 'L'esprit vit de différences, l'écart l'excite; le défaut l'illumine; la plénitude le laisse inerte' [citing Valéry, *Tel quel II*, in *Œuvres, tome II*, 672] [¶] En particulier: c'est quelquefois par nos lacunes que nous transformons œuvre dont nous subissons l'influence. 'Nous disons qu'un auteur est *original* quand nous sommes dans l'ignorance des transformations cachées qui changèrent les autres en lui' [citing Valéry, *Variété II*, in *Œuvres, tome I*, 634–35]" (*Recherches sur l'usage littéraire du langage*, [55](V3)) (Whatever an author shows that corresponds to an emptiness or gap in me makes me believe in a total fullness in him: 'Genius is sometimes an appearance due to this fact—that the *easiest* and *most favorable path* isn't the same for everyone' [¶] Further: it is sometimes precisely because of a lack that the other understands [¶] It's sometimes good for the mind to lack this or that, it only builds in absence. 'The mind lives on differences, gaps excite it, deficiency enlightens it, while fullness leaves it inert' [¶] In particular: it's sometimes through our gaps that we transform work that's influencing us. 'We say that an author is *original* when we're unaware of the hidden transformations that changed the others in him').

53. Expression of the art historian Henri Focillon quoted (without reference) by Gilbert Cohen-Séat, in his *Essai sur les principes d'une philosophie du cinéma, I. Introduction générale: Notions fondamentales et vocabulaire de filmologie* (Paris: Presses Universitaires de France, 1946), 130: "Le symbolisme de la caméra n'est peut-être pas irréductible. Il n'y a, pour l'essentiel, que noir et blanc, lumière et ombre, et suggestion de tout le reste. Ce support, emprunté à l'image des choses concrètes, accepte toujours assez de souvenirs, et d'assez simples, pour se ployer dans le sens de chaque vision intérieure, si pauvre soit-elle, ou si riche. Du lyrisme propre de la caméra—le 'lyrisme du noir et blanc' disait Focillon—naît ainsi une source de lyrisme selon chacun" (The symbolism of the camera is perhaps not irreducible. In essence, there is only black and white, light and shadow, and everything else is suggestion. This medium, borrowed from the image of concrete things, always admits enough memories, and sufficiently simple ones, to bend in the direction of every internal vision, however impoverished or rich it may be. From the lyricism of the camera—the "lyricism of the black and white" as Focillon used to say—thus emerges a source of lyricism in accordance with each individual).

54. Merleau-Ponty is referring to Linschoten, "Experimentelle Untersuchung"—see note 44 in lecture 7.

55. Linschoten's experimentation concerning "so-called" induced movement involved the projection of numerous drawn pictures, but none, at least not in the article in question, seem to be of or otherwise make reference to a "scraper." If that reading is correct (the term *grattoir* is uncertain), it may be an arbitrary example on the part of Merleau-Ponty, or one drawn from some other source. Be that as it may, however, in §11 of Linschoten's article (71–76), there is an important discussion—which, incidentally, makes reference to Merleau-Ponty—concerning a drawing of a *Radler* (a cyclist) that seems very closely relevant (74): "Hinsichtlich der Realität der dargebotenen Figuren ist nun folgendes zu bemerken. Eine Vp. notiert z.B.: 'Der Radler bewegt sich', und der VI. fragt, inwieweit der Radler auch ein Radler ist. Die Vp. antwortet, daß der Radler wirk-

lich ein Radler ist, vielleicht nicht ganz richtig gezeichnet, aber doch ein Radler. 'Wenn er ein gezeichneter ist, ist er also doch kein reeller Radler', sagt der VI. Und deshalb überhaupt kein Radler. Solche Gespräche, die natürlich nur nach Beendigung des Versuches stattfinden dürfen, sind sehr einleuchtend. Es spricht für sich, daß die Vp. nie den gezeichneten Radler für einen wirklichen halten würde. Darin ist schon enthalten, daß die Vp. nicht erwartet, daß diese Figur sich unter allen Umständen wie ein reeller Radler verhalten wird. Wenn die 'Erwartung' in psychologischer Hinsicht auch ohne Einfluß bleibt (vgl. 14, S. 81f.), so gilt dies nicht für das unreflektierte Wissen um die Situation ('la conscience irréfléchie'; vgl. 18, S. 61), die sich als irreelle Situation konstituiert. Die Figur *ist* kein Radler, sondern *stellt einen dar.* Sie ist das *Sinnbild* eines Radlers, und es darf keine Verwunderung wecken, daß auch viele Vpn. auf Grund dieses Sinngehaltes den Radler bewegt sehen, viele andere aber ihn auf Grund seiner Unwirklichkeit unbewegt" (With regard to the reality of the presented figures the following is noteworthy. One subject writes, for example: 'The cyclist moves,' and the investigator asks to what extent the cyclist even is a cyclist. The subject answers that the cyclist really is a cyclist, perhaps not drawn fully correctly, but a cyclist nonetheless. 'If he's a drawn one, then he's not a real one after all,' the investigator says. And thus not a cyclist at all. Such conversations, which of course can only take place after the completion of the experiment, are very illuminating. It goes without saying that the subject would never consider the drawn cyclist to be a real one. This implies that the subject does not expect this figure to behave like a real cyclist under all circumstances. Even if 'expectation' in the psychological sense remains without effect [cf. Walter Krolik, 'Über Erfahrungswirkungen beim Bewegungssehen,' *Psychologischen Forschung* 20 (1935): 81–82], this is not the case for unreflective knowledge of the situation ('unreflective consciousness' [cf. Merleau-Ponty, *Phénoménologie de la perception*, 61]) that constitutes itself as an unreal situation. The figure *is* not a cyclist, but rather *presents one.* It is the symbol of a cyclist, and it is not surprising that on the basis of this meaningful content, many subjects see the cyclist move, while many others see it as stationary on the basis of its unreality). Note that Linschoten's reference to Merleau-Ponty appears mistaken; it could be to the phrase "la vie de conscience irréfléchie" (PhP 334/302). Note, too, that if the uncertain term were *racleur,* which also means "scraper," but which could more easily be mistaken for *Radler,* then the situation might be clearer. It's pure speculation, but perhaps in the course of Merleau-Ponty's consideration of Linschoten's article, *Radler* morphed in his notes into the orthographically similar term *racleur,* which then morphed into its synonym *grattoir.*

56. Note that in this sentence the term "habitus" is to be read in the plural.

57. As at other points, Merleau-Ponty is presumably alluding to Sartre's notion of "analogon" in the account he gives of the imaginary and its relation to the real in *L'imaginaire: Psychologie phénoménologique de l'imagination* (Paris: Gallimard, 1940).

58. Presumably a reference to Russian filmmaker Lev Kuleshov's 1919 montage experiments, in which a close-up shot of a well-known actor, Ivan Mozhukin, was interspliced with various scenes: a child playing, a bowl of soup, a person in

a coffin (there were variations—e.g., a woman on a divan, a child in the coffin—but the experiments were not rigorously documented). The first illegible word thus almost certainly refers (or, at any rate, should refer) to Kuleshov, while the second, given the grammatical structure, would likely refer to Mozhukin, either by name or simply qua actor. Note, however, that the experiment had been most widely discussed and promoted by Kuleshov's (well-known) student Vsevolod Pudovkin (who may well have been involved in it in some way), and it was often misattributed to him—indeed, Merleau-Ponty himself had done so in the late 1940s in "The Film and the New Psychology" (SNS 96–97/54). As François Albera has noted ("Maurice Merleau-Ponty et le cinéma," 144n65), it was not until 1951 that the outcome of the experiment was recognized as the "Kuleshov effect," so it is possible that Merleau-Ponty still had Pudovkin in mind in 1953. In any case, the experiment showed how Mozhukin's basically expressionless face—and it was always the same identical shot—was interpreted in completely different ways by viewers who took it as an affective response to the various scenes. For Kuleshov, the point was that cinematic significance is more a function of the edited sequence or arrangement of shots than of the individual shots themselves. As he once put it, "The content of the shots in itself is not so important as is the joining of two shots of different content and the method of their connection and their alteration" (*Kuleshov on Film*, trans. and ed. Ronald Levaco [Berkeley: University of California Press, 1974], 46–47). Here Merleau-Ponty links this to the corporeality of the viewer, and so we may see a connection between the experience of montage in the cinematic context and its sense as the "schematic typology" (see note 8 in lecture 4) that shapes the body schema's role in perception, and thus how the latter may both enable as well as constrain the former (i.e., cinematic montage cannot create just any response whatsoever).

59. The reference is to David Efron, *Gesture and Environment: A Tentative Study of Some of the Spatio-temporal and "Linguistic" Aspects of the Gestural Behavior of Eastern Jews and Southern Italians in New York City, Living Under Similar as Well as Different Environmental Conditions* (New York: King's Crown Press, 1941); reprinted, with the same subtitle, as *Gesture, Race, and Culture* (The Hague: Mouton, 1972).

60. Merleau-Ponty used the word "pattern" in English.

61. Merleau-Ponty used the expression "parental care" in English.

Bibliography

Merleau-Ponty's own bibliographic notes are found on pages [137] and [157]–[173] of the BNF dossier. In the words of the editors of the French volume, however, these notes are "burgeoning, redundant, often illegible and incomplete," and to them it seemed that these notes referred to far more works than were actually consulted and used by Merleau-Ponty during the course. Rather than simply transcribing them, then, the editors decided to assemble selectively a more judiciously streamlined bibliography, which they did in two parts: the first includes everything of which there is at least a clear and explicit trace in Merleau-Ponty's notes, while the second lists further references (including other works by Merleau-Ponty) that are mentioned in their editorial introduction and notes.

I have taken a different approach here. For there are some cases (e.g., sources that are directly relevant but which are not explicitly mentioned) in which it is not self-evident into which category a certain work should be placed. So given that the text and the notes already identify with sufficient clarity those sources to which Merleau-Ponty refers explicitly, in the following bibliography I take a unified all-in-one approach, including the sources that Merleau-Ponty explicitly used, along with all other texts referred to in the introduction and the annotative notes. Relevant works by Merleau-Ponty himself are also included here.

Ajuriaguerra, Julien de, and Henry Hécaen. *Le cortex cérébral: Étude neuro-psychopathologique.* Paris: Masson, 1949.

———. *Méconnaissances et hallucinations corporelles: Intégration et désintégration de la somatognosie.* Paris: Masson, 1952.

Albera, François. "Maurice Merleau-Ponty et le cinéma." *1895: Revue d'histoire du cinéma* 70 (2013): 121–53.

Auersperg, Alfred Prinz von, and Harry C. Buhrmester. "Experimenteller Beitrag zur Frage des Bewegtsehens." *Zeitschrift für die Sinnesphysiologie* 66 (1936): 274–309.

Ayouch, Thamy. "Lived Body and Fantasmatic Body: The Debate between Phenomenology and Psychoanalysis." *Journal of Theoretical and Philosophical Psychology* 28, no. 2 (2009): 336–55.

Behrens, Roy R. "Camouflage, Art and Gestalt." *North American Review* 265, no. 4 (1980): 8–18.

Benary, Wilhelm. "Studien zur Untersuchung der Intelligenz bei einem Fall von Seelenblindheit." *Psychologische Forschung* 2 (1922): 209–97.

Benoist, Jocelyn. "Une première naturalisation de la phénoménologie?" In *L'itinéraire de Tran Duc Thao: Phénoménologie et transfert culturel*, edited by Jocelyn Benoist and Michel Espagne, 25–46. Paris: Armand Colin, 2013.

Berenson, Bernard. *Aesthetics and History in the Visual Arts*. New York: Pantheon, 1948.

———. *Esthétique et histoire des arts visuels*. Translated by Jean Alazard. Paris: Albin Michel, 1953.

Bergson, Henri. *Creative Evolution*. Translated by Arthur Mitchell. New York: Holt, 1911.

———. *The Creative Mind*. Translated by Mabelle L. Andison. New York: Philosophical Library, 1946.

———. *La pensée et le mouvant*. Paris: Félix Alcan, 1934.

———. *L'évolution créatrice*. Paris: Félix Alcan, 1908.

———. *Matière et mémoire*. Paris: Félix Alcan, 1896.

———. *Matter and Memory*. Translated by Nancy Margaret Paul and William Scott Palmer. London: Allen and Unwin; New York: Macmillan, 1911. Reprint, New York: Zone Books, 1991.

Beyle, Marie-Henri [Stendhal]. *De l'amour*. Paris: Pierre Mongie, 1822.

Bogaert, Ludo van. "Sur la pathologie de l'image de soi (Études anatomo-cliniques)." *Annales médico-psychologiques* 92 (1934): 519–55, 744–59.

Brain, W. Russell. "Visual Disorientation with Special Reference to Lesions of the Right Cerebral Hemisphere." *Brain* 64 (1941): 244–72.

Bréhier, Émile. *La théorie des incorporels dans l'ancien stoïcisme*. Paris: A. Picard, 1907.

Brunschvicg, Léon. *Le progrès de la conscience dans la philosophie occidentale*. Paris: Félix Alcan, 1927.

Bruzina, Ronald. "Eugen Fink and Maurice Merleau-Ponty: The Philosophical Lineage in Phenomenology." In *Merleau-Ponty's Reading of Husserl*, edited by Lester Embree and Ted Toadvine, 173–200. Dordrecht: Kluwer, 2002.

Bühler, Karl. *Sprachtheorie: Die Darstellungsfunktion der Sprache*. Jena: Gustav Fischer, 1934.

———. "Über den Begriff der sprachlichen Darstellung." *Psychologischen Forschung* 3 (1923): 282–94.

Busche, Hubertus. "Mind and Body in the Young Leibniz." In *Individuals, Minds and Bodies: Themes from Leibniz*, edited by Massimiliano Carrara, Antonio-Maria Nunziante, and Gabriele Tomasi, 141–58. Stuttgart: Franz Steiner, 2004.

Byerley, Amy K., and Andrew S. Davis. "Constructional Apraxia." In *Encyclopedia of Clinical Neuropsychology*, edited by Jeffrey S. Kreutzer, John DeLuca, and Bruce Caplan. New York: Springer, 2011.

Cairns, Dorion. *Guide for Translating Husserl*. The Hague: Martinus Nijhoff, 1973.

Cassin, Barbara, ed. *Dictionary of Untranslatables: A Philosophical Lexicon*. Translated by Steven Rendall, Christian Hubert, Jeffrey Mehlman, Nathanael Stein, and Michael Syrotinski. Translation edited by Emily Apter, Jacques Lezra, and Michael Wood. Princeton, N.J.: Princeton University Press, 2014.

———, ed. *Vocabulaire européen des philosophies: Dictionnaire des intraduisibles.* Paris: Le Seuil / Le Robert, 2004.

Cassirer, Ernst. *Philosophie der symbolischen Formen. Dritter Teil: Phänomenologie der Erkenntnis.* Berlin: Bruno Cassirer, 1929.

———. *The Philosophy of Symbolic Forms, Volume Three: The Phenomenology of Knowledge.* Translated by Ralph Manheim. New Haven, Conn.: Yale University Press, 1957.

Christian, Paul. "Wirklichkeit und Erscheinung in der Wahrnehmung von Bewegung." *Zeitschrift für Sinnesphysiologie* 68 (1940): 151–84.

Claudel, Paul. *Art poétique.* Paris: Mercure de France, 1913.

———. *Poetic Art.* Translated by Renée Spodheim. New York: Philosophical Library, 1948.

Cohen-Séat, Gilbert. *Essai sur les principes d'une philosophie du cinema, I. Introduction générale: Notions fondamentales et vocabulaire de filmologie.* Paris: Presses Universitaires de France, 1946.

Coole, Diana. "The Aesthetic Realm and the Lifeworld: Kant and Merleau-Ponty." *History of Political Thought* 5, no. 3 (1984): 503–26.

Corsini, Ray. *The Dictionary of Psychology.* New York: Routledge, 2016.

Courville, Denis. "La naissance de l'espace moderne: Merleau-Ponty et Panofsky sur la perspective linéaire." *Ithaque: Revue de philosophie de l'Université de Montréal* 7 (2010): 21–46.

Crawley, Greer. "Strategic Scenography: Staging the Landscape of War." PhD diss., University of Vienna, 2011.

Denes, Gianfranco, Maria Christina Mantovan, Alessandra Gallana, and Jee Yun Cappelletti. "Limb-Kinetic Apraxia." *Movement Disorders* 13 (1998): 468–76.

Dorval, Marie. *Lettres à Alfred de Vigny.* Edited by Charles Gaudier. Paris: Gallimard, 1942.

Duncker, Karl. "Induced Motion." In *A Sourcebook of Gestalt Psychology,* edited and translated by Willis D. Ellis, 161–72. New York: Harcourt, Brace, 1939.

———. "On Problem-Solving." Translated by Lynne S. Lees. *Psychological Monographs* 58, no. 5 (1945): 1–113.

———. "Über induzierte Bewegung: Ein Beitrag zur Theorie optisch wahrgenommener Bewegung." *Psychologische Forschung* 12 (1929): 180–259.

Efron, David. *Gesture and Environment: A Tentative Study of Some of the Spatio-temporal and "Linguistic" Aspects of the Gestural Behavior of Eastern Jews and Southern Italians in New York City, Living Under Similar as Well as Different Environmental Conditions.* New York: King's Crown Press, 1941. Reprinted, with the same subtitle, as *Gesture, Race, and Culture.* The Hague: Mouton, 1972.

Epstein, Jean. *The Intelligence of a Machine.* Translated by Christophe Wall-Romana. Minneapolis: Univocal Publishing, 2014.

———. *L'intelligence d'une machine.* Paris: Jacques Melot, 1946.

Fink, Eugen. "L'analyse intentionnelle et le problème de la pensée spéculative/ Die intentionale Analyse und das Problem des spekulativen Denkens." In *Problèmes actuels de la phénoménologie,* edited by H. L. Van Breda, 53–87. Paris: Desclée de Brouwer, 1952. Reprinted in *Proximité et distance: Essais et conférences phénoménologiques*, edited and translated by Jean Kessler, 113–27. Grenoble, Fr.: Jérôme Millon, 1994.

———. *VI. Cartesianische Meditation: Teil 1, Die Idee einer transzendentalen Methodenlehre.* Edited by Hans Ebeling, Jann Holl, and Guy van Kerckhoven. Dordrecht: Kluwer, 1998.

———. *Sixth Cartesian Meditation: The Idea of a Transcendental Theory of Method.* Translated by Ronald Bruzina. Bloomington: Indiana University Press, 1995.

Francastel, Pierre. "Espace et illusion." *Revue internationale de filmologie* 2, no. 5 (1949): 65–74.

Freud, Sigmund. "Some Neurotic Mechanisms in Jealousy, Paranoia and Homosexuality." In *The Standard Edition of the Complete Psychological Works of Sigmund Freud, Volume 18: Beyond the Pleasure Principle, Group Psychology and Other Works, 1920–1922*, edited by James Strachey (in collaboration with Anna Freud, assisted by Alix Strachey and Alan Tyson), 221–35. New York: Vintage, 1999.

———. "Über einige neurotische Mechanismen bei Eifersucht, Paranoia und Homosexualität." *Internationale Zeitschrift für Psychoanalyse* 8, no. 3 (1922): 249–58. Reprinted in *Gesammelte Werke*, vol. 13, edited by Anna Freud, Marie Bonaparte, E. Bibring, W. Hoffer, E. Kris, and O. Osakower, 195–207. Frankfurt am Main: S. Fischer, 1940.

Fröhlich, Friedrich W. *Die Empfindungszeit: Ein Beitrag zur Lehre von der Zeit-, Raum- und Bewegungsempfindung.* Jena: Gustav Fischer, 1929.

———. "Über die Messung der Empfindungszeit." *Zeitschrift für Sinnesphysiologie* 54 (1923): 58–78.

Gelb, Adhémar. "Grundfragen der Wahrnehmungspsychologie." In *Bericht über den VII. Kongreß für experimentelle Psychologie*, edited by Karl Bühler, 114–26. Jena: Gustav Fischer, 1921.

Gerstmann, Josef. "Fingeragnosie und isolierte Agraphie—ein neues Syndrom." *Zeitschrift für die gesamte Neurologie* 108 (1927): 152–77.

———. "Syndrome of Finger Agnosia, Disorientation for Right and Left, Agraphia and Acalculia: Local Diagnostic Value." *Archives of Neurology and Psychiatry* 44, no. 2 (1940): 398–408.

Goldenberg, Georg. "Apraxia and Beyond: Life and Work of Hugo Liepmann." *Cortex* 39 (2003): 509–24.

———. *Apraxia: The Cognitive Side of Motor Control.* Oxford: Oxford University Press, 2013.

Goldstein, Kurt. *The Organism: A Holistic Approach to Biology Derived from Pathological Data in Man.* 1934. Reprint, New York: Zone Books, 1995.

———. "Remarques sur le problème épistémologique de la biologie." In *Selected Papers/Ausgewählte Schriften*, edited by Aron Gurwitsch, Else M. Goldstein Haudek, and William E. Haudek, 439–442. The Hague: Martinus Nijhoff, 1971.

———. "Über Zeigen und Greifen." *Nervenartzt* 4 (1931): 453–66. Reprinted in Kurt Goldstein, *Selected Papers/Ausgewählte Schriften*, edited by Aron Gurwitsch, Else M. Goldstein Haudek, and William E. Haudek, 263–81. The Hague: Martinus Nijhoff, 1971.

———. "Zur Lehre der motorischen Apraxie." *Journal für Psychologie und Neurologie* 11 (1908): 169–87, 270–83.

Goldstein, Kurt, and Adhémar Gelb. "Psychologische Analysen hirnpathologischer Fälle auf Grund von Untersuchungen Hirnverletzer." *Zeitschrift für die gesamte Neurologie und Psychiatrie* 41 (1918): 1–142.

———. "Über Farbennamenamnesie: Nebst Bemerkungen über das Wesen der amnestischen Aphasie überhaupt und die Beziehung zwischen Sprache und dem Verhalten zur Umwelt." *Psychologische Forschung* 6 (1924): 127–86.

Gorbman, Claudia. *Unheard Melodies: Narrative Film Music.* Bloomington: Indiana University Press, 1987.

———. "Vigo/Jaubert." *Cine-Tracts* 1, no. 2 (1977): 65–80.

Gottschaldt, Kurt. "Gestalt Factors and Repetition." In *A Sourcebook of Gestalt Psychology*, edited and translated by Willis D. Ellis, 109–22, 123–35. New York: Harcourt, Brace, 1939.

———. "Über den Einfluss der Erfahrung auf die Wahrnehmung von Figuren, I: Die Wirkung gehäufter Einprägung von Figuren auf ihre Sichtbarkeit in umfassenden Konfigurationen." *Psychologische Forschung* 8, no. 1 (1926): 261–317.

———. "Über den Einfluss der Erfahrung auf die Wahrnehmung von Figuren, II: Vergleichende Untersuchungen über die Wirkung figuraler Einprägung und den Einfluss spezifischer Geschehensverläufe auf die Auffassung optischer Komplexe." *Psychologische Forschung* 12, no. 1 (1929): 1–87.

Grünbaum, Abraham Anton. "Aphasie und Motorik." *Zeitschrift für die gesamte Neurologie und Psychiatrie* 130 (1930): 385–412.

Guterman, Norbert, and Henri Lefebvre. *La conscience mystifiée.* Paris: Gallimard, 1936.

Halbwachs, Maurice. *Les cadres sociaux de la mémoire.* Paris: Félix Alcan, 1925.

———. *On Collective Memory.* Edited and translated by Lewis Coser. Chicago: University of Chicago Press, 1992.

Hartmann, George Wilfried. *Gestalt Psychology: A Survey of Facts and Principles.* New York: Ronald Press, 1935.

Hartmann, Heinz, and Paul Schilder. "Zur Psychologie Schädelverletzter." *Archiv für Psychiatrie und Nerven-krankheiten* 75, no. 1 (1925): 287–300.

Head, Henry. "Aphasia and Kindred Disorders of Speech." *Brain* 43, no. 2 (1920): 87–165.

———. *Aphasia and Kindred Disorders of Speech.* 2 vols. Cambridge: Cambridge University Press, 1926.

———. "Disorders of Symbolic Thinking and Expression." *British Journal of Psychology* 11, no. 2 (1921): 179–93.

———. "Sensation and the Cerebral Cortex." *Brain* 41, no. 2 (1918): 57–201.

———. *Studies in Neurology.* 2 vols. Oxford: Oxford University Press, 1920.

Head, Henry, and Gordon Holmes. "Sensory Disturbances from Cerebral Lesions." *Brain* 34, no. 2/3 (1911): 102–254.

Hécaen, Henry. "La notion de schéma corporel et ses applications en psychiatrie." *L'évolution psychiatrique* 2 (1948): 75–122.

Hécaen, Henry, and Julien de Ajuriaguerra. "L'apraxie de l'habillage: Ses rapports avec la planotopokinésie et les troubles de la somatognosie." *Encéphale* 35 (1942): 113–44.

Hécaen, Henry, Wilder Penfield, Claude Bertrand, and Robert Malmo. "The Syndrome of Apractognosia Due to Lesions of the Minor Cerebral Hemisphere." *Archives of Neurology and Psychiatry* 75, no. 4 (1956): 400–434.

Heidegger, Martin. *Being and Time.* Translated by John Macquarrie and Edward Robinson. Oxford: Blackwell, 1962.

———. *Sein und Zeit.* 1927. 8th ed. Reprint, Tübingen: Max Niemeyer, 1957.

Heilman, Kenneth M. "Anosognosia." In *Encyclopedia of Clinical Neuropsychology*, edited by Jeffrey S. Kreutzer, John DeLuca, and Bruce Caplan. New York: Springer, 2011.

Hier, Daniel, Philip Gorelick, and Andrea Gellin Shindler. *Topics in Behavioral Neurology and Neuropsychology: With Key References.* Stoneman, Mass.: Butterworths, 2013.

Husserl, Edmund. *The Crisis of European Sciences and Transcendental Phenomenology: An Introduction to Phenomenological Philosophy.* Translated by David Carr. Evanston, Ill.: Northwestern University Press, 1970.

———. *Die Krisis der europäischen Wissenschaften und die transzendentale Phänomenologie: Eine Einleitung in die phänomenologische Philosophie.* Edited by Walter Biemel. 1954. Reprint, The Hague: Martinus Nijhoff, 1962.

———. *Erfahrung und Urteil: Untersuchungen zur Genealogie der Logik.* Edited by Ludwig Landgrebe. 1939. Reprint, Hamburg: Felix Meiner, 1997.

———. *Experience and Judgment: Investigations in a Genealogy of Logic.* Translated by James S. Churchill and Karl Ameriks. Evanston, Ill.: Northwestern University Press, 1973.

———. *Ideas Pertaining to a Pure Phenomenology and to a Phenomenological Philosophy: First Book, General Introduction to a Pure Phenomenology.* Translated by Fred Kersten. Dordrecht: Kluwer, 1982.

———. *Ideen zu einer reinen Phänomenologie und phänomenologischen Philosophie. Erstes Buch: Allgemeine Einführung in die reine Phänomenologie.* Halle: Max Niemeyer, 1913.

———. *Idées directrices pour une phénoménologie et une philosophie phénoménologique pures. Tome premier: Introduction générale à la phénoménologie pure.* Translated by Paul Ricœur. Paris: Gallimard, 1950.

Jastrow, Joseph. "Studies from the Laboratory of Experimental Psychology of the University of Wisconsin.—II." *American Journal of Psychology* 4, no. 3 (1892): 381–428.

Jaubert, Maurice. "Le cinéma: La musique." *Esprit* 43 (1936): 114–19.

Jeanneret, Charles-Édouard [Le Corbusier]. *Toward an Architecture.* Translated by John Goodman. Los Angeles: Getty Research Institute, 2007.

———. *Vers une architecture.* Paris: Georges Crès, 1923.

Kant, Immanuel. *Critique of the Power of Judgment.* 1790. Edited by Paul Guyer.

Translated by Paul Guyer and Eric Matthews. Cambridge: Cambridge University Press, 2000.

———. *Critique of Practical Reason.* 1788. Translated by Mary J. Gregor. Cambridge: Cambridge University Press, 1997.

———. *Critique of Pure Reason.* 1781, 1787. Edited and translated by Paul Guyer and Allen W. Wood. Cambridge: Cambridge University Press, 1998.

Keller, Helen. *Sourde, muette, aveugle: Histoire de ma vie.* Translated by Antoinette Huzard. Paris: Payot, 1915.

———. *The Story of My Life.* New York: Doubleday, 1903.

Kenkel, Friedrich. "Untersuchungen über den Zusammenhang zwischen Erscheinungsgrösse und Erscheinungsbewegung bei einer sogenannten optischen Täuschungen." *Zeitschrift für Psychologie* 67 (1913): 358–449.

Klein, Elmer, and Paul Schilder. "The Japanese Illusion and the Postural Model of the Body." *Journal of Nervous and Mental Disease* 70, no. 3 (1929): 241–63.

Kleist, Karl. *Gehirnpathologie.* Leipzig: Ambrosius Barth, 1934.

———. "Kortikale (innervatorische) Apraxie." *Jahrbuch fur Psychiatrie and Neurologie* 28 (1907): 46–112.

Koffka, Kurt. "Die Wahrnehmung von Bewegung." In *Receptionsorgane II,* vol. 12/2 of *Handbuch der normalen und pathologischen Physiologie, mit Berücksichtigung der experimentellen Pharmakologie,* edited by Albrecht Bethe, Gustav von Bergmann, Gustav Embden, and Alexander Ellinger, 1166–1214. Berlin: Springer, 1931.

———. *Principles of Gestalt Psychology.* New York: Harcourt, Brace, 1935.

Köhler, Wolfgang. *Gestalt Psychology: An Introduction to New Concepts in Modern Psychology.* New York: Liveright, 1947.

———. "Tonpsychologie." In *Handbuch der Neurologie des Ohres,* vol. 1, edited by Gustav Alexander and Otto Marburg, 419–64. Vienna: Urban & Schwarzenberg, 1924.

Kohnstamm, Oskar. "Demonstration einer katatonieartigen Erscheinung beim Gesunden (Katatonusversuch)." *Neurologisches Zentralblatt* 34 (1915): 290–91.

Kraepelin, Emil. *Über Sprachstörungen im Traume.* Leipzig: Wilhelm Engelmann, 1906.

Krolik, Walter. "Über Erfahrungswirkungen beim Bewegungssehen." *Psychologischen Forschung* 20 (1935): 47–101.

Kuleshov, Lev. *Kuleshov on Film.* Translated and edited by Ronald Levaco. Berkeley: University of California Press, 1974.

Lachièze-Rey, Pierre. *Le moi, le monde et dieu.* Paris: Boivin, 1935.

Lalande, André, ed. *Vocabulaire technique et critique de la philosophie,* vol. 2. 4th ed. Paris: Félix Alcan, 1932.

Lange, Johannes. "Agnosien und Apraxien." In *Handbuch der Neurologie,* vol. 6, edited by Oswald Bumke and Otfrid Foerster, 807–960. Berlin: Springer, 1936.

———. "Probleme der Fingeragnosie." *Zeitschrift für die gesamte Neurologie und Psychiatrie* 147, no. 1 (1933): 594–610.

Le Corbusier. *See* Jeanneret, Charles-Édouard.

Leibniz, Gottfried Wilhelm. *Specimen inventorum de admirandis naturae generalis arcanis.* In *Die philosophischen schriften von Gottfried Wilhelm Leibniz*, vol. 7, edited by Carl Immanuel Gerhardt, 309–18. Berlin: Weidmann, 1890.

Leibniz, Gottfried Wilhelm, and Bartholomew Des Bosses. *The Leibniz–Des Bosses Correspondence.* Translated and edited by Brandon C. Look and Donald Rutherford. New Haven, Conn.: Yale University Press, 2007.

Leonardo da Vinci. *Traité de la peinture, traduit intégralement pour la première fois en français sur le codex vaticanus (urbinas) 1270, complété par de nombreux fragments tirés des manuscrits du maître, ordonné méthodiquement et accompagné de commentaires.* Edited by Joseph-Aimé Péladan. Paris: Delagrave, 1910.

———. *Trattato della pittura di Lionardo da Vinci, tratto da un codice della Biblioteca Vaticana e dedicato alla maestà di Luigi 18. re di Francia e di Navarra.* Edited by Guglielmo Manzi. Rome: Nella stamperia De Romanis, 1817.

———. *Treatise on Painting, Volume 1: Translation.* Translated by Amos Philip McMahon. Princeton, N.J.: Princeton University Press, 1956.

Lewin, Kurt. "Das Problem der Willensmessung und das Grundgesetz der Assoziation. I." *Psychologische Forschung* 1 (1922): 191–302.

———. "Das Problem der Willensmessung und das Grundgesetz der Assoziation. II." *Psychologische Forschung* 2 (1922): 65–140.

———. "Kriegslandschaft." *Zeitschrift für angewandte Psychologie* 12 (1917): 440–47.

———. "The Landscape of War." Translated by Jonathan Blower. *Art in Translation* 1, no. 2 (2009): 199–209.

———. "Untersuchungen zur Handlungs- und Affekt-Psychologie. I: Vorbemerkungen über die psychischen Kräfte und Energien und über die Struktur der Seele." *Psychologische Forschung* 7 (1926): 294–329.

———. "Will and Needs." In *A Sourcebook of Gestalt Psychology*, edited and translated by Willis D. Ellis, 283–99. New York: Harcourt, Brace, 1939.

Lewis, Hannah. "'The Music Has Something to Say': The Musical Revisions of *L'Atalante* (1934)." *Journal of the American Musicological Society* 68, no. 3 (2015): 559–603.

Lhermitte, Jean. *L'image de notre corps.* Paris: Éditions de la Nouvelle revue critique, 1939.

Lhermitte, Jean, and Jean Mouzon. "Sur l'apractognosie géométrique et l'apraxie constructive consécutives aux lésions du lobe occipital." *Revue neurologique* 73 (1941): 415–31.

Libera, Alain de, and Irène Rosier-Catach. "Dictum." In *Vocabulaire européen des philosophies: Dictionnaire des intraduisibles*, edited by Barbara Cassin. Paris: Le Seuil / Le Robert, 2004.

Liepmann, Hugo Karl. "Apraxie." *Ergebnisse der gesamten Medizin* 1 (1920): 516–43.

———. *Drei Aufsätze aus dem Apraxiegebiet.* Berlin: Karger, 1908.

Linke, Paul Ferdinand. "Die stroboskopischen Täuschungen und das Problem des Sehens von Bewegungen." *Psychologische Studien* 3, no. 5/6 (1907): 393–545.

Linschoten, Johannes. "Experimentelle Untersuchung der sog. induzierten Bewegung." *Psychologische Forschung* 24 (1952): 34–92.

Maak, Niklas. *Le Corbusier: The Architect on the Beach.* Munich: Hirmer, 2011.

The Man in the White Suit. Directed by Alexander Mackendrick. London: Ealing Studios, 1951.

Marx, Karl. *Morceaux choisis.* Edited by Paul Nizan and Jean Duret. Paris: Gallimard, 1934.

Mayer, Felix. "Die Struktur des Traumes." *Acta Psychologica* 3, no. 1 (1937): 81–136.

Mayer-Gross, Wilhelm. "Some Observations on Apraxia." *Proceedings of the Royal Society of Medicine* 28 (1935): 1203–12.

McFie, John, Malcolm Piercy, and Oliver Zangwill. "Visual-Spatial Agnosia Associated with Lesions of the Right Cerebral Hemisphere." *Brain* 73, no. 2 (1950): 167–90.

Mendoza, John E. "Allesthesia," "Asomatognosia," "Autotopagnosia," "Gerstmann's Syndrome," in *Encyclopedia of Clinical Neuropsychology*, edited by Jeffrey S. Kreutzer, John DeLuca, and Bruce Caplan. New York: Springer, 2011.

Menninger-Lerchenthal, Erich. *Das Truggebilde der eigenen Gestalt: Heautoskopie, Doppelgänger.* Berlin: Karger, 1935.

Merleau-Ponty, Maurice. *Child Psychology and Pedagogy: The Sorbonne Lectures, 1949–1952.* Translated by Talia Welsh. Evanston, Ill.: Northwestern University Press, 2010.

———. *Éloge de la philosophie: Leçon inaugurale faite au Collège de France le jeudi 15 janvier 1953.* Paris: Gallimard, 1953.

———. "Eye and Mind." Translated by Carleton Dallery. In *The Primacy of Perception: And Other Essays on Phenomenological Psychology, the Philosophy of Art, History, and Politics,* edited by James M. Edie, 159–90. Evanston, Ill.: Northwestern University Press, 1964.

———. *Humanism and Terror: An Essay on the Communist Problem.* Translated by John O'Neill. Boston: Beacon Press, 1969.

———. *Humanisme et terreur: Essai sur le problème communiste.* Paris: Gallimard, 1947.

———. *In Praise of Philosophy and Other Essays.* Translated by John O'Neill. Evanston, Ill.: Northwestern University Press, 1988.

———. *Institution and Passivity: Course Notes from the Collège de France, 1954–1955.* Translated by Leonard Lawlor and Heath Massey. Evanston, Ill.: Northwestern University Press, 2010.

———. *La prose du monde.* Edited by Claude Lefort. Paris: Gallimard, 1969.

———. *La structure du comportement.* Paris: Presses Universitaires de France, 1942.

———. *Le monde sensible et le monde de l'expression: Cours au Collège de France, Notes, 1953.* Edited by Emmanuel de Saint Aubert and Stefan Kristensen. Geneva: MétisPresses, 2011.

———. "Le primat de la perception et ses conséquences philosophiques." 1946. In *Le primat de la perception et ses conséquences philosophiques, précédé de Projet de travail sur la nature de la perception, 1933, La Nature de la perception, 1934,* edited by Jacques Prunair, 41–104. Lagrasse, Fr.: Verdier, 1996.

———. *L'institution. La passivité: Notes de cours au Collège de France, 1954–1955.*

Edited by Dominique Darmaillacq and Stéphanie Ménasé. Paris: Belin, 2003.

———. *L'œil et l'esprit.* Paris: Gallimard, 1964.

———. *Parcours deux, 1951–1961.* Edited by Jacques Prunair. Lagrasse, Fr.: Verdier, 2000.

———. *Phénoménologie de la perception.* Paris: Gallimard, 1945.

———. *Phenomenology of Perception.* Translated by Donald A. Landes. London: Routledge, 2012.

———. "The Primacy of Perception, and Its Philosophical Consequences." Translated by James M. Edie. In *The Primacy of Perception: And Other Essays on Phenomenological Psychology, the Philosophy of Art, History, and Politics,* edited by James M. Edie, 12–42. Evanston, Ill.: Northwestern University Press, 1964.

———. *The Prose of the World.* Translated by John O'Neill. Evanston, Ill.: Northwestern University Press, 1973.

———. *Psychologie et pédagogie de l'enfant: Cours de Sorbonne, 1949–52.* Edited by Jacques Prunair. Lagrasse, Fr.: Verdier, 2001.

———. *Recherches sur l'usage littéraire du langage: Cours au Collège de France, Notes, 1953.* Edited by Benedetta Zaccarello and Emmanuel de Saint Aubert. Geneva: MétisPresses, 2013.

———. *Résumés de cours: Collège de France, 1952–1960.* Paris: Gallimard, 1968.

———. *Sense and Non-Sense.* Translated by H. L. Dreyfus and P. A. Dreyfus. Evanston, Ill.: Northwestern University Press, 1964.

———. *Sens et non-sens.* Paris: Nagel, 1948.

———. *Signes.* Paris: Gallimard, 1960.

———. *Signs.* Translated by Richard C. McCleary. Evanston, Ill.: Northwestern University Press, 1964.

———. *The Structure of Behavior.* Translated by Alden L. Fisher. Boston: Beacon Press, 1963.

———. *Themes from the Lectures at the Collège de France, 1952–1960.* Translated by John O'Neill. Evanston, Ill.: Northwestern University Press, 1970.

Metzger, Wolfgang. *Psychologie: Die Entwicklung ihrer Grundannahmen seit der Einführung des Experiments.* Leipzig: Steinkopff, 1941.

Meyer, Linda. "Paraphasia." In *Encyclopedia of Clinical Neuropsychology,* edited by Jeffrey S. Kreutzer, John DeLuca, and Bruce Caplan. New York: Springer, 2011.

Michotte, Albert. *La perception de la causalité.* Louvain: Éditions de l'Institut Supérieur de Philosophie; Paris: Vrin, 1946.

———. *The Perception of Causality.* Translated by Tim R. Miles and Elaine Miles. London: Methuen, 1963.

Mitchell, Silas Weir. "The Case of George Dedlow." *Atlantic Monthly* 18, no. 105 (1866): 1–11.

———. *Des lésions des nerfs et de leurs conséquences.* Translated by Albert Dastre. Paris: G. Masson, 1874.

———. *Injuries of Nerves and Their Consequences.* Philadelphia: Lippincott, 1872.

———. "Phantom Limbs." *Lippincott's Magazine of Popular Literature and Science* 8 (1871): 563–69.

Morlass, Joseph. *Contribution à l'étude de l'apraxie.* Paris: Amédée Legrand, 1928.
Müller-Lyer, Franz Carl. "Optische Urteilstäuschungen." *Archiv für Physiologie* (1889 suppl.): 263–70.
Muncie, Wendell. "Concrete Model and Abstract Copy: A Psychobiological Interpretation of the 'Closing-in' Symptom of Mayer-Gross." *Journal of Nervous and Mental Disease* 88 (1938): 1–11.
Noble, Stephen. "Maurice Merleau-Ponty, or the Pathway of Philosophy: Desiderata for an Intellectual Biography." *Chiasmi International* 13 (2011): 63–122.
Nurmikko, Turo. "Paresthesia." In *Encyclopedia of Pain,* edited by Gerald F. Gebhart and Robert F. Schmidt. Berlin: Springer, 2013.
Ombredane, André. *Études de psychologie médicale, tome I: Perception et langage.* Rio de Janeiro: Atlantica Editora, 1944.
———. *Études de psychologie médicale, tome II: Geste et action.* Rio de Janeiro: Atlantica Editora, 1944.
———. *L'aphasie et l'élaboration de la pensée explicite.* Paris: Presses Universitaires de France, 1951.
Paliard, Jacques. *Pensée implicite et perception visuelle: Ébauche d'une optique psychologique.* Paris: Presses Universitaires de France, 1949.
Panofsky, Erwin. *Perspective as Symbolic Form.* Translated by Christopher S. Wood. New York: Zone Books, 1991.
———. "Perspektive als 'symbolische Form.'" In *Vorträge der Bibliothek Warburg 1924/1925,* edited by Fritz Saxl, 258–330. Leipzig: B. G. Teubner, 1927.
Parviel, Armand. *Le roman douloureux d'Alfred de Vigny.* Paris: Les éditions de France, 1934.
Paterson, Andrew, and Oliver Zangwill. "Disorders of Visual Space Perception Associated with Lesions of the Right Cerebral Hemisphere." *Brain* 67, no. 4 (1944): 331–58.
Paulhan, Jean. *The Flowers of Tarbes; or, Terror in Literature.* Translated by Michael Syrotinski. Urbana-Champaign: University of Illinois Press, 2006.
———. "La peinture moderne ou l'espace sensible au cœur." *La table ronde* 2 (February 1948): 267–80.
———. *Les fleurs de Tarbes.* Paris: Gallimard, 1941.
Pearce, J. M. S. "Hugo Karl Liepmann and Apraxia." *Clinical Medicine: Journal of the Royal College of Physicians* 9, no. 5 (2009): 466–70.
Piaget, Jean. *The Child's Conception of Movement and Speed.* Translated by G. E. T. Holloway and M. J. Mackenzie. New York: Basic Books, 1970.
———. *The Child's Conception of Time.* Translated by Arnold Julius Pomerans. New York: Routledge, 1969.
———. *Le développement de la notion de temps chez l'enfant.* Paris: Presses Universitaires de France, 1946.
———. *Les notions de mouvement et de vitesse chez l'enfant.* Paris: Presses Universitaires de France, 1946.
Piaget, Jean, and Marc Lambercier. With the collaboration of B. Bergert-Demetriades, H. Aebli, and M. Gantenbein. "La perception d'un carré

animé d'un mouvement de circumduction (effet Auersperg et Buhrmester)." *Archives de psychologie* 33, no. 130 (1951): 131–95.

Pick, Arnold. "Störung der Orientierung am eigenen Körper: Beitrag zur Lehre vom Bewußtsein des eigenen Körpers." *Psychologische Forschung* 1 (1922): 303–18.

———. *Über Störungen der Orientierung am eigenen Körper: Arbeiten aus der deutschen psychiatrischen Universitätsklinik in Prag.* Berlin: Karger, 1908.

Piéron, Henri. *Principles of Experimental Psychology.* Translated by James Burt Miner. 1929. Reprint, London: Routledge, 1999.

———. *Psychologie expérimentale.* Paris: Armand Colin, 1927.

Plessner, Helmuth, and Frederik Buytendijk. "Die Deutung des mimischen Ausdrucks: Ein Beitrag zur Lehre vom Bewußtsein des anderen Ichs." *Philosophischer Anzeiger* 1, no. 1 (1925): 72–126. Reprinted in Helmuth Plessner, *Gesammelte Schriften in zehn Bänden. VII: Ausdruck und menschliche Natur,* edited by Günter Dux, Odo Marquand, and Elisabeth Ströker, 65–129. Frankfurt am Main: Suhrkamp, 2003.

Poeck, Klaus. "Ideational Apraxia." *Journal of Neurology* 230, no. 1 (1983): 1–5.

Porcile, François. *Maurice Jaubert: Musicien populaire ou maudit?* Paris: Les Éditeurs Français Réunis, 1971.

Pötzl, Otto. "Über die Herderscheinungen bei Läsion des linken unteren Scheitellappens." *Medizinische Klinik* 19 (1923): 7–11.

Pritchard, Colin. "Type and Eidos—Schutz and Husserl." *Journal of the British Society for Phenomenology* 15, no. 3 (1984): 307–11.

Ravaisson, Félix. "Dessin." In *Dictionnaire de pédagogie et d'instruction primaire,* part 1, vol. 1, edited by Ferdinand Buisson, 669–97. Paris: Hachette, 1887.

Renzi, Ennio De, and Pietro Faglioni. "Apraxia." In *Handbook of Clinical and Experimental Neuropsychology,* edited by Gianfranco Denes and Luigi Pizzamiglio. Hove, U.K.: Psychology Press, 1999.

Revue philosophique de Louvain (Chronique générale) 45, no. 6 (1947): 289–300.

Ricœur, Paul. *A Key to Husserl's* Ideas I. Edited by P. Vandevelde. Translated by Bond Harris and Jacqueline Bouchard Spurlock. Milwaukee, Wis.: Marquette University Press, 1996.

Rodin, Auguste. *Art: Conversations with Paul Gsell.* Translated by Jacques de Caso and Patricia B. Sanders. Berkeley: University of California Press, 1984.

———. *L'art: Entretiens réunis par Paul Gsell.* Paris: Grasset, 1911.

Romero, Maryellen. "Paresis." In *Encyclopedia of Clinical Neuropsychology,* edited by Jeffrey S. Kreutzer, John DeLuca, and Bruce Caplan. New York: Springer, 2011.

Ross, Nathaniel. "The Postural Model of the Head and Face in Various Positions (Experiments on Normals)." *Journal of General Psychology* 7, no. 1 (1932): 144–62.

Rostand, François. "Grammaire et affectivité." *Revue française de psychanalyse* 14 (1950): 299–310.

Rubin, Edgar. "Kritisches und Experimentelles zur 'Empfindungszeit' Fröhlichs." *Psychologische Forschung* 13, no. 1 (1930): 101–12.

———. *Visuell wahrgenommene Figuren: Studien in psychologischer Analyse.* Berlin: Boghandel, 1921.

———. "Visuell wahrgenommene wirkliche Bewegung." *Zeitschrift für Psychologie* 103 (1927): 384–92.

Ruyer, Raymond. *Éléments de psycho-biologie.* Paris: Presses Universitaires de France, 1946.

———. *La conscience et le corps.* Paris: Presses Universitaires de France, 1937.

———. *Neofinalism.* Translated by Alyosha Edlebi. Minneapolis: University of Minnesota Press, 2016.

———. *Néo-finalisme.* Paris: Presses Universitaires de France, 1952.

Sack, Martin. *Von der Neuropathologie zur Phänomenologie: Alfred Prinz von Auersperg und die Geschichte der Heidelberger Schule.* Würzburg: Königshausen & Neumann, 2005.

Sadoul, Georges. *Dictionary of Films.* Translated by Peter Morris. Berkeley: University of California Press, 1972.

———. *Dictionnaire des films.* Paris: Seuil, 1965.

Saint Aubert, Emmanuel de. "Au croisement du réel et de l'imaginaire: Les 'ultra-choses' chez Merleau-Ponty." In *Est-ce réel? Phénoménologies de l'imaginaire,* edited by Annabelle Dufourcq, 240–58. Leiden: Brill, 2016.

Sartre, Jean-Paul. "La transcendance de l'ego: Esquisse d'une description phénoménologique." *Recherches philosophiques* 6 (1936–37): 85–124.

———. *L'imaginaire: Psychologie phénoménologique de l'imagination.* Paris: Gallimard, 1940.

———. *Transcendence of the Ego: An Existentialist Theory of Consciousness.* Translated by Forrest Williams and Robert Kirkpatrick. New York: Noonday Press, 1962.

Schilder, Paul. *Das Körperschema: Ein Beitrag zur Lehre vom Bewußtsein des eigenen Körpers.* Berlin: Springer, 1923.

———. *The Image and Appearance of the Human Body: Studies in the Constructive Energies of the Psyche.* 1935. Reprint, New York: International Universities Press, 1950.

Schilder, Paul, and Hans Hoff. "Der Verlauf der Lagebeharrung." *Monatsschrift für Psychiatrie und Neurologie* 66 (1927): 356–59.

———. "Lagebeharrung und Körperschema." *Monatsschrift für Psychiatrie und Neurologie* 61 (1926): 109–13.

———. "Über Lagebeharrung." *Monatsschrift für Psychiatrie und Neurologie* 58 (1925): 257–64.

Schütz, Alfred. "Type and Eidos in Husserl's Late Philosophy." *Philosophy and Phenomenological Research* 20, no. 2 (1959): 147–65.

Simon, Gerard. "Eidôlon." In *Vocabulaire européen des philosophies: Dictionnaire des intraduisibles,* edited by Barbara Cassin. Paris: Le Seuil / Le Robert, 2004.

Slock, Ken. *Corps et machine: Cinéma et philosophie chez Jean Epstein et Maurice Merleau-Ponty.* Sesto San Giovanni, It.: Éditions Mimésis, 2016.

Smyth, Bryan. "Heroism and History in Merleau-Ponty's Existential Phenomenology." *Continental Philosophy Review* 43 (2010): 167–91.

———. "The Meontic and the Militant: On Merleau-Ponty's Relation to Fink." *International Journal of Philosophical Studies* 19 (2011): 669–99.

———. *Merleau-Ponty's Existential Phenomenology and the Realization of Philosophy.* New York: Bloomsbury Academic, 2014.

———. "The Primacy Question in Merleau-Ponty's Existential Phenomenology." *Continental Philosophy Review* 50, no. 1 (2017): 127–49.

Spinnler, Hans. "Alzheimer's Disease." In *Handbook of Clinical and Experimental Neuropsychology*, edited by Gianfranco Denes and Luigi Pizzamiglio. Hove, U.K.: Psychology Press, 1999.

Stendhal. *See* Beyle, Marie-Henri.

Stockert, Franz Günther von. "Lokalisation und klinische Differenzierung des Symptoms der Nichtwahrnehmung einer Körperhälfte." *Deutsche Zeitschrift für Nervenheilkunde* 134 (1934): 1–13.

Stratton, George Malcolm. "Some Preliminary Experiments on Vision Without Inversion of the Retinal Image." *Psychological Review* 3, no. 6 (1896): 611–17.

———. "The Spatial Harmony of Touch and Sight." *Mind* 8 (1899): 492–505.

———. "Vision Without Inversion of the Retinal Image." *Psychological Review* 4 (1897): 341–60, 463–81.

Svare, Helge. *Body and Practice in Kant.* Dordrecht: Springer, 2006.

Temple, Michael. *Jean Vigo.* Manchester: Manchester University Press, 2005.

Ternus, Josef. "Experimentelle Untersuchungen über phänomenale Identität." *Psychologische Forschung* 7 (1926): 81–136.

———. "The Problem of Phenomenal Identity." In *A Sourcebook of Gestalt Psychology*, edited and translated by Willis D. Ellis, 149–60. New York: Harcourt, Brace, 1939.

Tolstoy, Leo. *La guerre et la paix, traduit avec l'autorisation de l'auteur par une Russe*, vol. 3. Paris: Hachette, 1885.

———. *War and Peace.* Translated by Constance Garnett. New York: Modern Library, 1931.

Trần Đức Thảo. *Phénoménologie et matérialisme dialectique.* Paris: Minh-Tân, 1951.

———. *Phenomenology and Dialectical Materialism.* Translated by Daniel J. Herman and Donald V. Morano. Dordrecht: D. Reidel, 1986.

Turkstra, Lyn, and Cynthia Thompson. "Agrammatism." In *Encyclopedia of Clinical Neuropsychology*, edited by Jeffrey S. Kreutzer, John DeLuca, and Bruce Caplan. New York: Springer, 2011.

Uexküll, Jakob von. *Bedeutungslehre.* Leipzig: J. A. Barth, 1940.

———. *A Foray into the Worlds of Animals and Humans: with* A Theory of Meaning. Translated by Joseph D. O'Neil. Minneapolis: University of Minnesota Press, 2010.

———. *Streifzüge durch die Umwelten von Tieren und Menschen: Ein Bilderbuch unsichtbarer Welten.* Berlin: Springer, 1934.

Valéry, Paul. *Collected Works of Paul Valéry, Volume 2: Poems in the Rough.* Translated by Hilary Corke. Princeton, N.J.: Princeton University Press, 1969.

———. *Degas, Danse, Dessin.* Paris: Gallimard, 1938. Reprinted in *Œuvres, tome II*, 1163–1240.

———. *Eupalinos, ou L'architecte. Précédé de l'âme et la danse.* Paris: Éditions de la Nouvelle revue française, 1923. Reprinted in *Œuvres, tome II,* 79–147.
———. *Introduction à la méthode de Léonard de Vinci.* Paris: Éditions de la Nouvelle revue française, 1919.
———. "La politique de l'esprit: Notre soverain bien." In *Œuvres, tome I,* 1014–40.
———. "Les deux vertus d'un livre." In *Œuvres, tome II,* 1246–50.
———. *L'idée fixe, ou deux hommes à la mer.* Paris: Les Laboratoires Martinet, 1932. Reprinted in *Œuvres, tome II,* 195–275.
———. "Mémoire sur l'attention." In *Cahiers (1894–1914), tome 6: 1903–1904,* edited by Nicole Celeyrette-Pietri, 223–41. Paris: Gallimard, 1997.
———. *Œuvres, tome I.* Edited by Jean Hytier. Paris: Gallimard, 1957.
———. *Œuvres, tome II.* Edited by Jean Hytier. Paris: Gallimard, 1960.
———. "Philosophie de la danse." In *Œuvres, tome I,* 1390–1403.
———. "Poésie et pensée abstraite." Oxford: Clarendon Press, 1939. Reprinted in *Variété V,* 127–62; *Œuvres, tome I,* 1314–39.
———. "Poésie perdue." In *Œuvres, tome II,* 656–62.
———. "Poetry and Abstract Thought." In *The Art of Poetry,* translated by Denise Folliot, 52–82. Princeton, N.J.: Princeton University Press, 1958.
———. *Tel quel I.* Paris: Gallimard, 1941. Reprinted in *Œuvres, tome II,* 471–594.
———. *Tel quel II.* Paris: Gallimard, 1943. Reprinted in *Œuvres, tome II,* 595–781.
———. *Variété V.* Paris: Gallimard, 1944.
Vigny, Alfred de, and Marie Dorval. *Lettres pour lire au lit: Correspondance amoreuse d'Alfred de Vigny et Marie Dorval, 1831–1838.* Edited by Ariane Charton. Paris: Mercure de France, 2009.
Wahmhoff, Natalie, and Elaine Clark. "Acalculia." In *Encyclopedia of Clinical Neuropsychology,* edited by Jeffrey S. Kreutzer, John DeLuca, and Bruce Caplan. New York: Springer, 2011.
Wallon, Henri. *Les origines de la pensée chez l'enfant.* Paris: Presses Universitaires de France, 1945.
Wegener, Stephen T., and Mathew Jacobs. "Pain Asymbolia." In *Encyclopedia of Clinical Neuropsychology,* edited by Jeffrey S. Kreutzer, John DeLuca, and Bruce Caplan. New York: Springer, 2011.
Weizsäcker, Viktor von. *Der Gestaltkreis: Theorie der Einheit von Wahrnehmen und Bewegen.* Leipzig: Georg Thieme, 1940. Reprinted as vol. 4 of Viktor von Weizsäcker, *Gesammelte Schriften,* edited by Dieter Janz, Wilhelm Rimpau, and Walter Schindler, with the collaboration of Peter Achilles und Mechthilde Kütemeyer. Frankfurt am Main: Suhrkamp, 1997.
Wertheimer, Max. *Drei Abhandlungen zur Gestalttheorie.* Erlangen: Verlag der Philosophischen Akademie, 1925.
———. "Experimental Studies on Seeing Motion." Translated by Michael Wertheimer and K. W. Watkins. In Max Wertheimer, *On Perceived Motion and Figural Organization,* edited by Lothar Spillmann, 1–91. Cambridge, Mass.: MIT Press, 2012.
———. "Experimentelle Studien über das Sehen von Bewegung." *Zeitschrift für Psychologie* 61, no. 1 (1912): 161–265.

———. "On Truth." *Social Research* 1, no. 2 (1934): 135–46.
———. *Productive Thinking*. New York: Harper and Row, 1945.
———. *Über Schlussprozesse im produktiven Denken*. Berlin: De Gruyter, 1920.
Westra, Adam. *The Typic in Kant's* Critique of Practical Reason*: Moral Judgment and Symbolic Representation*. Berlin: De Gruyter, 2016.
Wilkins, Robert, and Irwin Brody. "Gerstmann's Syndrome." *Archives of Neurology* 24, no. 5 (1971): 475.
Wölfflin, Heinrich. *Kunstgeschichtliche Grundbegriffe: Das Problem der Stilentwicklung in der neueren Kunst*. 1915. 5th ed. Reprint, Munich: Hugo Bruckmann, 1921.
———. *Principes fondamentaux de l'histoire de l'art: Le problème de l'évolution du style dans l'art moderne*. Translated by Claire Raymond and Marcel Raymond. Paris: Plon, 1952.
———. *Principles of Art History: The Problem of the Development of Style in Early Modern Art*. Translated by Jonathan Blower. Los Angeles: Getty Publications, 2015.
———. *Principles of Art History: The Problem of the Development of Style in Later Art*. Translated by Marie Donald Mackie Hottinger. New York: Dover, 1932.
Wundt, Wilhelm. *Die geometrisch-optischen Täuschungen*. Leipzig: B. G. Teubner, 1898.
Zéro de conduite. Directed by Jean Vigo. Paris: Argui-Films, 1933.
Zietz, Karl, and Heinz Werner. "Über die dynamische Struktur der Bewegung." *Zeitschrift für Psychologie* 105 (1927): 226–49.

Index

acalculia, xxxiii, 110, 113, 156, 215n29, 216n4
Achilles, 53
action, 13, 14, 45, 87, 88, 90, 97, 98, 100, 101, 104, 109, 111, 113, 114, 124, 138, 159; Bergson's notion of, 16, 29, 100; reflective, 116, 120; symbolic, 119. *See also* praxis
agnosia, xxxii–xxxiii, 28, 29–30, 31, 86, 87, 101, 105, 107, 109, 110, 113–17, 119, 155, 156, 201n13, 212n17, 214n18; finger, xxxiii, 113, 119–20, 156, 215n29, 219n6, 220n13
agrammatism, 158, 233n48
Ajuriaguerra, Julien de, 105, 113, 156, 211n17, 214nn21–22, 217n15, 217nn17–18, 218n21, 219nn2–3, 232nn43–45
allesthesia, 87, 97, 200n10
alteration, 124, 132
ambiguity, xiv, xviii, xxiii, xxviii, xxix, l, 26, 131, 132, 133, 135, 140, 149, 162, 229n3
ambivalence, 26, 131, 163. *See also* ambiguity
animism, 150
anosognosia, 87, 89, 97, 201nn10–11, 213n18
aphasia, xxxii–xxxiii, 28, 48, 105, 109, 110, 113, 119, 132, 133, 155, 156, 158, 172n12, 221n16, 229n5; agrammatic (*see* agrammatism)
apparent size, 42, 44, 46, 47, 49–50, 70, 75, 180n5
apractognosia, 105, 107, 114, 212n17, 213n18
apraxia, xxxii–xxxiii, xxxiv, 15, 28, 30, 31, 86, 87, 99, 104–5, 107, 109–17, 119, 131, 132, 155, 156, 158, 210–11nn10–13, 211nn12–13; constructional, 87, 105, 107, 114–16, 119, 201n20, 216n15; dressing, 105, 114, 212n17, 214n18, 214n22; ideational, 104, 114, 210n11; innervatory, 104, 114, 211n13; motor, 104, 114, 211n12; total, xxxiv, 110, 123, 222n24
Aristotle (and Aristotelianism), 18, 33, 131. *See also* illusion: Aristotle's
asomatognosia, 200–201nn10–11
attention, 58, 211n12; Valéry on, xxv, 48, 179n3
Auersperg, Alfred Prinz von, 169n9
auto-locomotion: phenomenon of, 62–63, 66, 192nn41–42, 231n25
autotopagnosia, 86, 95, 200n9, 206n13
awakening (and wakefulness), xxix, xxxiv, xxxvii, xlii n121, 12, 43, 49, 101, 110–11, 121–22, 159, 160, 163, 164

background, of perception, xix–xx, xxiv–xxvi, xxvii, xxx, 14–15, 20, 22–23, 24–27, 45, 50, 57, 58, 61, 63, 69, 70, 71, 119, 132, 133, 136, 138, 145, 150–51, 154, 159, 161, 165, 184n3, 193n47 (*see also* figure); intermodal, 32 (*see also* field: intermodal). *See also* body schema: as background of praxis
Beaufret, Jean, xl n46
being, xiii, xxvi, xxvii, xxviii, xxxii, 9, 10–11, 13, 19, 20, 22, 26, 35, 37, 45, 46, 50, 63, 65, 91, 112, 113, 123, 126, 131, 132, 134, 135, 138, 140, 153, 155, 159, 163, 164; of sense, xvi, 10–11; movement as disclosive of, 61–63, 67, 131; toward the world, xxxvi, 50, 97, 126, 127, 138, 163
Benary, Wilhelm, 182n6
Berenson, Bernard, xxxv, 123, 124–25, 222n26, 224nn37–38
Bergson, Henri, xix, xxvi, xxx, xxxiv,

xxxix n36, 134, 141–43, 147, 164, 173n15; failure to thematize body, xxvi, xxx, 54, 139; on movement, 31, 53–54, 58, 73, 79, 139–40, 142–43, 144; notion of action, 16, 29, 100; sugar cube example, 40, 175n3. *See also* duration
Beyle, Marie-Henri. *See* Stendhal
Binswanger, Ludwig, 212n17
body, xviii, xxi, xxiii, xxiv, xxv, xxix–xxx, 13, 15, 20, 21–22, 27, 28, 35, 73, 81, 84, 86–87, 89–90, 92–98, 110, 111, 118, 131, 132, 143, 146, 147, 153, 159, 165, 166; double function of, 15, 28; as expressive, 21, 27, 30, 45, 49, 86, 107, 117, 159; functioning, 58; as machine for living (*see* machine); mobility of, xxxiv, 15, 28, 45, 49, 53, 73, 79–80, 92, 112, 114, 115, 117, 131, 142, 143 (*see also* motility; motricity; movement, of my body); as organ of mimicry, xviii–xxi, 15, 28; and orientation, 35, 39, 40–41; perceiving, xxvi, xxx, 32, 54, 73, 139; and perception, 39–46, 48–49, 53–54; presence of, xxxiii, 41–42, 98, 99, 101, 102, 104, 106, 107, 109, 111; spatiality of, xxiii, 42, 54, 81, 89, 112; sublimation of, in cultural expression, 86; *Umweltintentionalität* of (*see* intentionality, toward the environment); unity of, 89–90, 131; virtual, 41. *See also* body schema
body schema, xxii–xxiii, xxix–xxxiv, 74, 86–91, 92–99, 100–104, 106–8, 109, 110–11, 114, 116, 117, 118–21, 123, 132, 154, 155, 156–57, 158 , 159, 160, 163, 164, 165, 202n23, 203n31, 213n17, 236n58; as background of praxis, xxxi, 87, 90, 93, 97–98, 99, 100–103, 109
Bogaert, Ludo van, 96, 207n20
Bosses, Bartholomew Des, 215n2
Brain, W. Russell, 214n22
Bréhier, Émile, 175n1
Brunschvicg, Léon, 27, 171n9
Bühler, Karl, 172n11
Buhrmester, Harry C., 169n9
Buytendijk, Frederik, 170n6

Cairns, Dorion, xlvi
camouflage, 68, 194n3
Cassirer, Ernst, 147, 172nn11–12, 229n4
Cézanne, Paul, 21, 125
Christian, Paul, 155, 232n42
cinema, xvii, xxii, xxxv–xxxvi, 16, 30, 31, 32, 57, 58, 61, 86, 108, 123, 126–28, 132, 134, 136, 161, 162; three-dimensional, 42, 45, 49. *See also* expression (and expressivity): in visual arts
Claudel, Paul, 147, 231n30
closing-in (symptom), 115, 216n15, 217n16, 217n18
Cohen-Séat, Gilbert, 234n53
configuration, xxiv, xxvi, xxvii–xxviii, xxxv–xxxvi, 13, 14, 57, 62, 63, 70–73, 76, 111, 138, 144, 145, 147, 149, 153, 154. *See also* organization: of the field
consciousness, xvi, xix, xxi, 9–16, 19, 22–23, 24–26, 28–30, 38, 46, 76, 91, 103, 110, 123, 128, 132–34, 159, 160, 163–64; ambiguous, 26, 133; of body, 53, 86, 90, 98, 139; cross-eyed, 22, 25, 169n8; false, 25; indirect, 22, 24, 30, 32, 131, 160; inverted, xx, 15, 22, 24–25, 28, 131; linguistic (or speaking), 12, 16, 133; monadic, 12, 19; and movement, 37, 52, 53–54, 55, 73, 76, 79, 84, 110–12, 115, 117, 139, 140, 141, 142–43, 152, 153; mystified, xx, 25, 131; perceptual, xix–xx, 12–15, 19–22, 24, 26, 28, 131, 133, 134, 158, 163, 165; situational, 155; symbolic, 86, 116, 155; and time, 147, 164
constancy: perceptual, 46, 49
convergence: visual, 42, 43, 47–49, 83, 138, 180n5 (Lecture 5)
culture, xii–xvii, xxi, xxxiv–xxxvi, 9, 15, 16, 17, 27–28, 45, 50, 86, 91, 127, 132, 134, 137, 138, 147, 153, 159, 161, 166; and nature, xii, xiv, xv, xvi, xxi, 17, 27

depth, 29, 31, 38, 42–43, 45, 47, 50, 137, 152, 176n5; perception, xxiii, xxv, xlii n121, 42–45, 47–48. *See also* relief
Descartes, René, 9, 18, 124
diacritical: language as, 122; perception as, xix, xxviii, xxxv, xxxvi, 159, 160 (*see also* reading, perception as); sense as, 21; signs, 71, 78, 83, 135, 138, 147, 152, 158–59, 160, 161; structure as, 137; systems, 72, 78, 126, 131, 132
dialectic: of expression, xxv, xxvii–xxix,

xxxii, xxxiv, xxxvi, xxxviii n2, 86, 110, 117, 131 (*see also* exchange: dialectical, in perception); of nature, 27
dimensions, 14, 20–22, 35, 39–40, 45, 72, 152
distance, as aspect of intentionality, xix, 12, 13, 19–20, 44, 49, 67, 70, 71, 75, 78, 84, 134–35, 137–39, 162, 165. *See also* intentionality; proximity, as aspect of intentionality
Dorval, Marie, 23, 170n8
dream, 110, 121–22
Duncker, Karl, 60, 63, 68, 71, 81, 188n16, 191n38
duration, xxvi, 53–54, 73, 79, 126, 139, 142–43, 152, 156, 164, 175n3
dyscalculia. *See* acalculia

Efron, David, 166, 236n59
Einfühlung ("feeling into" or empathy), 132, 146, 153, 166
encroachment, xix, xxv, xxvi, xxix–xxxii, 13, 20, 52, 53, 67, 150
Epstein, Jean, xlviii, 74, 77, 131, 148, 153, 196n19, 197n5
exchange: dialectical, in perception, xxv, xxviii–xxix, l, 43, 44, 48, 63, 70–71, 75–76, 131, 147, 152, 154. *See also* dialectic: of expression
expression (and expressivity), xiv–xvii, xviii–xix, xx, xxi, xxix, 9, 11–14, 15, 18–19, 21–22, 24, 26–31, 45, 123, 127, 131, 132, 134, 140, 150, 157; body as expressive, 21, 27, 30, 45, 49, 86, 117, 159; creative, 15, 158 (*see also* productivity); cultural, xv, xxi, xvi, xvii, xviii, xxxiv, xxxv, 28, 86; dialectic of, xxv, xxvii, xxviii, xxix, xxxii, xxxiv, xxxvi, xxxviii n2, 86, 110, 117, 131; expressive function, xv–xvi, xvii, xxiii, 9, 163, 172n11; history as creative, 158; linguistic, xv, xxxiii, xxxv, xxxvi, 27, 30, 32, 86, 134, 158 (*see also* language; speech); and movement, 30, 57, 107, 110, 117, 123, 126, 131, 139, 140, 144, 145, 150, 151; mute, 30, 32; natural, xvii, xix, xxxiv, xxxv, 28, 45, 50, 57; perceptual consciousness as, 19, 131, 133; sublimation of, 131, 132; in visual arts, xxxv–xxxvi, 31–32, 57, 85, 86, 108, 124, 132, 161

feedback, xxv, 43, 48, 67. *See also* exchange: dialectical, in perception
field, 10, 20, 28–29, 31–32, 40, 55–56, 58, 60–63, 65, 66–68, 71, 81, 133, 136, 140, 145, 148, 150, 152, 154, 164, 165; cultural, 127, 138; intermodal, 148; linguistic, xxix, 152, 160; mental, 29, 31, 154; organization of, xxvii, 56, 67–69, 75–76, 78, 131, 147, 150; perceptual, xxvi, xxvii, xlix, 29, 31, 55, 67, 152, 160; sensory, 15, 20, 28, 72–73, 78, 86, 102, 127; spatial, 29, 31, 136, 145; tactile, 102; temporal, 77–78, 164; visual, xxix, 34, 40, 58, 72
figure (and figural moments), xix–xx, xxiv, xxvi–xxviii, 14–15, 22–23, 24–27, 32, 35, 45, 50, 57, 58–61, 63–65, 66–71, 72–73, 75, 81, 91, 131–33, 136, 145–46, 149–54, 159, 161, 165, 184n3, 193n47. *See also* background: of perception
finalism (and finality), 131, 158, 159
Fink, Eugen, 10, 167n3, 168n6
Focillon, Henri, 161, 234n53
Francastel, Pierre, 126, 133, 227nn49–51, 228n54
Freud, Sigmund (and Freudianism), xx, 15, 22–23, 24–25, 133, 170n7, 208n21, 229n3. *See also* psychoanalysis
Fröhlich, Friedrich, 231n27

Gelb, Adhémar, xxx, 101, 182n6, 188n19, 202n24, 215n27, 217n19
George, David Lloyd, 222n24
Gericault, Theodore, 124, 223n33
Gerstmann, Josef, 215n29, 219n6; Gerstmann's syndrome, xxxiii–xxxiv, 108, 110, 119, 215n29
Gestalt theory, xix–xxi, xxv–xxx, xxxv, 10, 14, 22–23, 49, 54–56, 63–64, 67–69, 75, 131, 140, 143–45, 150, 159; abstractness of, 64, 74, 81, 148, 197n21
gnosia, 16, 28–29, 30, 31, 87, 104–6, 110, 112–13, 114–16, 119, 131, 155, 201n13
Goldstein, Kurt, xiii, xxv, xxx, xxxii, xxxiii, 87, 98, 101–2, 115, 116, 120, 166, 182n6, 201n17, 202n24, 211n12, 215n27, 217n19, 218n21
Gottschaldt, Kurt, 194n3
Gris, Juan, 125, 227n48

Grünbaum, Abraham Anton, 120, 220nn11–12
Guterman, Norbert, 171n2

haecceity, 135
Halbwachs, Maurice, 147, 231n28
Hamlet, 158
hand (as element of body schema), xxxiii–xxxiv, 96, 106, 110, 111, 119–21, 132, 156–57, 216n15, 220n9. *See also* illusion: Japanese
Hartmann, Heinz, 195n3, 208n31
Head, Henry, xxx, xxxii, 87, 88, 89, 90, 95, 96, 97, 100, 105, 113, 152, 156, 164, 165, 172n12, 209n2. *See also* taximeter (analogy)
Hécaen, Henry, 87, 88, 105, 113, 118, 156, 211n17
Heidegger, Martin (and Heideggerians), xl n46, 11, 167n4
heterosexuality, 23, 24–26, 170n7
history, xii, xvii, 17, 29, 30, 32, 45, 50, 66, 112, 121, 155; as creative expression, 158; personal, 69, 136. *See also* sedimentation: historical
Hoff, Hans, 90, 98, 102, 204n33
homosexuality, 23, 24–26, 170n7
horizon (and horizonality), xviii, xxxi, 12, 19, 22, 44–46, 49–50, 100, 102, 136, 138, 164, 227n52
Hume, David, 62
Husserl, Edmund, xiii, xl n46, 10, 12, 19, 33, 136, 163, 168n6, 231n27; on typicality, 177n8
Hyppolite, Jean, xvi, 10, 167n2

ideology, 25–26, 171n2, 171n4
illusion, xx, xxvii, 45, 52, 55, 58, 96, 97, 126, 133, 227n46; in anaglyph, 81–82, 84, 200n5; Aristotle's, 87, 88, 99, 103–4; Japanese, xxxiii, 87, 88, 106–7, 109, 111, 201n13, 214nn24–25, 216n6; Jastrow, 61, 188n19; retrospective, xxiii, 137
imagination (and imaginary), 90, 95, 134, 157, 161–63, 164
imperception, xix, xx, xxxvii, 15, 20, 22, 159
inhabiting: as bodily praxis, xxiv–xxv, xxvi, xxix, xxxi, 22, 35–36, 42, 45, 50, 96, 121
intentionality, 20, 23, 43, 48, 111, 124, 134, 155; toward the environment (*Umweltintentionalität*), xviii, 21, 136, 170n6

Jackson, Hughlings, 96
Jastrow, Joseph, 61, 188n19
Jaubert, Maurice, 74, 80, 131, 148, 153, 196n18, 196n20, 198n9
jealousy, 22–23, 24, 170n7
Jeanneret, Charles-Édouard. *See* Le Corbusier

Kant, Immanuel, 9, 32, 45, 62; Kantian form, 50, 174n17; on *Typik*, 178n8
Keller, Helen, 133
Kenkel, Friedrich, 189n21
Klein, Elmer, 214nn24–25, 216nn6–7
Kleist, Karl, 211n13
Koffka, Kurt, 47, 61, 62, 66, 68, 71, 76, 149, 183n3, 187nn12–13, 188n16, 188n19, 189nn20–21, 189n23, 195n3
Köhler, Wolfgang, 145, 192n47, 194–5n3, 231n24
Kohnstamm, Oskar, 204n32; Kohnstamm's phenomenon, xxxi, 90, 98, 102, 203n32
Kraepelin, Emil, 121, 221n15
Krolik, Walter, 235n55
Kuleshov, Lev, xlviii, 165, 235n58

Lachièze-Rey, Pierre, 18, 158
Lange, Johannes, xxxiii, 110, 120, 207n16, 219n6, 220nn7–8, 220nn10–13
language, xii–xiii, xvii, xxi, xxxii, xxxiv, 9, 10, 12, 15–16, 22, 27–30, 32, 45, 48, 50, 78, 86, 88, 93, 105, 108, 110, 113, 116–17, 121–23, 127–28, 132, 135, 138, 140, 152, 157, 158, 160, 161; automatic, 80; creative, 80; as diacritical, 103, 121–22; gestural, 122, 221n21; indirect, 161; literary, 161; natural, xviii, 14, 72, 79, 90, 153, 161; in Schneider, 107, 116; and sleep, 121–22. *See also* expression: linguistic; speech
Lavelle, Louis, xxxvii n1
Le Corbusier (Charles-Édouard Jeanneret), 181n5
Lefebvre, Henri, 171n2
Leibniz, Gottfried Wilhelm, 110, 215n2, 230n18

Leonardo da Vinci, 31, 173n15
level, xix, xxiv–xxvi, xxx–xxxi, 13–14, 20–21, 24, 29–32, 35, 42, 45, 50, 61, 87, 133, 134, 158–59; body schema as privileged, 90, 98, 103; of all levels, 45, 50; levels of motility and praxis, xxxii, 87, 105, 107, 110, 113, 116–17, 131, 155
Lewin, Kurt, 68, 193n3
Lhermitte, Jean, 105, 114, 208n21, 214nn19–20
Liepmann, Hugo Karl, 210n10, 211nn12–13
Linke, Paul Ferdinand, 29, 61, 151, 189nn22–23
Linschoten, Johannes, xxvii, xxviii, 63–65, 69, 154, 162, 192–93nn47–50
logic, 37, 72, 78; linguistic, xxxvi, 57; perceptual, 18, 29, 31, 37, 43, 57, 63–64, 68, 72, 78, 131, 144, 152, 153, 154; of sleeping consciousness, 163; transcendental, 38
Lukács, Georg, 158

machine: for living, xxx, xxxi, 54, 137–38, 143, 146, 147, 180n5 (Lecture 6); for living or making time, xxxi, 146, 147; for perceiving, 154; for thinking, 121
The Man in the White Suit (film), 127, 228n53
Marx, Karl (and Marxism), xx, 15, 25, 27, 131, 158, 171nn2–3
Mayer, Felix, 122, 221n17
Mayer-Gross, Wilhelm, 15, 216n15. *See also* closing-in (symptom)
McFie, John, 213n17, 214nn21–22
Menninger-Lerchenthal, Erich, 208n21
Merle, Jean-Toussaint, 23
Merleau-Ponty, Maurice: election to Collège de France, xii–xiv, xxxvii n1; *The Adventures of the Dialectic*, xi; "Eye and Mind," xxxvi; *Humanism and Terror*, xiii; "In Praise of Philosophy," xxxvii n1; "Man and Adversity," 133; *Phenomenology of Perception*, xi, xii–xvi, xix, xxii, xxiii–xxiv, xxxii, xxxix n26, xl n46, 9–11, 137, 194n3, 208n21; "The Primacy of Perception," xii–xiii, xl n46; *The Prose of the World*, xiii, xxxvi; *Sense and Non-Sense*, xiii; *The Structure of Behavior*, xi, xii, xiv–xv, xxi, xxxix n26; *The Visible and the Invisible*, xi
Metzger, Wolfgang, 191n38
Michelangelo, 174n15
Michotte, Albert, xxvii, 62, 66–68, 73, 79, 145–46, 147, 148, 149, 151, 153, 154, 184n3, 190–92nn24–42, 193n2, 231n25
mimicry (and mimesis), xix, xxi, 121; body as organ of, xviii–xix, 15, 28; mimetic method, 166
Minkowski, Hermann, 191n38
Mitchell, Silas Weir, 96, 207n20
mobility, 60, 73, 81, 111, 145; of body, xxxiv, 79, 112, 114, 115, 117. See also motility; motricity
Morlass, Joseph, 211n12, 211n16
motility, xxxii, xxxiv, 107, 110, 116, 117. *See also* level: levels of motility and praxis; mobility: of body; motricity
motricity, xxix, 74, 81, 85–86, 111, 117, 121. *See also* mobility: of body; motility
Mouzon, Jean, 105, 114, 214nn19–20
movement, xxii, xxiii–xxix, xxx–xxxiv, 16, 20, 25, 29–31, 32–33, 41, 51–57, 58–65, 66–74, 77, 79–80, 110, 112–17, 131–32, 138–46, 149–55, 156, 160; as disclosive of being, 61–63, 66–67, 131, 154; as figural moment, 59–61, 131; grounded in body schema, 87, 92, 110, 140, 156; illusion of, in anaglyph, 81–82, 84, 200n5; and language, 160; and meaning, 75, 77, 131, 144, 152; of my body, 31, 43, 44, 48, 53, 92, 111–12, 132, 139, 141, 142, 146; objective, 31, 51–52, 58, 73–74, 85, 131, 138–40, 141, 146; perception of, xxiii, xxvi–xxix, xxx–xxxiv, 30, 33, 53–54, 55, 58–65, 66–71, 73, 80, 81, 86, 152, 153, 155; perception of, as reading, xxviii, 71, 152 (*see also* reading, perception as); phenomenal, 32, 51, 52, 54–57, 58–59, 73, 131, 143–44, 147, 148, 149, 192n44; pre-movement, 81, 148; pure, xx, xxvii, 29, 31, 55, 59, 140, 143, 144, 184n4 (*see also* phi phenomenon); in Schneider, 87, 98, 101, 202n24; and space, 29, 31, 32–33, 36, 55, 76, 228n2, 232n41;stroboscopic, xxvii, 30–31, 55, 56, 58, 67, 70–72, 75, 78, 144, 149, 150, 153–54; subject implicated in,

53–54, 131; as tracing, xxviii, 32–33, 70, 73, 79, 115, 141, 146, 153, 155; in visual art, xxxv–xxxvi, 16, 30, 31–32, 57, 108, 123–27, 132, 222–23nn26–35, 224–26nn41–44, 227n46. *See also* mobility; motricity; motility
Mozhukin, Ivan, 165, 235n58
Müller-Lyer, Franz Carl, 188n19
Muncie, Wendell, 115, 217nn16–20
mutism: of perception, xviii, 22, 24; mute expression, 30, 32

nature, xiii, xxxvi, 17, 44, 77, 83, 91, 100, 159, 161; and culture, xii, xiv, xv, xvi, xxi, 17, 27; dialectic of, 27

Ombredane, André, 96, 133, 207n20, 229n5
organization: figural, 61, 63, 65, 66; of the field, xxvii, 56, 67–69, 75–76, 78, 131, 147, 150. *See also* configuration
orientation, xxiii–xxiv, 17, 35, 38, 39–42, 64, 85, 107, 116, 134–36, 155, 156

pain asymbolia, 88, 202n21
painterly (style, *das Malerische*), xxxv, 125–26, 134, 224n40, 225–26nn42–44, 227n46
painting, xvii, xviii, xxii, xxxv–xxxvi, 11, 13, 21, 30, 31, 45, 57, 80, 85, 86, 108, 132, 134; movement in, 123–25, 132, 156, 223n36; Paulhan on, 76. *See also* visual arts
Paliard, Jacques, 64, 74, 81–86, 131, 150, 192n45, 197n23, 199–200nn3–7
Panofsky, Erwin, 133, 229n6
pantheism, 18, 131
paraphasia, 221n16; sleep, 121–22
paresis, 97, 209n25
paresthesia, 96, 207n19
Paterson, Andrew, 105, 114, 214n21
Paulhan, Jean, 76, 131, 154, 197nn3–4, 223n29, 228n2, 232n41
perception, xii–xvi, 9–11, 18–19, 22, 27, 31, 35, 39, 44, 49, 65, 69, 70, 79, 81–86, 91, 131, 132; depth, xxiii, xxv, xlii n121, 43, 45, 47, 48 (*see also* relief); as diacritical, xix, xxviii, xxxv, xxxvi, 159, 160 (*see also* reading, perception as); and expression, 11–14, 15–16, 19–22, 24, 26, 30, 31, 57; miracle of, xxviii, 65, 67, 70; of movement, xxiii, xxvi–xxix, xxx–xxxiv, 30, 33, 53–54, 55, 58–65, 66–71, 73, 80, 81, 86, 152, 153, 155; mutism of, xviii, 22, 24; painterly, 134; primacy of, 10–11; of space, 33, 34, 45, 156; and symbols, 71, 131; synesthetic, 90; of time, 146. *See also* consciousness: perceptual
phantom limb, 88, 89, 96, 163, 202n25, 207n20
phasia, 28, 104, 113, 119, 121–22
phi phenomenon (Wertheimer), xx, xxvii, 59, 67, 140, 184n4. *See also* movement: pure
photography, 124
Piaget, Jean, 55, 73, 79, 133, 140, 146, 147, 148, 169n9, 231n29, 231n31
Pick, Arnold, 95, 206nn13–14
Piercy, Malcolm, 213n17, 214nn21–22
Piéron, Henri, 50, 180n5 (Lecture 5)
place, xxiii, xxiv–xxvi, 32–33, 35, 38, 51
plastic arts. *See* visual (and plastic) arts
Plessner, Helmuth, 170n6
postural schema, xxxi, 89, 97. *See also* body schema
Pötzl, Otto, 96, 206nn15–16
practognosia, 114
pragmatism, 100
praxia, xxi, 16, 28, 31, 106, 112–13, 114, 155
praxis, xxi, xxiv, xxviii, xxx, xxxi–xxxii, xxxiv, 16, 28–29, 87, 100, 104, 110, 112, 114, 116, 131, 155
productivity, xiv–xv, 15, 107, 139, 164
projection, xx, xxi, xxiv, xxx, xxxi–xxxii, xxxv, 107, 115
prolepsis, 16, 133, 145, 146, 149
Proust, Marcel, 170n7
proximity, as aspect of intentionality, xix, 12, 13, 19–20, 21, 135, 138. *See also* intentionality; distance, as aspect of intentionality
psychoanalysis, 26, 131, 158, 166. *See also* Freud, Sigmund (and Freudianism)
psychologism, 10, 56, 140
Pudovkin, Vsevolod, 236n58

rationality, xii, xvii, 27, 29, 158
Ravaisson, Félix, 172n15
reading, perception as, 78, 131, 132, 147, 152, 154, 160

regression: organic, 89, 96, 208n21. *See also* repression
relief, 42–43, 45, 47–49, 81–85, 133, 137, 156. *See also* depth
religion, xiii, 25–26
Rembrandt van Rijn, 125
repression, xx, 97; organic, 208n21. *See also* regression
Révész, Géza, 189n19
Ricœur, Paul, 168n6
right-left confusion, xxxiii, 87, 96, 119, 213n17
Rodin, Auguste, xxxv, 124, 125, 144, 222n27, 222–23nn29–32, 223nn34–35, 232n41
Rorschach test, 155
Ross, Nathaniel, 89, 202n27
Rostand, François, 137, 230n12
Rubens, Peter Paul, 125
Rubin, Edgar, 58, 150, 183n3, 231n27
Rude, Francois, 222n28, 232n41
Ruyer, Raymond, 12, 19, 167n5, 195n3

Sartre, Jean-Paul, 19, 138, 161, 162, 235n57
Saussure, Ferdinand de, 78. *See also* diacritical: signs; signs
schematic typology (*montage*), 43, 48, 133, 136, 137, 176n8
Schilder, Paul, xxx, xxxii, xxxiii, xli n87, xli n90, 86–88, 90, 93–98, 102, 104, 106–7, 114, 116–17, 165, 200n8, 201n10, 201nn12–15, 202nn23–25, 202n27, 202–4nn29–34, 205n3, 205nn5–8, 205–6nn10–11, 206–7nn13–16, 208n21, 209n23, 209nn26–28, 209nn31–33, 210n4, 210–11nn6–12, 211nn14–15, 215nn27–28, 216n10, 218n22, 232n44; Japanese illusion, 106, 216nn6–7, 214–15nn24–26; organic regression, 89, 96
Schneider (patient of Gelb and Goldstein), xxx, xxxiii, 56, 64, 98, 101–2, 107, 110, 115, 116, 146, 182n6
Schütz, Alfred, 178n8
science, xx, 9, 11, 27, 37, 55, 112–13, 134, 165
screen effect, 58, 61, 154, 184n3
sculpture, xxxv–xxxvi, xlii n116, 124
sedimentation, xlix, 64, 73, 79, 107, 110, 146, 157; historical, 44, 116, 155 (*see also* history)
sexuality, 119. *See also* heterosexuality; homosexuality
signs, 32, 42, 43, 47, 65, 70–71, 78, 98, 102, 122, 123–24, 126–27, 135, 145, 152, 154, 159, 160, 163. *See also* diacritical: signs
silence, 30, 32, 135, 136, 157
Sinngebung (bestowal of sense), xxi, xxv, xxvii, xxviii, 10, 19, 39, 44, 45, 48, 64, 146, 147
situation, xxiii–xxvi, xxvii–xxviii, 14, 16, 28, 35, 41, 56, 59, 65, 69, 81, 86, 89, 99, 101, 110, 112, 116–17, 134–35, 137, 147, 149, 152, 154, 155, 162, 164; bodily, 15, 96; *Situationserfassung* (grasping of the situation), xxiv, xxvii, xxviii, 64, 69, 70, 75
sleep, xxxiv, 87, 110–11, 121–23, 132, 163–64
somatognosia, 106, 154
sound, 13, 30, 32, 62, 65, 72–74, 79–80, 127, 136, 145, 148, 153, 154, 191n38, 193n51, 196n18, 198n9
space (and spatiality), xxii, xxiii–xxix, 16, 28, 29, 31, 34, 35, 37–50, 52, 55, 66, 71, 75–76, 88, 90, 98, 103, 122, 131, 135, 136, 139, 144, 145, 146; bodily (and primordial), xxiii, xxvi, 36, 42, 54, 90, 98, 106, 146, 147, 154, 213n17; in cinema, 126–27; cultural (and anthropological), 15, 45, 50, 132, 140, 146 (*see also* culture); ultra-spatial meaning, 126; virtual, xxiii–xxiv, 15–16, 28. *See also* orientation
speech, xxxiii, xxxvii, 30, 32, 119, 121, 123, 127–28, 132, 135, 138, 158
Stendhal (Marie-Henri Beyle), 233n51
stereoscope, 34, 42–45, 47–49
Stockert, Franz Günther von, 118, 218n2
Stratton, George Malcolm, xxiv, xxv, 34, 39–41, 87, 174n19, 174n21, 201n18, 205n10
structure, 13, 14, 18–21, 78, 90, 137, 146, 149, 154; of body (and body schema), 90, 104, 118, 120, 166; of consciousness, 23, 25; horizon as, 49, 50; of perceived figures (and move-

ment), 60, 62, 67, 75, 115, 116, 149, 151, 154; of perceived world (and field), xxxi–xxxii, 68, 76, 104, 137, 150, 154, 164, 184n3, 190n23; of sound, 145, 154. *See also* truth: structural theory of
style, 26, 43, 48, 71, 75, 76, 109, 110, 111, 138, 149
subject (and subjectivity), xxi, xxii, xl n46, xlii n98, 12, 18, 76, 137; embodied (and moving), 79, 85, 86, 138; epistemological (and thinking), 27, 65, 146; implicated in movement, 53–54, 131; perceiving, xiii–xiv, xxi, xxii, xxiv, xxv–xxvi, xxvii–xxix, xxxiv, 20, 56–57, 65, 69, 71–73, 85, 137, 138, 149, 150, 155; speaking, 157, 159; spectative, 52
symbol (and symbolism), xxxiv, 9, 15–16, 37, 70, 83, 105, 107, 114–15, 119, 131, 134, 145, 147, 154, 156, 157, 158, 162, 164, 234n53, 235n55; and body (and body schema), xxxiv, 118, 120–21; Cohen-Séat and cinema, 234n53; and dream, 122; indirect, 160; and Kant on *Typik*, 179n8; and language, 158; and perception, 71, 131; and Schneider, 64, 116; sedimented, 64; and signs, 70; and space, 89, 145; symbolic consciousness, 86, 116, 155; symbolic thinking, 28, 172n12; and time, 147
synthesis, 10, 16, 31, 46, 47, 144, 145, 149, 200n4; existential (and lateral), xxiv, 16, 46, 50; intellectual (and frontal), xxiv, 46, 50, 51, 87, 140, 141; and Paliard, 82–84, 86; passive, 10, 32; perceptual, xxiv–xxv, 145, 177n8; temporal, 46; of transition, 49

taximeter (analogy), xxx, 64, 90, 95, 152, 154, 156, 202n29, 232n44
ter Borch, Gerard, 125
Ternus, Josef, 59, 149, 150, 187n12
time (and temporality, temporalization), xxxi, 77, 79, 146, 147, 148, 153, 156, 164
Tolstoy, Leo, 181n5
tools, 11, 17, 21, 120, 220n9, 220n13
totality: body schema as, xviii, xxx, xxxi, 88, 93–97, 101, 109, 120; movement as, 59, 150; of perceptual field, 55, 78; space as, 38
tracing (*le tracé*), xxviii–xxx, 32–33, 51, 66, 73, 79, 115, 139, 141, 142, 146, 153, 155, 223n36
Trân Dúc Tháo, 27, 171n8
truth, xii, xiv, xvii, xviii, xxi, xxviii, xxxiv, 12, 15, 26–27, 29, 46, 49, 121, 135, 141; retrograde movement of, xix, xxxiv, xxxix n36, 27, 45; structural theory of, 16–17, 30, 32, 172n14; teleology of, 15

Uexküll, Jakob von, 170n6
unconscious, 23, 24, 25, 26, 97, 159, 163
use value, 71, 72, 78

Valéry, Paul, xxv, xxix, xxx, 43, 48, 136, 137, 160, 161, 179n3, 180n5 (Lecture 6), 229n11, 233n50, 233n52
Vigny, Alfred de, 23, 157, 170n8
Vigo, Jean, 196n18, 196n20, 198n9
visual (and plastic) arts, xvii, xxxiv–xxxvi, 57, 80, 127–28. *See also* cinema; painting; sculpture

wakefulness. *See* awakening (and wakefulness)
Wallon, Henri, 227n52
Weizsäcker, Viktor von, 134, 169n9, 193n50
Werner, Heinz, 65, 72, 79, 131, 148, 151–52, 153, 154, 193n51
Wertheimer, Max, xx, xxiv, xxv, xxvii, xl n66, 20, 21, 29, 31, 32, 35, 39–42, 55, 59, 67, 71, 135–36, 152, 172n14, 184–6nn4–8, 186–7nn10–11
Wölfflin, Heinrich, xxxv, 125–26, 224–27nn39–47
Wundt, Wilhelm, 189n19

Zaccarello, Benedetta, 179n3
Zangwill, Oliver, 105, 114, 213n17, 214nn21–22
Zeno of Elea, xxvi, xxvii, 52–53, 58, 139, 141–42
Zéro de conduite (film), 74, 80, 196n18, 196n20, 198n9
Zietz, Karl, 65, 72, 79, 148, 151–52, 153, 154, 193n51